CW00793551

"Present-Centered Group Therapy for PTSD: E, important new evidence-based approach for t therapists of virtually all theoretical orientatic based treatment can be readily applied to all sources of trauma from military combat, sexual assault, and domestic violence, to moving vehicle accidents. Its success rates parallel those found in all other effective treatments for PTSD."

Terence M. Keane, PhD, director, Behavioral Science Division, National Center for PTSD, professor and assistant dean for research, Boston University School of Medicine

"Drawing upon years of research findings, academic rigor and clinical practice, authors Melissa Wattenberg, Dan Gross, Barbara Niles, Bill Unger, and M. Tracie Shea bring Present-Centered Group Therapy to the forefront as an evidenced-based and clinically sustaining group treatment for addressing PTSD. Their book, *Present-Centered Group Therapy for PTSD: Embracing Today*, is as comprehensive as it is a clear and compelling. The chapters move from the origins, components, and evidence of PCGT to a complete three chapter manual which invites the reader to learn from experts who have spent years helping veterans open a space and place for their present self in a trusted group. Followed by chapters which expand the readers understanding of 'present' in PCGT, the efficacy of group in trauma treatment and the effective application of PCGT to other treatment contexts, this book is a unique contribution to trauma survivors and those working with them. We have come to a place and time where research and treatment inform each other with a true understanding of what trauma takes and what treatment works to return. The book *Present-Centered Group Therapy for PTSD: Embracing Today* epitomizes that place and time."

Suzanne B. Phillips, PsyD, ABPP, is a licensed psychologist, psychoanalyst, diplomate in Group Psychology, Certified Group Therapist, fellow of the American Group Psychotherapy Association

"Present Centered Group Therapy (PCGT) is an excellent alternative to trauma-focused treatment for PTSD that focuses on the here-and-now and not on traumatic memories. Through a combination of psychoeducation, problem solving, and group support, participants develop a better understanding of their PTSD symptoms and themselves, and learn how to embrace today by directly facing and overcoming the challenges in their lives. With over 20 years of research supporting its efficacy, PCGT is an effective, low stress option for treating PTSD, and helping people affected by trauma move on with their lives."

Kim T. Mueser, PhD, professor, Departments of Occupational Therapy and Psychological and Brain Sciences Center for Psychiatric Rehabilitation, Boston University

Present-Centered Group Therapy for PTSD

Present-Centered Group Therapy for PTSD integrates theory, research, and practical perspectives on the manifestations of trauma, to provide an accessible, evidence-informed group treatment that validates survivors' experiences while restoring present-day focus.

An alternative to exposure-based therapies, present-centered group therapy provides practitioners with a highly implementable modality through which survivors of trauma can begin to reclaim and invest in their ongoing lives. Chapters describe the treatment's background, utility, relevant research, implementation, applications, and implications. Special attention is given to the intersection of group treatment and PTSD symptoms, including the advantages and challenges of group treatment for traumatized populations, and the importance of member-driven processes and solutions in trauma recovery.

Compatible with a broad range of theoretical orientations, this book offers clinicians, supervisors, mentors, and students a way to expand their clinical repertoire for effectively and flexibly addressing the impact of psychological trauma.

Melissa S. Wattenberg, PhD, is a clinical psychologist, co-developed PCGT, and supervises VA Boston's Psychosocial Rehabilitation & Recovery Center. She is assistant professor of psychiatry, Boston University.

Daniel Lee Gross, LICSW, is a clinical social worker at the Veterans Administration Hospital and in private practice in Seattle. He is an associate professor at Seattle University's Master of Social Work program.

Barbara L. Niles, PhD, is a psychologist at VA Boston National Center for PTSD and assistant professor of psychiatry, Boston University, and investigates impact of psychotherapy and health enhancement for veterans with PTSD.

William S. Unger, PhD, is a psychologist in the Trauma Recovery Services at Providence VA Medical Center and associate clinical professor in the Department of Psychiatry and Human Behavior, Brown University. He served as the chief of the PTSD Program for 16 years.

M. Tracie Shea, PhD, is a psychologist in the Trauma Recovery Services, Providence VA, and professor, Department of Psychiatry and Human Behavior, Brown University, developed PCGT, and has played a key role in many clinical trials of PTSD psychosocial treatments.

Present-Centered Group Therapy for PTSD
Embracing Today

**Melissa S. Wattenberg,
Daniel Lee Gross,
Barbara L. Niles,
William S. Unger, and
M. Tracie Shea**

Routledge
Taylor & Francis Group

NEW YORK AND LONDON

First published 2021
by Routledge
52 Vanderbilt Avenue, New York, NY 10017

and by Routledge
2 Park Square, Milton Park, Abingdon, Oxon, OX14 4RN

Routledge is an imprint of the Taylor & Francis Group, an informa business

© 2021 Taylor & Francis

The right of Melissa S. Wattenberg, Daniel Lee Gross, Barbara L. Niles, William S. Unger, M. Tracie Shea to be identified as authors of this work has been asserted by them in accordance with sections 77 and 78 of the Copyright, Designs and Patents Act 1988.

All rights reserved. No part of this book may be reprinted or reproduced or utilized in any form or by any electronic, mechanical, or other means, now known or hereafter invented, including photocopying and recording, or in any information storage or retrieval system, without permission in writing from the publishers.

Trademark notice: Product or corporate names may be trademarks or registered trademarks, and are used only for identification and explanation without intent to infringe.

Library of Congress Cataloging-in-Publication Data
Names: Wattenberg, Melissa S., author.
Title: Present-centered group therapy for PTSD: embracing today / Melissa S. Wattenberg [and four others].
Description: New York, NY: Routledge, 2021. | Includes bibliographical references and index. | Summary: "Present-Centered Group Therapy for PTSD integrates theory, research, and practical perspectives on the manifestations of trauma, to provide an accessible, evidence-informed group treatment that validates survivors' experiences while restoring present-day focus. An alternative to exposure-based therapies, present-centered group therapy provides practitioners with a highly implementable modality through which survivors of trauma can begin to reclaim and invest in their ongoing lives. Chapters describe the treatment's background, utility, relevant research, implementation, applications, and implications. Special attention is given to the intersection of group treatment and PTSD symptoms, including the advantages and challenges of group treatment for traumatized populations, and the importance of member-driven processes and solutions in trauma recovery. Compatible with a broad range of theoretical orientations, this book offers clinicians, supervisors, mentors, and students a way to expand their clinical repertoire for effectively and flexibly addressing the impact of psychological trauma." – Provided by publisher
Identifiers: LCCN 2020048631 (print) | LCCN 2020048632 (ebook) | ISBN 9780367257439 (hardback) | ISBN 9780367338831 (paperback) | ISBN 9780429322617 (ebook)
Subjects: LCSH: Post-traumatic stress disorder--Treatment. | Group psychotherapy.
Classification: LCC RC552.P67 W38 2021 (print) | LCC RC552.P67 (ebook) | DDC 616.89/152--dc23
LC record available at https://lccn.loc.gov/2020048631
LC ebook record available at https://lccn.loc.gov/2020048632

ISBN: 978-0-367-25743-9 (hbk)
ISBN: 978-0-367-33883-1 (pbk)
ISBN: 978-0-429-32261-7 (ebk)

Typeset in Times
by MPS Limited, Dehradun

As therapists and researchers who have worked in VA settings for many years, we dedicate this book to the veterans, from whom we have learned so much. We extend appreciation to the many individuals, veterans and non-veterans, who have participated in PTSD treatment over the past decades, who have selflessly shared their insights and experiences toward the furtherance of treatments that will continue to benefit survivors of trauma.

Contents

About the Authors

Foreword Author
Matthew J. Friedman, MD, PhD, served for 24 years as executive director of the US Department of Veterans Affairs' National Center for PTSD. He stepped down in 2014 to become a senior advisor to the Center as well as founder and director of the National PTSD Brain Bank. In addition, he remains professor and vice chair for research in the Department of Psychiatry at the Geisel School of Medicine at Dartmouth. He has over 45 years of experience as a clinician and researcher, with approximately 350 publications, including 28 books. Dr. Friedman is a Distinguished Lifetime Fellow of the American Psychiatric Association, past president of the International Society for Traumatic Stress Studies, past chair of the APA's DSM-5 and DSM-5-TR PTSD Work Groups, and past chair of the Scientific Advisory Board of the Anxiety Disorders Association of America. He has served on many national research, education, and policy committees. Past honors include the ISTSS Lifetime Achievement Award in 1999 and Public Advocacy Award in 2009. He was a finalist for the 2011 Samuel J. Heyman Service to America Medal.

Author-Editors
Melissa S. Wattenberg, PhD, Dr. Wattenberg is a clinical psychologist who has worked with PTSD and persistent psychiatric conditions for over 30 years at Veterans Affairs Boston Healthcare System. She has presented and published on group therapy for PTSD. She has been program manager of the VA Boston Healthcare's Psychosocial Rehabilitation and Recovery Center (PRRC) for individuals with lived experience with serious mental health conditions (including severe and prolonged PTSD) since 2006, and collaboratively incorporated VA Boston's first peer support providers. Prior to initiating the PRRC, she developed and ran a short-term intensive program for veterans with significant mental health conditions. She has trained in a variety of evidence-based practices, including behavioral family therapy, integrated behavioral couples therapy, illness management and recovery, and motivational interviewing. She is also a tele-mental-health practitioner co-facilitating PCGT virtually for veterans with PTSD and significant lived

experience with co-occurring mental health conditions. Dr. Wattenberg was clinical supervisor of present-centered group therapy (PCGT) in VA Cooperative Study 420 across ten VA sites, and participated in development of its manual in collaboration with its originator, M. Tracie Shea, PhD. She is a primary mental health supervisor for physician assistant trainees at VA Boston as adjunct clinical professor at Mass. College of Pharmacy and Health Sciences, and is assistant professor of psychiatry at Boston University School of Medicine. She received her doctorate in clinical and cognitive psychology from the University of Illinois at Chicago. She is a focusing practitioner and trainer, and has a small private practice north of Boston.

Daniel Lee Gross, LICSW, Daniel Gross received his bachelor's degree in psychology from Cornell College in 1988, and his MSW from University of Washington in 1999. A licensed independent social worker, he has worked in various mental health settings, serving youth, older adults, and veteran clients. Mr. Gross has worked at the Veterans Affairs Puget Sound Healthcare System since 2012, where he introduced present-centered group therapy to the mental health clinic for veterans coping with significant PTSD symptoms. He currently holds the position as clinical social worker in the Intensive Outpatient Program. In his role as clinical social worker, Mr. Gross also designed and initiated Seattle VA hospital's first LGBTQ support group. He is versed in a variety of evidence-based interventions, including present-centered group therapy (PCGT) for PTSD, motivational interviewing, and cognitive processing therapy for PTSD. Mr. Gross also has a private practice and teaches as an associate professor at Seattle University's MSW Program. He has presented PCGT workshops on both a local and national level.

Barbara L. Niles, PhD, Dr. Niles is a staff research psychologist at the Behavioral Sciences Division of the National Center for PTSD at Veterans Affairs Boston Healthcare System, and an assistant professor of psychiatry at the Boston University School of Medicine. She has extensive experience providing treatment to veterans with PTSD as well as investigating the impact of psychotherapy and health enhancement for these veterans. Dr. Niles is well versed in state-of-the-art methods of assessment and current best practices for carrying out clinical trials to address PTSD. She has been a member and supervisor in the VA Boston PTSD Clinic Treatment Team for over 25 years and has served as PI or Co-PI on several randomized trials of interventions for veterans with PTSD. She has worked closely with the developers of present-centered group therapy (PCGT), served as a clinician on two trials of this treatment, and has led several workshops at national conferences. Dr. Niles received her doctorate in clinical psychology from Rutgers, the State University of New Jersey.

William S. Unger, PhD, Dr. Unger has worked as a clinical psychologist at the Providence Veterans Administration Medical Center for 31 years. He served as the clinical director of the PTSD Program for six years and as the chief of the PTSD Program for 15 years. Dr. Unger was selected as a VA regional PTSD Program Mentor to other VA program leaders to assist with the management of administration, program development, and treatment. Dr. Unger currently serves as the Evidence-based Psychotherapy Coordinator for the Providence VA Medical Center and as a VA national training consultant for cognitive behavioral conjoint therapy for PTSD. He works in the Trauma Recovery Service at the Providence VA Medical Center. He is an associate clinical professor in the Department of Psychiatry and Human Behavior at Brown University. Dr. Unger has extensive experience conducting clinical trials through involvement with multiple VA Cooperative Studies, including the VA Cooperative Study that examined the efficacy of trauma-focused group therapy for PTSD compared with present-centered group therapy (PCGT). During the past ten years, he has been involved in the development of peer-to-peer services for veterans in the PTSD program at the Providence VA Medical Center. He has been offering PCGT to veterans in both inpatient and outpatient settings via face-to-face and telehealth formats. Dr. Unger completed his doctorate in clinical psychology at State University of New York at Binghamton, and his masters in experimental psychology from Villanova University.

M. Tracie Shea, PhD, Dr. Shea is a staff psychologist in the Trauma Recovery Clinic, director of PTSD Research at the Providence Veterans Administration Medical Center, and professor in the Department of Psychiatry and Human Behavior at Brown University. In addition to 30 years of clinical work with veterans, she has extensive experience in conducting multi-site clinical trials, including investigations of the efficacy of trauma-based therapies for veterans with PTSD. Dr. Shea, together with Dr. Wattenberg and Dr. Dolan, developed the present-centered group therapy (PCGT) model and manual for use as a nonspecific therapy control for examining the effectiveness of trauma-focused group therapy in VA Cooperative Studies Program (CSP)-420, the largest randomly controlled trial of group treatment for PTSD. As a training site PI, she oversaw therapist training and supervision in PCGT at ten participating sites. Dr. Shea also developed and oversaw training and supervision of an individual therapy version of present-centered therapy (PCT) for CSP-494, a subsequent multisite VA CSP study. Dr. Shea was formerly at the National Institute of Mental Health, where she was chief of the Personality Disorders Program, and associate coordinator of the NIMH Treatment of Depression Collaborative Research Program. She was a member of the work group on personality disorders for DSM-IV; has served on numerous advisory and monitoring boards; and on review committees for NIMH,

DOD, and VA. Her recent research includes two VA merit-funded randomized clinical trials (RCTs) testing the effectiveness of treatments for veterans. These include an RCT testing the efficacy of a cognitive behavioral intervention for the treatment of anger problems in veterans returning from Iraq and Afghanistan, and an RCT comparing interpersonal therapy and prolonged exposure for treatment of PTSD in veterans. She has also received funding from the National Institute of Mental Health and the Department of Defense and has approximately 180 peer-reviewed publications. Dr. Shea received her PhD in psychology from Catholic University.

Authors on Specific Chapters
Scott D. Litwack, PhD, Dr. Litwack is the director of the PTSD Clinical Team at the Jamaica Plain VA Medical Center of the Veterans Administration Boston Healthcare System, and is an assistant professor of psychiatry at the Boston University School of Medicine. Dr. Litwack has had extensive training in a number of evidence-based practices for PTSD, including achieving VA certification status for cognitive processing therapy, prolonged exposure, and motivational interviewing. Over the past decade he has been a project coordinator, clinician, and supervisor in multiple randomized clinical trials comparing present-centered therapy to other evidence-based treatments for PTSD and related disorders. He received his doctorate from University of Connecticut.

Regina Dolan-Sewell, PhD, Following her work on the Treatment of Depression Collaborative Research Program at the National Institute of Mental Health, Dr. Dolan Sewell's research career continued at Brown University on the research faculty in the Department of Psychiatry. There she contributed to the Collaborative Longitudinal Study of Personality Disorders as well as a number of other longitudinal studies in mood and anxiety disorders. Dr. Dolan-Sewell also served as director of the Mood, Anxiety, Eating and Sleep Disorders Program in the Division of AIDS and Treatment Development at the NIMH and was the NIMH-wide coordinator for both the Sleep Disorders Research and Eating Disorders Research portfolios. At the NIMH, Dr. Dolan-Sewell received Director's Leadership and Merit awards. The Academy for Eating Disorders Research awarded Dr. Dolan-Sewell the Power of Action Award and twice awarded her special recognition for contribution to research. Dr. Dolan-Sewell is currently a volunteer for the Virginia Medical Reserve Corps with the Virginia Department of Health and serves on the board of Rush Homes. She graduated from the University of Virginia with a degree in psychology and completed her PhD at the Catholic University of America.

Daniel H. Grossman, BS, Daniel Grossman is a research assistant working under Dr. Barbara Niles at the Behavioral Science Division of the National Center for PTSD, VA Boston Healthcare System. Prior to this position, Mr. Grossman conducted research at Tel Aviv University and Yale School of Medicine. His work in psychology and neuroscience has spanned several research topics, including neural markers of decision-making processes, the impact of mindfulness training on stress-related symptoms of chronic liver disease, and most recently, a clinical trial of Tai Chi for Gulf War veterans with multi-symptom illness. He holds a BS in neuroscience from Union College in Schenectady, NY.

Foreword

Matthew J. Friedman

In the early 1990s the Department of Veterans Affairs (VA) Cooperative Studies Program (CSP) directed the National Center for PTSD to conduct a multi-site, randomized clinical trial (RCT) of the best treatment for PTSD. It was CSP's first RCT (CSP-420) on PTSD treatment. At the time we really didn't know what that treatment might be. A recently published meta-analysis (Solomon, Gerrity, & Muff, 1992) had shown that among the few rigorous studies that had been published up to that time, psychotherapy produced better results than pharmacotherapy, and treatments utilizing direct therapeutic exposure seemed to have the best outcomes. It should also be noted that, at that time, there were still great misgivings about the safety of exposure therapies because of concerns that they might precipitate relapse through therapy-induced exacerbation of PTSD symptoms.

Paula Schnurr and I convened a meeting of the top PTSD treatment experts in VA who concluded that group, rather than individual, therapy, would be best. We all believed that in addition to promoting recovery through psychoeducation, cognitive restructuring, a developmental perspective, relapse prevention, and coping skills training, the cohesion and safety of the group would buffer veterans against any potential toxic side effects of exposure therapy (Schnurr, Friedman, Lavori, & Hsieh, 2001).

Since the presumed therapeutic ingredient in our experimental treatment, trauma-focused group therapy (TFGT), was to focus on details of the traumatic event through exposure and cognitive restructuring, we needed a strong comparison treatment in which processing of traumatic material is actively prevented while the focus is kept on here-and-now problems that have resulted from PTSD symptoms. We also needed a treatment that would control for the "nonspecific" effects that all group therapies have in common. These include: therapist contact, a supportive milieu, group cohesion, instillation of hope, and expectation of improvement (Yalom, 1995).

At that time, Edna Foa and Patricia Resick were beginning to publish and present their positive findings with prolonged exposure and cognitive processing therapy, respectively, showing the efficacy of trauma-focused treatment for PTSD. Therefore, we knew that in order to rigorously test the effectiveness of TFGT, present-centered group therapy (PCGT) had to be a very strong comparison treatment that would embody the best elements of non-trauma-focused supportive group therapies. In addition, PCGT had to be a credible treatment that therapists believed would be an effective treatment for PTSD.

Recognizing that we needed a strong, credible manualized PCGT treatment, everyone we asked said that we would be lucky if we could convince Tracie Shea to design and manualize PCGT. Tracie had played a major role in the National Institute of Mental Health's large multisite Treatment of Depression Collaborative Research Program (Elkin et al., 1989) that had randomized almost 250 patients to either psychotherapy, medication or placebo conditions. We were thrilled when Tracie said "yes." She quickly recruited Melissa Wattenberg and they have remained a creative, durable, and effective team for 25 years. Since the epicenter of this activity was at the Providence VA Medical Center, where Bill Unger was director of all PTSD programs, he became site director and therapist at the Providence VA, one of the ten sites included in CSP-420. Barbara Niles was also a PCGT therapist in the study and Dan Gross joined this group of PCGT experts some years later.

In order to control for therapist bias, we randomized all study therapists to deliver either TFGT or PCGT. In other words, some therapists who strongly believed that trauma-focused treatments were better, found themselves assigned to provide PCGT. After they started treating veterans, skeptical (pro-TFGT) therapists assigned to deliver PCGT came to not only believe in its efficacy but to also to believe that they might have better therapeutic outcomes than their colleagues who were providing TFGT. As it turned out, both treatments were associated with modest improvements and neither was significantly better than the other.

Some years later, Paula and I called upon this same group to convert the PCGT manual from group to individual present-centered therapy (PCT) for our 15-site RCT (CSP-494) of prolonged exposure versus PCT (Schnurr, Friedman, Engel, Foa, Shea, et al., 2007). In this study of individual psychotherapy, PCT competed directly with PE, one of the most effective CBT treatments for PTSD. Although PE produced significantly better outcomes, it was a real horse race and PCT did quite well. Indeed, among those who received PCT (based on intent-to-treat analysis), 58.7% had significant clinical improvement, 20% no longer met criteria for PTSD, and 7% had a complete clinical remission (Schnurr et al., 2007).

These results with PCT were much better than clinical outcomes with conventional psychotherapy for PTSD. More importantly, they raised the fundamental question of whether there were effective psychotherapies for PTSD that *did not* include a trauma-focused component. Earlier studies with stress inoculation therapy suggested that this might be the case (Foa et al., 1999).

Approximately ten years later, while participating in the 2017 revision of the clinical practice guideline for PTSD jointly sponsored by the Department of Veterans Affairs and Department of Defense (VA/DoD0), I was frankly surprised to discover how well PGCT had performed in a number of studies (that are thoughtfully reviewed in chapter two of this book). As both group and individual therapy, PGCT/PCT had also done well in other studies, replicating our CSP-494 results, reported above. In other words, although PGCT and PCT had been employed as the comparison therapy in every single RCT testing a variety of index treatments, it had performed quite well with regard to clinical improvement, loss of diagnosis and complete remission. As a result, the latest VA/DoD clinical practice guideline (VA/DoD, 2017) recommends PCT as an evidence-based treatment for PTSD. It should be noted that the recommendation for trauma-focused treatments is "strong" whereas that for PCT is "weak," but the bar is set pretty high for any treatment to receive even a "weak" recommendation in the VA/DoD guideline. Given that there are many fewer trials of PGCT/PCT than of PE, CPT, and other trauma-focused treatments, and given that PGCT/PCT has always been the comparison, rather than the index, treatment in these RCTS, I agree strongly with the authors that the time has come to recognize PGCT/PCT as a treatment, in its own right, and that future research should test the efficacy of PGCT/PCT as the index, rather than as the comparison treatment.

It is also important to keep in mind that all participants in all RCTs with trauma-focused treatments gave informed consent to receive that treatment. We don't really know how many PTSD patients declined to do so because they didn't want to be randomized to a treatment in which they would have to focus intensely on their traumatic memories. Nor do we know how many of those who declined a trauma-focused therapy would have consented to receive a non-trauma-focused treatment such as PGCT/PCT.

Indeed, treatment preference is a very important factor that clinicians need to consider. There is emerging evidence that patients have better outcomes when they receive their preferred treatment, whether it is psychotherapy or pharmacotherapy (Zoellner, Roy-Byrne, Mavissakalian, & Feeny, 2018). In my own experience, some treatment-seeking patients would much rather focus on here-and-now PTSD-related problems instead of revisiting the traumatic material that dominates their conscious thoughts during the day and nightmares when they are asleep. Clinically, it would be of great value to know how well patients can be expected to benefit from PGCT/PCT when they strongly prefer such treatment to a trauma-focused approach.

Another major benefit of PGCT/PCT is that dropout rates are considerably lower than with trauma-focused treatments. So, even if we accept the VA/DoD guideline's conclusion that trauma-focused treatments are more efficacious than PGCT/PCT, a major trade-off for a clinician to consider is the relative utility of assignment to a stronger treatment with higher dropouts versus assignment to an effective, but less efficacious, treatment such as PCGT/PCT with fewer dropouts. A related question is the potential benefit of reassigning trauma-focused dropouts to PGCT/PCT.

There are also some very interesting clinical and theoretical issues to consider with regard to treatment matching and mechanism of action, respectively. Right now, we don't have very much information to guide optimal treatment assignment. Besides patient preference, there is very little data to help us identify the round pegs for the round peg therapeutic options versus the square pegs for square peg treatments. We have argued elsewhere that, given the heterogeneity of PTSD, as we identify future types, subtypes, phenotypes, and endophenotypes of posttraumatic psychopathology (Friedman, 2016; Friedman, Schnurr & Keane, in press), we will discover that the best treatment for one type may not be optimal for others. For example, we already know that the best trauma-focused treatments for patients with PTSD's dissociative subtype are not the best for non-dissociative-type PTSD patients (Lanius et al., 2013). In short, it is entirely possible that non-trauma-focused therapy will prove to be the treatment of choice for some posttraumatic syndromes while trauma-focused treatment (or pharmacotherapy) are best for others.

These speculations also suggest that the mechanism of action for PGCT/PCT may differ greatly from that for trauma-focused treatments (and from different types of pharmacotherapy). Using brain imaging, as an example (although the same arguments can be made with psychological indices or biomarkers), a few studies have shown that alterations in neurocircuitry activity and neuronal connectivity are associated with improvement with trauma-focused psychotherapy (Fonzo et al., 2017; Zantvoord, Diehle, & Lindauer, 2013). It would be of great interest to find out whether non-trauma-focused psychotherapy (or pharmacotherapy) works through the same or different mechanisms. Such research would not only help us understand how PGCT/PCT achieves positive therapeutic outcomes but would also advance our fundamental understanding of post-traumatic psychopathology itself. For example, concurrent benzodiazepine use suppressed the efficacy of PCT, whereas it did not reduce the effectiveness of PE (Rosen, et al., 2013). This may indicate that PE is a more potent treatment with an efficacy that cannot be blunted by benzodiazepines, although an alternative explanation is that PCT is mediated by a distinct benzodiazepine-sensitive pathway in contrast to PE, which is mediated by an entirely different mechanism of action.

As a godparent who was present at the births of both PGCT and her little sister, PCT, it is very exciting to see that non-trauma-focused treatments are finally being considered as index, rather than comparison, treatments for PTSD. I commend the authors of this book and of the PGCT manual for persevering with this important work. At a time when trauma-focused therapy has commanded the lion's share of PTSD treatment research, it is extremely important to consider alternate treatment approaches, especially in view of the heterogeneity of PTSD, variation in patient preference, low dropout rates, and optimal treatment matching. Finally, learning more about PGCT/PCT's mechanism of action will enable us to learn much more about the etiology of PTSD, itself.

Preface

Present-Centered Group Therapy for PTSD: Embracing Today was written to offer a flexible, present-oriented, evidence-based treatment for survivors of trauma. A number of factors have suggested a growing need for, and receptiveness to, this modality. Among these factors are:

- A distinctly thoughtful and generative period[1] in PTSD research and theory (as reflected on in the foreword), that has resulted in not only questioning and debate regarding the pre-eminent role of trauma-focused approaches (Steenkamp et al., 2020a; Litz et al., 2019; Hoge et al., 2018; Niles et al., 2018; Najavits, 2015; Schnurr et al. response to Steenkamp et al., 2020, and Steenkamp et al. (2020b) reply), but also a call for individualized, collaborative, and tailored approaches to treating the sequelae of trauma. While there are differences, there is agreement that there is not a "one-size-fits-all" treatment for PTSD. This discourse is consonant with a general call for broader and more nuanced approaches to psychotherapy research and evidence-based practice (Wachtel, 2010).
- As noted in chapter eight, DSM-5's (American Psychiatric Association, 2013) expansion of disorders related to trauma
- Acknowledgment of a potential role of trauma in previously non-trauma-identified disorders, at least as an exacerbating factor (see chapter eight)
- Clinician interest and requests over the years (personal communications with authors)
- Responses from presentations to national conferences (especially American Group Psychotherapy Association (AGPA) over the past 18 years)
- The publisher's inquiry leading to this publication, in response to a PCGT workshop offering at American Group Psychotherapy Association (AGPA)
- Developing evidence for this therapy from the mid-1990s through 2020 (as delineated in chapters one and two)

The Authors

Present-centered group therapy (PCGT) brought this team of authors together. We have among us researchers, clinical consultants, clinical administrators, trainers, teachers, and practitioners, each uniquely connected to PCGT. We owe much to a number of marvelous connectors: our colleagues and projects and organizations that support work in the field. We have acknowledged many of them at the beginning of this book, and apologize if there are any we have left out inadvertently.

Several of the authors were connected at the outset through the Veterans Health Administration's National Center for PTSD, in Cooperative Study Program 420 (CSP-420), a groundbreaking ten-site randomly controlled trial of PTSD treatment for Vietnam veterans with longstanding PTSD (Schnurr et al., 2003; detailed in chapter one). Others of us connected through the American Group Psychotherapy Association (AGPA), including during the period of training of practitioners in the days after the 9/11 attack on New York's World Trade Towers, and in the years afterward.

Our five major authors are trauma treatment providers and trainers. Geographically we span the country, hailing from three VA sites (two in New England, one on the West Coast). Three of our authors are currently providing PCGT virtually during the COVID-19 pandemic (described in chapter eight). In creating this book, we have drawn on our varied clinical backgrounds, and our range of theoretical orientations (from behavioral to cognitive-behavioral to analytic to person-centered to psychosocial rehabilitation). We have common ground in our interest in this treatment for PTSD, and in our wish to make it understandable and accessible for practitioners and trainers. Ultimately, we would like survivors of trauma to have PCGT among their options when they make choices about their treatment.

Context of This Time in the Field

A confluence in a number of forces in the field make this treatment particularly relevant:

- There is ongoing work in fields from brain science to psychotherapy to social justice regarding the impact and meaning of human suffering, and how to treat it across cultural contexts, across the many challenges of making things better for the survivors. This work calls for meeting people and cultures where they are, individualizing interventions, inclusion, and support for diverse communities (e.g., *Black Advocacy, Resistance & Empowerment for Mental Health and Wellness* website for trainings, articles and other resources (Graham-LoPresti & Abdullah-Swain, 2020; https://www.baremhw.com/)).

- The Recovery Movement in mental health (Resnick 2005, 2019; Smith et al., 2016), and the psychosocial rehabilitation approach for "lived experience" with potentially disabling psychiatric diagnoses (Anthony, 1993; Gagne, White, & Anthony, 2007) have been increasingly accepted by medical and treatment institutions, from departments of mental health to major hospital systems, and have been widely implemented. These approaches are strengths-based, focused on functional goals, empowerment, and community involvement, aimed at countering stigma and fostering inclusion.
- In synchrony with the recovery movement and psychosocial rehabilitation, person-centered care and whole health approaches are moving the needle toward broader and more personalized care. Each of these movements contributes to shifting the traditional medical model toward flexibility and inclusivity in two major ways:

  - Through an array of additional treatment options understood collectively as "complementary and integrative medicine," which includes interventions such as acupuncture, chiropractic treatment, massage therapy, as well as practices such as yoga, Tai Chi, mindfulness, and meditation
  - Through identifying the person served as the center of treatment decisions, in a collaborative approach that:
    - Emphasizes personal choice
    - Acknowledges the whole person
    - Incorporates functional and health goals across many domains of human experience.

Most major medical centers have mind-body medicine approaches to pain management. And the Veterans Health Administration (VHA), through its national Office of Patient Centered Care and Cultural Transformation, has implemented a Whole Health Initiative[2] promoting yoga, Tai Chi, and health behavior counseling across primary care and mental health services.

These movements and programs, while their details are beyond the scope of this book, have had and are having significant influence that will take the field beyond this moment (and likely into the next edition of this book). Present-Centered Group Therapy for PTSD: Embracing Today is consonant with these movements and the philosophies behind them. PCGT's flexibility, opportunity for expression, and practice of both self-determination and collaboration allows individuals to identify and pursue a broad array of goals driven by personal choice.

Updates in the PCGT Manual Since the Original Manual Was Developed

While this may be the reader's first exposure to the PCGT manual (chapters three through five), it is important to state that, given the evidence for PCGT, the targeted revisions in this book were made with an eye to preserving the structures and processes on which that evidence is based. While revising aspects of the PCGT manual to acknowledge developments in the field, the authors have been consistent concerning PCGT's essential therapeutic elements. The updates include the following:

*   Recovery Language and Attitude: While the original manual was created with Yalom's (1995) therapeutic factors in mind, and was largely consistent with a humanistic perspective, the field has become even more egalitarian in terms of recovery language, empowerment, and inclusivity. Some of the language, and perspective concerning the survivors of trauma who are in treatment, have been honed to reflect the respect and acceptance needed to deliver this treatment effectively and collaboratively.
*   Diagnostic Criteria: The Diagnostic and Statistical Manual (DSM-5, American Psychiatric Association [APA], 2013) has significantly refashioned the diagnosis of PTSD. Specifically relevant to the PCGT manual are: the articulation of PTSD-related feelings and actions that were recognized previously in treatment but not explicitly stated in the prior diagnostic manual; and the separation of avoidance and numbing as distinct criteria. Accordingly, in the updated manual and related chapters:
    *   Some of the "secondary features" of PTSD identified in the original manual (which were included additionally because DSM-IV (APA, 1994) did not include them) are now listed as primary symptoms of PTSD.
    *   Our references to PTSD symptoms and diagnostic criteria have been updated to reflect the current (DSM-5) criteria. Currently, Avoidance, Criterion C, "Persistent avoidance of stimuli associated with the traumatic event(s)" (page 271), is listed separately from numbing. Meanwhile, the quality of 'numbing' formerly included DSM-IV's Criterion C ("...numbing of general responsiveness") is now included in DSM-5's Criterion D, "Negative alterations in cognition and mood" (pages 271–272), and is described as the symptom of "Persistent inability to experience positive emotions" (page 272). This shift in diagnostic criteria does not substantially change the treatment itself, and is represented in chapter six when discussing potential mechanisms behind PCGT and interventions.

- Developing Concepts in the Field: Concepts such as post-traumatic growth (Tedeschi & Calhoun, 2004) and moral injury (Litz et al., 2009, Griffin et al. 2019), developed further during the period since the original manual was created, and are incorporated or referenced where relevant in the manual. Both are considered important concepts on which facilitators may draw to understand the dynamics within their groups.
- New Evidence-Based Present-Centered Approaches: New treatments have become prominent in the field, whether developed for PTSD or adapted to serve a traumatized population. Most can be delivered in a group or individual format. Their formats are distinct from each other, and even more distinct from PCGT (in the extent to which PCGT enlists the group process, utilizing a less structured format). These therapies include: seeking safety for dual diagnosis of PTSD and substance dependence (Najavits, 2002); acceptance and commitment therapy (Walser & Westrup, 2007; Hayes et al., 2012; Hayes et al., 2013); dialectical behavioral therapy (Linehan, 2014) for borderline personality disorder, adapted for complex PTSD (Bohus et al., 2019); and cognitive processing therapy in some of its forms that may omit a trauma statement (Resick, Fontana, Lehman, & Rosenheck, 2015). Motivational interviewing (MI; Miller & Rollnick, 2014) has been included in the section on motivation in chapter five. This modality has been referenced by a variety of therapies as an approach to enhancing potential for behavior change. In the context of this book and the included manual, MI offers certain general tools compatible with PCGT (such as reflective listening, use of metaphor, and shifting emphasis toward potential rather than limitations).
- Conceptualizations of Trauma Treatment: In order to enhance the provider's understanding of trauma and recovery, especially as related to PCGT, some additional theory relevant to practice of PCGT is offered in chapter six.

Summary

How to Use This Book

This book is designed for flexible use across a variety of clinical, recovery, academic, and public health settings. Key uses are for trauma therapists across a variety of contexts. The book may be used as a guide in training and educational settings, including clinical supervision classes, practica, and internships. It may also be used in clinical research settings. The manual guide in chapters three through five covers the structure and interventions. The education provided in these chapters can be considered a unit in terms of implementation and delivery of services. Chapters one and two provide the practitioner or supervisor with the research background relevant to

PCGT, while chapters six and seven introduce PCGT's context through theoretical considerations and history. Chapter eight broadens the arena through suggestions and brief "how-to" on potential applications of PCGT in clinics, agencies, Department of Defense, first-responder and post-disaster response contexts, forensic settings, private practice, telehealth, and with diverse or heterogeneous populations.

Secondarily but importantly, this book is offered within a trauma field that is moving increasingly toward researching and implementing staging of treatment, and individualizing selection of treatment according to both choice of the client, and identification of indicators for a particular approach or set of approaches (Hoge, 2018; Litz, 2019; Steenkamp, 2020). The unique particulars of the development of PCGT, its growing evidence base (covered in chapters one and two), and its foundation in the "common factors" of group psychotherapy blended with trauma awareness and trauma education, may have implications for addressing the needs of survivors of trauma in an increasingly nuanced and articulated manner. In this sense, Present-Centered Group Therapy for PTSD: Embracing Today may be of interest not only to trauma research institutes, but also public health organizations, professional organizations, and academic settings.

Finally, this book is offered to underscore the needs and the right of survivors of trauma to have and to personally navigate a life in the present, and to be connected and present within that life.

Notes

1 It would be painting with too broad a brush to see this discourse as the ancient dialectic of "covering" vs "uncovering" described in chapter seven. There are now very few who would deny the importance of traumatic experience and the right of survivors to share their stories and create a personal narrative of healing for themselves and their culture. Nevertheless, the current field appears to be shifting toward an understanding in which these approaches are not in opposition to one another, and, as Dr. Friedman points out in the foreword, may instead serve in the interest of "optimal treatment matching." There is a sense of something not-yet-formed in the discourse in this literature, as though the field is reaching toward new definition. While Thomas Kuhn (1970) cautioned against social sciences adopting his ideas of paradigm competition (as he saw social sciences as inveterately pre-paradigmatic), we may be seeing at least the "shadow" of such a process. Or it may be that we are simply seeing exponential growth in this still relatively new field of trauma, in which the rapidly developing area of brain science (Friedman and Pitman, 2007) and the substantial field of trauma treatment research are leading into a period of recalibration and a shift in ideas and methodology. In any case, in

light of the broadening and tailoring trends in this field, we see an opportunity for present-centered group therapy to more fully "take a seat at the table," as both an available treatment, and a subject for additional inquiry regarding mechanisms of healing and recovery from trauma.

2 https://www.va.gov/wholehealth

References

American Group Psychotherapy Association. (n.d.). *American Group Psychotherapy Association*. Retrieved August 28, 2020, from https://www.agpa.org/

American Psychiatric Association. (1994). *Diagnostic and statistical manual of mental disorders* (4th ed.). Washington, D.C.: Author.

American Psychiatric Association. (2013). *Diagnostic and statistical manual of mental disorders* (5th ed.). Washington, D.C.: Author.

Anthony, W. A. (1993). Recovery from mental illness: The guiding vision of the mental health service system in the 1990s. *Psychosocial Rehabilitation Journal*, *16*(4), 11–23. https://doi.org/10.1037/h0095655

Bohus, M., Schmahl, C., Fydrich, T., Steil, R., Müller-Engelmann, M., Herzog, J., & Priebe, K. (2019). A research programme to evaluate DBT-PTSD, a modular treatment approach for complex PTSD after childhood abuse. *Borderline Personality Disorder and Emotion Dysregulation*, *6*(1), 1–16. https://doi.org/10.1186/s40479-019-0099-y

Department of Veterans' Affairs. (2013). *Whole health*. Retrieved August 28, 2020, from https://www.va.gov/wholehealth/

Elkin, I., Shea, M. T., Watkins, J. T., Imber, S. D., Sotsky, S. M., & Collins, J. F. (1989). NIMH treatment of depression collaborative research program: General effectiveness of treatments. *Archives of General Psychiatry*, *46*, 971–982.

Foa, E. B., Dancu, C. V., Hembree, E. A., Jaycox, L. H., & Meadows, E. A. (1999). A comparison of exposure therapy, stress inoculation training, and their combination for reducing posttraumatic stress disorder in female assault victims. *Journal of Consulting and Clinical Psychology*, *67*, 194–200.

Fonzo, G. A., Goodkind, M. S., Oathes, D. J., Zaiko, Y. V., Harvey, M., and Peng, K. K. (2017). PTSD psychotherapy outcome predicted by brain activation during emotional reactivity and regulation. *American Journal of Psychiatry*, *174*, 1163–1174.

Friedman, M. J. (2016). Deconstructing PTSD. In E. J. Bromet (Ed.) In: Long term outcomes in psychopathology research: Rethinking the scientific agenda (pp. 123–139). Oxford: Oxford University Press.

Friedman, M. J., & Pitman, R. K. (2007). New findings on the neurobiology of posttraumatic stress disorder. *Journal of Traumatic Stress*, *20*(5), 653. https://doi.org/10.1002/jts.20299

Friedman, M. J., Schnurr, P. P. & Keane, T. M. (in press). Key questions and an agenda for future research. In, M. J. Friedman, T. M. Keane & P. P. Schnurr (Eds.), Handbook of PTSD: Science and practice, (3rd ed.). New York, NY: Guilford Publications.

Gagne, C., White, W., & Anthony, W. A. (2007). Recovery: A common vision for the fields of mental health and addictions. *Psychiatric Rehabilitation Journal, 31*(1), 32–37. doi.org/10.2975/31.1.2007.32.3

Griffin, B. J., Purcell, N., Burkman, K., Litz, B. T., Bryan, C. J., Schmitz, M., Villierme, C., Walsh, J., & Maguen, S. (2019). Moral injury: An integrative review. *Journal of Traumatic Stress, 32*, 350–362.

Graham-LoPresti, J., & Abdullah-Swain, T. (2020). *Black advocacy, resistance and empowerment for mental health and wellness.* Retrieved August 28, 2020, from https://www.baremhw.com/

Hayes, S. C., Levin, M. E., Plumb-Vilardaga, J., Villatte, J. L., & Pistorello, J. (2013). Acceptance and commitment therapy and contextual behavioral science: examining the progress of a distinctive model of behavioral and cognitive therapy. *Behavior Therapy, 42*(2), 180–198.

Hoge, C. W., & Chard, K. M. (2018). A window into the evolution of trauma-focused psychotherapies for posttraumatic stress disorder. *JAMA, 319*(4), 343–345. https://doi.org/10.1001/jama.2017.21880

Kuhn, T. S. (1970). *The structure of scientific revolutions.* Chicago, IL: The University of Chicago Press.

Lanius, R. A., Vermetten, E., Loewenstein, R. J., Brand, B., Schmahl, C., Bremner, J. D., & Spiegel, D. (2010). Emotion modulation in PTSD: Clinical and neurobiological evidence for a dissociative subtype. *American Journal of Psychiatry, 167*, 640–647.

Linehan, M. (2014). *DBT Skills training manual.* New York, NY: Guilford Publications.

Litz, B. T., Stein N., Delaney, E., Lebowitz, L., Nash, W. P., Silva, C., & Maguen, S. 2009. Moral injury and moral repair in war veterans: a preliminary model and intervention strategy. *Clinical Psychology Review, 29*(8), 695–706.

Litz, B. T., Berke, D. S., Kline, N. K., Grimm, K., Rusowicz-Orazem, L., Resick, P. A., ... Peterson, A. L. (2019). Patterns and predictors of change in trauma-focused treatments for war-related posttraumatic stress disorder. *Journal of Consulting and Clinical Psychology, 87*(11), 1019–1029. https://doi.org/10.1037/ccp0000426

Miller, W. R., & Rollnick, S. (2012). *Motivational interviewing: Helping people change.* New York, NY: Guilford Publications.

Najavits, L. (2002). *Seeking safety: A treatment manual for PTSD and substance abuse.* New York, NY: Guilford Publications.

Najavits, L. M. (2015). The problem of dropout from "gold standard" PTSD therapies. *F1000prime Reports, 7*, 43–43. https://doi.org/10.12703/P7-43

Neisser, U. (1976). *Cognition and reality: Principles and implications of cognitive psychology.* New York, NY: W H Freeman/Times Books/Henry Holt & Co.

Niles, B. L., Polizzi, C. P., Voelkel, E., Weinstein, E. S., Smidt, K., & Fisher, L. M. (2018). Initiation, dropout, and outcome from evidence-based psychotherapies in a VA PTSD outpatient clinic. *Psychological Services, 15*(4), 496–502. doi:10.1037/ser0000175

Resnick, S. G., Fontana, A., Lehman, A. F., & Rosenheck, R. A. (2005). An empirical conceptualization of the recovery orientation. *Schizophrenia Research, 75*(1), 119–128.

Resnick, S. G., & Goldberg, R. W. (2019). Psychiatric rehabilitation for veterans and the evolution of the field. *Psychiatric Rehabilitation Journal, 42*(3), 207.

Rosen, C. S., Greenbaum, M. A., Schnurr, P. P., Holmes, T. H., Brennan, P. L. & Friedman, M. J. (2013). Do benzodiazepines reduce the effectiveness of exposure therapy for posttraumatic stress disorder? *Journal of Clinical Psychiatry*, *74*, 1241–1248.

Schnurr, P. P., Friedman, M. J., Lavori, P. W. & Hsieh, F. Y. (2001). Design of Department of Veterans affairs cooperative study No. 420: Group treatment of posttraumatic stress disorder. *Controlled Clinical Trials*, *22*, 74–88.

Schnurr, P. P., Friedman, M. J., Engel, C. C., Foa, E. B., Shea, M. T., & Chow, B. K. (2007). Cognitive behavioral therapy for posttraumatic stress disorder in women: A randomized controlled trial. *Journal of the American Medical Association, 297*(8), 820–830.

Schnurr, P. P., Norman, S. B., & Hamblen, J. L. (July 2020). PTSD treatments for veterans (comment and response). *Journal of the American Medical Association, 324*(3), 301.

Solomon, S. D., Gerrity, E. T. & Muff, A. M. (1992). Efficacy of treatments for posttraumatic stress disorder. *JAMA, 268* (5), 633–638.

Steenkamp, M. M., Litz, B. T., & Marmar, C. R. (Jan. 2020a). First-line psychotherapies for military-related PTSD. *JAMA.* Insights: Update, https://doi.org/10.1001/jama.2019.20825

Steenkamp, M. M., Litz, B. T., & Marmar, C. R. (2020b). (Comment and Response, Reply). *Journal of the American Medical Association, 324*(3), 301–302.

Tedeschi, R. G., & Calhoun, L. G. (2004). Posttraumatic growth: Conceptual foundations and empirical evidence. *Psychological Inquiry, 15*(1), 1–18.

US Department of Veterans Affairs. (2017). VA/DOD Clinical Practice Guideline for the Management of Posttraumatic Stress Disorder and Acute Stress Disorder. VA/DOD Website. Retrieved from: https://www.healthquality.va.gov/

Wachtel, P. L. (2010). Beyond "ESTs": Problematic assumptions in the pursuit of evidence-based practice. *Psychoanalytic Psychology*, *27*(3), 251–272. https://doi.org/10.1037/a0020532

Walser, R. D., & Westrup, D. (2007). *Acceptance and commitment therapy for the treatment of post-traumatic stress disorder and trauma-related problems: A practitioner's guide to using mindfulness and acceptance strategies.* (foreword by S. Hayes). Oakland, CA: New Harbinger Publications.

Yalom, I. D. (1995). *The theory and practice of group psychotherapy.* New York, NY: Basic Books.

Zantvoord, J. B., Diehle, J. & Lindauer, R. J. L. (2013). Using neurobiological measures to predict and assess treatment outcome of psychotherapy in posttraumatic stress disorder: Systematic review. *Psychotherapy and Psychosomatics*, *82*, 142–151.

Zoellner, L. A., Roy-Byrne, P. P., Mavissakalian, M. & Feeny, N.C. (2018). Doubly randomized preference trial of prolonged exposure versus sertraline for treatment of PTSD. *American Journal of Psychiatry*, *176*, 287–296. doi:10.1176/appi.ajp.2018.17090995

Acknowledgments

The authors would like to extend thanks and appreciation to the following organizations that create a solid foundation for sharing of ideas and connection:

- The National Center for PTSD within the Veterans Administration's Healthcare System has been a force since its inception for acknowledging the impact of human suffering, and supporting research, assessment, and treatment to better the lives of trauma survivors. Among the many contributions of the National Center, Cooperative Study Program 420 in the late 1990s brought together many of this book's authors in a highly collegial and ambitious study on group therapy for longstanding PTSD in Vietnam veterans. There have been many studies since that time that built on the example of this seminal project. The National Center continues to be a beacon shedding light not only on combat trauma, but military sexual trauma, and the many other forms of trauma to which veterans may be subject. Many of these sources of trauma are shared by nonveterans, for whom the National Center's work provides important information on recovery from trauma.
- The American Group Psychotherapy Association (AGPA) has long been a purveyor of training, advancement, and professional support for group therapy practitioners, and was a point of contact for dissemination of many group treatments for trauma (including PCGT) following the 9/11 attack on the World Trade Towers in New York in 2001. Many of this book's authors have presented on group therapy for PTSD within this organization, which offers group practitioners a professional home and a network of connections.
- The International Society for Traumatic Stress Studies (ISTSS) has been an organization that helped put trauma on the map before it was widely accepted. ISTSS has also been a professional home for many of our authors, and a far-ranging resource on research and practice that advances an understanding of and response to trauma.

We wish also to extend thanks and appreciation to these valued colleagues who have been an inspiration for us and have been a force for present-centered group therapy, PTSD treatment, or both:

- David W. Foy, PhD, professor emeritus of psychology, Graduate School of Education and Psychology, Pepperdine University, was member of the CSP-420 Executive Committee who played a key role in recruiting Dr. Wattenberg for her role in this study. He is the author of many professional publications on PTSD, and has been involved in research and training of graduate students at a variety of educational institutions. He was instrumental in creating a link between several of us from the CSP-420 team and the post-9/11 dissemination of group treatments for PTSD. While an advocate for exposure-based therapies, his open-minded, empirically interested approach led to his embracing present-centered group therapy as well, promoting its utility for PTSD treatment. Ever a connector, Dr. Foy engaged several of the authors (Drs. Wattenberg, Unger, and Niles) in presenting at AGPA, as well as at its post-9/11 conference (May 2002), and eventually co-authored chapters on group treatment of trauma with Drs. Unger, Wattenberg, and Glynn. Dr. Foy's intellectual curiosity and broad-ranging professional interests have been hallmarks of his presence in the field, extending to his mentorship with the above authors and his encouragement of dissemination of PCGT.
- Suzanne Phillips, PsyD, ABPP, CGP, FAGPA, is adjunct full professor of clinical psychology at LIU Post, N.Y., the Trauma/Disaster Chair for the Suffolk County Psychological Association, a clinician for The Soldiers Project Long Island, and fellow and board member for AGPA, who has written many books and chapters about trauma, and who has been a catalyst for collaborations among group therapy professionals, including among our authors. She connected with a subset of our team originally through Dr. Foy and maintained a strong collegial and supportive relationship with those of us involved in AGPA (Drs. Wattenberg, Unger, and Niles). She introduced Melissa Wattenberg and Daniel Lee Gross around their shared interest in PCGT, spurring a broader collaboration that resulted in this book. Her energy, thoughtfulness, inclusivity, and far-reaching community involvement make her a force within this field, and we would like to thank her for that and for her vibrant presence in this field.
- Shirley M. Glynn, PhD, is a research psychologist at the Semel Institute for Neuroscience and Human Behavior at UCLA, as well as a clinical psychologist in private practice. She has been prolific in her research in the areas of schizophrenia, PTSD, and family therapy, and is program manager of the Department of Veterans Affairs Family Services National Evidence-based Clinician Training Program. Dr. Glynn was the trauma-focus group therapy consultant in

CSP-420 and, along with Dr. Foy, recruited Dr. Wattenberg to be the present-centered group therapy consultant. Dr. Glynn has co-presented on group therapy with Drs. Foy, Unger, Niles, and Wattenberg at ISTSS and AGPA, and co-authored chapters on group therapy for PTSD with Drs. Foy, Unger, and Wattenberg. She has a strong commitment to the dissemination of evidence-based practices, and brings a thoughtful, reasoned presence to the field. Her grasp of the "big picture" (as well as details) is highly appreciated, as is her sense of humor. She is a valued colleague to many of the authors, and is a major contributor to the field.

- Terence M. Keane, PhD, is director of the National Center for Posttraumatic Stress Disorder Behavioral Science Division; professor of psychiatry and clinical psychology, Boston University; assistant dean of research, Boston University School of Medicine; and associate chief of staff, Research & Development, VA Boston Healthcare System. He has been instrumental in the development of the field of PTSD research and practice (including the acceptance of PTSD as a disorder), and has been a supportive colleague and leader in the field of PTSD, including to Drs. Niles, Wattenberg, Unger, and Shea. We appreciate the important role that Dr. Keane has played and continues to play in this field, which has been pivotal to the understanding and treatment of survivors of trauma.

- CSP-420 Colleagues and Leadership: Co-principal investigators and executive leadership of the National Center for PTSD, Matthew J. Friedman, MD, PhD, and Paula P. Schnurr, PhD, steadily steered the very large ship of CSP-420 (ten VA sites, each with two conditions and three iterations). We thank them for their vision, responsiveness, and genuineness. They have had profound impact on the field of PTSD, as well as on the careers of the many VA practitioners and researchers involved in CSP-420 and the studies that built on it. They were instrumental in recruiting one of our authors, M. Tracie Shea, PhD, into the field of PTSD research and practice.

We thank the entire Executive Committee of CSP-420: Bruce Rounsaville, PhD; David W. Foy, PhD (as above); Fred D. Gusman, M.S.W.; Charles R. Marmar, M.D.; Daniel S. Weiss, PhD; Terence M. Keane, PhD (as above); M. Tracie Shea, PhD (see author biographies); and Daniel Weiss, PhD. We thank as well the statisticians involved with CSP-420: Philip Lavori, PhD; Frank Hsieh, PhD; and Yajie Wang, M.S. We thank, also, Project Coordinator Nancy Bernardy, PhD, and Administrative Officer Veronica Thurston, MPH. These individuals (in conjunction with the Co-PIs, above) formed an inspirational "think tank," bringing together some of the best minds in the field of PTSD.

• We would like to thank the American Group Psychological Association's leadership, including those who initiated the original post-9/11 conference, *The Psychological Effects of Terrorist Disasters* (May 2–4, 2002), and the subsequent edited text that developed from it. These respected colleagues "took the bull by the horns" after 9/11, and after Hurricane Katrina as well, creating resources to address these disasters and to disseminate group treatments for trauma. Among them are: Leon A. Schein, EdD, LCSW; Henry I. Spitz, MD; Gary M. Burlingame, PhD; and Philip R. Muskin, MD. Drs. Shein, Spitz, and Burlingame welcomed the team of Drs. Foy, Unger, and Wattenberg to AGPA, and also engaged them in presenting at the post-9/11 symposium on group treatment for PTSD. Their efforts enhanced the commitment to group treatment for trauma at AGPA, as well as in the field.

Personal and Professional Individual Acknowledgments:
Melissa S. Wattenberg: I would like to thank my husband, Ric Amante, for his love and support throughout the work on this book and in life.

I would like to thank my family for their valuing of writing and their literary advice, including my parents, Jacqueline and Morris; my sister, Valerie; my husband, Ric; and my son, Vinny. I acknowledge the influence of my father's World War II experience investigating war crimes committed by the Nazis, from which he derived these two principles: do not go along with the crowd; and you cannot judge what someone may do under extreme circumstances unless you have been there yourself. Finally, I credit my son Vinny for bringing into my life his gentleness, creativity, humor, and courage. I again thank the veterans who have shared their stories, struggles, and triumphs with us, and I offer appreciation for their ongoing contributions as citizens in everyday life.

Daniel Lee Gross: It is with gratitude that I acknowledge the lasting impact of Suzette Astley, PhD, from my undergraduate days at Cornell College. Recognition must also go to the gifted colleagues I've known through my career, including William and Janet Solan, M.D., and Kristen Strack, PhD. Suzanne Phillips, PsyD, played a major role through the American Group Psychotherapy Association for her mentorship and introducing me to Melissa. To Rose Quiello, PhD, John Allemand, PsyD, and Mary Kay Brennan , PhD, for their valued feedback and encouragement while writing this book.

Many thanks go to my spouse, Brian, for being my Rock of Gibraltar, and my family for their love and inspiration, including a courageous and inspirational mother. I am indebted to the inspiring veterans I've had the privilege to know, foremost my father and brother, Michael, who continue to leave an indelible touch on my life and work.

William S. Unger: To my wife, Susan, for a life filled with hope, happiness, and heart.

Barbara L. Niles: To my husband, Jay, for providing the respite of laughter through these dark days of the pandemic with his very "bad dad" jokes, and for his love, support, and wonderful parenting of our two boys. To David (born in the middle of CSP-420) and Michael for providing me inspiration and great hope for the future. I want to thank my parents for instilling the value of scholarship, with special gratitude to my father for encouraging clarity in writing. To the veterans who have courageously allowed me to witness their stories of pain and resilience, thank you.

Introduction: Present-Centered Group Therapy and Embracing Today

Melissa S. Wattenberg, Daniel Lee Gross, Barbara L. Niles, William S. Unger, and M. Tracie Shea

This book offers clinicians, supervisors, mentors, training programs, and students a way to expand their clinical repertoire for effectively and flexibly addressing the impact of psychological trauma. Present-centered group therapy (PCGT) is compatible with a broad range of theoretical orientations, providing practitioners with a highly implementable modality through which trauma survivors can begin to reclaim and invest in their current lives, experience current relationships and events, and progress through phases of adult development that psychological trauma may have disrupted. Since its inception over 20 years ago, its lessons are increasingly in demand.

PCGT originated in a study on group treatment of longstanding PTSD in Vietnam veterans (see chapter one). Designed to control for "non-specific" effects or "common factors" of group psychotherapy, PCGT incorporated solid treatment principles – accessing the essential therapeutic factors of group psychotherapy identified by Yalom (1995) – as well as education on PTSD, and a generally trauma-aware stance. With its inclusion subsequently in a variety of research protocols (see chapter two) for this same purpose, PCGT emerged as a "user-friendly" form of group treatment for trauma survivors, generally "in the running" with other effective group treatments, typically with less attrition. PCGT uses the group process itself (rather than structured content that can overburden group process) to maintain a focus on the present in the face of intrusions, reliving, and loss of engagement. In this way, PCGT offers experience with interacting interpersonally in the present.

The need for PTSD treatment becomes heightened in our collective awareness during and following major traumatic world events. There is an immediate need for a response, not only in the days following an event (which have unique demands, such as blankets, comfort, and safety, typically before psychotherapy), but in the weeks and months following. Yet there is ongoing need in response to trauma that unfortunately occurs continually in the world and in our local communities, often exacerbated during "anniversaries" of tragic events. In addition, there are the long-term sufferers and survivors, who may wait years to seek help, or struggle for decades to find the right treatment and gain access to it. Long-term survivors may find themselves triggered by recent world events, and need intervention many years past the original trauma. A case in point was the 50th anniversary of D-Day, at which time many World War II veterans were activated by the public remembrances and sought therapy for the first time (Snell & Padin-Rivera, 1997).

For trauma survivors, being drawn into (and, often, encased in) the traumatic past can compromise the capacity for accurate social judgment, emotional awareness, relationships, enjoyment, thoughtful planning, achievement of goals, and hope for the future. PCGT embeds an understanding of trauma into a group model that embraces current life rather than reviewing the past. Its modest structure allows it to harness the essential healing elements of group psychotherapy, including empowerment, for survivors who experienced loss of power and control during traumatic experience. It is consistent with a recovery model, supporting survivors' strengths and honoring their choices, preferences, and participation in life.

For providers, the treatment of trauma can present compelling and challenging work. Following the 9/11 attacks in New York, and after Hurricane Katrina in New Orleans in 2005, the need for PTSD interventions gained particular prominence in the treatment community. Providers with little prior experience in treating trauma found themselves called upon to see new clients with PTSD, and to treat current clients who now appeared clearly traumatized. Diverse needs emerged, and present-based treatment was among the important options available to providers shifting into trauma treatment mode. For example, in New York following the 9/11 attacks on the World Trade Towers, the American Group Psychotherapy Association (AGPA) and Eastern Group Psychotherapy Society (EGPS), with funding from the New York Times Foundation, brought together experts in a variety of trauma interventions, training therapists across the city (May 2002 Conference, American Group Psychotherapy Association and Eastern Group Psychotherapy Society). PCGT (as well as trauma-focused group therapy (TFGT)) was incorporated in the initial training conference, and subsequently, in trainings for the Mental Health Association of New York City on both PCGT and TFGT. Both treatments were subsequently incorporated in a post-9/11 /post-Katrina text on group treatments for PTSD (in Schein et al., 2006) stemming from this pivotal conference.

The year 2020 marked the 40th anniversary of the establishment of PTSD in the Diagnostic and Statistical Manual of Mental Disorders, Third Edition (in DSM-III, 1980). Over the last few decades, interventions focusing on exposure to and processing of trauma have been widely researched and disseminated. In addition, structured skills-building groups have been developed to assist individuals in managing the often-debilitating symptoms of PTSD (as noted in the preface, these include: seeking safety for dually diagnosed survivors [Najavits, 2002]; mindfulness; dialectical behavior therapy [Linehan, 2014]). PCGT adds to this body of work an accessible, trauma-aware treatment supporting consistent attention to and experience of the present. This model includes problem solving, attention to and expression of "mid-range" affects, and a foundation in ongoing interpersonal interactions that counter alexithymia, alienation, and social isolation.

The upcoming sections I and II offer coordinated chapters describing this treatment's background, relevant research, manual, history, mechanisms, implications, implementation, and applications. The five book authors have written and substantively edited these chapters, with collaboration from additional authors on selected chapters.

- Section I (Origins, Evidence, and the Guide & Manual) describes the arc of PCGT's development, from its origins to its emergence as an efficacious treatment for PTSD (chapters one and two). The manual in three parts offers: step-by-step procedures for PCGT sessions (chapter three); integrating group therapy interventions into PCGT (chapter four); and strategies for addressing symptoms and trauma-based patterns (chapter five).
- Section II (Present-Centered Group Therapy Practice: Theory, History, and Applications) offers a framework for understanding and utilizing PCGT, including: mechanisms and functions of PCGT (why and how it works, chapter six); an overview of the intersecting histories of group psychotherapy and the treatment of psychological trauma (chapter seven); and a guide to implementation and application of PCGT in an array of clinical contexts, from outpatient settings to inpatient mental health to *telementalhealth* (chapter eight).

References

American Group Psychotherapy Association & Eastern Group Psychotherapy Society. (May 2–4, 2002). *Conference on Psychological Effects of Terrorist Disasters*, New York City.

American Psychiatric Association. (1980). *Diagnostic and statistical manual of mental disorders* (3rd ed.). Washington, D.C.: Author.

Linehan, M. (2014). *DBT skills training manual*. New York, NY: Guilford Publications.

Najavits, L. (2002). *Seeking safety: A treatment manual for PTSD and substance abuse*. New York, NY: Guilford Publications.

Schein, L. A., Spitz, H. I., Muskin, P. R., & Burlingame, G. (2006). *Psychological effects of catastrophic disasters: Group approaches to treatment*. Abingdon, UK: Psychology Press.

Snell, F. I., & Padin-Rivera, E. (1997). Post-traumatic stress disorder and the elderly combat veteran. *Journal of Gerontological Nursing, 23*(10), 13–19.

Yalom, I. D. (1995). *The theory and practice of group psychotherapy*. New York, NY: Basic Books.

Part I

Origins, Evidence, and the Guide & Manual

1 Present-Centered Group Therapy: Origins, Theoretical Influences, and Overview of Components

M. Tracie Shea

Present-centered group therapy (PCGT) was originally developed to control for the "nonspecific" effects of group psychotherapy in order to test the specific benefits of trauma-focused group therapy (TFGT) for the treatment of PTSD in Vietnam veterans (VA Cooperative Studies Program 420 – CSP-420; Schnurr, Friedman, Lavori, & Hsieh, 2001; Schnurr et al., 2003). Subsequently, several additional studies have used PCGT for the same purpose in trials of other treatments. Although developed as a nonspecific therapy control, PCGT has performed better than expected in most of the trials that have used it (reviewed in chapter two). Of note, an individual format of present-centered therapy (PCT) was developed for the same purpose and has similarly shown better than expected results (Belsher et al., 2019; Schnurr et al., 2007). This chapter describes the origins of PCGT, including the context, purpose, and considerations influencing its development, theoretical influences, and key components.

CSP-420 was motivated by the large number of Vietnam veterans with chronic PTSD receiving care from the VA healthcare system, and the absence of clear guidelines for the treatment of these veterans. Cognitive behavioral approaches, including those using exposure, had the most empirical evidence for PTSD treatment in civilians, and to a lesser extent in veterans. While effective, exposure therapy was challenging and sometimes difficult to tolerate. Given concerns about the feasibility of using exposure in this population of veterans with chronic combat-related PTSD, the CSP-420 chose to use a group rather than individual format for delivering exposure therapy (TFGT; Foy, Glynn, Ruzek, Riney, & Gusman, 1997). This was based on the idea that the development of support and cohesion in the group setting would enhance tolerability and increase compliance with exposure (Schnurr et al., 2003).

Much has been written about the challenges of defining control conditions for psychotherapy. The randomized clinical trial (RCT) design, historically used for pharmacotherapy research, has provided many methodological benefits that have enhanced the rigor of psychotherapeutic treatment research.

A limitation of the RCT for these studies, however, is that unlike drug studies that can use an inert pill as a control, there is no clear placebo for psychosocial treatment studies – a condition that would need to be both inert and credible (Parloff, 1986). As noted, the approach taken by the CSP-420 was to use a nonspecific comparison design; more specifically, using a comparison group that included features that are present in most forms of psychotherapy but excluded the hypothesized "active ingredients" of the treatment being tested (Borkovec, 1993; Schnurr, 2007; Schnurr et al., 2001). For CSP-420, this meant excluding exposure and other formal cognitive behavioral interventions from PCGT. The task was to develop a condition that would clarify and operationalize the "nonspecific" factors present in most forms of psychotherapy, provide good clinical care, and be credible to both therapists and veterans with PTSD, while excluding elements of cognitive behavioral therapy or other theoretically based interventions.

Non-Specific/Common Factors

Non-specific factors have also been referred to as common factors, and there is debate about the use of the term non-specific. It has been argued that nonspecific has additional meanings, and at times has been used to describe aspects of psychotherapy that are either unspecified or unspecifiable and thus not observable, and that the use of the term should be dropped (e.g., Castonguay, 1993). From this perspective, the term *common factors* more accurately describes the approach taken in developing PCGT.

Saul Rosenzweig (1936) first introduced the idea that factors common to different forms of psychotherapy may play an important role in outcome; an idea that was further developed by Jerome Frank. Frank (1971, 1986) proposed that all forms of psychotherapy introduce new concepts and information that help the individual in treatment to make connections between symptoms and experiences, and to change the meaning of the symptoms and problems in a way that increases their sense of hope, self-efficacy, and ability to tolerate their symptoms. "All forms of psychotherapy ... include, first, an emotionally charged, confiding relationship with a helping person; second, a setting identified in the patient's eyes as a place of healing; third, a therapeutic rationale that explains the causes of the patient's symptoms, and fourth, prescribes a procedure for relieving them that requires active participation by both the patient and the therapist" (Frank, 1986, p. 342).

Over time, different conceptualizations of common factors have evolved; the most consistent factors include the therapeutic alliance (which involves both a confiding relationship, and active collaboration by the therapist and client), provision of a psychotherapeutic rationale, the experience of talking about problems in a safe environment, the acquisition and practice of new behaviors, creation of positive expectations and hope for improvement, and beneficial therapist qualities and interventions (Grencavage & Norcross, 1990). Beneficial therapist interventions that are common to most forms of psychotherapy include, for example, conveying interest through verbal and non-verbal reactions, providing appropriate praise, encouragement, and reassurance, and providing statements that help the client feel understood and validated.

Most of the literature on common factors has focused on individual therapy, but they play an important role in group therapy as well. Yalom's classic book on group psychotherapy (Yalom, 1995) includes a description of therapeutic factors provided by groups (see chapter six for additional discussion of such therapeutic factors), and we drew upon aspects of this work in the development of the manual. One factor, instillation of hope, is described: "The instillation and maintenance of hope is crucial in any psychotherapy" (p. 4). Noting that faith in a treatment approach can itself be effective, Yalom discusses specific efforts to enhance belief and confidence in the efficacy of the group. This includes reinforcing positive expectations, removing negative preconceptions, providing a persuasive explanation of the beneficial effects of the group, and calling attention to the improvement that group members have made.

A second factor, universality, refers to the relief associated with discovering that others have similar experiences, helping the individual to feel less isolated and alone. This can be particularly relevant for those with PTSD, so often characterized by isolation and absence of social support. In addition to learning about PTSD symptoms (discussed next), hearing others in a group talk about similar experiences can help alleviate this sense of isolation.

Yalom (1995) also discusses the significance of psychoeducation as a therapeutic factor. Providing information about the symptoms and common associated features is an important source of validation of one's experience, facilitates universality, and can help establish connections among members early on in the group. Yalom proposes that didactic information can also have a direct therapeutic effect – with increasing understanding of painful experiences comes reduced uncertainty and confusion and increased sense of control. This point regarding the significance of psycho-education is similar to Frank's point that the introduction of new concepts and information that helps individuals connect their experiences with their symptoms and change the meaning of their problems can increase hope and self-efficacy.

An important difference for group therapy in the consideration of common factors is that rather than a single bond between a client and therapist, well-functioning groups involve the creation of bonds among group members (reflected in the term *group cohesion*). As noted by Yalom (1995) "... group cohesion is the analogue of relationship in individual therapy" (p. 47). Hearing about other group members' experiences (universality) likely enhances the power of other common factors such as normalization and validation. Given the strong sense of isolation from society and people that is often present among those with PTSD, the creation of bonds within the group, as well as the experience of normalization and validation of their experiences, may be particularly therapeutic. Successful development of group cohesion, like the therapeutic alliance in individual therapy, creates the conditions that allow other therapeutic elements to occur. As noted, the strong sense of support that evolves in a group setting is what motivated the use of the group format for TFGT in the CSP-420 – with the idea that the bonds and support that develop might make the experience of exposure more tolerable. For the study to be able to draw conclusions about the effects of exposure, these common aspects of group therapy were critical to the development of PCGT as the active control.

Components and Session Content of PCGT

The broad objective of PCGT as developed for CSP-420 was to help veterans with PTSD to better understand and cope with current life problems and difficulties. The use of the term *present-centered* was intended to contrast with the focus on past (trauma) in TFGT, and is distinct from current mindfulness approaches that encourage being present and aware in the moment. As described in the original PCGT manual overview, "The central elements of the PCGT condition include: 1) psycho-education about the typical symptoms and features associated with PTSD in Vietnam veterans, particularly those affecting interpersonal relationships; and 2) the use of a group format to decrease isolation, normalize symptoms, provide the experience of giving and receiving support and feedback, and offer opportunities for positive interpersonal interactions." These two components are particularly relevant to prominent themes that characterize PTSD – feeling overwhelmed and helpless, and feeling disconnected and isolated. Psycho-education directed at increased understanding of how overwhelming and confusing personal experiences may be connected to PTSD symptoms may reduce the sense of helplessness and increase a sense of efficacy, and the experience of positive interpersonal interactions in the group may decrease feelings of disconnection and isolation.

Early sessions of PCGT were designed to develop feelings of comfort, trust, and group cohesion. Session one includes presenting a rationale for PCGT, describing the structure and process of the group, presenting group rules and expectations of group members, discussing potential benefits and gains from the group, and encouraging positive expectations. In addition to providing the necessary information about the group, session one's content encourages the mobilization of hope and motivation. The rationale provided in session one includes acknowledgement of the strong pull towards the past, specifically group members' Vietnam experiences, at the expense of their current lives. By focusing on the present, the group is intended to help them shift the pull from the past to the present, for example, by investing in more meaningful relationships with the people in their lives, and engaging in meaningful activities. PCGT is also described as an opportunity to develop a clearer understanding of how their symptoms may be related to some of their problems, and to learn to identify, talk about, and deal with their problem areas. The importance of participation and support of each other to the benefits of the group, and the development of a feeling of support and trust among the members, are explicitly discussed in order to promote the process of group cohesion.

Two sessions are devoted to psycho-education about PTSD symptoms, associated disorders, and common problems areas. In addition to increasing understanding of their experiences and how their difficulties may be related to PTSD, these interactive discussions help to normalize their experiences, to provide a common framework for the group, and to increase the sense of connection and trust among group members by highlighting the experiences they have in common. It also helps to identify problems areas that they can work on in the group.

The fourth session focuses on helping group members to identify and discuss the problems they may want to work on and their goals for the group. When appropriate, the group facilitators try to connect the problems described with PTSD symptoms. The goals of subsequent sessions are to continue the development of trust and cohesion among group members, to facilitate identification and clarification of day-to-day difficulties and their relationship to PTSD, and to facilitate problem solving around problems identified by group members. As the end of the group approaches, sessions address additional themes. One is the consolidation and reinforcement of gains made by group members, and the importance of maintaining gains to their lives outside the group. Another is preparing for transitioning and termination. This involves helping the group members to discuss their thoughts and feelings about termination, including discomfort and negative feelings. Attention is paid to identifying symptoms and behaviors that may be serving the purpose of avoiding feelings about termination.

The Role of Facilitators in PCGT

Broadly speaking, the role of facilitators is to provide information and guidance to group members, to create a structure that allows a sense of safety in the group, to support the development of group cohesion, and to support members' work on their individual goals. Facilitators open each session with a check-in, and lead a ten-minute session review prior to ending the session. The check-in starts in session two, and allows group members to bring up any reactions, questions, comments, problems or concerns from the previous session. The session review provides an opportunity for members to discuss what they got out of the group, any difficulties they may have had, and suggestions for how things might have worked better.

Facilitators are more active in the early sessions, when the structure and framework of the group are being established. During this phase, facilitators work on helping group members to feel comfortable with the group, and in learning how the group process works. They identify potential conflicts and work towards their resolution. Starting in session four, facilitators help group members to identify and discuss their problems and goals for the group, and help to make the transition to a less structured format. In this and subsequent sessions, facilitators encourage feedback among group members, and also try to identify common themes that may emerge across the kinds of issues described by group members, with the goal of increasing the sense of connection among group members and the relevance of the discussion for each member. They help to facilitate problem solving around problems raised by group members, help the group stay focused on topics raised, address any deviations from the established ground rules, note similarities and differences among issues that members raise, and continue development of group cohesion by encouraging feedback and support among members. In the final sessions, facilitators help members process the ending of the group. This includes reinforcing gains made by members and consideration of how to maintain gains and continue moving forward, and encouraging members to talk about their feelings about ending the group.

Summary

This chapter has described the history of PCGT including the reason for, objectives of, and considerations involved in its development, the theoretical influence of the common factors in psychotherapy research literature, and a summary of its basic components as delivered in the original trial for which it was developed. As noted, PCGT has since been used in numerous studies, resulting in an evidence base reviewed in chapter two. It has also been applied clinically, primarily within VA clinics. Over time, this cumulative experience has led to expansions and improvements to PCGT. While part I of the manual (chapter three) has only minor revisions from the original manual, the two guidance chapters (chapters four and five) have been revised and updated. The expanded conceptualization of mechanisms that may be operative and responsible for the benefits of PCGT (described in chapter six) is new, as is the material about the potential adaptations and uses of the basic PCGT framework discussed in chapter six. This book has presented the opportunity for the authors to elaborate on the initial PCGT framework, incorporating broader principles of group therapy, and speculations about the mechanisms and process of groups provided within this framework. While chapter three describes the original PCGT manual, chapters four and five benefit from further experience, reflection, and theoretical integration to optimize the use of the original framework. As such, therapist training for research uses of PCGT did not include the breadth of the material included in these later chapters that expand upon the original manual. It is also important to note that although the PCGT framework is clearly applicable to PTSD treatment in different populations, at present research findings are based upon veteran and active duty military samples.

With these caveats, the accumulating findings (chapter two) suggest that PCGT, developed in an attempt to control for common factors that characterize group therapy, performs comparably to trauma-focused and mindfulness group therapies for PTSD in veterans, with at best modest differences in outcome. These findings would not be surprising to proponents of the common factors model, who argue that common factors, rather than being "necessary but not sufficient" for change, are themselves therapeutic (e.g., Wampold, 2015). On a practical level, PCGT provides a useful framework and an alternative approach to treatment for PTSD.

References

Belsher, B. E., Beech, E., Smolenski, D. J., Shea, M. T., Otto, J. L., Rosen, C. S., & Schnurr, P. P. (2019). Present-centered therapy (PCT) for posttraumatic stress disorder (PTSD) in adults. *Cochrane Data Base of Systematic Reviews*. DOI: 10. 1002/14651858.CD012898.pub2

Borkovec, T. D. (1993). Between-group therapy outcome research: design and methodology. *NIDA Research Monograph, 137*, 249–289.

Castonguay, L. G. (1993). "Common factors" and "non-specific variables": Clarification of the two concepts and recommendations for research. *Journal of Psychotherapy Integration, 3*, 267–286.

Foy, D. W., Glynn, S. M., Ruzek, J. L., Riney, S. J., & Gusman, F. D. (1997). Trauma focus group therapy for combat-related PTSD. *In Session: Psychotherapy in Practice, 3*, 59–73.

Frank, J. D. (1971). Therapeutic factors in psychotherapy. *American Journal of Psychotherapy, 25*(3), 350–361.

Frank, J. D. (1986). Psychotherapy – The transformation of meanings: Discussion paper. *Journal of the Royal Society of Medicine, 79*, 341–346.

Grencavage, L. M., & Norcross, J. C. (1990). Where are the commonalities among the therapeutic common factors? *Professional Psychology: Research and Practice, 21*, 372–378.

Parloff, M. B. (1986). Placebo controls in psychotherapy research: A sine qua non or a placebo for research problems? *Journal of Consulting and Clinical Psychology, 54*(1), 79.

Rosenzweig, S. (1936). Some implicit common factors in diverse methods of psychotherapy: At last the Dodo said, "Everybody has won and all must have prizes." *American Journal of Orthopsychiatry, 6*, 412–415.

Schnurr, P. P. (2007). The rocks and hard places in psychotherapy outcome research. *Journal of Traumatic Stress, 20,* 779–792.

Schnurr, P. P., Friedman, M. J., Engel, C. C., Foa, E. B., Shea, M. T., Chow, B. K., ... Bernardy, N. (2007). Cognitive behavioural therapy for posttraumatic stress disorder in women. *JAMA, 28,* 820–830.

Schnurr, P. P., Friedman, M. J., Foy, D. W., Shea, M. T., Hsieh, F. Y., Lavori, P. W., ... Bernardy, N. C. (2003). Randomized trial of trauma-focused group therapy for posttraumatic stress disorder. *Archives of General Psychiatry, 60,* 481–489.

Schnurr, P. P., Friedman, M. F., Lavori, P. W., & Hsieh, F. Y. (2001). Design of Department of Veterans Affairs Cooperative Study No. 420: Group treatment of posttraumatic stress disorder. *Controlled Clinical Trials, 22,* 74–88.

Wampold, B. E. (2015). How important are the common factors in psychotherapy? An update. *World Psychiatry, 14,* 270–277.

Yalom, I. D. (1995). *The theory and practice of group psychotherapy* (4th ed.). New York, NY: Basic Books.

2 Review of the PCGT Literature: What is the Evidence?

Barbara L. Niles, Scott D. Litwack, and Daniel H. Grossman

Review of the PCGT Literature: What is the Evidence?

In the U.S. general population, the lifetime risk of developing PTSD is estimated to be 8.7% (Kessler, Chiu, Demler, & Walters, 2005). For individuals with high exposure to traumatic events, the risk can be much higher. For example, it is estimated that nearly a quarter of veterans exposed to combat trauma in recent military conflicts (Fulton et al., 2015) and one-fifth of women who experienced sexual assault (Scott et al., 2018) experience subsequent PTSD. PTSD is characterized by four symptom clusters that cause significant distress: intrusions, avoidance, negative alterations to cognition and mood, and hyperarousal (American Psychiatric Association, 2013). PTSD and subthreshold symptomatology are associated with diminished functioning in many meaningful life areas such as physical health, financial and employment stability, intimate partner and social relationships, and psychological well-being (Elbogen, Johnson, Wagner, Newton, & Beckham, 2012; Engelhard, van den Hout, Weerts, Hox, & van Doornen, 2009; Franz et al., 2020; Mota et al., 2016; Sareen et al., 2007; Smith, Schnurr, & Rosenheck, 2005). In some cases, symptoms persist for years or even decades (Lee et al., 2020). Although empirically supported and efficacious treatments for PTSD are available, success rates are modest and a substantial proportion of individuals who access treatment either drop out or are not substantially helped by PTSD treatment (Niles et al., 2018; Schottenbauer, Glass, Arnkoff, Tendick, & Gray, 2008; Steenkamp, Litz, Hoge, & Marmar, 2015; Steenkamp et al., 2020a). Given the difficulty of treating PTSD, it is important to understand the evidence base of available treatments in order to have the greatest impact on improving the lives of survivors of trauma.

This chapter reviews empirical support for present-centered group therapy (PCGT) in clinical trials for PTSD. In chapter one, Shea detailed the origins of PCGT and how it was developed and codified in the late 1990s for a Veterans Health Administration (VHA) Cooperative Studies Program (CSP). Known as "CSP-420," this large randomized trial of Vietnam veterans with PTSD related to their deployment to Southeast

Asia compared two treatments for PTSD: trauma-focused group therapy (TFGT) and PCGT (Schnurr et al., 2003). As noted in chapter one, there is no true placebo for psychotherapy trials for PTSD (Schnurr, 2007). The choice of PCGT as a treatment condition against which to compare TFGT in CSP-420 was developed with the aim to examine whether the specific elements of TFGT provided additional benefit beyond the benefits provided by "most types of psychotherapy" (Schnurr et al., 2003, p. 482). Thus, the goals of PCGT were to (1) include and match the "non-specific" or common factors of psychotherapy, such as therapist contact, support, and expectation of improvement, and (2) omit elements hypothesized to be therapeutic mechanisms of action specific to TFGT, such as exposure to past trauma-related stimuli and memories, and cognitive restructuring. Both groups were designed to include the therapeutic factors of group therapy identified by Yalom (1995): Instillation of hope, recognition of universality, psychoeducation, and development of group cohesion.

In the current chapter, we first review seven randomized controlled trials (RCTs) comparing PCGT to other treatments for PTSD: CSP-420 (Schnurr et al., 2003) and six subsequent trials (Bremner et al., 2017; Davis et al., 2019; Polusny et al., 2015; Ready et al., 2018; Resick et al., 2015; Sloan, Unger, Lee, & Beck, 2018). In addition to examining the PTSD outcomes for these studies, we also examine the dropout rates, as dropout is often considered an indicator of tolerability and acceptability of treatment. Next, we consider information provided by reviews and meta-analyses of PCGT and then summarize treatment guidelines for PTSD that examined PCGT. Finally, we summarize the main findings from these various sources and provide some suggestions for future research directions for PCGT.

Randomized Controlled Trials of PCGT

Studies that met the following criteria were included in this review: (1) study aims were to evaluate treatment efficacy on PTSD outcomes; (2) PCGT was compared to one or more other treatment conditions; (3) eligibility criteria explicitly included a minimal level of symptoms of PTSD or a diagnosis of PTSD; (4) individuals were randomly assigned to condition; (5) the interventions were adequately developed and described; (6) valid quantitative measures were used to evaluate outcomes; and (7) dropout rates were reported. The valid PTSD outcome measures discussed below from these studies include both self-reported (a paper-and-pencil or computerized scale completed by the client) and clinician-assessed (symptoms assessed by a clinician using a semi-structured diagnostic interview) assessment instruments. Self-report scales, such as the PTSD Checklist (PCL; Weathers et al., 2013), are easier and faster to administer than clinician-assessed instruments, but also have a higher likelihood of error and thus cannot be used to establish a diagnosis (National Center for PTSD, 2013b). Clinician-assessed scales administered by trained interviewers are generally considered to yield more valid results and can render a diagnosis. The Clinician-Administered PTSD Scale (CAPS; Weathers et al., 2018) is the clinician-assessed scale most commonly used in RCTs for PTSD and is considered the "gold-standard" PTSD assessment tool (National Center for PTSD, 2013a).

Since no singular manual has been published and consistently utilized, we first examined these studies to see the degree to which the versions of PCGT used in these trials had common prescribed and proscribed elements. As noted in Table 2.1, these elements were largely consistent, with two studies offering the option for therapists to incorporate structured problem-solving training, and one of these studies incorporating the instruction of grounding. In Table 2.2, we have summarized the results of the studies and further discuss the major findings from each of these below.

PCGT Compared to Trauma-Focused Group Therapies

PCGT has been used as a comparison group treatment in four randomized controlled trials of trauma-focused group treatment for PTSD (Ready et al., 2018; Resick et al., 2015; Schnurr et al., 2003; Sloan et al., 2018). Since the 1990s, published studies and reviews in aggregate have indicated that cognitive behavioral therapy that includes a direct focus on the traumatic events, or "exposure" to the trauma, accrued the most empirical support in the treatment of PTSD (Foa, Keane, Friedman, & Cohen, 2010). While the proposed mechanisms of change for the four trauma-focused group treatments reviewed in this section vary somewhat, there are fundamental similarities among them. They all incorporate processing of trauma-related thoughts and beliefs, exposure to trauma memories, and introduction of specific skills for approaching and managing these trauma-related thoughts, beliefs, and memories. We therefore review the results of these trauma-focused group treatments together below.

In the first trial examining PCGT, CSP-420, Schnurr et al. (2003) studied a large sample of 360 Vietnam veterans across ten sites and compared PCGT with trauma-focused group therapy. Groups of six or fewer veterans met once weekly for 30 weeks in 90-minute sessions with two facilitators, with the trauma-focused groups meeting for an additional 30 minutes (2 hours total) for the exposure sessions. After weekly sessions were completed, the groups shifted to monthly booster sessions for 5 months, with 15-minute monthly check-ins by phone for the TFGT group. This study employed intention-to-treat analyses, considered the gold standard for clinical trials (Yelland et al., 2015). In this type of

Table 2.1 Prescribed and Proscribed Elements of Present-Centered Group Therapy (PCGT) Treatments

	Schnurr et al., 2003	Polusny et al., 2015	Resick et al., 2015	Bremner et al., 2017	Davis et al., 2019	Ready et al., 2018	Sloan et al., 2018
PRESCRIBED							
Topics of discussion based on clients' present difficulties and reactions	Yes	Yes	Yes	Yes	Yes	Yes	Yes
Structured Problem-Solving Training	No	Optional	No	No	No	Optional	No
Assign Journal/Diary	No	No	Yes	Yes	Yes	No	Yes
PROSCRIBED							
Discussions of trauma details	No	No	No	No	No	No	No
Imaginal exposure	No	No	No	No	No	No	No
In *vivo* exposure	No	No	No	No	No	No	No
Breathing retraining	No	No	No	No	No	No	No
Structure Cognitive Restructuring	No	No	No	No	No	No	No
Structured skills training (other than problem solving) led by therapists (e.g., mindfulness, relaxation, anger management)	No	No	No	No	No	Grounding	No

Note: Manuals were retrieved for all of these studies except Polusny et al., 2015 and were used to complete this table.

Table 2.2 Randomized Clinical Trials of Present-Centered Group Therapy

Source	Population	Present-Centered Group Therapy (Frequency & Duration)	Comparison Intervention (Frequency & Duration)	Pre-to-Post Effect Sizes on PTSD Measures (Bold Indicates Statistically Significant Greater Symptom Reduction)	Dropout & Attendance (or Comparable Statistic)
Schnurr et al. (2003)	Male Vietnam veterans with PTSD $N = 360$ (0% women) Mean age = 50.7	Weekly 1.5-hour sessions for 30 weeks, then 5 monthly booster sessions	Trauma-focused group therapy (TFGT) (Weekly 1.5- to 2-hour sessions for 30 weeks, then 5 monthly booster sessions, plus monthly 15-minute phone calls [absent in PCGT])	Between Groups (ITT): CAPS: TFGT vs PCGT (no sig. effect) PCL: TFGT vs PCGT (no sig. effect) Within Groups: CAPS: TFGT (effect size not reported, sig. effect); PCGT (effect size not reported, sig. effect) PCL: TFGT (effect size not reported, sig. effect); PCGT (effect size not reported, no sig. effect)	PCGT: $N = 8.6\%$ dropout Mean sessions attended = 9.8 (SD = 2.3) TFGT: $N = 22.8\%$ dropouts Mean sessions attended = 8.4 (SD = 3.5)
Polusny et al. (2015)	Veterans with PTSD $N = 116$ (16% women) Mean age = 58.5	9 weekly 1.5-hour group sessions	MBSR (8 weekly 2.5-hour sessions plus a 6.5-hour retreat)	Between Groups (ITT): CAPS: **MBSR** vs PCGT ($d = 0.41$, sig. effect) PCL: **MBSR** vs PCGT ($d = 0.40$, sig. effect) Within Group: CAPS: (not reported) PCL: (not reported)	PCGT: $N = 4$ (6.9%) dropouts Mean sessions attended = 8.08 (SD = 1.84) MBSR: $N = 13$ (22.4%) dropouts Mean sessions attended = 6.96 (SD = 2.56)

(Continued)

Table 2.2 (Continued)

Source	Population	Present-Centered Group Therapy (Frequency & Duration)	Comparison Intervention (Frequency & Duration)	Pre-to-Post Effect Sizes on PTSD Measures (Bold Indicates Statistically Significant Greater Symptom Reduction)	Dropout & Attendance (or Comparable Statistic)
Resick et al. (2015)	Active Duty US Army soldiers $N = 108$ (7% women) Mean age = 32.1	Twice a week 1.5-hour sessions for 6 weeks	Cognitive Processing Therapy (CPT) (twice a week 1.5-hour sessions for 6 weeks)	Between Groups (ITT): PSS-I: CPT vs PCGT ($d = .21$, not sig.) PCL: **CPT** vs PCGT ($d = -0.4$, sig. effect) Within Group: PSS-I: CPT ($d = 0.66$, $p = .001$); PCGT ($d = 0.45$, sig. effect) PCL: CPT ($d = -1.1$, effect size not reported); PCGT ($d = -0.7$, effect size not reported)	PCGT: $N = 7$ (13.4%) non-completers Mean sessions attended = 9.8 (SD = 2.3) CPT: $N = 15$ (26.8%) non-completers Mean sessions attended = 8.4 (SD = 3.5)
Bremner et al. (2017)	Combat veterans with PTSD $N = 26$ (0% women) Mean age = 34	Total hours same as comparison, frequency, and duration not reported	MBSR (8 weekly 2.5-hour sessions plus a 6-hour retreat)	Between Groups (modified ITT): CAPS: (not reported) Within Group: CAPS: **MBSR** (effect size not reported, sig. effect); PCGT (effect size not reported, no sig. effect)	PCGT: (not reported) MBSR: (not reported)

Davis et al. (2019)	Veterans with PTSD $N = 214$ (16% women) Mean age = 51	8 weekly 1.5-hour sessions plus 2-hour group lunch	MBSR (8 weekly 1.5-hour sessions plus a 6-hour retreat)	Between Groups (modified ITT): CAPS: **MBSR** vs PCGT (effect size not reported, no sig. effect) PCL: **MBSR** vs PCGT (effect size not reported, sig. effect) Within Group: CAPS: (not reported) PCL: (not reported)	PCGT: $N = 19\%$ did not attend week 9 assessment MBSR: $N = 32\%$ did not attend week 9 assessment
Ready et al. (2018)	Vietnam Veterans $N = 81$ (0% women) Mean age = 61.4	PCGT (Two 1.5-hour sessions per week for 16 weeks, plus five 1.5-hour booster sessions spaced every 3 weeks)	Group-Based Exposure Therapy (GBET) (Two 4-hour sessions per week for 16 weeks)	Between Groups (ITT): CAPS: GBET vs. PCGT ($d = 0.25$, no sig. effect) PCL: GBET vs. PCGT ($d = 0.38$, no sig. effect) Within Groups: CAPS: GBET ($d = 0.59$, sig. effect); PCGT ($d = 0.30$, sig. not reported) PCL: GBET ($d = 0.96$, sig. effect); PCGT ($d = 0.48$, sig. not reported)	PCGT: $N = 4$ (10%) dropouts CPT: $N = 4$ (9.7%) dropouts
Sloan et al. (2018)	Male Veterans $N = 198$ (0% women) Mean age = 55.82	14 2-hour sessions over 16 weeks	Group Cognitive-Behavioral Therapy (GCBT) (Fourteen 2-hour sessions across 16 weeks)	Between Groups (ITT): CAPS: GCBT vs PCGT (effect size not reported, no sig. effect) PCL: GCBT vs PCGT (effect size not reported, no sig. effect)	Adequate dose defined as attending at least 10 of 14 sessions PCGT: $N = 10$ (10%) dropouts 21.2% inadequate dose

(Continued)

Table 2.2 (Continued)

Source	Population	Present-Centered Group Therapy (Frequency & Duration)	Comparison Intervention (Frequency & Duration)	Pre-to-Post Effect Sizes on PTSD Measures (Bold Indicates Statistically Significant Greater Symptom Reduction)	Dropout & Attendance (or Comparable Statistic)
				Within Groups: CAPS: GCBT (d = 0.97, sig. effect); PCGT = 0.61, sig. effect) PCL: (not reported)	GCBT: PCGT (d N = 31 (32%) dropouts 38.4% inadequate dose

MBSR = Mindfulness-Based Stress Reduction, CAPS = Clinician Administered PTSD Scale, PCL = PTSD Checklist, PSS-I = Posttraumatic Symptom Scale - Interview, ITT = Intention to Treat Effect size interpretation: small (d = 0.25), medium (d = 0.50), and large (d = 0.80) analysis, all participants who were randomized to a group are included in analyses regardless of whether the participants completed treatment, dropped out early, or never began. The average improvements on PTSD measures for both the PCGT and the trauma-focused groups were statistically significant but modest, and a minority of the participants (approximately 40% in both groups) achieved a clinically effective reduction in symptoms (defined as a drop of ten points or more on the clinician-assessed PTSD scale). No significant differences between groups on PTSD measures were found and a statistically significant higher rate of dropout was noted in the trauma-focused group (22.8%) than in the PCGT group (8.6%), with PCGT participants attending more sessions on average. The investigators were also interested in examining the results for the subset of individuals who received an "adequate dose" of treatment (defined as attendance to 24 or more of the sessions). In a post-hoc analysis limited to the approximately 60% of participants who received an adequate dose of treatment, the trauma-focused condition performed better than PCGT at all follow-ups on clinician-assessed PTSD. These findings suggested that trauma-focused treatment may be better for those who can tolerate it, but that dropout and attendance rates indicated it may be more difficult to tolerate than PCGT.

Resick et al. (2015) compared group cognitive processing therapy and PCGT in a sample of 108 active duty service members. Cognitive processing therapy is a treatment for PTSD primarily focused on identifying and challenging unhelpful thoughts that develop after trauma. Sessions for both treatments were 90 minutes in length and held twice weekly for six weeks. Both treatment groups demonstrated large reductions in PTSD severity up to the 12-month follow-up. A significant between-group difference favoring the cognitive processing condition was found on self-reported PTSD ($d = -0.4$), but no significant differences were found between the two groups on clinician-assessed PTSD. In terms of clinically significant change (defined as a ten-point or greater drop on self-reported PTSD), almost half (49%) of the participants in the cognitive processing condition achieved a clinically significant change at post-treatment compared to only a third (34%) in PCGT. However, by the 12-month follow-up this difference diminished (to 56% and 50%, respectively) and overall there were no significant differences between conditions on this metric. In addition, twice as many participants in the cognitive-processing groups did not complete the intervention (26.8%) than in PCGT (13.4%), with participants in the cognitive processing group completing fewer sessions on average, suggesting that cognitive processing may be more difficult for participants to tolerate than PCGT.

Sloan et al. (2018) compared 14 two-hour sessions of PCGT to a group cognitive-behavioral treatment that included psychoeducation and implementation of in vivo and written exposure, progressive muscle relaxation, cognitive restructuring of post trauma dysfunctional thoughts, assertion training, behavioral activation, and prevention of symptom recurrence. Male veterans with PTSD ($N = 198$) were randomized, and participants in both conditions exhibited significant reductions in PTSD severity on both clinician-assessed and self-report measures, as well as significant reductions in PTSD diagnostic status. These gains were found to be maintained at 12 months' post-treatment. Notably, there were no significant differences between the two treatments in any of these outcomes at any time point. The authors noted that, "Consistent with a growing body of evidence, the findings also suggest [PCGT] is as equally efficacious as group trauma-focused treatment" p. 886. As with the studies described above, there were substantial differences between the treatments with regards to treatment dropout: 31 out of 98 participants (32%) in the cognitive-behavioral condition dropped, whereas only 10 out of 100 participants (10%) randomized to the PCGT condition dropped out of treatment. In addition, a significantly greater proportion of participants in PCGT completed an adequate dose of treatment (71.4%) than those in the cognitive-behavioral condition (62.6%), indicating again that PCGT may be more easily tolerated than trauma-focused treatments.

PCGT was compared to group-based exposure therapy in veterans by Ready et al. (2018). The core component of the exposure treatment was the sharing and reviewing of trauma narratives as a group. Notably, as highlighted in Table 2.1, the version of PCGT used in this trial also incorporated active teaching of grounding skills and allowed for the option to introduce other active skills training (e.g., relaxation, thought-stopping, problem solving). However, as with the other studies in this review, sharing of trauma details was prohibited. Eighty-one Vietnam era veterans were randomly assigned to these two conditions. Participants in both treatments exhibited significant reductions in PTSD symptoms at post-treatment that were maintained 12 months later. No significant differences between the PCGT and exposure therapy conditions were found with regards to changes in PTSD symptoms at post-treatment, four-month follow-up, or one-year follow-up. In contrast to the other studies reviewed in this section, in this study there were no differences between groups in dropout rates (both 10%). However, there were substantial differences in the structure of the two treatments. PCGT consisted of 90-minute sessions twice per week for 16 weeks, followed by five 90-minute booster sessions once every three weeks. The exposure treatment consisted of four-hour sessions twice per week (including lunch and an afternoon break) for 16 weeks. Thus, an important characteristic to consider for this study is that there was a large difference in the dose of treatment in the two groups: 128 hours of treatment for the exposure group compared to 55.5 hours for the PCGT group. Even though participants in the PCGT group received far less total treatment, the outcomes were not significantly different.

Overall, the studies comparing trauma-focused treatments with PCGT do not provide compelling evidence for the superiority of either treatment over the other. Of the studies reviewed above, only one reported an adequate dose analysis (Schnurr et al., 2003) and suggested that trauma-focused treatment was more effective when enough sessions are administered. However, a general pattern of higher dropout rates and/or lower session attendance for trauma-focused conditions was present in all studies but one (Ready et al., 2018), a study that did not detect between-group differences on PTSD outcomes despite participants in the PCGT condition receiving far fewer hours of total treatment.

PCGT Compared to MBSR

To date, PCGT has been used as a comparison group in three studies examining the efficacy of mindfulness-based stress reduction (MBSR) with veterans with PTSD (Bremner et al., 2017; Davis et al., 2019; Polusny et al., 2015). Mindfulness is often defined as "an openhearted, moment-to-moment, nonjudgmental awareness" (Kabat-Zinn, 2005, p. 24) and MBSR is an intervention designed to cultivate the state of mindfulness. This intervention is typically delivered in nine sessions (eight weekly 2.5-hour sessions plus one day-long retreat). It uses a combination of meditative practices and techniques (e.g., body scanning, walking meditation, sitting meditation, yoga). Decades of research indicate that MBSR is efficacious in reducing depression and anxiety as well as improving quality of life and physical functioning (Grossman, Niemann, Schmidt, & Walach, 2004; Khoury, Sharma, Rush, & Fournier, 2015), with minimal adverse reactions.

Polusny et al. (2015) compared PCGT with MBSR with a large sample of veterans with PTSD ($N = 116$). Researchers used the same version of PCGT in this study as used in Ready et al. (2018), with the exception that grounding skills and relaxation were disallowed given their potential overlap with mindfulness. Clinicians were allowed the option to introduce other active skills training (e.g., thought-stopping, problem solving) while keeping to the structure of the PCGT modality. Using intention-to-treat analyses, both conditions were found to lead to significant improvements in self-reported and clinician-assessed PTSD symptoms. The authors reported that these improvements were significantly greater in the MBSR group than in PCGT and that participants in the MBSR condition were more likely than those in PCGT to experience clinically significant change in self-reported PTSD at the two-month follow-up, suggesting that MBSR may be more efficacious. However, a notable characteristic of this study was a substantial difference in treatment dosage between those in MBSR

(26.5 hours) and PCGT (13.5 hours). In addition, for those in the MBSR condition, home practice was highly encouraged while those in the present-centered therapy condition were not given home practice assignments. This trial design did not allow the investigators to disentangle how much the MBSR approach compared to the greater quantity of treatment contributed to the superior results for MBSR. Given the important differences between the two experimental groups in this study, it is unclear whether MBSR would be superior if the treatments were matched for dose. Additionally, the treatment dropout was notably higher in the MBSR group (22.4%) than in PCGT (6.9%) in this study.

A small pilot study ($N = 26$) focused on changes in brain regions associated with PTSD also compared PCGT to MBSR in veterans with PTSD (Bremner et al., 2017). In this study, the two groups were matched on dose for the eight 2.5-hour study sessions and a social event (barbeque) was provided for the PCGT group to match the one-day retreat of the MBSR group. MBSR was found to be superior to PCGT in reducing symptoms of PTSD and these differences persisted through the six-month follow-up. However, the authors' use of completer analyses rather than intention-to-treat may have skewed the results, especially as dropout rates were quite different in this study: 48% in the MBSR group compared to 11% in PCGT, something that is much better adjusted for by intention-to-treat-analyses.

Davis et al. (2019) compared MBSR to PCGT in a large, methodologically rigorous, multisite study ($N = 214$). In this trial the MBSR sessions were shortened from the typical 2.5 hours to 90 minutes so that the two conditions matched for dosage of treatment. Using modified intention-to-treat analyses (i.e., all participants who attended at least one session were included in analyses), these authors found that both the MBSR and PCGT groups showed significant improvement on the primary outcome (clinician-assessed PTSD) with no statistically significant differences between groups. The MBSR group achieved greater reductions in self-reported PTSD symptoms at post-treatment, but these differences were not maintained at the follow-up seven weeks later. In addition, although a greater number of participants in the PCGT group completed the post-treatment assessments (81%) than in the MBSR group (68%), this difference was not significant. Also, on average, participants in the PCGT group attended 5.66 group sessions, while participants in the MBSR condition attended 4.58 sessions, although this difference was not significant.

Considering these three studies comparing MBSR to PCGT, the evidence appears consistent that both interventions are efficacious, as they are associated with significant reductions in PTSD symptoms. Differences between these two treatments in efficacy are not apparent. In terms of dropouts from the trials, the evidence is somewhat mixed.

Dropouts were significantly and substantially lower for those in the PCGT group in the earlier trials (Bremner et al., 2017; Polusny et al., 2015), while the later trial (Davis et al., 2019) indicated no significant differences.

In all seven of the trials reviewed above, PCGT has been studied only as a comparison treatment in studies using a "superiority design." In a superiority design, the study's statistical approach tests only whether or not one treatment is superior to another but cannot determine whether or not the treatments are equivalent: "the absence of evidence is not evidence of absence" (Alderson, 2004). Thus, even though no significant differences were found between PCGT and the study's target treatment in most of these trials, the superiority design does not allow us to conclude that the treatments have equal efficacy. Future clinical trials using "non-inferiority designs" may determine that PCGT is not inferior to other treatments and can be considered equivalent in efficacy.

Importantly, all of the RCTs of PCGT reviewed here were completed in veteran or active duty military populations with a focus on combat-related PTSD. Four of the study samples did not include any women and the others included only small numbers of women. Thus, the degree to which findings from these studies can be generalized to women and to other trauma populations is unknown. As noted in the previous chapter and discussed in chapter eight, the PCGT framework can be applied to different populations though there are few research findings at this time to directly speak to efficacy in non-military settings.

Reviews and Meta-Analyses of Present-Centered Therapies

Over that last decade, several researchers have conducted systematic reviews and meta-analyses of the randomized trials that used present-centered therapies for PTSD. A meta-analysis is a statistical analysis that examines and pools data from a number of independent studies of the same subject in order to determine conclusions about the body of research. Most of these meta-analyses (Belsher et al., 2019; Frost, Laska, & Wampold, 2014; Imel, Laska, Jakupcak, & Simpson, 2013; Kitchiner, Lewis, Roberts, & Bisson, 2019; Steenkamp et al., 2015) aggregated the results from trials examining both individual and group present-centered therapy. There are important similarities between group and individual present-centered therapy – most notably the focus on problem solving current issues rather than review of past experiences. However, a fundamental distinction between group and individual treatment is, of course, the critical role of the group and group process. As described in chapter one, interaction among group members is considered to be an important vehicle for therapeutic resolution in PCGT. Although key differences between group and individual therapy are not always accounted for in these reviews, they do provide important information about the present-centered approach to PTSD treatment and how this approach differs from other approaches, such as trauma-focused treatment.

Dropout from treatment was the focus of two meta-analyses of clinical trials for PTSD (Imel et al., 2013; Lewis, Roberts, Gibson, & Bisson, 2020). In both studies, findings revealed dropout rates exceeding 15% on average across all studies examined, with a large amount of variability. There was little evidence of consistent differences among interventions with two notable exceptions: the first study found that present-centered therapy had lower dropout rates compared to trauma-focused treatments and the second study found trauma-focused treatments had higher dropout rates compared to non-trauma-focused treatments. Over three large-scale clinical trials that compared trauma-focused to present-centered treatments, Imel et al. (2013) found that trauma-focused treatments were associated with an average of 36% odds of dropout and present-centered associated with 22%, a significant difference. Lewis et al. (2020) found the trauma-focused treatments to have a significantly higher dropout rate (18% on average) compared to treatments without a trauma focus (14% on average). These authors also found that there was no evidence that group interventions had higher dropout rates than individual treatments.

An early meta-analysis of PCT as a treatment for PTSD (Frost et al., 2014) included five studies and found no significant differences in efficacy between PCT and other evidence-based treatments, though PCT had considerably lower dropout rates. Of note, two of the studies examined used PCT as an individual therapy intervention and three examined PCGT, yet all of the results were aggregated for the meta-analysis. Additionally, one of the group trials included in the meta-analysis, Classen et al. (2011), enrolled individuals with histories of childhood sexual abuse but did not evaluate or report how many of these individuals met diagnostic criteria for PTSD. Nonetheless, in publishing this meta-analysis, Frost et al. (2014) drew well-deserved attention to considering the evidence base for present-centered therapy for PTSD.

Steenkamp et al. (2015) performed a systematic review of randomized controlled trials examining the efficacy of individual and group trauma-focused treatments for military-related PTSD. They found that, despite large within-group reductions in symptoms among participants in the trauma-focused conditions, approximately two-thirds retained a PTSD diagnosis at post-treatment, and a generally similar degree of efficacy was noted in present-centered active treatment control groups. The authors concluded that the trauma-focused treatments they examined (cognitive processing therapy and prolonged exposure) were "marginally superior" compared to active treatment control groups, including present-centered therapy.

Belsher et al. (2019) completed a rigorous systematic review and meta-analysis of the individual and group randomized clinical trials of present-centered therapy to treat PTSD. In contrast to many other reviews examining the efficacy of the target treatments in clinical trials – most often trauma-focused treatments – this meta-analysis focused on present-centered therapy and used a non-inferiority design. These authors reported that there is moderate evidence that present-centered therapy is more effective in reducing PTSD severity than non-active control conditions (e.g., wait list, standard care, minimal attention, or repeated assessment). In the comparison of present-centered therapy and trauma-focused cognitive behavioral therapy, the evidence did not support the hypothesis that PCT has comparable effectiveness or is "non-inferior" to trauma-focused cognitive behavioral therapy; in other words, there was some evidence of superiority of trauma-focused therapy. The authors concluded that "Findings are generally consistent with current clinical practice guidelines that suggest that PCT may be offered as a treatment for PTSD when TF-CBT is not available" (Belsher et al., 2019, p. 2). However, several caveats were offered that temper this conclusion. First, the authors rated the quality of evidence for this analysis to be low. Second, the findings from the subset of studies that conducted follow-up assessments up to 12 months' post-treatment suggest a different conclusion. Findings from these studies indicate that the differences between present-centered and trauma-focused groups attenuated over time such that no clinically meaningful differences were detected by the final assessments. Third, this meta-analysis determined there was moderate quality evidence that the dropout rates for present-centered therapy were 14% lower than for trauma-focused treatments. Finally, the authors reported that, since all the included studies were designed to test the effectiveness of trauma-focused treatments, there was potential bias in favor of those treatments. The authors also conducted a subgroup analysis to examine differences in outcomes between individual and present-centered group therapy (PCGT) found no significant differences, indicating that the subgroup findings were consistent with the main findings. Thus, this rigorous review supported trauma-focused treatment as possessing a clinically meaningful advantage in efficacy compared to present-centered treatment at post-treatment. It is important to note, however, that this advantage did not persist through the 12-month follow-up, and that present-centered therapy was found to be superior with regards to lower dropout rates.

Aggregating data from three clinical trials examining trauma-focused treatments in active duty military samples, Litz et al. (2019) examined symptom change trajectories. Two of the included trials used a present-centered approach as a comparison treatment, one of which was a study of group treatments (Resick et al., 2015, reviewed above). These investigators found that the trauma-focused treatments were not associated with better slope change (i.e., greater symptom change) than present-centered therapy. These authors suggested "It can be argued that PCT should be used as a first-line treatment for war-related PTSD" (Litz et al., 2019, p. 8). While acknowledging that present-centered therapy requires rigorous training (as do other manualized treatments), they note that it is "arguably simpler to learn, easier to use, and less invasive and demanding of therapists and patients" (Litz et al., 2019, p. 8).

Most recently, Kitchiner et al. (2019) completed a meta-analysis examining the efficacy of PTSD treatments, including present-centered approaches, among veteran and active-duty military samples. Seven studies that examined present-centered treatment were included in this meta-analysis: five that delivered therapy in an individual format and two that delivered PCGT (Resick et al., 2015; Schnurr et al., 2003). Consistent with the review in this chapter, Kitchiner et al. (2019) found that when comparing PCGT to group trauma-focused therapies across these two studies, there was no difference in reduction of PTSD symptoms at post-treatment. While they go on to report that group trauma-focused therapies had greater reductions at 6- and 12-month follow-ups, this is based solely on a subset of results from one study: self-reported PTSD in the Resick et al. (2015) study. As noted previously, while Resick et al. (2015) did find significantly greater reductions among trauma-focused therapy participants on a self-report measure of PTSD symptoms, PCGT was found to be equally effective when using a clinician-administered measure of PTSD and when considering the percentage of participants who achieved a clinically significant change in symptoms.

Meta-Analysis of Group Versus Individual Treatments for PTSD

On a different note, treatment providers have been interested in the question of modality of treatment – group versus individual – and whether or not one modality has an advantage over the other. Indeed, chapter one and later chapters of this book discuss the unique benefits offered by a group approach to PTSD treatment. Unfortunately, there are no published randomized trials that compared PCGT to individual present-centered therapy to directly examine this question for present-centered approaches. However, the Kitchiner et al. (2019) review included a comparison of group and individual treatments for PTSD. They identified only one study that addressed this issue: Resick et al. (2017) compared individual and group cognitive processing therapy in an active-duty military population and found that the individual format was more efficacious at post-treatment, but that this difference did not persist to the six-month follow-up. Thus, there is very little research examining the relative benefits of group compared to individual treatment. The single study available shows no advantage for one modality over the other at follow-up, so this finding should not be considered evidence that group approaches are any less powerful or efficacious than individual.

Clinical Practice Guidelines Conclusions and Caveats

Several organizations have conducted large-scale reviews of clinical trials for PTSD to synthesize the extant evidence in order to offer treatment guidelines for clinicians (e.g., the American Psychological Association [APA; 2017], the International Society for Traumatic Stress Studies [ISTSS; 2019], the U.S. Departments of Veterans Affairs and Defense [VA/DoD; 2017]). As a recent example, in 2018 the ISTSS released the results of a comprehensive evaluation of high-quality research for PTSD as the *ISTSS Prevention and Treatment Guidelines*. Given the large number of trials reviewed and analyses performed in this effort, researchers were able to examine the outcomes for studies of PCGT separately from those for individual present-centered therapy. Due to specific inclusion criteria developed for this ISTSS review, only two studies (Resick et al., 2015; Schnurr et al., 2003) were included in the meta-analysis comparing group trauma-focused CBT with PCGT. Although the results indicated that group trauma-focused CBT showed a positive effect compared to PCGT, the small number of studies and quality of the evidence led the investigators to state that further research is very likely to change the estimate of this effect. In addition, this meta-analysis only considered effects at post-treatment so did not reflect that in both of these studies the differences between groups diminished during the follow-up periods. Another meta-analysis conducted for these treatment guidelines examined differences between MBSR and PCGT and included the three studies described above with the conclusion that there is "no evidence of a difference" between MBSR and PCGT.

In a "guide to the guidelines," Hamblen et al. (2019) highlighted some of the similarities and differences among five sets of treatment guidelines examined. All guidelines gave strong recommendations for individual trauma-focused treatments and three recommended individual present-centered therapy. Only three of the five sets of guidelines addressed group treatments. ISTSS (2019) gave a moderate recommendation for group trauma-focused CBT, but no recommendation was made for PCGT. The VA/DoD guidelines provided a moderate recommendation for group therapy over no treatment and noted that the quality and quantity of evidence is insufficient to recommend any specific type of group therapy over another. The 2013 guidelines offered by the Phoenix Australia Centre for Posttraumatic Mental Health (Phoenix Australia Centre for Posttraumatic Mental Health, 2013) gave a low recommendation for group treatment in general and did not distinguish between trauma-focused or other types of treatment. As noted previously, PCGT was used only as a comparison treatment in all of the trials reviewed and no evidence of superiority or non-inferiority of PCGT compared to another treatment is available. Thus, despite the encouraging evidence offered in this chapter, the current treatment guidelines do not provide support for PCGT as a recommended treatment for PTSD.

However, several researchers – including those involved in development of some of these guidelines – have noted shortcomings with published clinical practice guidelines and urged caution in interpreting recommendations. Norcross and Wampold (2019) offered a critique of the American Psychological Association (2017) clinical practice guidelines in which they emphasized the importance of the therapist–client relationship: "the relationship is the heart of healing trauma" (Norcross & Wampold, 2019, p. 394). They expressed that the APA guidelines were overly focused on the specifics of therapeutic methods while neglecting a wealth of evidence that therapist–client relationships, treatment adaptations, and individual therapist effects better account for therapy outcomes than the treatment method per se. Further, they cited numerous meta-analyses demonstrating roughly equivalent outcomes for recommended trauma therapies, suggesting the specifics of the treatment method matter far less than the APA implicitly suggested. They cautioned: "the most studied therapy is not the most effective therapy. Cognitive–behavioral therapies are obviously the most frequently studied treatments in RCTs .... Identifying them as 'first line' or 'strongly recommended' therapies because they are the most studied is not compelling" (Norcross & Wampold, 2019, p. 397). Courtois and Brown (2019) levelled a similar criticism of the APA's guidelines and concluded that "'the jury is still out' and any foreclosure around one or more treatment or method is premature" (Courtois & Brown, 2019, p. 338).

Clear clinical guidelines with succinct and unambiguous recommendations likely lack the nuance needed to identify the most effective treatment for any given situation. As noted by Hamblen et al. (2019), practice guidelines provide information that should be used "as a starting place for a conversation about treatment choice" (Hamblen et al., 2019, p. 372). Steenkamp et al. (2020b) emphasized the importance of monitoring non-response to and potential dropout from treatment and suggested that switching to new treatments may be warranted in such cases; they noted that there are "multiple roads to symptom improvement" (p. 302). Thus, guidelines do not hold "the answer," rather they should be used to guide decision making in combination with other important considerations: client preferences and characteristics (e.g., comorbidities, symptom severity, response to treatment), clinician experience, and availability of resources.

Conclusion

Although more research is needed, the extant literature provides preliminary support for the use of PCGT to treat PTSD. No consistent differences were found between PCGT and evidence-based trauma-focused group treatments, with most of the differences detected immediately post-treatment. Studies that followed participants for six months or more suggest that post-treatment differences attenuate over time. Additionally, evidence has accrued from three studies showing no differences between PCGT and MBSR. Given the superiority design of the published RCTs and the fact that PCGT was used as a comparison group that was hypothesized to be inferior to the target treatments studied, we cannot currently conclude that PCGT is "as good as" other types of therapy. We feel it is time to recognize PCGT as a legitimate treatment in its own right and recommend that future studies examine PCGT as a primary focus of research. Non-inferiority designs should be employed to test whether this treatment can be considered comparable or equivalent to other evidence-based treatments. In addition, as all of the RCTs examined here were conducted with veteran or active-duty military samples, studies including women and non-veteran/military populations are needed to determine if this treatment will work as well or perhaps better with other populations.

One consistent finding in this literature is that dropout rates for PCGT are lower than for the group treatments against which it has been compared. This speaks to high tolerability and acceptability of PCGT to clients. This is critical to consider in the context of consistently high rates of dropout even for the most celebrated and evidence-based treatments for PTSD (Imel et al., 2013; Lewis et al., 2020). A present-centered approach may also be more appealing to therapists as it has been identified as easier to learn and less demanding for therapists than trauma-focused treatments (Litz et al., 2019).

Another potential advantage of PCGT over other treatments is the focus on socialization and social support. Recent evidence emphasizes the importance of social support in the long-term trajectory of PTSD (Lee et al., 2020). Given the focus on group interaction and cohesion, PCGT may have a particular ability to enhance socialization – to foster mutual support among group members in the short run and to boost skills that will augment friendships and family relationships in the long run. As there is scant empirical evidence that evaluates whether group treatments are more efficacious than individual, future research should examine whether PCGT has advantages over individual treatments in terms of social functioning and other outcomes.

Although current published treatment guidelines for PTSD did not include PCGT as a first-line therapy, we agree with Courtois and Brown (2019) that "the jury is still out" (Courtois & Brown, 2019, p. 338). While we await further research and a verdict, we offer this book to make PCGT available to clinicians who wish to utilize it. The following chapters of this book provide the PCGT manual along with clinical examples and wisdom to educate therapists about how to provide this treatment. The evidence supports that PCGT is a viable treatment with the potential to reduce suffering and enhance functioning for individuals with PTSD. PCGT is an accessible and useful tool to be included in the toolbox for clinicians who treat PTSD.

References

Alderson, P. (2004). Absence of evidence is not evidence of absence. *BMJ*, *328*(7438), 476–477. https://doi.org/10.1136/bmj.328.7438.476

American Psychiatric Association. (2013). *Diagnostic and statistical manual of mental disorders* (5th ed.). Washington, D.C.: American Psychiatric Association.

American Psychological Association. (2017). *Clinical practice guideline for the treatment of posttraumatic stress disorder (PTSD) in adults.* Retrieved from https://www.apa.org/ptsd-guideline

Belsher, B. E., Beech, E., Evatt, D., Smolenski, D. J., Shea, M. T., Otto, J. L., … Schnurr, P. P. (2019). Present-centered therapy (PCT) for posttraumatic stress disorder (PTSD) in adults. *Cochrane Database of Systematic Reviews, 2019* (11). DOI:10.1002/14651858.CD012898.pub2.

Bisson, J. I., Berliner, L., Cloitre, M., Forbes, D., Jensen, T. K., Lewis, C., … Shapiro, F. (2019, Aug). The International Society for Traumatic Stress Studies new guidelines for the prevention and treatment of posttraumatic stress disorder: Methodology and development process. *Journal of Traumatic Stress, 32*(4), 475–483. https://doi.org/10.1002/jts.22421

Bremner, J. D., Mishra, S., Campanella, C., Shah, M., Kasher, N., Evans, S., … Davis, L. L. (2017). A pilot study of the effects of mindfulness-based stress reduction on post-traumatic stress disorder symptoms and brain response to traumatic reminders of combat in Operation Enduring Freedom/Operation Iraqi freedom combat veterans with post-traumatic stress disorder. *Frontiers in Psychiatry, 8*, 157.

Classen, C. C., Palesh, O. G., Cavanaugh, C. E., Koopman, C., Kaupp, J. W., Kraemer, H. C., … Spiegel, D. (2011). A comparison of trauma-focused and present-focused group therapy for survivors of childhood sexual abuse: A randomized controlled trial. *Psychological Trauma: Theory, Research, Practice, and Policy, 3*(1), 84.

Courtois, C. A., & Brown, L. S. (2019). Guideline orthodoxy and resulting limitations of the American Psychological Association's Clinical Practice Guideline for the Treatment of PTSD in Adults. *Psychotherapy, 56*(3), 329–339. https://doi.org/10.1037/pst0000239

Davis, L. L., Whetsell, C., Hamner, M. B., Carmody, J., Rothbaum, B. O., Allen, R. S., … Bremner, J. D. (2019). A multisite randomized controlled trial of mindfulness-based stress reduction in the treatment of posttraumatic stress disorder. *Psychiatric Research and Clinical Practice, 1*(2), 39–48. https://doi.org/10.1176/appi.prcp.20180002

Department of Veterans' Affairs. (2017). *VA/DOD clinical practice guideline for the management of posttraumatic stress disorder and acute stress disorder.* Retrieved from https://www.healthquality.va.gov/guidelines/MH/ptsd/VADoDPTSDCPG Final012418.pdf

Elbogen, E. B., Johnson, S. C., Wagner, H. R., Newton, V. M., & Beckham, J. C. (2012). Financial well-being and postdeployment adjustment among Iraq and Afghanistan war veterans. *Military Medicine, 177*(6), 669–675.

Engelhard, I. M., van den Hout, M. A., Weerts, J., Hox, J. J., & van Doornen, L. J. (2009). A prospective study of the relation between posttraumatic stress and physical health symptoms. *International Journal of Clinical and Health Psychology, 9*(3), 365–372.

Foa, E. B., Keane, T. M., Friedman, M. J., & Cohen, J. A. (2010). *Effective treatments for PTSD: Practice Guidelines from the International Society for Traumatic Stress Studies* (2nd ed.). New York, NY: Guilford Publications.

Franz, M. R., Kaiser, A. P., Phillips, R. J., Lee, L. O., Lawrence, A. E., Taft, C. T., & Vasterling, J. J. (2020). Associations of warzone veteran mental health with partner mental health and family functioning: Family Foundations Study. *Depression and Anxiety.* DOI:10.1002/da.23083.

Frost, N. D., Laska, K. M., & Wampold, B. E. (2014). The evidence for present-centered therapy as a treatment for posttraumatic stress disorder. *Journal of Traumatic Stress, 27*(1), 1–8.

Fulton, J. J., Calhoun, P. S., Wagner, H. R., Schry, A. R., Hair, L. P., Feeling, N., ... Beckham, J. C. (2015). The prevalence of posttraumatic stress disorder in Operation Enduring Freedom/Operation Iraqi Freedom (OEF/OIF) Veterans: A meta-analysis. *Journal of Anxiety Disorders, 31*, 98–107. https://doi.org/10.1016/j.janxdis.2015.02.003

Grossman, P., Niemann, L., Schmidt, S., & Walach, H. (2004). Mindfulness-based stress reduction and health benefits: A meta-analysis. *Journal of Psychosomatic Research, 57*(1), 35–43.

Hamblen, J. L., Norman, S. B., Sonis, J. H., Phelps, A. J., Bisson, J. I., Nunes, V. D., ... & Schnurr, P. P. (2019). A guide to guidelines for the treatment of posttraumatic stress disorder in adults: An update. *Psychotherapy, 56*(3), 359–373. https://doi.org/10.1037/pst0000231

Imel, Z. E., Laska, K., Jakupcak, M., & Simpson, T. L. (2013). Meta-analysis of dropout in treatments for posttraumatic stress disorder. *Journal of Consulting and Clinical Psychology, 81*(3), 394.

Kabat-Zinn, J. (2005). *Coming to our senses: Healing ourselves and the world through mindfulness.* UK: Hachette .

Kessler, R. C., Chiu, W. T., Demler, O., & Walters, E. E. (2005). Prevalence, severity, and comorbidity of 12-month DSM-IV disorders in the National Comorbidity Survey replication. *Archives of General Psychiatry, 62*(6), 617–627.

Khoury, B., Sharma, M., Rush, S. E., & Fournier, C. (2015). Mindfulness-based stress reduction for healthy individuals: A meta-analysis. *Journal of Psychosomatic Research, 78*(6), 519–528. https://doi.org/10.1016/j.jpsychores.2015.03.009

Kitchiner, N. J., Lewis, C., Roberts, N. P., & Bisson, J. I. (2019). Active duty and ex-serving military personnel with post-traumatic stress disorder treated with psychological therapies: Systematic review and meta-analysis. *European Journal of Psychotraumatology, 10*(1), 1–17. https://doi.org/10.1080/20008198.2019.1684226

Lee, D. J., Lee, L. O., Bovin, M. J., Moshier, S. J., Dutra, S. J., Kleiman, S. E., … Marx, B. P. (2020). The 20-year course of posttraumatic stress disorder symptoms among veterans. *Journal of Abnormal Psychology.* https://doi.org/10.1037/abn0000571

Lewis, C., Roberts, N. P., Gibson, S., & Bisson, J. I. (2020). Dropout from psychological therapies for post-traumatic stress disorder (PTSD) in adults: systematic review and meta-analysis. *European Journal of Psychotraumatology, 11*(1), 1709709. https://doi.org/10.1080/20008198.2019.1709709

Litz, B. T., Berke, D. S., Kline, N. K., Grimm, K., Rusowicz-Orazem, L., Resick, P. A., … Peterson, A. L. (2019). Patterns and predictors of change in trauma-focused treatments for war-related posttraumatic stress disorder. *Journal of Consulting and Clinical Psychology, 87*(11), 1019–1029. https://doi.org/10.1037/ccp0000426

Mota, N. P., Tsai, J., Sareen, J., Marx, B. P., Wisco, B. E., Harpaz-Rotem, I., … Pietrzak, R. H. (2016). High burden of subthreshold DSM-5 post-traumatic stress disorder in US military veterans. *World Psychiatry: Official Journal of the World Psychiatric Association (WPA), 15*(2), 185.

National Center for PTSD. (2013a). *Clinician-administered PTSD scale for DSM-5 (CAPS-5).* Retrieved from https://www.ptsd.va.gov/professional/assessment/adult-int/caps.asp

National Center for PTSD. (2013b). *PTSD checklist for DSM-5 (PCL-5).* Retrieved from https://www.ptsd.va.gov/professional/assessment/adult-sr/ptsd-checklist.asp

Niles, B. L., Polizzi, C. P., Voelkel, E., Weinstein, E. S., Smidt, K., & Fisher, L. M. (2018). Initiation, dropout, and outcome from evidence-based psychotherapies in a VA PTSD outpatient clinic. *Psychological Services, 15*(4), 496–502. https://doi.org/10.1037/ser0000175

Norcross, J. C., & Wampold, B. E. (2019). Relationships and responsiveness in the psychological treatment of trauma: The tragedy of the APA Clinical Practice Guideline. *Psychotherapy (Chic), 56*(3), 391–399. https://doi.org/10.1037/pst0000228

Phoenix Australia Centre for Posttraumatic Mental Health. (2013). *Australian guidelines for the treatment of acute stress disorder and posttraumatic stress disorder.* Victoria: Phoenix Australia.

Polusny, M. A., Erbes, C. R., Thuras, P., Moran, A., Lamberty, G. J., Collins, R. C., … Lim, K. O. (2015). Mindfulness-based stress reduction for posttraumatic stress disorder among veterans: a randomized clinical trial. *JAMA, 314*(5), 456–465.

Ready, D. J., Mascaro, N., Wattenberg, M. S., Sylvers, P., Worley, V., & Bradley-Davino, B. (2018). A controlled study of group-based exposure therapy with Vietnam-era veterans. *Journal of Loss and Trauma, 23*(6), 439–457. https://doi.org/10.1080/15325024.2018.1485268

Resick, P. A., Wachen, J. S., Mintz, J., Young-McCaughan, S., Roache, J. D., Borah, A. M., … Peterson, A. L. (2015). A randomized clinical trial of group cognitive processing therapy compared with group present-centered therapy for PTSD among active duty military personnel. *Journal of Consulting and Clinical Psychology, 83*(6), 1058–1068. https://doi.org/10.1037/ccp0000016 doi:10.1001/jamapsychiatry.2016.2729

Resick, P. A., Wachen, J. S., & Dondanville, K. A. (2017). Effect of group vs individual therapy in active-duty military seeking treatment for posttraumatic stress disorder: A randomized clinical trial. *JAMA Psychiatry, 74*(1), 28–36.

Sareen, J., Cox, B. J., Stein, M. B., Afifi, T. O., Fleet, C., & Asmundson, G. J. (2007). Physical and mental comorbidity, disability, and suicidal behavior associated with posttraumatic stress disorder in a large community sample. *Psychosomatic Medicine, 69*(3), 242–248.

Schnurr, P. P. (2007). The rocks and hard places in psychotherapy outcome research. *Journal of Traumatic Stress, 20*(5), 779–792. https://doi.org/10.1002/jts.20292

Schnurr, P. P., Friedman, M. J., Foy, D. W., Shea, M. T., Hsieh, F. Y., Lavori, P. W., ... Bernardy, N. C. (2003). Randomized trial of trauma-focused group therapy for posttraumatic stress disorder: Results from a Department of Veterans Affairs cooperative study. *Archives of General Psychiatry, 60*(5), 481–489.

Schottenbauer, M. A., Glass, C. R., Arnkoff, D. B., Tendick, V., & Gray, S. H. (2008). Nonresponse and dropout rates in outcome studies on PTSD: Review and methodological considerations. *Psychiatry, 71*(2), 134–168. https://doi.org/10.1521/psyc.2008.71.2.134

Scott, K. M., Koenen, K. C., King, A., Petukhova, M. V., Alonso, J., Bromet, E. J., ... Kessler, R. C. (2018). Post-traumatic stress disorder associated with sexual assault among women in the WHO World Mental Health Surveys. *Psychological Medicine, 48*(1), 155–167. https://doi.org/10.1017/S0033291717001593

Sloan, D. M., Unger, W., Lee, D. J., & Beck, J. G. (2018). A randomized controlled trial of group cognitive behavioral treatment for veterans diagnosed with chronic posttraumatic stress disorder. *Journal of Traumatic Stress, 31*(6), 886–898. https://doi.org/10.1002/jts.22338

Smith, M. W., Schnurr, P. P., & Rosenheck, R. A. (2005). Employment outcomes and PTSD symptom severity. *Mental Health Services Research, 7*(2), 89–101.

Steenkamp, M. M., Litz, B. T., Hoge, C. W., & Marmar, C. R. (2015). Psychotherapy for military-related PTSD: A review of randomized clinical trials. *JAMA, 314*(5), 489–500.

Steenkamp, M. M., Litz, B. T., & Marmar, C. R. (2020a). First-line psychotherapies for military-related PTSD. *JAMA.* https://doi.org/10.1001/jama.2019.20825

Steenkamp, M. M., Litz, B. T., & Marmar, C. R. (2020b). PTSD treatments for veterans – Reply. *JAMA, 324*(3), 301–302.

Szafranski, D. D., Smith, B. N., Gros, D. F., & Resick, P. A. (2017). High rates of PTSD treatment dropout: A possible red herring? *Journal of Anxiety Disorders, 47*, 91–98. https://doi.org/10.1016/j.janxdis.2017.01.002

Weathers, F. W., Bovin, M. J., Lee, D. J., Sloan, D. M., Schnurr, P. P., Kaloupek, D. G., ... Marx, B. P. (2018). The clinician-administered PTSD scale for DSM-5 (CAPS-5): Development and initial psychometric evaluation in military veterans. *Psychological Assessment, 30*(3), 383–395. https://doi.org/10.1037/pas0000486

Weathers, F. W., Litz, B. T., Keane, T. M., Palmieri, P. A., Marx, B. P., & Schnurr, P. P. (2013). *The PTSD checklist for DSM-5 (PCL-5).* Retrieved from www.ptsd.va.gov/professional/assessment/adult-sr/ptsd-checklist.asp

Yalom, I. D. (1995). *The theory and practice of group psychotherapy.* New York, NY: Basic Books.

Yelland, L. N., Sullivan, T. R., Voysey, M., Lee, K. J., Cook, J. A., & Forbes, A. B. (2015). Applying the intention-to-treat principle in practice: Guidance on handling randomisation errors. *Clinical Trials, 12*(4), 418–423. https://doi.org/10.1177/1740774515588097

3   Guide for Present-Centered Group Therapy: The Manual Part I

M. Tracie Shea, Melissa S. Wattenberg, and Regina Dolan-Sewell

Guide for Present-Centered Group Therapy: The Manual Part I

This chapter provides the basic building blocks for understanding, implementing, and delivering present-centered group therapy.[1,2] Each session's objectives, rationale, and procedures are described, as indicated below.

Sections

- Overview of Present-Centered Group Therapy
- Session One: Orientation to Present-Centered Group Therapy
- Session Two: Education and Discussion: PTSD Symptoms and Associated Disorders
- Session Three: Education and Discussion: Common Issues Associated with PTSD
- Session Four: Identification and Discussion of Individual Issues and Goals
- Intermediate Sessions: Discussion of Current Life Issues
- Ending/Termination Sessions: Consolidating Gains, and Transition
- If Using Five Monthly Booster Sessions
- Summary

As discussed in chapter one, the didactic components of PCGT are "front-loaded" in the early sessions, identifying not only symptoms, but common themes, such as isolation, guilt, low self-esteem and anger, with attention to the reasons why these features develop when exposed to traumatic events. One purpose of the educational component is to normalize the associated features as well as the symptoms of PTSD. Another purpose is to offer a shared framework for awareness of PTSD and related themes in the individual's current day-to-day life. This awareness serves as a foundation for symptom management and other recovery strategies toward pursuit of functional personal goals. Appendix B at the end of this chapter outlines a 30-minute orientation meeting prior to the group. Clinics will vary in their intake procedures and length of screening, including whether they screen for group in person ahead of the group. This orientation tool is flexible for use by clinics with a variety of policies for group intake. Chapter eight further discusses elements of the assessment process for entering PCGT.

Overview of Present-Centered Group Therapy

Present-centered group therapy (PCGT) offers the essential therapeutic factors of group treatment (Yalom, 1995), adapted specifically for survivors of trauma. The central elements of PCGT include: 1) education about the typical symptoms and features associated with post-traumatic stress disorder (PTSD), particularly those affecting interpersonal relationships; and 2) the use of group format to decrease isolation, normalize symptoms, provide the experience of giving and receiving support and feedback, and offer opportunities for positive interpersonal interactions. The educational element includes a didactic component in the early sessions, identifying and describing common themes, such as isolation, guilt, low self-esteem, anger, etc., as well as impact of PTSD symptoms. One goal of this aspect of the education is to normalize the associated features as well as the symptoms of PTSD. Another goal is to develop a framework for the ongoing focus of the group, targeted at increasing awareness of the manifestations of PTSD-related themes in the individual's current day-to-day life, and increasing mastery and ability to cope with such issues. Finally, as discussed previously, the group naturally provides the opportunity to practice being in the present, contrasting with life dominated by traumatic memories.

The group format provides an opportunity for members to have positive experiences with relationships, an area that can be compromised in their current lives. The group offers opportunities for positive group cohesion, and development of an atmosphere of safety and trust through involvement in the group itself. Having an opportunity to discuss current life difficulties and ongoing emotional experiences in this receptive environment allows survivors of trauma to gain perspective regarding their current relationships, and life more generally. In addition, the group provides shared practice at concentrating on life in the present, contrasting with the trauma-based experience of intrusions of the past trauma into their everyday lives.

Group members have primary input into the agenda for the sessions. Facilitators enlist the group itself as one of the main interventions, along with therapeutic trauma-informed comments and guidance (see chapters four and five for interventions utilized in PCGT).

What PCGT Is Not, and What It Is

- While facilitators may offer suggestions about coping with symptoms and stress, they refrain from over-structuring the group through, for

example, systematic training in behavioral skills, relaxation training, or thought stopping.
- PCGT does not include disclosure, discussion, or exposure of individual traumatic events. Instead, the focus is on manifestation of the sequelae of traumatic experience in behavior and feelings in current day-to-day life. For example, a group member may be struggling with isolation and inability to form connections with others. In contrast to exposure-based models, PCGT emphasizes, in the initial education and brief education in ongoing sessions as relevant, how PTSD and traumatic experience may generally result in trauma-based ways of being in the world (e.g., avoiding attachments, difficulty trusting). This discussion remains in the present, without review of the individual's specific traumatic experiences, utilizing the group, and targeted facilitator comments, to address issues that arise. PCGT interventions are focused on helping the group members identify patterns in current feelings and behavior resulting from history of traumatic experience, while encouraging development of new, more effective responses that are less trauma-based, more relevant to the current situation. The goal is to develop and apply a broader framework for understanding the consequences of trauma and PTSD, so that the group members can recognize more clearly where their limitations and vulnerabilities lie, as well as their strengths and post-traumatic growth (Tedeschi & Calhoun, 2004). The aim is for group members to increase their ability to identify and modify trauma-based reactivity to current events and situations, with practice and support within the therapeutic group process. While basic interventions are incorporated in this chapter, chapters four and five elaborate further concerning materials and interventions useful with this modality.

Flexibility of PCGT

Present-centered group therapy is adaptable to the needs and logistics of the clinic, practice, or program in which it is implemented, as well as to the needs of the specific trauma population for which a clinic intends it.

Variations in Session Count and Length of Sessions

As discussed in chapters one and two, the original manual called for 30 weekly 90-minute sessions and five monthly "booster" sessions. In other contexts, this group has been limited to anywhere from eight or nine, to 16 sessions (see chapter two). PCGT has also been offered twice a week in some contexts. It has been run with 50-minute and 60-minute session durations. As a flexible treatment, PCGT can be tailored to the needs of the particular clinic or program (or research). The structure of the groups remains essentially the same, irrespective of the session length and number of groups, within the parameters described. Sessions under 50 minutes have not been researched but have been offered in clinical settings; shorter than 45 minutes is not recommended given the tasks of the group. Fewer than nine sessions (or eight with one introductory session) is not recommended given the phases of the group. Rolling admission is not recommended, as the group builds from the initial educational sessions and also develops rapport and cohesion through the group process; starting and ending as a cohort is recommended (see chapter eight for adaptations in settings that need to have rolling admissions). In the upcoming section on the intermediate sessions of this group, further potential variations are discussed. While the session numbers are flexible, for convenience this chapter will use a 12-week model.

Standards for Missed Sessions

Clinics may set their own standards as to number of visits or number of visits in a row that may be missed before members are no longer able to return to the group. In the context of the original study, members could miss no more than three sessions in a row. In a non-research context, the decision will be a matter of clinical judgment, although it is useful to have a standard at the outset of the group and to inform the members of it. The key in determining this standard is to consider both number of visits that will allow members to benefit, and the impact of more than a certain number of missed visits on the group as a whole (and its membership) in terms of group cohesion and emotional safety in the group. Timing is a factor, in that missed visits at the start means that a member is not sharing in the collective knowledge base of the group (and therefore, it may be beneficial for all members to start by the second session, and to not include members who miss more than one of the educational sessions). Missing three sessions in the middle section of the group may be more workable than three at the start, depending on the stage of group development and number of sessions included in the group.

Session One: Orientation to Present-Centered Group Therapy

Objectives

1. Explain PCGT rationale and goals
2. Introduce group members to each other
3. Explain structure and process of group
4. Discuss need for group cohesion and support
5. Explain ground rules

6. Encourage and address questions/reactions
7. Explain session review/checkout procedure

Rationale for Facilitators

The early sessions of present-centered group therapy (PCGT) are directed towards development of the trust, comfort, and group cohesion that are critical to group work. The goals of these early sessions are:

1. To help members begin to feel comfortable with each other and with the group format
2. To provide an understanding of how the group process will work, and how it is related to their issues with PTSD.

Facilitators play a more active role in the early sessions than in subsequent sessions, and the early sessions are more structured than later sessions. It is during the first three to four sessions that the framework, structure, and norms of the group are established. There is more work on the part of the facilitators in these sessions to help develop a structure that allows members to feel that the group is a safe place, with flexibility, but with appropriate boundaries. Early sessions include facilitators helping the group members in:

a. Getting to know one another
b. Working to resolve potential conflicts
c. Exploring expectations
d. Discussing symptoms and associated features of PTSD
e. Exploring a variety of present-day issues, determined by the group members' needs and concerns

In this first session, facilitators introduce the group as a collaborative process between facilitators and group members. This session includes:

1. Introduction of facilitators to the group members and group members to each other
2. Presentation and discussion of the rationale for PCGT
3. Description of how the group will work
4. Presentation of ground rules and what is expected from group members
5. Discussion of potential gains from the group experience, and encouragement of realistic, positive expectations about potential benefits from the group
6. Encouragement of motivation and active participation from group members.

Procedures

1. Overview of Session One
    During our time today we will do two main things. First, we want to tell you about the present-centered group, how it will work, and what you can expect. We'll also talk about some rules of the group, and what we will expect of you. We will also spend time with introductions, to begin the process for all of us getting to know each other.

2. Introduction
    Facilitators introduce themselves and briefly describe their background/training etc., then ask members to introduce themselves. Note that members will be asked to say more about themselves later on in today's session, but for now just names will do.

3. Group Rationale and Goals
    Facilitators describe the rationale behind the present-centered group:

    The present-focus in this group means that you are making an investment in your current life. Many survivors of trauma with PTSD find that the past has monopolized their lives, leaving a sense of emptiness, or even unreality, about the present. Some express that their traumatic experiences seem much more real to them than everyday life around them. Many see themselves as monuments to the past, unable to connect with spouses, children, grandchildren, and other family and friends, despite a deep devotion to these individuals in their everyday lives.

    Many survivors of trauma express a need to assert themselves in their current lives, rather than being relegated to the past and the trauma. Yet this process of refocusing on the present can be very challenging for those with traumatic experience.

    This group is devoted exclusively to that process of living in the present. The overall goal is to help you establish a meaningful relationship with the world around you and the important people in it – family, friends, and (last but not least) yourself. You may also want to work on developing more meaningful activities in your life. This focus also means working to reduce stress, anxiety, and depression that may be associated with problems in your current life.

    PTSD is very often associated with difficulties in managing stress, in feeling unable to adequately deal with problems in life, and particularly, with difficulties in interpersonal relationships. There are several reasons for this, which we will talk about in later sessions. While each of you may experience different kinds of problems, most likely all of you have had some difficulty in establishing and maintaining close and satisfying relationships with others. It may often be difficult for you to understand what is going on in your relationships, to talk about your positive and negative feelings, and to listen to feedback from others. There may be frequent misunderstandings, hurt feelings, or even a total breakdown in communication. Some of you may have isolated yourselves from other people as a result; others of you may be struggling with relationships but finding a lot of challenges in doing so.

PTSD is often associated with feeling overwhelmed by these and other typical tensions, frustrations, and problems of life. There is often a tendency to shut down emotionally when problems occur, or to feel hopeless and defeated. Sometimes there is a tendency to overreact to these problems, to blow up, to blow things out of proportion, or to withdraw.

The purpose of this group is to provide an opportunity to get a better understanding about the ways in which PTSD symptoms and features may be creating obstacles for you, to identify more clearly where these issues are arising, and to see if there are alternative ways of thinking about and responding to these trauma-based patterns that may work better for you. We will ask you to talk about the challenges you are experiencing currently in your lives, and to provide support and feedback to each other, toward overcoming these challenges and moving toward the life you want. The group also provides an opportunity to talk about your interactions with each other here in the group. This might feel difficult at times; however, if you learn to talk about your feelings and reactions to each other in the group, it may help you to do this with others in your life outside of the group.

So, the goals of the group include helping you to learn to identify and discuss problem areas, and to improve your ability to deal with such problems. In this way, the group may help to decrease feelings of isolation, and increase your satisfaction with your relationships and with life more generally.

Note: What the group will not be talking about (i.e., traumatic experiences)

It is important that the group members do not unintentionally get the message that facilitators do not appreciate the importance of the traumatic material, or that they are afraid of hearing about the trauma, or don't want to hear about it. So it is important to clarify from the beginning the reasons why the group will not include discussions of trauma, and to check out whether the reasons for the limits on talking about trauma make sense to the group members. The more that they understand and accept the reasons for present focus and avoidance of traumatic material up front, the easier it will be to keep the group present focused.

While we will talk a lot in this group about how PTSD continues to affect your life, we will not be talking here about your individual, specific traumatic experiences.

We recognize the significance of the past, and the profound impact traumatic experiences have had on members of this group. We know that these experiences have been and continue to be critically important for you; they are why you are here today, and they affect much of your day-to-day experience. We want to be clear that by focusing on the present and by asking you to avoid getting into descriptions and discussions of your traumatic experiences, we are not suggesting that these experiences are unimportant, or that you should try to forget them. We know that would be impossible; nor would many of you want to forget even if you could. At the same time, we believe in the importance of your trying to live the best you can in the present, and to improve the quality of your current lives and your personal interactions with others. Our strategy in this group will be to reduce the painful experiences and feelings you have, and move your life forward, by working on the issues you are dealing with in your current life, and increasing your ability to cope with current problems and difficulties.

There is a second very important reason why we need to avoid discussions of individual traumatic events, and why we will try to shift you back to the present if this should occur. Hearing about traumatic events experienced by another person may be triggering or disturbing to members of the group if they are not expecting or are not prepared to hear or talk about such experiences. Some of you may have had this experience of being triggered in the past. Similarly, use of trauma-related words and phrases may be a trigger for members. Even if you believe that it would not bother you to hear others' events, it is important to remember that this may not be true for other members of the group. Since the focus of this group is on present-day experiences, none of you will be expecting to hear about traumatic events that could well remind you of your own. If trauma recollections should come up spontaneously, we will need to redirect the discussion to bring the focus back to the present. Sometimes, it can happen that discussion of PTSD and related symptoms may unintentionally remind you of specific trauma memories. If you experience distressing memories while in group, please let the group know that you feel "triggered," and we will help you refocus on the present.

Part of our job as facilitators will be to help the group with this – if someone begins to digress into past traumatic events, we will remind you and help you to refocus. We also ask that members help each other with this effort.

This is a good time to ask for reactions from the members, particularly to see if there are any feelings associated with being assigned to the present-centered group (e.g.,

How are you feeling about being in this group, that is, the treatment focusing on the present vs. the past? Did anyone have any hopes or preferences? What were they?)

If there are negative reactions expressed, or comments about wanting to be in a group that allows discussion of trauma experiences, it may be helpful to empathize with these feelings, while revisiting the rationale for this group (of course, members can opt for alternate or concurrent treatment at any time). This is also a good time to emphasize positive expectations about what members will get out of the group, noting that many survivors of trauma have expressed getting much help from this type of group, and that the group has a good track record in PTSD treatment research.

4.   Structure and Process of the Group

Each clinic, practice, or program will make a determination of members' needs and clinic capacities regarding number, length, and frequency of sessions, and share this information during (and often prior to) the initial session. Members are also informed of the basic group structure:

- Check-In
- Structured group content initially, then agenda setting by members
- Group Discussion
- Checkout

Participation

Each member's participation is highly valued and contributes to feelings of group cohesion; thus, members are asked to arrive on time and remain for the entire session if possible. This being said, given members' PTSD, it is important for them to have the ultimate control over staying and leaving. Facilitators take an encouraging rather than a controlling approach to this concern, offering welcome and acceptance toward members negotiating capacity to stay through groups.

Absences

Members are asked to notify the group ahead of time, whenever possible, if they will miss a session, and to call the facilitators to let them know they will miss the group if something comes up between sessions. Again, facilitators take a welcoming and accepting approach.

Overview of the Group Content/Process

In the first few sessions of the group, we will spend a lot of time talking about the symptoms of PTSD, and about other kinds of features that are frequently associated with PTSD in general. We will address problems with self-esteem, excessive guilt, difficulty trusting people – which may be interfering with your getting the most you can out of your life now. Many of you probably are familiar with the symptoms of PTSD, but this will be a chance to increase your understanding of your own experiences with these symptoms, and to hear how others are experiencing and dealing with these symptoms.

We will spend some time talking about how PTSD in survivors of trauma has frequently affected relationships – with family, partners, children, friends. Again, the purpose of these sessions is to give you a chance to understand more clearly the nature of your own ongoing difficulties, and how they may be related to PTSD. Talking about your experiences with PTSD and hearing others talk about theirs may help you to think about your problems differently, and may help you to think of different ways of approaching them.

Following these early sessions, the group will shift to a focus on current issues in your life. Each member will have the opportunity to define the areas that are most important, or that present the greatest challenges – which you may then choose to focus on and work on in this group. In these sessions, you will be doing most of the talking, and our role will be to help you with this process. We'll talk more about how these later sessions will work, later on.

Discussion of Need for Group Cohesion and Support

The benefits that each of you will get out of the group depend upon how much all of you participate and support each other. This is really the most important element of the group – building a feeling of support and trust among all of you. Support from each other helps you to cope with difficult and painful issues and experiences in your current life, and trust makes it possible for each of you to talk about your own personal issues. We are all here to understand, not evaluate or justify. We are not here to judge one another, but to give support and feedback in order to help you look at your experiences in more detail and understand them better.

Explaining Ground Rules

[Provide a Group Guidelines handout for your own group or clinic – the exact ground rules will vary by clinic, but will include at least these basic standards.]

We've just talked about the need for a supportive atmosphere in this group. One way of helping achieve this is through setting up some rules that we will ask you to follow, in order to make the group feel safe for each other and help make support happen.

Confidentiality

By participating in this group, each member agrees not to disclose the contents of the group discussion outside of the group session. Confidentiality is essential if members are going to speak freely and have confidence that their statements will remain in the group. Facilitators note 1) the exceptions to confidentiality for clinical reasons, and then 2) the protection of confidentiality for any materials that may apply in your specific group circumstances, which could include recordings, assessments, homework, supervision of therapists, and/or research-related information (if your group is held within a research project).

Exceptions to Confidentiality

For the facilitators, include legal responsibility of risk of danger to self or others, and risk to a minor child, or to an elderly or handicapped person. Facilitators will also record necessary information in the medical treatment record, and share relevant information with other members of the group member's treatment team, in the interest of coordinating good clinical care.

Other ground rules include that the group guidelines are based on respect and co-creating a recovery-oriented therapeutic environment in which members can learn from each other; therefore:

- Keep regular attendance (*provide numbers to call*)
- Attend group free from influence of non-prescribed substances
- Limit distractions, for example:

  - No food during session
  - No smoking during the session (while most settings do not allow smoking, this rule applies to telementalhealth sessions as well)
  - Cell phones/pagers off

- Try to stay in the room during the session unless it is absolutely necessary to leave (in which case, alert facilitators/group to reason for leaving, and level of safety)
- Respect for safety: no violence, threats of violence, intimidation, or bullying
- Standard of respect to the group and its members
- No use of demeaning names in reference to any group of people
- Limit political discussion to describing personal activities (e.g., volunteering for a campaign or organization – no advocating for a political point of view)
- Limit discussion of religion to spiritual life as a personal support for you (no "preaching" a particular religion or religious point of view)
- If participating in a virtual or telehealth group, provide your location and emergency contacts

Further Introductions and Discussions of Expectations

Members are asked to further introduce themselves by saying something about themselves, for example what their current situation is (e.g., marital status, living arrangements, employment status, and/or area of important involvement in their lives). This is an invitation to say what they want; but encourage all to address the question:

What do you hope or expect to get out of the group?

Explain and Conduct Session Review (Checkout)

We'll leave about ten minutes at the end of each group to reflect on the session. This is an opportunity to comment briefly about the session, including any of the following:

1. *What you got out of the group this session*
2. *How the group discussion related to your own issues*
3. *Any difficulties you may have experienced in group*
4. *Any suggestions as to how the group might have worked better.*

For example, if you experienced difficulty getting "floor time," or felt the discussion was especially meaningful (or not meaningful) for you this week, you may use this time to give this feedback to the group. This checkout will also be a chance to let the group know how you're doing as you are leaving the session.

Facilitators ask if there are any questions or reactions, and begin the Checkout by asking for comments, reactions, questions, etc. This should be an invitation to the group as a whole, rather than going around to each member. The Checkout is a chance for the facilitators to raise observations and check them out as well. For example, inquiring about a member who has been unusually silent, asking if everyone feels that they did get enough floor time, how might the process be improved, etc. The purpose of the Checkout will be repeated in the next couple of sessions.

Session Two: Education and Discussion: PTSD Symptoms and Associated Disorders

Objectives

1. Familiarize members with both today's group and group structure
2. Educate members about the check-in procedure
3. Increase level of comfort in group setting among group members
4. Increase knowledge about symptoms of PTSD (as discussed in Appendix A)[3], in order to develop a shared understanding and language for addressing issues related to PTSD
5. Increase group member's understanding of their own and others' personal experiences with PTSD symptoms.

Rationale for Facilitators

This session is devoted to providing group members with information regarding the nature of PTSD, including symptoms and associated features. This information is essential background for helping group members understand what is happening to them, to normalize their experiences, and to provide a common framework for the work of the group. A second reason for discussion of PTSD symptoms is to increase the sense of connection among the group members by highlighting the experiences that they have in common. While this discussion highlights the potential problems and barriers posed by PTSD, the intent is to utilize this shared knowledge in the interest of expanding personal capacity and movement toward cherished goals, meaningful involvement, and fuller investment in current life.

Procedures

1. Group Check-In (approximately ten minutes of group time; may be slightly longer in this group due to need for members to re-introduce themselves)

    After greetings and noting any absences, if relevant, facilitators may want to have the members reintroduce themselves by going around and repeating their names. If there are any new members (i.e., anyone who missed the first session), the introduction process should of course be repeated for each member.

    Facilitators next ask the group for any reactions, comments, or questions from the last session, and address any that are raised. It is important to educate members about the purpose of the check-in and intended content.

    The check-in, rather than a review of the week for each member, is an opportunity to raise any issues, concerns, reactions, or comments "left over" from the prior week's group (positive, negative, or neutral), especially if there are lingering needs for clarification. Reactions to the prior group may include: extending appreciation; taking exception to something stated in the group; an observation spurred by the discussion in the group; efforts to apply learning in group to current life; need for closure on an issue that was not resolved in the group; and /or clarifying questions.

    Facilitators do not "call on" each member of the group; rather, members are encouraged to respond either about the prior week's group, or anything they feel will affect their participation in the current group. Facilitators may sometimes call on a specific member (e.g., if that member has been unusually quiet, or appears to have something to say but has not spoken). The majority of group time is spent in discussion on group topics, whether formal (as in the first few sessions), or open-ended (the remainder of the sessions).

    Note to Facilitator: The reason that a lengthy member-by-member check-in is not conducted is that it would take up group time that needs to be allocated to more lively group discussion. Keeping the check-in topic to "anything left over from last week's group" (rather than a check-in on how each member is doing, or a week in review for each member) will keep the check-in on-point and within its intended time frame of approximately ten minutes. Members will have an opportunity to share personal aspects of their lives in subsequent sessions, and in this session in the context of discussion of symptoms.

Group members are next reminded about group ground rules (e.g.,: *"As we said last week, in order to be the most helpful for you, there needs to be a supportive atmosphere in this group. One way of helping achieve this is through setting up some rules which we will ask you to follow, in order to make the group safe for each other and help make support happen."*).

2.   Review the Ground Rules (i.e., confidentiality, food/smoking, leaving the room, politics, violence/threats, respect)

It may also be important to remind members that this group will not be focusing on the trauma that they have experienced, but rather on current life issues, and that it will be necessary for the facilitators to bring the discussion back to the present if there is a shift into talking about their trauma experiences. Depending upon the need (i.e., the extent to which wandering into trauma topics occurs), this reminder may be repeated periodically at the beginning of sessions and throughout the group. Stating this policy at the beginning of the session can be helpful in keeping the content focused on the present.

3.   Overview of Session

Remind the group that today and next week are devoted to education and discussion about PTSD, while the rest of the meetings will focus on their current concerns.

We will spend today and the session next week talking about PTSD and problems that are often associated with PTSD. This week we will be talking about some of the symptoms you may be experiencing, and how these are considered part of PTSD. We will also discuss some commonly associated problems that you may be experiencing, like depression, panic attacks, and/or alcohol or substance abuse. In the following week, we will discuss some more general life difficulties, particularly in terms of relating to others, that survivors of trauma often describe as interfering with a full life and sense of involvement. Some relate to relationships with friends and family, and some relate to how you may be feeling inside. After next week, we will switch gears and begin to talk about specific problems, issues, and aspirations in your current life that you would like to work on.

Members may well differ in their own knowledge of PTSD, and some are likely to have been exposed to such education in the past. Facilitators should probe for the level of knowledge among the members regarding PTSD, and acknowledge that some of the material presented may not be new for some members. It can be noted that even for those who are knowledgeable about PTSD, it is still important to review, as there are often misunderstandings about the symptoms of PTSD. The more accurate the understanding that members have about their own personal experiences with such symptoms, the better position they will be in to cope with and manage such symptoms, in the interest of working toward personal goals and aspirations.

Note: The text that follows illustrates the information to be provided to the group. Most facilitators will have their own experience providing education about PTSD, and will use their own style to do the education piece. It is also important to gauge where the group members are in terms of their knowledge of PTSD symptoms, and adjust the discussion accordingly. In addition to providing information, the goal of this session is to get the members talking about their own lived experiences, including how PTSD has affected and continues to affect their lives. Education should be delivered at a level that all group members can understand, using clear vocabulary and multiple ways of explaining the concepts. Members usually experience the sharing of the diagnostic concepts as empowering, as it demystifies the clinical terms, and makes treatment more accessible. Yet members may feel intimidated at first if they are not yet knowledgeable about PTSD, or have had negative or limited educational experiences.

4. Education and Discussion of PTSD
   Part 1: Symptoms of PTSD
   While some of you may know a lot about PTSD, others of you may not be clear about what it is, or may have questions. In addition, there is often misinformation about what PTSD is, so we want to take some time today to make sure you have an accurate knowledge of PTSD, and give you time to ask whatever questions you may have. In general, PTSD is a name for a group of symptoms that are commonly experienced after being exposed to life-threatening situations, or witnessing horrifying events. While often associated with military combat, or with sexual assault, it can occur following any traumatic experience, such as earthquakes, floods, hurricanes, and other natural disasters, physical assault, or automobile accidents. In general, the worse or the more prolonged the exposure to a traumatic event, the more symptoms people are likely to have. For some people, the symptoms get better over time. For others, they don't; or they recur off and on. Sometimes the symptoms arise immediately after a traumatic event, but in other cases, the symptoms can take months, years, or even decades to surface. For many people affected by PTSD, other disorders like depression, panic attacks, and substance abuse are common. We'll be talking about those disorders a little later, but first we will focus on the symptoms of PTSD.

   To begin, PTSD is a normal emotional and psychological response to trauma – that is, to a severe, painful, shocking experience. After experiencing trauma, many people feel that their lives have changed, or that they have changed and will never be the same. The world or other people may seem dangerous and unpredictable. And, very often survivors of trauma feel lonely and misunderstood by others. Often survivors of trauma are told to "get over it" or "forget about it," and may feel that others do not want to hear about their distressing incidents. That is why learning about PTSD, and talking about what makes life difficult as a result of PTSD, with others who can and want to understand, is the focus of this group. Often, people who have similar experiences can share their strategies for coping and overcoming the effects of trauma, including symptoms of PTSD, or their impact in your life.

So, what are the symptoms that define PTSD?

Let the group offer their suggestions as to what the symptoms are, and provide any others that are not brought up by the members. The symptoms can be listed on a board or flipchart to help organize the discussion. The handout (Appendix A) can be handed out during the group, or, alternatively, given to the members to take with them at the end of group, after discussion. It contains educational material for sessions two and three. Session one covers the symptoms of PTSD, and can lead into associated features if there is time. Usually PTSD symptoms will take up the entire session, however, and the remaining material on the handout can be reserved for session three.

As noted, facilitators should encourage discussion of personal experiences with PTSD symptoms, for example:

What experiences have been especially troubling for you?

How does your PTSD affect you? How has it most affected your life?

The emphasis is on sharing experiences, learning about experiences that members may have in common with others in the group (as well as differences among them), and gaining a better understanding of their experiences and how they relate to PTSD.

Talking about PTSD symptoms may unintentionally lead some into discussion of their own trauma (e.g., talking about intrusive thoughts or flashbacks could lead into discussion of the content of those memories). If disclosure of a traumatic event begins, facilitators should tactfully shift the discussion back to current experiences. This shift to the present requires both "catching" the disclosure quickly to reduce potential for group members to be "triggered," and validating the discloser's experience. It is important to keep the group focused in a positive and supportive manner, rather than abruptly interrupting or shaming the member making the disclosure. As disclosure of a traumatic event can be a sensitive issue for group members, the facilitators do not want to give the impression that they consider the trauma "taboo" or "unspeakable." The facilitators strike a balance between respecting the experience of the individual making the disclosure, and maintaining the group expectations and frame. Over time, members will take on the role of shifting back to the present; however, in the early sessions, facilitators model this process.

Facilitators may make this shift directly or indirectly. For example, they may say:

So, in what ways does this relate to what's happening in your life right now?

Or they may comment directly, for example:

You seem to be getting into some pretty heavy experiences here. These are important experiences, but I'm concerned we may be getting beyond your comfort level, and the comfort level of the group. How are you feeling right now? Did something in the group discussion trigger this memory? How are other group members feeling? What can we do to shift ourselves back to the present?

It may also be useful to discuss how group members experience the refocusing to the present, either during the main part of the group, or during the Checkout.

Part 2: Associated Disorders (see again handout in Appendix A, which covers associated disorders as well as PTSD symptoms that were covered in session two).

After thoroughly discussing the symptoms and answering any questions the group members have, facilitators next discuss the often comorbid disorders of depression, panic, agoraphobia (intense discomfort in open or crowded spaces), and substance abuse.

Sometimes in addition to PTSD, people have other difficulties as well. For example, they may try to rid themselves of or forget painful emotions or disturbing thoughts, numb themselves, struggle with controlling feelings of hatred or violent impulses, or try to help themselves numb the pain through use of alcohol or other drugs.

Others may have sudden attacks of panic that seem to come out of the blue and that cause the person to feel very afraid, have physical symptoms like heart racing, irregular heartbeats, sweating, trembling or shaking, shortness of breath or hyperventilation or choking feelings, chest pain, nausea, or abdominal distress, feeling dizzy, lightheaded or faint, feelings of unreality or being unattached to oneself, fear of losing control or going crazy, fear of dying, numbness or tingling, chills or hot flashes, and may have thoughts like, "I am going crazy," "I am having a heart attack," or "I am going to die." Sometimes people have these symptoms when they try to leave their homes, or in crowds, wide-open spaces, closed places, or while traveling in buses, planes, or trains, or even while going over bridges or through tunnels.

Very commonly, people diagnosed with PTSD also have depression. Symptoms of depression include feeling down or blue, lack of interest or pleasure in all or most of activities, significant weight loss not due to dieting, or weight gain, sleep problems (either not sleeping enough or sleeping too much), feeling keyed up and restless or the opposite – slowed down like moving through jello, fatigue and lack of energy, feelings of worthlessness, or extreme guilt, difficulty concentrating, problems with memory, indecisiveness, recurrent thoughts of death or suicide, and/or suicide attempts. Sometimes, people don't actually think of themselves as suicidal, but they put themselves in dangerous situations repeatedly (for example, drinking and driving, driving too fast, getting into fights, or neglecting serious health concerns).

The important thing to remember is that although these symptoms and problems can be extremely unpleasant, they are not uncommon reactions to traumatic experiences, and they can improve. Understanding them can inform the work of recovery. The notion of recovery as defined by the SAMHSA (Subsatnce Abuse and Mental Health Services Administration) website and associated brochure (2020) is: "A process of change through which individuals improve their health and wellness, live a self-directed life, and strive to reach their full potential." *What this approach indicates is that recovery is not simply about symptoms, but about change ultimately in the direction of the life you choose for yourself. So today's discussion of symptoms and issues is one of the starting points of present-centered group therapy, but not the end point. [Note to Facilitator: continue review of associated features in handout]*

Again, facilitators encourage group discussion about the group members' experiences with these symptoms in the context of normalizing and sharing, and discussing how the symptoms have an impact on their current lives.

5. Checkout: Leave about ten minutes at the end of the session for discussion about how hearing this information affected members of the group. One way to approach the Checkout is to ask if members learned anything new, and if any misunderstandings about PTSD and other symptoms were clarified or corrected for them. In addition, facilitators may ask how group members felt about hearing other members' experiences with symptoms that they might be experiencing. General reactions to the group process and specific reactions to the material presented are all encouraged during the Checkout.

Session Three: Education and Discussion: Common Issues Associated with PTSD

Objectives

1. Increase intimacy and trust among group members
2. Educate group members about common issues with which survivors of trauma may struggle (please refer to handout in Appendix A, second section of handout; copies may be provided to group members, or the materials may be used by facilitators as points of discussion)
3. Increase understanding among group members about how their own challenges in day-to-day living may be related to PTSD.

Rationale for Facilitators

This session is devoted to discussions about other consequences of PTSD in survivors of trauma. Some of these features overlap with symptoms of PTSD; others are not part of the diagnosis but are recognized as secondary consequences of the trauma or of PTSD symptoms, or as associated features that are commonly present. The goal is to normalize these experiences as well as to target them as appropriate problem areas to work on in PCGT. Both PTSD symptoms and associated features may be tied to interpersonal difficulties and barriers to full involvement in present-day life. Examples include: difficulty participating in or tolerating close interpersonal relationships (particularly with spouses or partners – which may include difficulty with sexual intimacy – and also with children, where distancing, numbing, or overly high expectations can interfere with parenting); inability to feel emotions such as love, affection, pleasure etc.; anger; increased potential for aggressiveness or violence; isolation – feeling as if one doesn't "fit in" or have a place in society; alienation from friends and family members; guilt about both the past, and the impact of PTSD symptoms on their families, friends, and at work; concerns about physical safety of self and loved ones; feelings of worthlessness; feelings of lack of empowerment/control; sleep disturbances; loss of spirituality or a sense of meaning in life; loss of dreams, innocence, and goals for future.

Procedures

1. Group Check-In
    After greetings and noting any absences or returns to the group, facilitators ask whether any of the members have comments, reactions, or questions following last week's session. Facilitators can also briefly ascertain how the members feel about participating in the group, and whether there are any problems or concerns regarding the group, in order to encourage members' development of comfort within this setting. Members may have lingering questions about the educational materials, which facilitators can clarify. Again, this session opening is intended to give members a chance to raise any leftover issues from previous weeks, to resolve any questions, and, similar to the Checkout, to make comments or suggestions regarding participation in the group or about the group process.
2. Overview of Session
    Remind the group that today is the last session devoted to education, and that beginning next week, the rest of the meetings will be spent talking about current issues in their lives.
    Last week we discussed PTSD in general. We talked about the symptoms and about some other difficulties that often accompany

PTSD, such as depression, panic disorder, and substance abuse. Today we will discuss some general life issues, particularly difficulties with relationships, that often accompany PTSD and that survivors of trauma often describe as problematic. Some relate to relationships with friends and family, and involvement in the world in general; some relate to how you may be feeling inside. This is the last session focused on education; next week we will switch gears and begin to talk about specific experiences or issues that may be occurring in your current life, and your personal aspirations and goals.

3. Discussion of Associated Features of PTSD and Common Problem Areas

Begin the discussion of material by giving out the handout in Appendix A once again, focusing on the second section of the handout as an outline for the session, which group members can take home as reference material. Facilitators begin the discussion by choosing one of the topics and briefly discussing it in relation to PTSD. Then group members are asked to talk about if and how they have experienced the problem under discussion. Facilitators try to relate group members' experiences to each other (i.e., note what is common and what is different). If not clear, members can be asked to expand upon how the issue affects their lives, or presents a barrier to investment in current life or relationships.

The points made in the handout are likely to be very familiar to most facilitators; it is included here to provide a common framework for this session of the group. Not all of the material included in the handout will actually be discussed in detail in the group; the intent is to have a reminder of some of the factors that may underlie these concerns. For example, facilitators do not encourage discussion by members of how an individual's specific actions during a traumatic event may be related to current anger or guilt. Rather, the facilitators' comments are general (e.g., that traumatic events may contribute later to ongoing difficulty with guilt, or with experiencing and expressing anger). The general principle is to normalize the experiences by emphasizing the very common links between trauma and the kinds of life difficulties that the group members are experiencing, but not to explore specific traumatic experiences.

The list is not exhaustive, but can help members understand that all these difficulties are common responses. Some items on the list indicate ways that PTSD symptoms can play out. Some of the problem areas are interconnected; and members may identify additional issues to the list of concerns. Members should be encouraged to add to the list, to talk about what they have experienced. The discussion provides a means for members to reflect on their own experiences with such issues, and to begin to share and discuss personal material to which most group members will be able to relate. Facilitators encourage discussion and may start to frame some of what members raise as possible areas for focus in subsequent sessions of the group.

4. Checkout

    As in previous and all subsequent sessions, the last ten minutes are reserved to reflect on the process of the session. Group members are encouraged to comment on their reactions to the session, positive or negative, and to make any suggestions they may have for addressing problems or improving the process of the group.

    Before we close, we want to take some time for each of you to comment on your experience in the group today, that is, how it was for you, what you may have learned or gotten out of the group, or what you didn't get out of it that you hoped that you might.

As noted previously, facilitators can also use this time to make their own comments on the group process, or to check in with individual members if relevant. For example, if the group process was dominated by one or a few members, facilitators may note this and see how others feel about it, and whether any one has suggestions about how the discussion can be more balanced in the future. Or if a member was unusually silent or withdrawn and this had not been commented on during the group, facilitators could take this opportunity to inquire about the member's reticence and whether the group could have helped with this.

Session Four: Identification and Discussion of Individual Issues and Goals

Objectives

1. Help members make transition to less structured group format
2. Educate members about agenda setting procedure that begins in next group (in this session, the agenda is pre-set as members work on their goals and aspirations)
3. Facilitate the identification and discussion of individual members' goals for the group and any barriers or obstacles identified, as well as strengths, interests, and abilities that may be marshaled toward goals and aspirations
4. Facilitate feedback and support among group members.

Rationale for Facilitators

This is the first of the less structured sessions, in which the amount of talking by members increases and that of the facilitators decreases. This session differs from subsequent sessions in that the focus here is on helping members to identify areas of personal aspiration, barriers, specific impact of symptoms, and strengths more broadly; in subsequent sessions, the focus shifts to more specific examples from their own lives occurring week to week.

Procedures

1. Group Check-In
   Open with usual group check to see if there are comments or reactions from the previous session (ten minutes).
2. Overview of Session
   Today, we will be shifting gears from the last meetings, in which we have talked about PTSD symptoms, to talk more about what is going on in your current life. In our subsequent meetings, we will be asking you about specific events or issues that have occurred, related to either PTSD, or your personal goals and aspirations, or both, which you may want to discuss. Today, we would like to get a more general sense from each of you about what you see as areas in your life that are the most important areas of focus for you – these may be the areas causing you the most distress, or where you find yourself repeating the same actions and not getting anywhere, or where you are most intent on progressing. Identifying general areas of difficulty and areas of striving may be helpful in providing a framework for understanding some of your day-to-day challenges and rewards. Some of you may have a good idea of the areas that concern you most; for others there may be more than one area, or it may be difficult to identify a specific area of focus. We see this as a starting point, and there will be lots more time in future meetings to clarify, modify, or change your descriptions and your focus, so don't worry about getting it right. Just beginning to talk about the issues you see as most significant may help you to define your barriers and strengths more clearly, and to help you focus your efforts to gain the most from the group. It will also help the other members to understand more about what's going on with you, allowing each of you to be better able to support each other in your work here.
   Facilitators ask if there are any questions or reactions at this point.
3. Discussion of Personal Challenges, Issues, and Aspirations
   Facilitators then ask if anyone would like to start. If members are reluctant to begin, facilitators can encourage them with statements such as *It's hard to begin – you can start with as little or as much as you want – today we're just trying to begin the process of identifying goals, aspirations, and obstacles to your progress.* Facilitators may note some common themes such as anger or isolation that may have emerged in prior sessions, and ask whether anyone sees such issues as playing a central role affecting current life (e.g., interfering with relationships or aspirations). Facilitators encourage focus on functional goals, which

are likely to be areas in which symptoms interfere. Once members begin to identify issues and areas of interest, facilitators encourage members to be as specific as possible regarding how the identified endeavor or concern manifests in day-to-day life. For example, if a member states that the biggest problem is anger, facilitators may ask questions such as: *What is the impact of your anger on everyday life, and how you would like things to go? What kinds of situations is this most likely to occur in? Are there certain people with whom this is more of a problem? Are there some situations where this is less of a problem? What are some of the things that are most likely to trigger your anger? Where would you like to see yourself in regard to how you experience and express anger? Do you see a relationship between anger and your ultimate needs and wishes for your future?*

Facilitators also try to connect member-identified barriers to goal achievement with PTSD symptoms and related issues. For example, given a stated problem involving anger, the connection might be noted as follows:

As we have discussed, feelings of anger and difficulty controlling anger are very commonly associated with PTSD. We've discussed some of the reasons that this is so – including the initial advantages to reacting with anger, possible biochemical changes, sense of helplessness common for survivors of trauma, feeling triggered or reminded of the trauma, and so on. So we can certainly understand where the anger comes from. The challenge for you is working on this problem as it comes up in your current life, and to trying to sort out how much of the anger you are feeling comes from the old experiences, versus what seems to be causing the anger in the present. For example, when your son doesn't listen to you, you blow up. How much does this have to do with your PTSD symptoms (for example, feeling tense, wired, and irritable from not being able to sleep) and perhaps reminders of past events, versus the present incident? Focusing on this question may help you to gain some distance from your anger and the events triggering it.

(Note: This is an area where it is important to be careful to not encourage discussion of specific traumatic events. The goal is to make the connection between the experience of traumatic experiences in general with PTSD symptoms, and to validate each member's experience.)

Facilitators also encourage feedback from other group members. The goal here is to validate each member's experience, to help members better understand some of the factors involved, and to experience support and insights from others.

The amount of time for this initial discussion of goals and concerns may vary for each member. When members have difficulty speaking or articulating their issues, the facilitators should try to draw them out with questions. At the same time, members should not be pushed too hard at this point if they are reticent or not ready to speak. Members may still be feeling wary about sharing; or a sense of helplessness may make it difficult to invest in working toward a goal. The message from facilitators is that these members will continue to have the opportunity in future sessions to discuss their issues and aspirations.

For others, it may be the opposite – talking excessively, without allowing opportunity for questions or feedback. Here, the facilitators will need to tactfully interrupt the member, try to summarize the main points, and then encourage feedback from other members. While the goal for this session is for all members to have identified an area or areas to focus on, it is fine to allow this process to continue into the next session.

The role of the facilitators in this session is, as noted, to help each member to identify a current goal area or area of focus, and to try to get examples of how related issues play out in the member's life now, especially as pertaining to barriers or obstacles to functioning related to PTSD. Facilitators summarize and reflect back their understanding of the issues for each member, and, as noted, encourage others in the group to comment and give feedback to the member speaking. Facilitators also identify and comment on common themes that emerge across the kinds of issues described by the different members, to increase the sense of connection among the group members and to increase the relevance of the group discussion for each individual. For example, the facilitator may note that a variety of members have voiced a sense of helplessness that is common in PTSD, while also voicing high standards and ideals that can also be common for people who have experienced trauma and are invested in making the world a better place.

4.   Checkout Facilitators repeat the rationale for the review at the end of the session.

Before we close, we want to take some time, as in past weeks, for each of you to comment on your experience in the group today. That is, how it was for you, what you may have learned or gotten out of the group, or what you didn't get out of it that you hoped that you might.

As noted previously, facilitators can also use this time to make their own comments on the group process, or to check in with individual members if relevant.

Intermediate Sessions: Discussion of Current Life Issues

Objectives

1.   Continue transition to less structured group sessions (session five)
2.   Educate members about the "agenda setting" process (session five)
3.   Increase trust and sense of cohesion among group members

4. Facilitate the continued development of a group atmosphere that encourages openness and support among members
5. Facilitate the continued identification and clarification of: current goals and aspirations; barriers or obstacles to fully functioning in day-to-day life stemming from PTSD and related issues; and occurrences in the lives of members that indicate a shift from trauma-based reactivity to present-oriented, non-trauma-based functioning
6. Facilitate problem solving around concrete issues raised by group members
7. Facilitate movement of members toward fully functioning in the areas of their chosen goals and aspirations.

Rationale for Facilitators

The structure of these weekly group sessions is essentially the same, although the nature of the interactions among the group members is likely to change from earlier to later sessions (see chapter four regarding group development). These sessions are the "heart" of the group, characterized by group interaction that addresses current concerns, and supports the work toward goals and aspirations identified in the previous session. The prior sessions' education about PTSD and related issues serves as a shared "platform" from which to understand trauma-related symptoms and related struggles. These earlier sessions prime the group work in these mid- to later sessions through establishing a shared knowledge base and language that supports ongoing group discussion – providing the raw materials needed to formulate plans, overcome barriers, and shift toward greater access to present-day life. Facilitators provide some structure for the group by opening the group, conducting an initial brief check-in with all members ("Anything left over from last group?"), facilitating the agenda or areas of focus for the session, and conducting the Checkout during the last ten minutes. Throughout the sessions, the role of the facilitators is to help the group stay focused on the topics raised at the beginning; to ensure that members adhere to the ground rules spelled out in the earlier sessions; to help members make connections between their current difficulties and PTSD where applicable; to note similarities and differences among issues with which members are struggling; and to facilitate the continued development of group cohesion by making process comments and encouraging feedback and support among members.

Procedures

As discussed in the opening of this chapter, PCGT has been offered with varying numbers of groups and lengths of sessions. The length of group phases will vary somewhat according to how many sessions the group will run. While in the original manual the group ran for 30 sessions with five additional monthly sessions, many study protocols and clinics appear to prefer a 12-week, weekly group. This chapter is mindful of this frequent preference in considering 12 weeks as a common length of groups. The variations in numbers of sessions are discussed briefly below. Regarding PCGT groups with varying numbers of sessions:

- In the 30-session group, these sessions will run from session 5 through session 25 or so, until the termination sessions (which continue with similar structure, but shift to addressing the group's ending, along with personal concerns – assisting with good-byes and closure for group members). Booster sessions are similarly formatted, but continue the focus on termination, and intensify the ongoing focus on application of gains from the group to current life (given the monthly interval, the content tends to be more of a "reporting in" on progress and any unexpected stressors encountered (problem solving how to handle the latter).

- In the 12-session versions, these intermediate sessions will run from session five to session ten, leading into termination in the last couple of sessions; however, facilitators will generally observe the "number" of each group session so that members are aware of how many sessions are left as they progress through the group. The pattern is similar for 16-session groups (again leaving the last few sessions for termination, and "numbering" groups to alert to group phase and endpoint).

- For eight- or nine-session groups, these "main" intermediate sessions are more limited; some treatment contexts have started this phase in session four, covering goals and aspirations "along the way" rather than devoting a group strictly to them. Some settings have also tried to combine sessions two and three, although the material is fairly extensive. "Numbering" the groups is also essential in a group that is this short term.

As referenced earlier, group lengths have varied from running for 50 minutes to one hour (also preferred in many clinics) to 90 minutes (as provided in the original version of this manual). Group sessions follow the same structure regardless of length of session.

1. Group Check-In: Open with usual check-in to see if there are comments or reactions from the previous session.
2. Review of Structure of Group (session five, and later if necessary)
   As we discussed last week, from now on in the group we will be talking about what's going on in your current life. Last week each

(some) of you talked about some areas that you see as needing attention. Starting this week we will try to address some of the events during the week that may have been important, distressing, or challenging – or that you were uncertain how to handle, or that you would just like to talk about, and hear feedback from others. We'll start out by opening the floor for anyone who wants to bring up an issue. We'll ask that you make the initial description brief, so that we can get a sense of how many of you have something you want to bring up, then we'll go back and decide as a group where to start. For example, if you want to talk about a fight you had with your wife, in the initial part you say just that – save the details for after we finish hearing from everyone who wants to bring something up – give us just the "headlines." After everyone has had a chance to speak, we will help you to set an "agenda," that is, to decide who will start and how the different issues that come up can be covered. Near the end of the session (last ten minutes or so), we will do the usual Checkout, giving everyone a chance to say something about how the session was for them, any feelings about the process of the group, about what did and did not get covered, and so forth.

Most people will have an opportunity to address issues, although some issues will take longer than others; it may occur from time to time that some issues will be tabled until the next week, depending on how we set the agenda and prioritize. That does not mean anyone's issues are less important; it just means that the group process itself will have a life of its own, and you all contribute to it by prioritizing and devoting time to issues as needed in the moment. [Note to Facilitators: This statement is important because some members new to groups may assume that each person is allotted a certain exact amount of time, or that everyone is allotted equal time in each group, while in fact, the group process, with guidance from facilitators, will result in somewhat variable time frames for discussion of issues raised. Negotiation of sharing the group and its time is part of the benefit of this group modality, in which learning the "give and take" of communication among others is key.]

Any questions?

3. Setting the Session Agenda (five to ten min.) – "Just the Headlines"
    Agenda setting is the prelude to group discussion, but is not the discussion itself. In session five it is important to educate members to this process, which began briefly in session four. Agenda setting can be formal or informal, but in either case involves the group members identifying issues to "put on the table," and prioritizing those issues (as, again, all may not fit within the group's time). Members therefore need not launch into an explanation of the entire issue, which is very common in groups; rather, they are educated about summarizing the

issue briefly (e.g., "argument with my son" or "applied to college"), versus telling the entire story. Once the agenda is set and the issues for discussion are identified, the members can proceed as determined, discussing these issues in depth, with exchange and feedback.

Facilitators ask if anyone would like to start, or ask someone to begin, and then continue until all who want to have spoken. Again, not all members need to offer an agenda item, and the facilitators do not need to go around the room eliciting a response unless there is a reason to do so (e.g., the group is very quiet, or certain members rarely initiate). Facilitators may reflect back to members the issues raised, clarifying or asking questions as necessary. Again, the goal is to focus on issues that are going on currently in members' lives; members may need to be reminded of this focus from time to time.

Facilitators then help the members determine how to start. The various issues raised are summarized, and if there are multiple issues raised, facilitators try to identify issues that may overlap (e.g., "*both Dave and Joe mentioned arguments with family members*"). The question of how to proceed is left to the members to determine, although facilitators may make suggestions if members are having difficulty, or if the balance of the time in previous sessions has been dominated by some of the members.

4. Discussion of Issues

The group can take a variety of directions at this point. Sometimes members may stay focused on the issues identified during agenda setting. On other occasions, the discussion of one member's issue may lead into a discussion of a general problem area that many of the group members have experienced. For example, if a member brings up a problem of feeling uncomfortable in anticipated social situations, this topic may turn into a general discussion of how members feel they are different from other people in society (e.g., those who are not survivors of trauma). If the discussion does not follow the agenda, facilitators remind the members of the selected topics, yet allow the group to determine where to go with it (assuming the group has a life of its own, and may go where the group process takes it).

There are some exceptions to this support of group discussion, which are detailed in chapter five. For one, the facilitators intervene if the group starts to segue into details of trauma. While a member may refer generally to personal trauma history within the PCGT group (e.g., "Ever since 9/11 I have had trouble sleeping") without disrupting the present-day focus, references to specifics of the event may trigger both the member who is speaking, and the other members who are listening. For the same reason, facilitators redirect references to specifics of violence, whether imagined or actual. For example, if a member speaks graphically about a wish for revenge ("If I had a gun I would...."), or even about a news story or a drama with similar characteristics to personal trauma ("I saw a TV drama about child abuse that was just like mine, where the parents..."), members of the group can be triggered, and may either withdraw or become hyperaroused. In these instances, it is important to respectfully acknowledge the trigger that led to the reference (or to ask what brought it up, if not clear), and to refocus on the impact of the reminder (and away from the details of the trauma, or the violent thought or image). It is generally helpful to check around the room to see if other members are triggered when a trauma reference occurs, or if expression of aggression triggered other members. Facilitators play an active role in acknowledging and discussing symptoms and reactivities related to being triggered, and to problem solve how to get back to the present.

Changes in facilitator and member roles over time: As time goes on, the facilitators shift much of the responsibility for the group to the members, taking a guiding rather than intervening role except as clinically useful to move the group and its members forward. It is also the role of the facilitators to remind the group what session they are at, and to remind them of the group's endpoint, so that members will be able to have enough time to terminate with the group (see next section). The facilitator's role also includes being mindful of "next steps" for the group members; while some members may end therapy as the group ends, others may go on to other groups, couples or family therapy, vocational services, substance dependence treatment, or individual therapy. They may also go on to make further use of community resources, such as self-help groups, job coaches, book clubs, senior centers, and other natural supports. The facilitator keeps a lookout for these natural resources and encourages them throughout the group; it is important to remember that the group is part of the person's journey and not an endpoint.

5. Checkout

The last ten minutes or so continue to be reserved for general comments and reactions to the content and process of the session.

Ending/Termination Sessions: Consolidating Gains, and Transition

Objectives

1. Consolidate progress group members have made
2. Encourage continued application of therapeutic gains
3. If booster sessions are planned (e.g., monthly), help prepare for the reduced contact, emphasizing the role of booster sessions in

continuity, and transition from the group to other therapeutic and/or natural supports

4. Engage in specific work of transition, preparing members for change in amount of contact, and emotional reactions to this change
5. Encourage continued and developing use of coping strategies and personal resources to sustain members once the group has concluded
6. Encourage expression of feelings about the group ending
7. Continue work on goals.

For Final Groups

1. Consolidate gains of the group by reviewing progress of group and members across the group "timeline"
2. Encourage carrying forward gains made in the group into the future
3. Obtain feedback from group members about the group experience thus far, including both positive and negative feelings about the group
4. If using "booster" follow-up sessions (e.g., monthly), help the group make this transition, discussing date of next sessions, coping in between sessions, etc.
5. Consolidate follow-up goals
6. Encourage acknowledgment of connections among members, including what they gained from each other (opportunity to express appreciation and affirm the meaningful nature of relationships that occurred within the group).

Rationale for Facilitators

The aim of these final weekly sessions is to further assist members in connecting their current group experience with the larger context of their own lives beyond the group. Members are encouraged to recognize gains and experiences that they will take with them. The focus of these sessions is also to establish a sense of closure. The group process acknowledges the relationships developed within the group, and how such relationships may apply to relationships outside the group. The structure continues with initial group check-in, agenda setting, and ending session review (checkout), with inclusion of discussion on the transition.

Given the difficulty survivors of trauma with PTSD often have with changes, facilitators strive to maintain a sense of continuity as the group prepares to come to a conclusion (or if booster sessions are used following the weekly groups, for reduced group contact). Members' work on transition and eventual termination is likely to be affected by PTSD-related symptoms such as avoidance, numbing, and alexithymia, as well as increased anxiety. Members may tend to "numb out," or avoid "goodbyes" by staying away from the group. Or they may divert from "goodbyes" by excessive joking, and moving away from serious topics.

Facilitators assist members in overcoming these symptoms and patterns during the termination, helping them discuss any difficulty identifying, acknowledging, and expressing feelings. Group members may also be reassured through discussion of coping strategies and problem solving toward continued transfer of therapeutic gains to life outside of group. Emphasis on emotional connection among members also will also facilitate a sense of continuity during this transition. Facilitators stress the importance of acknowledging the relationships among members, reinforcing the significance of the time the group has had together.

Procedures

1. Group Check-In

   The group opens with checking for comments and reactions from the previous session. Facilitators also remind the group of how many sessions are left before the group concludes (or reference booster sessions if reducing frequency of meetings, while discussing the intended role of booster sessions in aiding transition).

2. Review of Group Structure

   Group structure continues as it has for past weeks, with check-in, setting of agenda by members, discussion, and checkout.

3. Setting the Session Agenda

   Group members may set the agenda automatically at this stage; however, facilitators remind them to do so if they have difficulty starting, or get off track. Facilitators may frame the agenda setting in terms of number of sessions remaining (or if the final session, referencing it as such), and may offer this as a topic for the agenda. In this consolidation phase, facilitators work to reinforce gains the members have made, orienting members toward continuing with these gains. Ongoing focus on relationships and future goals is especially important at this phase.

4. Discussion of Issues

   As in previous weeks, facilitators assist the group process as members address issues identified in the agenda. Facilitators continue to support the group process by letting the group decide where to go with the issues identified in the agenda. As members address the issues identified in the agenda setting, facilitators help the members frame current issues in terms of progress made toward goals, and general therapeutic movement achieved within the group.

   At this stage, members may again tend to bring up issues about trauma as they consider the loss of the group, and any losses that may have occurred in the context of the trauma. Members may also feel triggered in response to the change entailed by the ending of the group, which may reflect loss of predictability and control harkening back to the trauma. Here, the facilitator has the opportunity to help the group address the sense of loss in the present, as well as the need for predictability and control going forward – while acknowledging the past experience in a general way as common for survivors of trauma. Again, while not going into trauma details, the facilitators may individualize the trauma-related reactions according to issues individual members may have discussed throughout the group. This phase is also an opportunity for members to experience a process of termination that embraces feelings, and values the individuals in the group, in contrast to endings that may have occurred under traumatic conditions (often characterized by abrupt or unacknowledged loss, followed by "numbing," loss of meaning, and shame/loss of worth). Maintaining the sense of relationship and continuity while preparing for the group's conclusion (or "tapering," if using booster sessions) can be a "corrective emotional experience" in this sense. In this phase, facilitators also reinforce the connection of members to the therapeutic and natural resources and supports in their ongoing lives, and continue to frame the group as a portion of their recovery journeys rather than an end in itself (i.e., something that serves its members and has its own time frame in the course of the person's life).

As issues arise that may be indirectly connected to change and eventual termination, the facilitators draw out this connection more explicitly, and encourage members to discuss their feelings and thoughts. Facilitators may need to help the group focus on discomfort and negative feelings, so that members don't simply provide what they think others want to hear. Facilitators model leave-taking by discussing their own feelings about the group ending, and by giving feedback to members.

Ending Sessions (last two in a group with limited number of sessions; final two or three sessions in groups of 16 weeks; in 30-week group, last five sessions).

During the final sessions, facilitators may comment on common themes, relating them to this transitional phase of group. Members are encouraged to review their group experience from the beginning of this group to the present. Members may recall and share specific anecdotes from the group that are particularly meaningful for them. They may also be encouraged to discuss this group experience in the context of the therapy they have had to date. Facilitators encourage members to discuss whether they have so far been able to really express what they want to express to each other, and facilitate feedback among members.

In request for feedback, facilitators assist members in identifying both the positive things they will take away from the group, and the things they have not as yet achieved which they hope to achieve in the future. Facilitators also elicit feedback about negative feelings or disappointments in the group, with suggestions about how future groups might be improved.

If a member appears to have difficulty managing the transition and does not have a planned follow-up, facilitators address this concern and problem solve with the member. If there is not another provider, the facilitator may offer to meet the member outside the group on a limited basis to collaboratively set up follow-up care. If the member has other primary providers, the facilitator will likely have been in ongoing contact and can enlist the primary providers, sharing observations from the group (depending on the system and permission from the member).

If booster sessions are used following the weekly group sessions (e.g., five monthly sessions, as in the PCGT original manual), facilitators emphasize continued focus on identified goals, as well as any new goals, for ongoing progress to track during the booster sessions. Facilitators identify number of weekly sessions left (or identify last weekly session), and remind members of the booster sessions and their significance in maintaining the continuity of treatment. The exact schedule of these groups is presented, and a written schedule of the booster sessions is provided. Booster sessions are generally characterized as transitional and goal-related, as well as providing opportunities to check in and update (and hear from) other members.

5. Checkout

The last ten minutes or so of the group are again devoted to checking with members on how the group session has gone for them. Facilitators continue to make observations on the group process. As appropriate, facilitators may comment on the developmental process within the group, comparing these later groups with earlier groups, as well as highlighting changes members have made. Facilitators may take particular care at this stage to aim the group forward to the next meeting, encouraging members to stay with the group.

If Using Five Monthly Booster Sessions

Objectives

1. Consolidate transfer of therapeutic gains to members' lives outside the group
2. Encourage ongoing work on goals, and maintenance of goals achieved
3. Utilize relationships among group members to support therapeutic gains
4. Facilitate and complete termination of group (last few sessions).

Rationale for Facilitators

Booster sessions taper from weekly to monthly meetings, in order to allow a more gradual ending process that maximizes maintenance of therapeutic gains and continued progress. When utilized, the purpose is to create a step-down process to enhance the sense of continuity, and utilize the group relationships, to counter a vulnerability toward alienation and disconnection that may occur in PTSD. If boosters are not used, this work of countering alienation and disconnection nevertheless remains part of the group agenda, especially in the last phase of the group.

The structure within the group continues with check-in, agenda setting, discussion, and review/checkout. Facilitators encourage members to share current life events, to update each other on the status of their therapeutic goals, to discuss and problem solve around any current symptoms or issues, and to identify new goals.

Procedures

1. Group Check-In

   The group continues to check in for comments and reactions from the previous session. Facilitators remind the group of how many booster sessions remain (e.g., *"This is our first booster session, and we will be meeting monthly for four more sessions after this."*). In the first booster session, facilitators comment on the change to monthly meetings, how members have experienced this change, and the goal of these meetings (supporting current gains and goals, continued group support among members, helping members to make changes in their lives).

2. Review of Group Structure

   Facilitators remind members that the group structure begins with a brief check-in, agenda setting, discussion, and checkout.

3. Setting the Session Agenda

   Facilitators allow members to set the agenda, prompting them if they get off track. Members prioritize the issues they bring up. With monthly group meetings, it is more important for each member to contribute, if possible.

4. Discussion of Issues

   Facilitators allow members to reconnect, and assist them in reconnecting if they have difficulty, by commenting on any awkwardness in reconvening after a month, noting common issues, relating current issues to past discussion in group, or asking the group for feedback about a member's issue. The group may take on a more informal character in this stage as the group is winding down. The group cannot be expected to delve into details of ongoing issues for each member, but can be helpful in identifying themes and processing emotions experienced by group members. The group should also continue to problem solve and reinforce coping between sessions.

Over the first two boosters, facilitators encourage continued discussion of members' feelings about the shift to monthly sessions, and review of goals achieved and progress made. Throughout the booster sessions, particular focus is put on relationships in members' personal lives, and meaningful activity in which they may be involved. By the third booster session, facilitators help members discuss the upcoming termination, and encourage group members to participate actively in this process. Throughout the boosters, there is increasing emphasis on use of other therapeutic and natural supports. If a member appears to have difficulty managing and does not have planned follow-up, facilitators address this concern and problem solve with the member. If there is not another provider, the facilitator may offer to meet the member outside the group to collaboratively set up follow-up care. If the member has other primary providers, the facilitator may have been in ongoing contact and can enlist the primary providers, sharing observations from the group.

Over the last two sessions, the final termination is discussed. Members are encouraged to acknowledge the attachments they have made in the group, and to give feedback to each other and to the facilitators, as well as discussing future plans. Facilitators model leave-taking by discussing their own feelings about the group ending, and by giving feedback to members. Emphasis is also placed on helping the group members problem-solve about coping with life problems and managing symptoms once the group has ended.

5. Checkout

Again, the last ten minutes or so of group are devoted to checking in with members regarding how that group session has gone. Facilitators again make comments about common themes in the group, and also make connections between previous groups, the current group, and upcoming groups. They also remind the group of the exact timing of the upcoming group, and how many group sessions are left. In the last group, facilitators and members finalize group "good-byes." Facilitators encourage a sense of closure of this phase, emphasizing the significance of the group experience, while encouraging a sense of continuity with upcoming life plans and treatment plan (e.g., ongoing case management sessions).

Summary

This chapter has outlined the building blocks of PCGT for implementation and essential aspects of the delivery of this therapy. It includes some of the updates in the field since the first iteration, in support of discussion in the early sessions, and an outline for a pre-group individual informational meeting. The next chapter incorporates the original clinical guide for the manual, with additional updates, and expanded guidance for conducting present-centered group therapy.

Notes

1 See chapter four, Invitation to the Present for Part II of Manual and Guide, and chapter five, Part III of Manual and Guide, offering strategies and further information on implementation and application of clinical interventions.
2 See Appendix C for summary of updates and modifications from CSP-420 original manual, made with an eye to maintaining its essential content and features while adapting for current treatment community, PTSD developments, and general use as a PTSD treatment. The manual itself is in the public domain and can be obtained through the book authors, or, regarding the original manual used in CSP-420, the Veterans Administration's National Center for PTSD Executive Division in White River Junction, VT.
3 DSM-5 is the basis for this handout discussing symptoms of PTSD (Appendix A). At such time that DSM-5 symptoms are revised, please feel free to provide an updated version. This educational handout is from the Present-Centered Therapy (PCT) Manual, 2016, but is modeled after the earlier VA study CSP-494 Manual (Shea et al., 2003; Schnurr et al., 2007), both of which are in the public domain.

References

American Psychiatric Association. (2013). *Diagnostic and statistical manual of mental disorders* (5th ed.). Arlington, VA: American Psychiatric Association.

Shea, M. T., Bernardy, N., Howard, J., Key, F., Lambert, J. (2003).

Litz, B. T., Stein, N., Delaney, E., Lebowitz, L., Nash, W. P., Silva, C., Maguen, S. (2009). Moral injury and moral repair in war veterans: a preliminary model and intervention strategy. *Clin Psychol Rev. 29*(8), 695–706. doi: 10.1016/j.cpr.2009.07.003. Epub 2009 Jul 29. PMID: 19683376.

Schnurr, P. P., Friedman, M. J., Engel, C. C., Foa, E. B., Shea, M. T., Chow, B. K., ... Bernardy, N. (2007). Cognitive behavioral therapy for posttraumatic stress disorder in women: A randomized controlled trial. *Journal of the American Medical Association, 297*(8), 820–830.

Schnurr, P. P., Friedman, M. J., Foy, D. W., Shea, M. T., Hsieh, F. Y., Lavori, P. W., Glynn, S. M., Wattenberg, M., & Bernardy, N. C. (2003). Randomized trial of trauma-focused group therapy for posttraumatic stress disorder: Results from a Department of Veterans Affairs cooperative study. *Archives of General Psychiatry, 60*(5), 481–489.

Shea, M. T., Wattenberg, M. S., & Dolan, R. (1996). CSP-420 *present-centered group therapy manual: Training and instruction manual for VA Cooperative Study #420 on group treatment of PTSD*. National Center for PTSD, Veterans Healthcare Administration.

Shea, M. T., Bernardy, N., Howard, J., Key, F., & Lambert, J. Present-Centered Therapy (PCT) Manual, updated version, 2016.

Substance Abuse and Mental Health Services Administration. (2020). *Brochure.* Retrieved from https://www.samhsa.gov/

Tedeschi, R. G., & Calhoun, L. G. (2004). Posttraumatic growth: Conceptual foundations and empirical evidence. *Psychological Inquiry*, *15*(1), 1–18.

Yalom, I. D. (1995). *The theory and practice of group psychotherapy*, 4th edition. New York, NY: Basic Books.

Appendix A
Handout for Sessions Two and Three

Common Reactions to Trauma

A traumatic experience produces emotional shock and may cause many emotional problems. This handout describes some of the common reactions people have after a trauma. Because everyone responds differently to traumas, you may have some of these reactions more than others. Please read it carefully, and think about any changes in your feelings, thoughts, and behaviors since the trauma.

Remember, many changes after a trauma are normal. Becoming more aware of the changes you've undergone since your trauma is the first step toward recovery.

Some of the most common problems after a trauma are described below.[3]

1.   **Fear and anxiety**. Anxiety is a common and natural response to a dangerous situation. For many, it lasts long after the trauma ended. You may become anxious when you remember your trauma. But sometimes anxiety may come from out of the blue. Anxiety may occur in certain places, times of day, with particular smells or noises, or any situation that reminds you of the trauma.

2.   **Re-experiencing of the trauma.** People who have been traumatized often re-experience the traumatic event. For example, you may have **unwanted thoughts** of the trauma, and find yourself unable to get rid of them. Some people have **flashbacks**, or very vivid images as if the trauma is occurring again. **Nightmares** are also common.

3.   **Increased arousal** is also a common response to trauma. This includes feeling jumpy, jittery, shaky, being easily startled, and having trouble concentrating or sleeping. Continuous arousal can lead to **impatience** and **irritability**, especially if you're not getting enough sleep. The arousal reactions are due to the fight-or-flight response kicking up in your body.

4.   **Avoidance** is a common way of managing trauma-related distress. The most common is avoiding situations that remind you of the trauma, such as the place where it happened. Often situations that are less directly related to the trauma are also avoided, such as going out in the evening if the trauma occurred at night. Another way to reduce discomfort is trying to push away painful thoughts and feelings. This can lead to feelings of **numbness**, where you find it difficult to have

both fearful and pleasant or loving feelings. Sometimes the painful thoughts or feelings may be so intense that your mind just blocks them out altogether, and you may not remember parts of the trauma.

5. Many people who have been traumatized feel **angry** and **irritable**. If you are not used to feeling angry, this may seem scary as well. It may be especially confusing to feel angry at those who are closest to you. Sometimes people feel angry because of feeling irritable so often.

6. Trauma often leads to feelings of **guilt** and **shame**. Many people blame themselves for things they did or didn't do to survive. For example, some assault survivors believe that they should have fought off an assailant, and blame themselves for the attack. Others feel that if they had not fought back they wouldn't have gotten hurt. You may feel ashamed because during the trauma you acted in ways that you would not otherwise have done. Sometimes, other people may blame you for the trauma.

7. **Depression** is also a common reaction to trauma. It can include feeling down, sad, hopeless, or despairing. You may cry more often. You may lose interest in people and activities you used to enjoy. You may also feel that plans you had for the future don't seem to matter anymore, or that life isn't worth living. These feelings can lead to thoughts of wishing you were dead, or doing something to hurt or kill yourself. It is not unusual to feel sad and to grieve for what you lost because of the trauma.

8. **Self-image** often becomes more negative after a trauma. You may tell yourself, "If I hadn't been so weak or stupid this wouldn't have happened to me." Sometimes people see themselves as more negative overall after the trauma. It is also very common to feel that you can't **trust** anyone. Relationships with others can become tense and it is difficult to become intimate with people as your trust decreases.

9. **Sexual relationships** may also suffer after a traumatic experience. Many people find it difficult to feel sexual or have sexual relationships. This is especially true for those who have been sexually assaulted, since in addition to the lack of trust, sex itself is a reminder of the assault.

Many of the reactions to trauma are connected to one another. For example, a flashback may make you feel out of control, and will therefore produce fear and arousal. Many people think that their common reactions to the trauma mean that they are "going crazy" or "losing it." These thoughts can make them even more fearful. As you work on solving the problems that you are having in your day-to-day life, these symptoms should become less distressing.

Appendix B
Pre-Group Individual Orientation Meeting

The two co-facilitators meet with each potential member for approximately 30 minutes, covering the following issues:

1. Brief introduction to group rationale. PCGT involves:

    a. Education about PTSD symptoms and features in the early sessions
    b. Supportive group discussion of current personal issues
    c. Exchange of feedback with other members
    d. Non-trauma focus; investment in current life issues

2. Facilitators ask members why they are seeking treatment at this time, and what they hope to get from the group.
3. Explain the purpose of the group and potential benefits.
4. Review group structure and guidelines:

    a. Number of sessions, length of sessions, and whether there will be additional follow-up afterward (and if so, what that follow-up will be)
    b. Date, time, and place of sessions
    c. Encouragement for adherence to other treatment (as needed) (e.g., medication, case management, individual therapy, family/couples therapy – and explanation of coordination of care with other providers (including obtaining a release of information for providers outside the system)
    d. Encouragement to share any changes in other treatment, and status in relation to other treatment (e.g., medication changes, smoking cessation (or relapse), substance dependence treatment (e.g., established sobriety, episodic use, "slips," and significant relapse))
    e. Commitment to regularly attending group and maintaining a present-centered focus as crucial for achieving therapeutic gains from this group; members will benefit most if they can apply what they learn in group to life outside the group
    f. Address status of family relationships and close friendships, encouraging use of group for addressing interpersonal concerns (some programs may already involve family therapy and some may not; clinicians may refer group members for family therapy as needed)
    g. Any video- or audiorecording (with signed releases for use of picture and/or voice (or local release for recording), and specifying who will see/hear the session
    h. Any measurement instruments utilized, how often measures will be administered, and how long the measures will take, as well as

who will see the results, and how the group member will be informed of the results and their implications for treatment

  i. Group members are encouraged to keep their medical appointments, collaboratively maintain or amend medication regimens as needed (in consultation with provider), and address medical issues with their physicians as they arise

  j. Share programmatic expectations and guidelines for group, including status needed to maintain group membership:

- How risk to self/others, psychosis, and/or substance abuse will be addressed
- How many missed visits your clinic will allow (ask group members to call if they need to be out for any reason)
- Other treatment expectations
- Standards of confidentiality (including of other members) and limitations of confidentiality (e.g., regarding risk to self/others/children/elderly/handicapped persons); that records will be entered in treatment note (these are required in most systems)
- Adhere to group guidelines/sign informed consent (as applies): Guidelines are presented in writing during first group, as well as during the initial contact

5. Ask prospective group member for relevant, brief history, including:

- Psychosocial summary, current life status, and personal goals and aspirations
- Preferences regarding treatment and personal needs
- Psychiatric history (PTSD treatment history – inpatient, outpatient, intensive outpatient; Substance abuse history – inpatient, outpatient, residential; number of inpatient psychiatric hospitalizations); barriers/limitations
- Risk to self/others; risk history

6. Give the prospective group member a chance to raise any concerns; identify any potential barriers to commitment to participation in the group; problem solve as needed

7. If possible, provide written information explaining the group format, schedule, purpose, and expectations

Appendix C
Changes from Original Version of Present-Centered Group Therapy Manual (Shea, Wattenberg, & Dolan, 1996)

In order to keep consistency regarding the essential elements of the original manual from VA Cooperative Study CSP-420 (Schnurr et al., 2003) (i.e., to provide for the optimal evidence base in use of this manual and its extension in chapters four and five), the modifications in this chapter are made sparingly, based on needs that are largely:

- Cosmetic (for greater accessibility for providers)
- Informational, related to updates in the post-traumatic stress disorder research and practice field, and related fields (including DSM-5 changes in elements of PTSD, as well as concepts such as moral injury (Litz et al., 2009) and post-traumatic growth (Tedeschi et al., 2004) that have been topics of research increasingly since the original manual was developed in the mid-1990s)
- Adjustments made due to the broader purpose of this book (for general use of this manual as opposed to strictly for research study facilitators). For example:
  - References made specifically for research study staff have been removed.
  - This manual references survivors of trauma in general rather than only Vietnam combat veterans (note that some subsequent studies utilized a more varied trauma population, with similar results [see chapter two]).
  - This manual is intended for persons-served of any gender and gender-identity rather than an exclusively male client base (some subsequent studies and clinical settings have used this model with a gender-mixed client-base; see chapter two).
  - CSP-420 ran for 30 weeks, with five monthly "booster" sessions thereafter; other studies (see chapter two) have modified this manual to run for 9 to 12 sessions. The results of the studies suggest that PCGT is highly adaptable, and can be tailored to the needs of the clinic (as well as research study). Because of this variability in length of group across studies, the "stages of group" in this manual have been referred to generally rather than by specific session. See chapter two on the variations of PCGT in research studies. In the original manual, the groups ran for 90 minutes. This length of time has been reduced to 45 to 60 minutes in some clinical and research contexts, without apparent loss of efficacy.

- The handout for sessions two and three in this chapter replaces handouts one and two in the original manual, and was adapted to account for changes in the Diagnostic and Statistical Manual of Mental Disorders (DSM-5, American Psychiatric Association, 2013), developments in the field, and clarification of concepts. This handout was adopted from the Present-Centered Therapy (PCT, originally developed for VA Study CSP-494 individual therapy protocol) Manual, which was originally modeled on the PCGT Manual. This handout is from the 2016 version of the PCT Manual (Shea et al., 2016).

- Adaptations to reflect a person-centered approach that was intended originally in this manual are now updated to keep step with progress in the field regarding person-centered and recovery-oriented care, especially as related to respectful language regarding the person-served. Perspective and language have been modified in adherence to and in support of these positive changes in the treatment community. As this aspect of the field develops, further adaptations may be suitable for future manuals, without loss of the substance and context of this treatment approach.
- The modifications described previously do not substantially alter the content of the PCGT approach, its purpose, nor its basic treatment elements. They are incorporated to clarify the manual and make its implementation and application more "user-friendly" and "person-friendly." The Special Topics section included as a practice resource within the original manual, is now offered in the two upcoming chapters (chapters four and five), both in order to be more conveniently referenced, and to expand the practice-related updates, as discussed previously, while this portion (the basic manual) is relatively unchanged except for updates as indicated.

4 Present-Centered Group Therapy Guide & Manual Part II: Invitation to the Present

Melissa S. Wattenberg, M. Tracie Shea, Daniel Lee Gross, and William S. Unger

Overview[1]

The invitation to the present in this chapter offers consideration of group dynamics, including ways to respond respectfully and therapeutically to PTSD symptoms and trauma-related issues, as well as to patterns that can emerge in any group. Interventions in PCGT almost always include "enlisting the group" – the group as a whole being a key resource in any group therapy. This intervention is particularly accessible in PCGT, given the low to moderate structure. Techniques employed in PCGT are perhaps less "technique-ie" than those in many groups, and are always integrated into the process of the group, with any didactic being relatively brief, and discussion accentuated. In this sense the group itself is the primary intervention, and present-oriented techniques are embedded within it. As time goes on, the group itself will typically facilitate the present-oriented process, with facilitators guiding as needed, supporting and deepening this process. This chapter covers a variety of interventions within PCGT that are trauma-aware, that invite members to be connected in the present, and that move the group toward engagement, self-awareness, self-management, and personal choice. Characteristics and processes of PCGT are shown below.

PCGT Characteristics

- Low to moderate structure
- Structure secondary to process
- Re-orients toward current time-frame
- Emphasis on "mid-range affects" (hyperarousal kept to a minimum, as possible)
- Emphasis on acceptance and establishment of comfort in the group
- Group as a "safe place"
- Emphasis on respect and collaboration; low level of conflict
- Emphasis on social/interpersonal interaction
- Low to moderate level of confrontation

- Active facilitation (members know where facilitator stands; facilitator manages re-experiencing and acknowledges trauma triggers; less intervention is needed as the group progresses)
- Transference minimized, diffused, or kept at low to moderate level rather than intensified
- Little or no "homework"
- Emphasis on personal strengths
- Change seen as gradual and incremental

Processes That the PCGT Model Encourages

- Opportunities to change "mental set" from past to present
- Focus away from trauma details
- Opportunities to engage in problem solving on current life situations, interpersonal issues
- Opportunities to recover skills
- Initiative in members
- Feedback and role-modeling among members
- Social practice
- Attention to current feelings; counters "alexithymia"

The Content of the Group

Content will vary widely, depending on the group members and the status of their particular issues. Facilitators also contribute to the action of the group, as there is more room in a present-centered group for the facilitators' personal styles and theoretical orientations than in more structured groups. At the same time, facilitators may need to shift their styles away from being overly active, directive, or lecturing, and away from structured interventions characteristic of more scripted groups. A rule of thumb is to prioritize group discussion, with introduction of any more formal intervention occurring briefly and in the service of offering necessary information, fostering the discussion, or empowering the group. The group can begin to function as a relatively safe environment in which to experience and explore patterns emerging in the lives of members, and to introduce potentially corrective experiences through brief education, support, and encouragement of attention to current life. PCGT practitioners have noted that, as members utilize the group process for discussion of feelings and personal life, they become more able to experience and express emotion. The key aspects of PCGT conducive to allowing this practice of expression of emotion are the emphasis on lowering arousal in the group so that "mid-range emotions" can be experienced, and the modest group structure that allows ongoing practice at discussing, identifying feelings, and collaborative problem solving.

The Practice at Being in the Present

The lives of survivors of trauma are so commonly interrupted by trauma-based images, thoughts, and beliefs that the practice of being in the present for the duration of a group (and being redirected as intrusions occur) is an intervention in itself, a kind of informal "exposure" to what it is like to adhere to current life experiences and concerns. This effect of PCGT originally occurred by default, as a "side effect" of this treatment. Present-centered group therapy was enjoined to leave trauma-focused work to the target treatment, and as a corollary, to assure a safe and ethical protocol by minimizing potential risk from sudden unaddressed trauma references. While elements of this treatment have not been deconstructed, it is reasonable to consider this practice a likely source of benefit from PCGT.

Group Dynamics and the Present in PCGT

For any population in group therapy, the group process takes on a life of its own, in which "the whole is greater than the sum of its parts." While a group can be examined in terms of its individual members and facilitators, group therapists are aware of the powerful dynamics that occur at a group level, in which members act and take on roles to express something for the group as a whole (Yalom, 1995). Therefore, while certain group members may bring particular qualities into a group, the action of an individual in a group can be seen also as a product of the group process. The presence of a repetitive pattern within a group (whether or not originating in trauma) suggests some protective or expressive function of that pattern for the entire group. For example, the group process may express a fear of intimacy, a response against merging and losing individuality, or protection against vulnerability. If maintaining a particular pattern is central to the dynamics of a group, "role exchange" may occur. For instance, if a member who acts as a caretaker in the group is absent or "steps down" from this role, another member is likely to take on this function. In this sense, the group is an organism, and a dynamic environment. For survivors of trauma in particular, who may often be alienated from the current environment and feel more closely connected to a place in the past, the aim is for the group to become a lively reference point in which members can connect to others in a safe place.

In addressing group dynamics in PCGT, the therapeutic factors identified by Yalom (1995), listed below, are particularly relevant:

1. Instillation of hope
2. Universality
3. Imparting of information

4. Altruism
5. The corrective recapitulation of the primary family group
6. Development of socializing techniques
7. Imitative behavior
8. Interpersonal learning
9. Group cohesiveness
10. Catharsis
11. Existential factors

Facilitators, who are likely to be very familiar with these factors from their training and practice, may nevertheless find some review useful in considering how the effects of PTSD interact with these factors, detailed in chapter six.

PTSD and Group Dynamics

Group therapists will be familiar with the myriad of potential dynamics, and common patterns, a subset of which are discussed in detail later in this chapter. Even in a group for survivors of trauma, not all themes and patterns in the dynamics of a group can be assumed to be trauma-related. At the same time, in a trauma group there will be many opportunities for trauma-related patterns and themes to emerge. Pynoos et al. (2004) note several sources of impact on social group interactions that occur frequently for survivors of trauma: "(1) the human appraisal and response to danger; (2) the nature of trauma and the complexity of traumatic experiences; (3) the role of trauma reminders in posttrauma behavior; (4) posttraumatic stress disorder; (5) posttrauma adversities; and (6) traumatic expectations" (p. 1). These phenomena will emerge in any group process that encourages discussion and interaction among group members. Facilitators are aware of potential trauma-related phenomena, and at the same time, may expect some of the dynamics that may occur in any group (with an eye to trauma-related influences even with these occurrences).

A key function of PCGT involves addressing these patterns from a present-oriented perspective. Trauma themes may emerge independent of the original content, and can be identified as natural trauma-based re-activations that nevertheless have limited utility for current living. PCGT assures that the group does not segue from emergence of a trauma-based pattern into discussion of details of the original trauma; however, reference may be made to the trauma as an entity, as a source of re-enactment, or as an intrusion into the present. In this sense, trauma is "in the room" and acknowledged, while the members themselves and their current lives are the focus.

The Potential Character of Trauma-Related Dynamics in Group

SPECIFIC PTSD SYMPTOMS THAT MAY BE DRIVING THE GROUP PATTERN

PTSD symptoms may require management in the group, aided by clear group guidelines. For example, a group may be dominated by a sense that members are numb and disaffected, or struggling with anger and agitation, or strongly convinced of trauma-based beliefs. PCGT facilitators validate the members as survivors of trauma, while reminding members of group guidelines (e.g., respect-based standards in group, no intimidating behavior, etc.), and holding out hope for a landscape that is not wholly trauma-based. Facilitators enlist the group in developing a shared understanding. Members have the opportunity to address symptoms as they play out in everyday life with family, work, friends, and activities. With recognition of these occurrences, and shared problem solving in the group, members can develop new strategies for reducing symptom-based interruptions of life in the present.

THE REALITY OF TRAUMA

Trauma issues and PTSD symptoms weave through the group, along with the distinct personalities, strengths, frailties, and personal histories of the members, giving the group its unique character. The reality of trauma is part of the group's reality, even though the group does not examine the trauma itself. Facilitators, as collaborative leaders, acknowledge this reality (a reality that is also part of their own world) when they decide to facilitate a trauma group. The group is in no position to undo this reality, as both members and facilitators often wish were the case. The resulting anger, grief, and sense of loss are generally a backdrop in trauma groups, and reflect the "existential issues" that group therapy can help to address (Yalom, 1995). The early educational sessions in PCGT and ongoing awareness of the shared legacy of trauma supports the bond that group members develop with each other, which can be a solace in the face of this loss of meaning. Over time, through a supportive group process, members share present-oriented experiences in their lives that can help to create new meaning.

PERSISTENCE OF TRAUMA-BASED BELIEFS

It is not surprising that survivors of trauma often continue to operate from responses learned under traumatic conditions. Group members may not readily give up patterns learned in the interest of survival, under conditions of threat and danger. They may also be motivated secondarily by shame about the symptoms they are experiencing, (as well as about the trauma itself, and the fact that it happened to them (the "why me" of it)). Members may minimize problems and symptoms due to a sense of vulnerability, therefore feeling safer with the status quo. They may worry that their symptoms are "crazy," and so keep a low profile rather than reveal themselves. The helpless feeling from the original trauma may be disempowering when it comes to considering change. The structure of PCGT has an advantage in that it allows the group to meet people where they are. It contrasts in this way with more structured groups aimed specifically at beliefs. PCGT's approach is nonconfrontive, and allows the group to address issues as they arise. Beliefs are not specifically targeted, except as addressed in early sessions as part of PTSD education. The open-ended group process allows members to address issues that are interfering with their lives, at their own pace, and as needed, including beliefs that are not serving them well with family, friends, and coworkers. Fuller delineation of the dynamics and mechanisms behind persistence of trauma-based actions and beliefs can be found in chapter six.

Sustaining Present Focus

Present-centered group therapy offers an opportunity to remain in the present rather than be overtaken by traumatic experiences. At the same time, the nature of PTSD involves intrusions from the past that interrupt the present. It is natural for these intrusions to occur during groups as well. Some survivors of trauma easily segue into discussing details of trauma out of habit of thinking often about the trauma. For example, members may begin to discuss a nontraumatic situation, such as plans to avoid traffic on an upcoming trip, and drift into graphic description of a car accident one of them had in the past, which may then trigger other members. Or members may start mentioning place names associated with a particular trauma (especially if a shared trauma), leading easily into discussion of traumatic events, which the facilitator must then redirect. Members who are triggered by an anniversary of the trauma, ambient cues such as weather or noises, or a statement or conflict, may inadvertently begin speaking about the traumatic event. Early in the group sessions, just being in a trauma group can be a trigger to recall the trauma. A member may avoid details, but make broad declarations referencing trauma (e.g., "I've seen people killed!"). Or a member may not reference the past trauma but offer "trauma-adjacent" references, bringing trauma into the room through statements generally referencing violence, for example, "I'd like to punch that guy out!" or "I'd meet your boss in the parking lot if I were there!"

As members are not expecting to encounter traumatic references or reminders, they are more vulnerable to being triggered if another member crosses this threshold. Trauma references reduce the sense of safety in the group; it is important to address them expeditiously, while minimizing any shaming of the member making the statement. Priming members in the first group meeting about how trauma references will be handled (and including general references to violence in this context) will reduce the occurrences, and will empower group members to self-limit trauma-related references in group. When references do occur, facilitators are encouraged to use their own styles and techniques in redirecting groups, and to incorporate the techniques below and in the upcoming Interventions section. Because PCGT is not technique-oriented, it relies heavily on the essentials of group therapy, the therapeutic relationship between facilitators and the group, and the development of a therapeutic process among group members. Dynamics that may arise around present focus may include:

• Some survivors feel a press to talk about the trauma as a form of identity, or out of a need to validate the reality of their experience of extreme stress. Or subgroups may form from among those who experienced a certain kind of trauma (e.g., combat vs. noncombat, in a heterogeneous group), and may tend to reference their trauma source as a shared form of identity that distinguishes them from other group members. PCGT facilitators acknowledge and validate the experience of trauma but redirect from details. They refocus on triggers, symptoms, and feelings. They may also offer education as a way of generalizing and normalizing the survivor's experience.

• Present-day life can feel tenuous for survivors of trauma who are beset by intrusive memories and hyperarousal. After prolonged periods of intermittent intrusions, it may be hard to feel centered in the present, or even to believe it is possible. Current life can appear vague, pale, less vivid and less valid than the traumatic past, given the juxtaposition of intense intrusions from the past, and numbing in the present. Sleep loss can reduce energy and investment in everyday life, as well as making it less manageable, exacerbating the fogging over of daily life.

• While for many survivors, hyperarousal is very distressing, some also experience it as "a rush" of excitement (which also leaves everyday life appearing mundane in comparison). Further, for survivors of trauma, the mid-range emotions that make up most of daily living tend to drop out as hyperarousal favors orientation to rage and terror, and emergency functioning. As navigation of everyday life becomes less manageable, more tedious, and less central to the survivor's existence, it can be difficult initially to embrace the present. Dissociation and intrusions may validate the past experience of extreme stress. The symptoms themselves, while painful, may also become a source of identity for some survivors, especially as other sources of identity from connection in daily life appear inaccessible.

- Early in group, some members may challenge the facilitators' reliability and consistency regarding both present focus, and the group guidelines, in the process of evaluating how much to trust the facilitators and the group. Facilitators can provide explanation and help members process doubts and anxiety about starting the group, while continuing to restate the group's focus, and guidelines.
- If it appears that a group member is introducing "shock value" through disclosures and trauma-based references, the facilitator can gently redirect, while showing curiosity about this pattern. For example, does this pattern occur in the person's home or personal life? What is it like for the group member to make sudden mention of trauma in the group? How might this pattern function in the person's life? The potential for other group members to be "triggered" by sudden trauma disclosure means that the facilitator needs to address both the disclosing member, and the reactions of other members to the disclosure. The facilitator may also judiciously enlist the group for feedback on the impact of the disclosure (which can be expected to range from support for the member's "right of self-expression," to feeling "triggered" by the trauma reference). Each of these scenarios is an opportunity to discuss the importance of the survivors' current lives, and the challenges of dealing with intrusions – as well as the need for validation and community.
- Members may also be drawn to discussing trauma because they are actively re-experiencing – rarely finding themselves in the present for more than a short period of time. Or they may be triggered by something in the group. On such occasions, members are encouraged to reconnect with the group in the present. This instance is again an opportunity to explore how much reexperiencing symptoms are occurring in the person's life, what triggers them, and how the group member and other group members deal with it on an ongoing basis. It offers group members a chance to bond over shared experience in their current lives.
- Some survivors may be embroiled in crises in their current lives (e.g., going through divorce, financial crises/homelessness, medical concerns, family issues) that can reactivate traumatic memories. This emergence of traumatic memories can serve as an opportunity to provide validation and acknowledgment – as well as to enlist group in problem solving around both ways of managing the crisis, and ways to minimize reexperiencing and accompanying hyperarousal. When there are concrete issues affecting life functioning, it is also important for the facilitators to assess need for additional services. If it emerges as time goes on that "living in crisis" has become a life pattern for a group member (or members), there will be ongoing opportunities in the group to address this pattern, to collaboratively

weigh the costs and any value to the pattern, and to enlist the group in establishing ways to "walk down another street" (Nelson, 1993).

• As the group progresses, the group members themselves will intervene if someone starts to veer off into a trauma-related reference. A goal for this treatment is for members to become adept at bringing themselves and others back into the present.

The Facilitators

The present-centered facilitators are skilled therapists who have developed their own styles and psychotherapy techniques for working with survivors of trauma. The interventions discussed in this section are expected to support or augment the strategies that the facilitators tend to use already. Facilitators are encouraged to consider these methods as they integrate them with their own styles of conducting group.

The Therapeutic Relationship

The first order of intervention is the therapeutic relationship. Below are three aspects of relationship in these groups.

THE COTHERAPY RELATIONSHIP

Cotherapists work together to establish a relationship with the group that provides the foundation for the essentials of group therapy. It is important for cotherapists to plan with each other and to process the group after sessions. It is also important that therapists discuss their approaches and previous experiences doing therapy. Facilitators may come from a variety of backgrounds and professions, with differences in types of training and orientation. They may be of different genders, and have different preferences and identities regarding gender and sexuality. They may be of different ages or from different generations. They may be distinct from each other ethnically. And they may differ in their type of personal exposure to trauma, or intergenerational trauma within their families. Discussion of these differences is "grist for the mill" for coleadership pairs. Transparency in the cotherapy team allows greater mutual support and collaboration while working within the group, and greater spontaneity in responding to the group process. Cofacilitators need not overdisclose beyond their own comfort level; however, a modicum of disclosure within a comfortable professional level allows facilitators to field the intense emotions that facilitators typically encounter in a trauma group, and to experience each other's support.

Their styles of handling the task and socio-emotional leadership of groups differ; some therapists switch back and forth between these roles, while others split the roles between them, each focusing on one role or the other. If both are drawn to a similar role, they may need to process how to vary the roles so as to support each other and the group. Level of activity in group is another important cotherapist variable; if one is more active than the other, there is a risk that the quieter facilitator will feel excluded, while the more active facilitator will feel overworked and underappreciated. Planning a balance of responsibility can relieve the cotherapists of potential discord and make use of their respective styles. Facilitators may also want to plan specific roles ahead of time, for example: switching off as task leader vs. socio-emotional leader, so each has an opportunity to manage each of these roles; or taking turns as presenter (in early educational sessions) or check-in leader, versus attending to group interaction and engagement. Division of group leadership roles may take any form the facilitators prefer. They can choose to "go with the flow," or plan exactly who is taking what role in each group. They can split up roles during the group (e.g., one do the check-in, the other, the checkout). The main thing is to have the conversation about it and have a level of agreement that fits the styles of both facilitators.

Cotherapists can expect to go through stages of adjustment as they do therapy together. Even therapists who have worked together previously likely will develop a new cotherapy relationship in the context of PCGT. Cotherapy in a group for survivors of trauma can be a rich and inter-esting experience. As facilitators react to the group and process it after-ward, they use their own unique observations and distinctive responses to understand the group process and determine therapeutic actions. Members of the group may respond differentially to the two facilitators. A range of transferences and countertransferences can be expected, with each facilitator picking up on different aspects of the members and the group. Sharing and integrating this valuable information provides a unified and differentiated response to the group, and further develops the relationship as a cotherapy team. The more comfortable the cotherapists are with each other and each other's reactions, the more they can support each other in providing a foundation for the group.

THE MEMBERS' RELATIONSHIPS WITH EACH OTHER AND THE GROUP
AS A WHOLE

Members initially identify with each other as "fellow travelers," each with a history of trauma and the willingness to address their lives in the present in this group. PCGT fosters this identification in the early sessions' discussion of symptoms and issues. The "working group" aspect of the members' relationship is fueled by shared agenda setting, and partaking in responsibility for the group as members. Their differentiation over time in the group is fostered by giving and accepting feedback, gradually be-coming more adept at expressing and sharing feelings (developing a shared language), listening to each other with interest and empathy, and working toward perspective-taking. Group members often start out feeling that they are "all in the same boat," and even that "we are all the same." As the group continues, members deepen their connection while recognizing and accepting differences – which enhances the group's liveliness and spontaneity (and present orientation). While subgroups may develop, the members are encouraged to keep in touch across those subgroups. Secrets within the group are discouraged. If members have relationships with each other outside the group (which varies according to local clinic norms, and the particular makeup of each group), the fact of these relationships and their potential impact on interactions within the group are addressed within the group.

As membership in a trauma group can be a trigger in and of itself (and doubly, if the trauma occurred in a group setting), the ongoing everyday life focus of the group is important to resetting the group in the present and maintaining this time frame. The group check-in is a ritual that reinforces this connection in the present, and creates a sense of continuity from group to group. The checkout at the end of the group also allows the group to close down and switch gears to the next stop in the person's day (as well as to provide feedback to the group and facilitators).

THE FACILITATORS' RELATIONSHIPS WITH THE GROUP

The therapeutic relationship creates a supportive environment in which group members can establish a sense of safety and trust so that they can express themselves, process issues, receive feedback, and evolve emotionally and psychologically. Irrespective of style, one of the most important qualities in a therapist is genuineness (also referred to as "congruence" (Raskin & Rogers, 2005; Rogers, 1951)), "transparency," or "attunement" (Fonagy, Gergely, & Jurist 2018). Facilitators communicate to group members their real interest and therapeutic concern. They rely on their professional boundaries, while presenting themselves as human beings. They model communication, expression of their own emotion within therapeutic bounds as facilitators, and acceptance of their own imperfection. It is important, as facilitators consider interventions, that they pick those with which they feel comfortable, and present them with sincerity. It is almost never advisable for facilitators to share more than is comfortable, and it is important to model boundaries as well as accessibility.

Leadership Part of therapist "congruence" is assuming a legitimate (if flexible) leadership role. Facilitators maintain the boundaries and rules of the group. They are as clear as possible about these limits, making the group a safe place to which members can return. Facilitators are respectful of group members and of themselves. They are responsible to group members in the role of facilitator, but allow members to take responsibility for themselves.

Therapist Empathy Empathy is one of the facilitators' essential interventions. Empathic listening responses create a "holding" space in which members can grow and develop. Facilitators model real attention to feelings, and help members develop awareness within themselves, diminishing alexithymia (difficulty putting feelings into words; see chapter six). Their appreciation of a member's feelings enhances the member's sense of self. Empathy serves a rehumanizing function, providing the group with a model of human connectedness. From this foundation, the group can develop a norm of mutual acceptance and self-acceptance, which then supports exploration and change.

MAKING MISTAKES

Facilitators will encounter some challenges within the group, and will sometimes miss the mark. They cannot expect to always "ace" these challenges. It is important that therapists be open to processing members' disappointment without becoming overly defensive or excessively apologetic. It is OK for facilitators to acknowledge that they occasionally miss something, or need to revisit an issue from a different perspective, but can still remain "good enough" (Winnicott, 2005).

Reciprocal Feelings (Including Countertransference [McCann & Pearlman, 1990]) It is common for facilitators to feel very responsible for group members, to feel inadequate in the face of the members' problems, and to feel guilty in response to missed opportunities to help. Because shame can be a prominent experience in survivors of trauma, facilitators may absorb these feelings as well. Facilitators may make use of these feelings in understanding the group process and developing a therapeutic response. As indicated earlier in this chapter, facilitators may find that a sense of playfulness and humor (without sarcasm or "put-downs") can be useful in creating a spontaneous and vital environment. This approach cuts through shame, and allows group members to feel "rehumanized" as they learn or relearn to connect and express themselves, becoming more alive in the present.

In PCGT, facilitators are not trying to engender intense transference, but rather are working to reduce hyperarousal, and to engage and identify "mid-range" emotions, which then become the basis for connection to the present, and for operating more effectively with significant others and in valued activities. The facilitator stance and shared knowledge with the group members in the early sessions helps to diffuse personalized reactivity and "transference" (as recommended by Chu, 1988, for complex trauma). The relationship is deliberately collaborative, facilitative, and transparent, which helps to minimize dependency, suspicion, romanticized attachment, and resentment. A recovery approach emphasizing respect for members and their independence and empowerment is very helpful in this regard.

While members may still have strong reactions to facilitators (or to one or the other of the facilitators) at times, the focus is on the members themselves and their own lives. The exception is that facilitators may deliberately engage the whole-group process in relation to themselves (e.g., to address issues such as loss of trust ("How might you know if you can trust us?"), a divisive pattern in the group ("I notice that there have been some disrespectful comments between members; I wonder if we as facilitators are not coming across as respectful to you in this group"), or passivity in the group ("We have been noticing that the group has been very quiet lately. I wonder if we as facilitators are letting you down in some way")). These interventions take pressure off of any member who is being scapegoated in a divisive group process, and reduce potential shame of members by modeling shared responsibility for issues in the group.

A key decision for a facilitator in a trauma group is whether to share one's own story with the group, if one has also survived trauma (especially trauma similar to those of members of the group). In PCGT, clearly the details of a trauma story would not be shared. The question then becomes whether to share the fact of being a survivor. Unless a peer support provider, the facilitator is under no obligation to share personal information. Even peer facilitators are advised to use discretion in self-disclosure, to assure that disclosures are made within the peer role in order to help others in recovery. There may be times that the shared trauma is evident, such as when both group members and facilitators have shared the same event (e.g., a local flood or hurricane) or are known to have had a shared role (e.g., both were veterans in Afghanistan, or both had been first responders or caregivers in a local disaster). On the one hand, the opportunity to role-model recovery can be powerful; on the other hand, the discrepancy of being a provider while others are in recovery from trauma can be shame-inducing for the survivors, who may ask themselves why they have not done as well. When there is a shared trauma, survivors may feel automatically understood, which can facilitate a bond when trusting a provider or group can be difficult. However, someone with a shared survivor experience may assume too much similarity and not share feelings because the facilitator "already knows." It can also be complicated if one facilitator is a survivor, and the other is not; a discussion of how to handle this coleadership can be fruitful and beneficial for the group, although facilitators are likely to have to field responses from members "favoring" the facilitator who is a survivor of trauma.

Ultimately, it is a personal and professional decision on whether and when to disclose. Some settings will support and encourage disclosure, while others do not allow it. Most settings are somewhere in the middle, where decisions about disclosure can be made in consultation with a clinical supervisor, or at the facilitator's professional discretion. A general rule of thumb when disclosing is to only share experiences that the facilitator has in perspective and has fully processed and digested.

A corollary is to only disclose material that the facilitator would not mind having disclosed more generally (as the group members are not bound to keep facilitators' disclosures confidential).

Work with survivors of trauma can be meaningful and worthwhile for the facilitators. It can also be draining, disturbing, and frustrating. Facilitators will encounter the issues with which members are grappling: loss of meaning, sense of helplessness, fear, anger, and despair, among others. If hyperarousal can be contagious among members, facilitators are also susceptible to heightened arousal experienced in group. Even within a present-centered focus, trauma-related affects, themes, and issues are communicated indirectly. This secondary contact with trauma can result in vicarious traumatization, even if it also stimulates a broader understanding of the human experience. To restore themselves, facilitators can offer themselves respect for the significance of their work, can attend to their own feelings and reactions, and can strive to balance work life with "down time," recreation, social life, and meaningful personal activity. One such approach created by Pearlman and Saakvitne (1995) employed the ABCs of self-care as a means of mitigating the impact of vicarious trauma: **A**ssessment of needs/limitations, sustaining **B**alance in personal/professional life, and cultivating **C**onnections within professional personal circles. Therapist self-care is important both to the health of the therapist and to the health of the group members (as facilitators model and legitimize valuing of one's health and well-being).

Stages of Group

The interventions employed in PCGT aim to help members become aware of themselves and others in the present, both within and outside the group. The more members can be helped to connect with each other and with their current lives in a genuine way, the more they will be able to develop new patterns of relating, to replace those entrenched patterns learned during traumatic experience.

Early Stage of Group

Interventions will vary at different stages of the group process. In the early sessions, active intervention is needed in order to establish therapeutic group norms, to assure members of emotional safety in the group, and to model that group standards can be discussed upfront and upheld. Also, in the early phase, therapists are charged with balancing the tasks of:

- Establishing their positions in the group as collaborative persons with a guiding role (legitimate "authority," i.e., role as a collaborative leader rather than authoritarian role)

- Joining with members not only as reliable professionals, but as human beings within a professional role
- Acknowledging within themselves (and each other, as cofacilitators), then operating from the understanding, that the trauma to which the group members have been subject is also part of the world in which the facilitators live (whether or not the facilitators have experienced their own trauma). That is, that as facilitators working with survivors of trauma, our clients have survived, and are still surviving, real-life events to which we are not immune.
- Fielding and normalizing trust issues that crop up when the trauma undermines group members' sense of trust
- Understanding and managing authority issues that may occur:

  ○ Authority figures may have been implicated in either the trauma itself or in an unsupportive or damaging response following the trauma.
  ○ Survivors of trauma may question whether facilitators who have not shared the same degree of traumatic experience can truly understand or empathize with what they have endured both during and after the trauma.
  ○ Members may hesitate to give up patterns learned in extreme conditions, and may question the wisdom of therapists who encourage such changes.
  ○ Members may fear judgment from the facilitators, which may echo their own self-judgment, or judgment experienced from others, and may question authority out of a sense of trauma-based shame.

Trust, safety, and authority issues may be validated directly in group by the facilitator (e.g., asking members how they feel about therapy and the therapists) and normalizing these issues. Or, facilitators may keep aware of these issues as they arise, commenting respectfully. For example: *"I'm glad you brought that up, about not trusting us yet. It can often feel like that, being in therapy. You don't know us that well, and we are starting a group together in which we will be discussing personal things about your current lives. Does anyone else feel that way [Leave time for group response]? You don't have to trust us right away. At the same time, we are going ahead as facilitators, and you can let us know when you don't feel comfortable with something we say, or do, or ask of you. And we will try to be clear about why we are doing what we do. Does that make sense? [Leave time for group response]. We have a responsibility as your therapist. At the same time, in this group you have an important and powerful role. Your feelings, ideas, and feedback are the center of this group. Your participation is really important, both for yourselves, and for other members."* In this way, the facilitators find a means to embrace their legitimate roles as helping professionals, while validating and empowering members, and diffusing the trauma-based issues rather than intensifying them.

While facilitator styles vary widely, authenticity is key to developing trust with group members whose trust has been violated by traumatic experience. In the early sessions, the facilitators are walking a fine line between being active and genuine – setting the direction for the group and modeling empathy – while also being cautious and polite (establishing that the group is a respectful environment that gives group members space to be themselves as they are now, and to consider trying out present-day strategies without pressure). Respect, inclusion, and empathy are of particular value in trauma groups, given that the nature of trauma so often involves threat of annihilation, loss of esteem, loss of sense of agency, and alienation (e.g., a sense of not being completely human). While developing a trusting relationship takes time, members are encouraged to give facilitators and even other group members the benefit of the doubt, even if it is "in percentages" (e.g., allowing trust at 20%, 50%, 80%). Facilitators understand that members, in joining the group, are taking a leap of faith, making an act of courage in allowing themselves to trust (or at least to try something new). The facilitator's position in the first few sessions is to support members in *joining* the group in a meaningful way – that is, in a manner that supports both a sense of all being "in the same boat," and at the same time, acceptance of each group member's individuality. Opening the group in this manner permits a sense of shared humanity among group members while encouraging eventual individuation within the group. While early on in the group, members may experience their greatest connection to other survivors of trauma, the facilitators emphasize from the start the members' connection to their significant others and the world around them, representing members' lives outside the group as important and accessible. In terms of establishing the facilitators' shared humanity, use of humor can be a gentle way to "break the ice" that may be relatively nonthreatening (as long it is clearly not sarcastic or shaming).

While facilitators may early on observe patterns that could be the basis of an incisive comment, it can work better to file away the observation until a later session – or first test the waters with a mild and completely supportive comment in the general vicinity of the observed pattern. For example: *"Shane, I notice you have been quiet in the group. Is there anything you would like to add today?"* versus *"Shane, I notice that you shut down today when Alice started talking about taking guitar lessons. Is this what happens at home? You mentioned that your family members complain that you get quiet when they try to share their interests with you."*

PACING OF STRUCTURED PRESENTATIONS

Educational materials in the first few sessions structure these sessions and generate discussion. There are a variety of styles for presenting this material. Some facilitators may prefer a more relaxed discussion format, while others may want to put a lot of energy into presenting the didactic material briefly, up front, with clarifying questions and answers, leaving more time for general discussion afterwards. The most important thing is that the facilitators be comfortable with the presentation format, and to match the format to the group. Groups may vary in composition and knowledge about the material; more therapy-seasoned members can handle a more relaxed discussion, while members new to the material may prefer a straightforward presentation. Facilitator and group energy level are important variables in the pacing. Facilitators may do well to pick up the pace if the exploration of the material seems to be dragging. For example:

> *OK, so let's get back to our topic, and move through it, so we can discuss it. We have the main symptoms of PTSD, which define the diagnosis; and then we have common features that often go along with the diagnosis. Does this make sense to everybody? How familiar are you with these symptoms and secondary features?*

Members also may have varied educational levels and literacy levels. Facilitators present to a variety of levels, making sure to explain more technical terms, and allowing members to share their knowledge as well as questions. Members are considered "the experts" when it comes to their own experience of trauma and its impact, and have a lot to share with the group. It is worth it early on to share that understanding of the survivors' expertise. Doing so helps to establish the collaborative relationship, and empowers the survivors. In addition, group members are likely to sense when facilitators don't completely "get it" from an experiential standpoint, and it lends to facilitators' credibility and transparency to acknowledge and validate the survivors' personal experience.

There is also what amounts to a *translational* issue between lists of symptoms as diagnostic criteria, and survivors' actual experience of symptoms. While the lists can be validating and informative, they are linear; the experience of symptoms is often not. For that reason it is not uncommon to ask the group whether anyone has had intrusive memories, and hear back about startle response, hypervigilance, nightmares, or panic attacks. The list of symptoms is distilled from the experiences of survivors of trauma, and categorized in this linear fashion, while symptoms tend to occur simultaneously and not necessarily experienced as distinct. For some members, it may feel like parsing a grammatical sentence to separate symptoms one from the other. At the same time, understanding of the diagnostic criteria and definitions of symptoms is extremely useful as a shared language for the group, and may help members communicate more effectively with providers.

Middle to End Phase of Group

As the group continues, facilitators gradually encourage members to take greater responsibility for maintaining the group standards and norms, with back-up from the facilitators. Of course, facilitators maintain ultimate responsibility regarding violation of group rules and consequences, as well as for emergencies, risk, and other treatment issues. As the group structure becomes more open-ended and fluid by session five, the direction of the group rests largely on the members. Some members may take readily to this process and engage more actively. Other members may need guidance in order to adapt to the decreased formal structure and increasing level of intimacy in the group, as well as greater demand for interpersonal skill. Early in these sessions, members tend to stress their similarities and bond over them, especially their shared experience of symptoms and related life issues. They may feel better understood by each other than by family members and friends. As this bond becomes secure, members at this stage can be expected to start to differentiate, noticing differences in how they handle their symptoms, as well as life circumstances. This is an important phase of the group, and may need prompting by facilitators if it is not occurring. With differentiation, members acknowledge each other as persons, and are able to give each other more meaningful feedback, including on management of symptoms, relationships, and situations. One of the facilitators' roles in this phase is to help members distinguish between trauma-based feedback (e.g., to trust no one, to give up on relationships), and sharing of strategies that have worked out well (e.g., getting to know people before trusting them, communicating genuinely in relationships).

FACILITATOR STYLE IN THE MIDDLE TO END PHASES OF GROUP

Communication from facilitators may at times become more informal, playful, and direct, during the middle to later sessions. While facilitators are always present rather than remote, they become less active in this phase as members take a central role in setting the agenda and responding to one another, thereby allowing the group process to fully develop.

A good rule of thumb for level of activity in trauma groups is that therapists remain accessible – neither uncommunicative or distant (which can elicit paranoia, confusion, and sense of abandonment), nor over-involved, intrusive, or controlling (which can elicit over-dependence and passivity). The aim is for empowerment of group members through active involvement in the therapy process. Facilitators act in support of this process, according to the specific needs of the group. During the middle phase, members are encouraged to actively utilize group-related learning in the world outside the group, rather than use the group only as a refuge.

LATER PHASE/TERMINATION

During termination, facilitators guide the process and take an active role in structuring good-byes and review of gains and needs, as well as facilitating members' termination with each other. At the same time, the facilitators need to leave space for members to interact with each other and to express anticipation and concerns about the next phase of their lives (and therapy, if relevant) following the ending of the group. It can be useful to remind members throughout the group as to the number of the session, so that members stay aware themselves of the length of the group and to enhance transparency in the group process. Even so, members may be surprised by the ending and have strong feelings about wanting it to continue or feeling abandoned, given the role the group has played in supporting feeling more fully human, and in supporting progress. Facilitators attend to the valuing process throughout the group, and especially during termination, to assure that members continue to feel valued and effective as the group ends, and to carry gains into the next phase of their lives, whether further treatment or completion of treatment.

Interventions: Group Techniques as Applied in Present-Centered Therapy

This section summarizes basic group therapy interventions as adapted for PCGT. The techniques that follow represent those most frequently utilized and most accessible. They will, it is hoped, be familiar to many group therapists, and they do not represent the universe of all possible interventions. Facilitators are free to add to this repertoire. However, as reviewed in the next chapter, heavy use of confrontation, prolonged silences, and approaches that could be experienced as particularly intrusive would not be useful.

Enlisting the Group

Facilitators support the group's own healthy process. This support means turning issues over to the group whenever possible. Members may repeatedly direct issues to the facilitators, or direct questions and comments to them through eye contact and body language. The group process is enhanced when members can turn to each other, rather than valuing the therapists' input over their own and other members'. In the first several sessions, facilitators encourage a sense of empowerment and responsibility in group members by enlisting the group's help with maintaining group focus and group rules. Facilitators also actively encourage discussion and exchange of personal experiences and practical information among members. They make comments that return the process to the group. Some examples include:

> *"Let's get some feedback for you on that issue. Does anyone have any feedback for Jim? Has anyone had similar experiences?"*

> *"I notice members are pretty quiet today. What is the feeling in the group? What kind of feeling do you get from the group today?"*

When a question is directed to a facilitator: *"I can answer that question. But I wonder what the experience has been in the group. Does anyone have a response to that question? Does it ring a bell for anyone?"* The facilitator may choose to answer the question first, or may wait until after group members respond.

The facilitators indicate turning to the group nonverbally through eye contact and body language, such as gesturing back to the group.

Reframing

Facilitators may wish to come at a group issue from a different angle, to help the group or a member out of a "stuck" position. There are many ways of reframing, including shift of perspective, use of metaphor, and paradoxical interventions. Facilitators may use whatever means of reframing with which they are comfortable. Some facilitators will want to stay close to the members' own statements, whereas others may want to overtly disagree ("See, I look at it this way ..."), depending on therapist style. Some basic examples of reframing are as follows:

> *"Well, I know it can really seem like that sometimes. But then, if you really step back and look at the situation, sometimes you find it's like this ..."*

> *"Wow, that's a really good example of _____ (PTSD-related issue). A lot of people with PTSD feel that way. In this group, we're trying to expand our horizons, to see things a little differently. Can anyone help John with that?"*

> *"I can see that getting angry gets you what you want sometimes. That's what's tricky about anger. You know what it gets you; but sometimes it's hard to see what it's cheating you out of – like closer relationships with family and friends, trust, and acceptance."*

Paradoxical/Non-judgmentally Weighing a Dilemma

To a group member just out of rehab: *"Yeah – so everyone is telling you to stop drinking, and now you have a few weeks sobriety, and you are considering drinking at your sister's wedding this weekend. That's a really tough choice you have to make. You put so much into rehab, but drinking has been your best friend for so long."* Here, the emphasis is on the fact that the survivor has a choice, even though others are weighing in on the side of not drinking. The facilitator characterizes alcohol as a "best friend," giving voice to this side of the dilemma and amplifying its attraction. This intervention reflects the reality of the situation (the real appeal of drinking), and allows the member to consider what it might be like to give up this "best friend." The group may then weigh in on (or be asked to weigh in on) the relative value of drinking at a wedding, what it might be like to not drink at the wedding (the member might feel anxious and be less sociable, or not "fit in"), and what it might be like to drink (e.g., they might drink too much, get sick, get in an argument, be embarrassed afterward). This intervention takes the decision out of the realm of "shoulds," into serious consideration about impact of drinking on the member's life.

Reflective Listening and Listening "Between the Lines"

Reflective listening increases the level of empathy in group. It provides a mirror that validates the feelings that members are able to express, and can be especially helpful for alexithymia. While it may seem to be a very simple intervention, its power is often overlooked. It is a great lead-in to connection and an ongoing tool for therapeutic change, as well as a fall-back for therapists in confusing interactions. It is useful for managing countertransference (rather than acting on unclear feelings or assumptions). Listening "between the lines" for feelings, and reflecting feelings, helps members learn to find and identify their own feelings better. For members who really struggle with expression of affect, facilitators may want to offer choices of feelings that could possibly fit the situation (a "multiple-choice" approach):

> Member: *"I really lost it when my brother told me he couldn't go with me. So I got up and left."*

> Facilitator: *"You say you 'lost it' – do you mean – you were really angry – sort of like you felt cheated? Or was it more like feeling rejected?"*

Facilitators may also find reflective statements of body movements and postures useful in giving feedback:

"You're sitting with your arms crossed, and your foot is really going – are you feeling very anxious right now? What's happening?"

Redirecting

There are a variety of ways facilitators may redirect the group process. Sometimes the facilitators may want to redirect the group as a whole:

"It seems we're getting off our agenda here – how does the group feel about that? Do you want to get back to the issues we brought up, or continue with this?"

"You know, I notice there's a lot of joking going on here, and it reminds me how sensitive some of these issues are – I wonder if it's hard to stay with these feelings."

At other times, the redirection may address a particular member:

(Member brings up an issue, receives feedback, and continues talking without acknowledging the feedback) *"John, did you hear what Laura just said to you? Can you check it out with her? You might be able to get something from what she's saying to you."*

(Member begins preaching to the group) *"Evan, we can see how much your spirituality means to you. Spirituality can be a very important element in recovery. But it is a very personal subject – spiritual beliefs are very individual, and we need to respect these differences in the group. Let's hear how you felt, bringing your daughter to church with you for the first time."*

(Member digresses) *"I think I'm losing the thread here – can you go back to the part about your father?"*

(Member is hyperaroused and is speaking loudly, making group uncomfortable) *"Sam, can you take a deep breath and slow down a little? You seem kind of 'wired' today. Can you take a little time to tune in with the group, and then let us know what's getting to you?"*

Redirection can be either direct or indirect. Often facilitators can identify the reason for redirecting, and explain why it might be helpful to approach the group differently. A direct explanation serves as feedback, as well as maintaining the functioning of the group. Members develop an understanding of the facilitator's point-of-view, in the interest of enhanced perspective-taking. The direct approach may diminish control struggles, as the members feel respected when the facilitators take the time to share their rationale. They are also more likely to understand the benefit of the redirection. For example:

"I'm going to bring the group back to personal topics, because, while politics are important, we are all entitled to our opinions, and we cannot use the group to try to sway others. For the group to work well, we need to respect our differences, and focus on the ways the group can work to benefit everybody."

However, at times, an indirect approach is useful. The facilitator may find a thread in a series of tangential remarks and bring it back to a more focused topic, by connecting it to a larger theme, or by deepening the significance of the conversation. For example:

(Members move away from a "hot" issue, to giving each other advice about playing the lottery) *"You know, it strikes me as kind of funny – that advice you gave Nick about the lottery could apply to life, as well."*

(Members discuss car repair) *"You know, there's a lot of knowledge in this room. A lot of you sound very confident about this subject, and are able to help other people out. Can you just take a moment to notice what it feels like when you do that? What's the feeling you get, connecting to others through giving advice in an area where you have expertise?"*

Interrupting

Interrupting is among the most direct forms of redirecting. Therapists sometimes feel impolite when they interrupt, especially when working with clients who are older than they are. Nevertheless, judicious use of interrupting is part of the therapist's repertoire, and may help to establish the facilitators' role in guiding the group. Facilitators can let members know in the first session that they may at times interrupt. Interrupting is one of the effective interventions when members monopolize, become aggressive, delve into details of trauma, or violate the rules and norms of the group (e.g., issuing disrespectful remarks, or verbal threats). It also may be useful when a member is explaining something in a way that the group cannot grasp.

Facilitators may cue a group member through summarizing, using closed-ended comments, and offering subtle redirection. While these interventions will usually be effective, sometimes members may misinterpret these efforts as encouragement to continue. While members could take offense at interruption, there are ways to make it more acceptable, particularly if respect and interest are also communicated, and if the reason for the interruption is made clear. For example:

"Pat, I am going to interrupt you here, because I notice you seem to be getting triggered."

> *"Jan, hold on, I want to make sure the group understands what you are saying."*

There are a number of ways to introduce interruption. Often accompanying hand gestures and body language are important. The therapist typically shifts body posture, with hand/arm gesture indicating "hold on," "stop," or "wait a minute" (e.g., arm out, palm down). Often members may not respond immediately, and it may be necessary to repeat the interruption. Using a "time-out" hand gesture can be useful at times.

Very Direct Interruption

"Whoa, hold on a minute, there!! I have to stop you, Elaine and Paul, because it seems like we're getting into some pretty intense remarks between you. Just stop and take a breath, and we'll check back with you. I want to find out how other members are reacting." (Elaine and Paul start to protest; therapist gestures a 'hold it' message) *"No, I really want to get some feedback going for the group. You seemed to be getting into a struggle, where you can't really hear each other. See if you can get some feedback from the rest of the group. You'll get a chance to speak for yourselves, but it's important to remember everyone here can be pretty sensitive about these issues."*

Moderately Direct Interruption

"Wait – I'm confused. Can everyone follow what Edgar is saying? Edgar, why don't you try again – try to fill us in."
    (A member is dominating the group conversation) *"You know, I'm going to interrupt you right here, because I notice something happening. Pat, you seem to be carrying a lot of the load for the group today. I want to see if anyone else has a related issue to share. Can someone take Pat 'off the hook'?"*
    (Group digresses or is off on a tangent, hard to redirect) *"Oh, wow!* (Gesture of surprise) *Let's hold on a minute here, and pay attention to what's happening. What's the feeling in the group right now?"*
    (A member approaches making trauma references) *"Emily, I think we are getting pretty close to the trauma, the way we're headed. Can you take a moment to come back into the present? What is bringing this up now?"*

Representing or Intensifying the Negative Side of the Ambivalence

Facilitators may find themselves engaged in a struggle on the side of making positive changes. This dynamic leaves an opening, as with a seesaw, to be balanced out with the negative option. If the facilitator pulls for the advantages of the negative side (even amplifying it somewhat), it leaves the opening on the positive side. For example:

> (Members agree they do not want to go to family events) Facilitator: *"It sounds as though you agree about family events – that they are not enjoyable. In fact, for most of you they are miserable. What makes them as bad as they are? What is the worst of it?"*

Exploring the negative option has several advantages. First, it takes the facilitator out of a struggle. The facilitator gives up the "locked-in" position of insisting that family events have value. Second, it shows that the facilitator is not rigid, but is open to expression of opposing views (creating a more comfortable atmosphere, and modeling openness). Third, it encourages members to balance their own views. Once members have expressed the negative, they are more likely to consider the alternate possibility, which allows them to endorse the positive side of their own ambivalence. The intensification of the negative ("Family events are burdensome") opens a move toward a more moderate position ("There are some potentially good things about family events"), and supports members' individuality through being able to counter the facilitator's more extreme statement.

This intensification can also be framed in a more paradoxical intervention:

> (Members are supporting use of outbursts of anger) Member: *"You therapists are always telling us not to act on our anger. I've been trying to hold back my rage; so now people think I'm a wimp! My neighbors mistake my kindness for weakness. One of these days, I'll just lose it, and then they'll back off, and fast!!"*

> Facilitator: *"Yeah, that's what's so great about anger. If you scare people off, at least you can be sure no one's going to bother you!"*

The therapist's joining with the group on the issue of anger may diffuse the group's identification with anger. It leaves the issue for the members to explore and problem solve themselves, rather than identifying the therapists as champions of calm (in opposition to the group's rallying in favor of rageful outbursts). It also mirrors the group's position, and acknowledges the reality of the group opinion (anger can be effective). In addition, it relieves the facilitators of the position of "Pollyanna" or "preacher," allowing a more real relationship with the group. Members may become more willing to explore the downside of angry outbursts, without experiencing it as a restriction imposed by the facilitators.

Facilitators may also split the ambivalence:

> *"You know, Anna* (cotherapist) *and I were talking about family events and this group. Anna was wishing you all would be able to enjoy family events, and I was saying, 'Yeah, but those events can be so demanding, confusing, even annoying – what would it take to make it worth it to go anyway?'"* (Facilitators turn the discussion over to the group.)

If a member's or group's issue is unclear, or the process around a topic appears stalled, the facilitators may endorse opposite sides – especially if each has a slightly different take on the issue. They can model respectful disagreement in the group, and encourage discussion in a way that empowers the group and its members. It also models that the facilitators do not have all the answers and can have different reasonable perspectives – making it safe to express a viewpoint without having to be right. In the example below, Erin is considering whether to take a semester off from school. The group encourages Erin to stay in school but perhaps take fewer classes. Erin appears nonplussed, and shrugs. The group rallies to continue encouraging, citing the good grades Erin had managed in the previous semester. Erin is quiet. When facilitators inquire, Erin shrugs again.

> *John (facilitator): [to other facilitator, Jane] "What do you think, Jane? I think the group has made a good case for taking fewer classes rather than taking a break. Then Erin wouldn't lose the momentum from last semester."*

> *Jane (facilitator): "The group did make a good case. I understand about not losing momentum. But if Erin isn't 'into' it this term, then taking a break is a perfectly reasonable thing to do. A lot of people do take breaks from school, and go at their own pace – which can be a lot better than getting 'burnt out.'"*

> *John: "True, good point. Erin, is that it? Do you feel you are getting 'burnt out?'" [Erin nods "yes"; a group member asks what is causing the burn-out after a successful semester – was it too much work? Erin explains that the upcoming month is an "anniversary period." Group engages in problem around handling anniversary periods, providing Erin with additional options to consider regarding school versus taking a break. Erin gets more support around the anniversary period. Making either choice about school becomes clearly acceptable and within Erin's capacity to decide (especially once she processes her anniversary reaction), removing the "shoulds" around the matter.]*

In this instance, the facilitators engage each other when the group and Erin are at a stalemate, despite the encouraging tone of the group. The facilitators' friendly disagreement models that it is OK to take different perspectives (and therefore, acceptable for the group as a whole and a member to have different points of view). When the group uniformly suggested Erin stay in school, it was hard for Erin to counter the suggestion. Jane's opposing point of view made it safer for Erin to differ as well. The facilitators' taking opposite sides of the issue opened the discussion both for the group and for Erin. The brief stalemate ended and the group re-engaged in problem solving from a more connected perspective, with new information about Erin's anniversary period (also allowing Erin to get more support in the coming months).

Confronting

Facilitators may sometimes find occasion to directly confront an issue, especially where rule violations are involved (although the style of the group is generally not confrontational). There are a variety of ways to confront; the particular form the confrontation takes depends in part on therapist style. In the early stages of group, confrontation is typically more "soft-sell" or indirect, while later in group, both group and facilitators may have built up enough trust and comfort to tolerate a more direct, "hard-sell" approach. However, both styles may be appropriate at any stage, depending on the issue and how entrenched it is (and to what extent the group needs to be protected from the guideline violation), as well as on the relationship between group members and facilitators.

Example: Members engage in a struggle with each other, becoming increasingly loud and disrespectful.

Hard-Sell Approach to Confrontation

Facilitator: *"Whoa – James, Robert – this discussion is getting out of bounds for our guidelines of respectful communication. I would like you both to stop and take a breath."* [After leading the group in a breath so that everyone can recover from contagion of arousal; to group]: *"The discussion in the group just crossed the line, and you can see how the level of anger triggered the group. How can we keep this from happening again in the future?"* [The facilitator redirects from personal judgments of the group members who argued, and engages group in discussion and problem solving].

Soft-Sell Approach to Confrontation

Facilitator: *"Whoa, I am going to stop you, James and Robert – do you notice the tension in the room rising? [To group]: What's happening here?"*

[Followed by group discussion about what to do to prevent aggressive communication]

Example: Members repeatedly making inappropriate and offensive sexual remarks toward facilitator.

Hard-Sell Approach to Confrontation

"Hey, these remarks feel very disrespectful."

Soft-Sell Approach to Confrontation

"I wonder what's going on – are you feeling that we (the facilitators) are putting you down in some way? I notice we have some disrespectful comments going on in the group."

Setting Limits/Maintaining Group Boundaries

As with confronting, there are many ways facilitators may set limits, depending on style and situation. Facilitators generally take more responsibility for setting limits in the earlier sessions, when group members tend to be more tentative, needing facilitators to model how limits are set, and to establish how real the group standards are. As the group develops, members may be expected to participate more in setting certain limits (e.g., talking about trauma, aggressiveness/loudness, interruption by other members). However, facilitators always take responsibility on clinical issues (e.g., intoxication, risk of suicide or homicide (although member feedback may also be elicited afterward)), and boundary violations (e.g., threatening or intimidating behavior, statements targeting one group, scapegoating). The goal is to develop a sense of legitimate and reasonable, collaborative authority on which members can depend (one that contrasts with what they experienced during the trauma, and which is modeled, then shared with the group, rather than retained solely by the facilitators).

Setting limits requires that facilitators use their assertiveness skills. Messages to the group or to a group member may need to be repeated. Facilitators may tend to feel guilty when setting limits, and will often have that feeling reinforced by members' responses to any significant limits (e.g., member removed from group for coming in intoxicated). Facilitators cannot necessarily expect members to agree with their decisions; they can model "agreeing to disagree" when differences of opinion occur, and can communicate openness to critical feedback from group members. Members may show more understanding about the facilitators' decisions later, and appreciate the limits; or they may never express appreciation, but still show improvement in the group (even if the issue still comes up as a sore point).

Limits may be set by referring to group ground rules, by confronting a member or members, or sometimes by directly addressing and making a mild interpretation of a rule violation. Issues that threaten the sense of physical and emotional safety in the group are especially important to address.

Example: Member shows heightened arousal, gets up and paces while venting loudly, and gesticulating.

Facilitator: *"John – I have to tell you something. Can you sit down a minute? ... No, I really can't wait until you finish, it's important to talk about this right now. So please sit down – it's hard to see you while you're up and moving around, so we can't really tell where you're coming from .... Thank you. John, I'm concerned about how 'wired' you were getting just now. When you get up and pace, and speak loudly and move a lot, it can be intimidating .... I know I felt uneasy, and I noticed some of the other members here looked pretty edgy .... John, I'm going to ask you to slow down, and to stop for a moment to catch your breath, so we can all catch our breath. See if you can bring yourself into the present with us now, so we can help you out with this – you don't seem to really be with us. Can you join us? Try to tune in to the group, and see if the group can help you out."*

If after repeated efforts, a member does not respond to requests regarding group safety, or escalates, it may be necessary to remove the person from the room, if possible. The facilitator can either invite the member to "take a break," if safe for the member to do so, or invite the member to leave the room with one of the facilitators:

> *"Sally, I'm really concerned about how agitated you are right now – can you take a break and come back and tell us what's getting to you? Can you handle it if you run into someone in the hall? If you can't come back in, I'll catch you after group. Would it help if I go with you? (Facilitator gets up.) Let's go, I can talk with you out here."*

Some survivors of trauma with PTSD may tend to progress automatically in the years following the trauma, becoming less reactive except when specifically triggered. However, as in any treatment setting, facilitators should be aware of measures to take in case there is real risk of physical violence or threatening behavior in the group. In a worst-case scenario, if a member is agitated at a level suggesting risk, and won't leave (or is unsafe to leave), the facilitator can have the group take a break: *"OK, let's all take a five-minute break, and meet back here."* In a case in which there is real risk, police or agency security may be involved, as well as emergency services (in some settings, a "code green" may be called, for staff backup). Facilitators are encouraged to follow emergency procedures in their settings in cases of immediate risk. This intervention can be necessary in establishing an emotionally safe group environment. As members' responses may run the gamut if a member is hospitalized psychiatrically or removed from group, facilitators process any such event in the group as soon as possible (and potentially over several weeks).

Taking a "One-Down" Position

This strategy can be effective for dealing with issues of shame, and for diffusing struggles for control between members and facilitators. It also recognizes realities (e.g., that therapists can be off-base at times), and members really are the experts on their own trauma. For example, if the group tends to challenge ideas from facilitators:

> *Example: "Now I'm going to share something with you, but it just might be one of these weird ideas that therapists like us come up with ..."*

> *Example: "Well, you all are the real experts on PTSD, because you've been living with it. So maybe you can tell me what you think about this ..."*

Members may fault facilitators for not being aware of specifics of the traumatic context, if it was a communal trauma (e.g., terminology specific to the military and combat, or to situations specific to the 9/11 attack on the World Trade Towers in New York). In PCGT, these references will be at a minimum, but related issues can arise. Therapists can acknowledge that members have the primary knowledge about their trauma-related issues (while facilitators are knowledgeable about therapy for trauma).

> *Example: "You're right – we as facilitators of this group may not have that personal knowledge about the trauma that you have. You are definitely the expert in your experience of the trauma. But I know we do care a lot about how your experiences have affected you, and we have learned a lot from the survivors of trauma we have worked with."*

Process Comments

Speaking to the group as a whole can be powerful. Making simple process comments (simpler is more powerful, generally) in this context can be particularly useful when the group appears slow or "stuck" – for example, when it is dominated by shared trauma-based or depression-influenced thinking (e.g., general agreement that no one can be trusted; family events are to be avoided; life is only suffering). The facilitator may comment that the group seems depressed (and check this impression out with the group), or reflect that the group as a whole has determined that no one can be trusted (and elicit discussion). While one-to-one discussions within the group can also be fruitful (e.g., "Jenny, do you feel anyone at all can be trusted? How can you tell who to trust and not to trust?"), the facilitators will then bring the process back to the group level so that members interact with each other around the "stuck" topic. Some additional basic examples are listed below:

- *"The group seems quiet today – what's going on?"*
- *"What's the feeling in the group as we're discussing this?"*
- *"I get the feeling today as if we're on a carousel – the conversation keeps spinning around, and I'm not sure where it's going – any ideas?"*
- *"Looks like all our members are in their 'own corners' today – what does it feel like to be here?"*

Facilitators may also make interpretations around feelings and patterns in the group:

- *"Seems like the group is working hard today to keep things light – I wonder what the group is protecting us from."*
- *"It seems like the anger in the group is keeping us from feeling how sad this all is."*

Motivational Interventions

Motivation is an umbrella concept for the many factors contributing to facilitation of change, and, conversely, for the factors that maintain patterns that appear unproductive. In behavioral terms, motivation is governed by reinforcement contingencies. At the same time, in the context of treatment and recovery, in which the person served is regarded as having agency and choice, this description is limited. A major influence in the field (Prochaska, Norcross, & DiClemente, 1994) suggests meeting people where they are in relation to behavior change, using a non-judgmental yet proactive stance. As may be familiar, Prochaska et al. identify stages of readiness for change as precontemplation, contemplation, planning, action maintenance, and relapse-prevention. Different interventions are useful at different stages. For example, for someone at contemplation stage, the person served might engage in information gathering about a potential change, but not in planning and implementation. These concepts are useful therapeutically generally, including in PCGT, toward assuming a non-judgmental, individualized stance rather than imposing specific expectations on the person served. Motivational interviewing (MI; Arkowitz, Miller, & Rollnick, 2015; Miller & Rollnick, 2012) has built upon this approach in a multilayered yet accessible set of interventions. Many manuals on various topics have referenced motivational approaches identified in MI; while not part of the original versions of PCGT, the first of which predated the surge of MI, some of MI's informal strategies lend themselves well to use in PCGT. For example, reflective listening in MI ends on the "upswing"; rather than reflecting, "you'd like to go to the yard sale, but you may be too anxious," the facilitator reverses the order:

> *"You are afraid you will be too anxious, but you'd really like to go to the yard sale."* The emphasis on potential over-pathology weights the group toward progress and hope.

Motivation may also be understood in terms of trauma-based schemas (McCann & Pearlman, 1990) that present a set of contingencies based on experience of (and learning from) the trauma. PCGT, as an open-ended, supportive approach, offers the opportunity to develop a sense of agency and access to personal choice, which can counter contingencies that were overlearned during the trauma. As described in chapter six, PCGT offers opportunities for gradual recalibration of expectations and beliefs through the experience of working consistently in the present within the group, and encouragement of investment in current life outside the group. The collaborative and open-ended approach in PCGT is accessible to "readiness for change" at any level of the spectrum. There is no specific requirement in PCGT to engage in a predetermined set of exercises, lessons, or home assignments, nor to identify a set time frame in which specific aims must be accomplished. Goals may be as broad as "feeling better," "learning about PTSD," "getting support," or as narrow as "return phone calls" or "find out more about my new neighborhood." Beyond considering goals consistent with members' current lives, members must also be willing to participate within a group format, work within the present-centered modality, and agree to group guidelines.

From a recovery perspective (Davidson, Rowe, Tondora, O'Connell, & Lawless, 2009), "not motivated" can be considered a pejorative, in that it implies a judgment of where the person is at in the recovery process, rather than accepting people where they are. A member may say, "I feel unmotivated," in which case facilitators may consider this statement in terms of PTSD symptoms, barriers to engagement, and factors such as feeling personal aspirations are not within reach. PCGT can address such issues through reframing "motivation" and exploring the context of disengagement. Embracing the possibility of a broad array of personal goals (rather than terming some goals "unrealistic") can enhance motivation. The process of striving for a goal that does not pan out may lead to another goal that is more meaningful or more accessible. Supporting survivors of trauma in their goals may entail embracing the notion of "dignity of risk," which suggests that no aspiration is too large or too small, and that it is not the role of mental health professionals to protect the person served from disappointment or failure. Facilitators need not be overly cautious, nor discourage members from aspirations, even when the members may be at a high level of distress, recently out of rehab or psychiatric hospitalization, going through a divorce, or surviving cancer. The group also plays an active role in providing feedback on goals and ways to achieve them. Facilitators model acceptance of aspirations so that the group can participate in support of its members' goals.

Motivation Versus Avoidance

Group members do not always engage in the assistance offered by their peers or by the clinician. When group members notice this pattern, especially in circumstances where the offered suggestion or intervention appears simple, this member is often viewed by the other group members and even the facilitators as not being motivated to change. Suggestions from peers may be, "Just get off the couch and take a walk" or "Do your breathing exercise." However, the individual who is the target of these recommendations fails to engage in the offered activity. Such circumstances are usually a source of great frustration for everyone involved, including the identified member.

Even experienced clinicians may struggle to comprehend this behavior. They view themselves as professionals who have long worked at educating and training themselves to offer the best possible care and advice, yet this group member fails to adopt the presented suggestions. As indicated previously in the section on recovery, this individual may be characterized as "unmotivated to change." The failure to engage in the corrective strategies is seen as the "fault" of the identified member. The inability to initiate change or to follow up with the suggestions is seen as a lack of interest or low motivation.

However, the very nature of the symptom (avoidance) prevents change. The emotional numbing and avoidance behaviors associated with the trauma have created an interactive network of cognitions and feelings that inhibit change. The seemingly simple act of getting up from the couch and walking out the door often becomes a daunting task as it pushes the identified member to confront the avoided and overwhelming negative thoughts and feelings related to the index trauma. The PCGT clinician assists with guiding the group to a consideration of these inhibiting factors. Furthermore, the group is facilitated to address the mechanisms concerning the barriers to the implementation of the proffered activities.

Basic Grounding

Grounding (Kabat-Zinn, 2013) can be a key tool for interrupting and reducing reexperiencing or dissociation, which can be essential for responding to members who become triggered to trauma memories during the group. In PCGT, formally structured mindfulness protocols are not used and when used in research as a comparison to mindfulness-based stress reduction (MBSR; Carmody, 2015), as described in chapter two, all grounding was omitted in order to avoid overlapping the target treatment. However, in practice (outside of a study protocol), any group for trauma survivors would do well to have grounding in the "toolbox," given the reexperiencing symptoms of PTSD; and for PCGT in particular, basic grounding techniques are compatible with the group's present-day orientation. Care needs to be taken to choose grounding techniques that are not themselves triggering, and that are readily available to the group in the moment. Grounding techniques may include:

- *Verbal body reflection (e.g., "I notice you are looking away, you're tapping your foot, you seem far away.")*
- *Invitation to return to the present (e.g., "You seem far away, can you come on back to the room?")*
- *Redirecting attention to the room (e.g., "Take a look around the room, check out the other members.")*
- *Breathing out.* Individuals often hold their breath in when anxious or agitated (which tends to increase anxiety). Use of breath can be both empowering and convenient, as it is almost always available. Even members with specific breathing challenges (whether related to a medical condition, or past trauma), who may find elaborate breathwork distressing, can usually access this simple and straightforward strategy.
- *Smelling a pleasant scent.* Naturally based sources of aroma that are strong enough to engage attention, yet not overwhelming and preferably hypoallergenic (e.g., essential oils rather than deodorizers) may be provided by the facilitators, or brought into the group by members who prefer a specific aroma or are sensitive to certain scents. Sense of smell is especially powerful for "changing channels" from reexperiencing to the present. The olfactory sense is the most direct, "hard-wired" sense (i.e., there are fewer "way stations" in the brain required for smell than for vision and hearing). Just as olfactory triggers can be especially powerful, olfactory reminders of the present can be particularly effective for overriding the trauma-related sensations evoked in reexperiencing.
- *Feeling a pleasant object* (e.g., a smooth stone or ridged shell, marble, etc.). Facilitators may provide grounding objects, or encourage members to identify and bring in their own.
- *Member-initiated strategies*, which can vary widely according to member's preference (e.g., carrying a small stuffed animal in a purse or backpack that the survivor can touch; turning a ring on one's finger or a bracelet on one's wrist; wearing something connected with personal or spiritual meaning that can be touched for grounding).

These grounding strategies are brief and distinct from structured mindfulness and meditation interventions (e.g., MBSR or other courses in mindfulness). They allow the facilitators to maintain the open-ended group discussion format while facilitating the experience of returning to the present. One of the most useful ways grounding is introduced in PCGT is for members to engage in recommending grounding techniques to each other, which can foster a meaningful discussion, with sharing of painful, ameliorative, and peak experiences. Members' values emerge in discussions of choices of grounding, and those members who were embarrassed or uncomfortable about making use of these techniques may feel reassured that there are at least some techniques that might be acceptable, and might work for them.

Summary

This chapter has provided information on group therapy and its components, as well as basic group and therapeutic interventions. These interventions are readily utilized within the present-centered framework. While this treatment is accessible for use by providers, formal training in group psychotherapy can only enhance the quality of care and the experience of the provider, as well as the group. For facilitators interested in learning more about groups, there are professional education courses and organizations locally and nationally that are geared to providing this training.

This chapter has referenced provider self-care. Vicarious trauma is a topic in itself (Pearlman & Saakvitne, 1995; Figley & Ludick, 2017; see also chapter seven for history of trauma and self-care). Facilitators are encouraged to spend time processing the group, to make use of peer consultation or supervision as available, and to engage in whatever activities are personally enlivening and restorative.

The next chapter continues this manual with strategies for addressing the symptoms and issues common in PTSD that are likely to influence the group process in PCGT, as well as benefit from it.

Note

1 This and the following chapter incorporate updates and revisions of the Special Topics section of the original present-centered group therapy manual utilized in research. As indicated in chapter one, modifications to optimize the original framework have been based on developments in the field, further experience and reflection on the utility of PCGT, and theoretical integration. The manual itself is in the public domain and can be obtained through the book authors, or, regarding the original manual used in CSP-420, the Veterans Administration's National Center for PTSD Executive Division in White River Junction, VT.

References

Arkowitz, H., Miller, W. R., & Rollnick, S. (2015). *Motivational interviewing in the treatment of psychological problems.* New York, NY: Guilford Publications.
Carmody, J. (2015). Mindfulness as a general ingredient of successful psychotherapy. In B. Ostafin, B. Robinson, & B. Meier (Eds.), *Handbook of mindfulness and self-regulation* (pp. 235–248). New York, NY: Springer.
Chu, J. (1988). Ten traps for therapists in the treatment of trauma survivors. *Dissociation: Progress in the Dissociative Disorders, 1,* 24–32.
Davidson, L. J., Rowe, M., Tondora, J., O'Connell, M. J., & Lawless, M. A. (2009). *A practical guide to recovery oriented practice: Tools for transforming mental health care.* Oxford, UK: Oxford University Press.
Figley, C. R., & Ludick, M. (2017). Secondary traumatization and compassion fatigue. In S. N. Gold (Ed.), *APA handbooks in psychology®. APA handbook of trauma psychology: Foundations in knowledge* (pp. 573–593). Washington, DC: American Psychological Association.
Fonagy, P., Gergely, G., & Jurist, E. L. (2018). *Affect regulation, mentalization and the development of the self.* Abingdon, UK: Routledge.
Kabat-Zinn, J. (2013). Full catastrophe living: Using the wisdom of your body and mind to face stress, pain, and illness. New York, NY: Bantam Books.
McCann, I. L., & Pearlman, L. A. (1990). *Brunner/Mazel psychosocial stress series, No. 21. Psychological trauma and the adult survivor: Theory, therapy, and transformation.* Levittown, PA: Brunner/Mazel.
Miller, W. R., & Rollnick, S. (2012). *Motivational interviewing: Helping people change.* New York, NY: Guilford Publications.
Nelson, P. (1993). *There's a hole in my sidewalk: The romance of self-discovery.* Hillsboro, Oregon: Beyond Words Publishing, Inc.
Pearlman, L. A., & Saakvitne, K. W. (1995). *Trauma and the therapist: Countertransference and vicarious traumatization in psychotherapy with incest survivors.* New York, NY: W. W. Norton & Company.
Prochaska, J., Norcross, J., & DiClemente, C. (1994). *Changing for good: A revolutionary six-stage program for overcoming bad habits and moving your life positively forward.* New York, NY: William Morrow & Company.
Pynoos, R. S., Steinberg, A. M., Dyb, G., Goenjian, A. K., Chen, S.-H., & Brymer, M. J. (2004). *Reverberations of danger, trauma, and PTSD on group dynamics.* In B. Sklarew, S. W. Twemlow, & S. M. Wilkinson (Eds.), Analysts in the trenches: Streets, schools, war zones (pp. 1–22). El Dorado Hills, CA: Analytic Press.
Raskin, N. J., & Rogers, C. R. (2005). Person-centered therapy. In R. J. Corsini & D. Wedding (Eds.), *Current psychotherapies* (pp. 130–165). New York, NY: Thomson Brooks/Cole Publishing Company.
Rogers, C. R. (1951). *Client-centered therapy.* Oxford, UK: Houghton Mifflin.
Winnicott, D. W. (2005). *Playing and reality.* Abingdon, UK: Routledge Classics.
Yalom, I. D. (1995). *The theory and practice of group psychotherapy.* New York, NY: Basic Books. p 1.

5 Guide & Manual Part III: Addressing PTSD Symptoms, Trauma-Related Issues, and Group Patterns in PCGT

Melissa S. Wattenberg, M. Tracie Shea, William S. Unger, and Daniel Lee Gross

Overview and Format

This chapter reviews symptoms and patterns that may occur for survivors of trauma, and how they can be approached effectively in PCGT.[1] It also examines group therapy patterns as they may emerge in any group, and how these patterns may intersect with trauma, as well as how they may be effectively addressed in a group for survivors of trauma. The symptoms, patterns, and therapeutic responses are described in each subsection using the following format:

- *Potential function* of the pattern, which may include:
  - Reasons the pattern may have developed originally
  - Ways the pattern may be adaptable in some circumstances, and therefore take on a life of its own once established. That is, whether there may be reinforcers that maintain the status quo – despite the disruption it causes for the survivor, or the limitations it imposes on the survivor's way of life.
  - Ways the pattern may be protective in the individual's life, and in the group
  - Ways the pattern may serve a momentarily protective function for the group itself

- *Potential challenges to the group* (and individuals within it) – the possible limitations posed by the pattern (and occasions for intervention) – including:
  - Impact on the survivor, for example, interference with goals and/ or everyday life
  - Ways the pattern may play out in the group, for example, introduction of trauma-based actions, feelings, interactions, or themes
  - Potential barriers to recovery within the group

- Possible representation of the trauma itself without awareness or directly discussing it (e.g., the trauma may be "in the room" in some ways, as an intrusive pattern or reenactment)
- Possible ways the pattern may affect the facilitators as well as the group, for example, countertransference, reciprocal reaction

- *Interventions to consider* for addressing trauma-based reactivity (whether a symptom picture, or an established pattern of action), and/or group patterns intersecting with trauma-based reactivity.

These interventions in PCGT, while not tied to any one orientation, are largely person-centered, recovery-based, non-confrontational, and facilitative of the group as a primary resource for support and personal change. They promote a present-centered focus, while acknowledging the presence of trauma and its sequelae in the lives of group members. The use of these interventions requires that facilitators understand that the trauma is present for group members (and therefore, the group as a whole), and that PCGT moves the members into attention to their current lives rather than past events, addressing the time frame in which the impact of trauma is playing out.

The group, as a force of healing for survivors, forms the overall context in which interventions are embedded. While some examples suggest an interchange between a facilitator and a group member, all address the group as well (even if a comment is delivered to a specific individual within the group). Anthony (1968) advised group therapists, "If you look after the group, the individual will look after himself" (p. 300).

The techniques described here do not constitute the universe of all interventions possible within this group. Facilitators will have their own repertoire of group treatment interventions, some overlapping the ones provided here, and some unique. While facilitators in PCGT have considerable leeway in use of their own personal styles and reliance on their own orientations, PCGT does exclude:

- Focus on details of traumatic events
- Borrowing heavily from structured protocols
- Lecture format rather than discussion (didactic material is presented only in the early sessions and is limited to 20–30 minutes in order to accentuate discussion)
- Highly directive or confrontational approaches
- Approaches emphasizing therapist silence. It should be noted that, while a brief silence can be a tool in groups as an invitation to members to take an active role, prolonged silences in a trauma group can:

- Mystify group members, provoking uncertainty and therefore, trust and safety issues
- Reify a sense of abandonment reminiscent of the trauma (and secondary trauma that may have occurred in the aftermath of the original event)
- Exalt the facilitators while disempowering group members, due to a sense that the facilitators are withholding their input from the group – a reversal of the intention of a short silence
- Open a portal for "time-traveling" into the trauma (see chapter six)

Impact of PTSD Symptoms and Trauma-Related Issues

While PCGT offers therapeutic factors that can be particularly useful for the effects of trauma, combined with trauma-awareness aimed at addressing these effects, the expression of PTSD symptoms and trauma-related issues will have impact on the character of the group, the concerns presented, and the challenges and needs of group members as well as the group as a whole. These symptoms and patterns as they intersect with PCGT are discussed in the subsections below.

Hyperarousal Symptoms

Under conditions of hyperarousal, it is particularly difficult for group members to attend to feelings or to take in verbal information, which is ultimately essential in group therapy. Members may experience alexithymia, which can contribute to frustration and sense of inadequacy in response to the demands of the group.

Potential Function

In emergency situations, physiological arousal prepares the body for the familiar fight-or-flight response, and shuts down "non-essential" processes (including higher cognitive processes). As hyperarousal recurs in nonemergency conditions, it may maintain a sense of physical power that protects against the sense of helplessness inherent in the original trauma. Some members may rely on aggressive, angry actions as a counterpoint to the helplessness experienced during trauma. Others reference experiencing a "rush" during hyperarousal, preferable to numbing and disaffection. The manifestations of hyperarousal, such as tension, appearing restless or on edge, and irritability, may communicate an automatic, nonverbal message: "Back off! Don't mess with me!" – which can act as protection against threat.

Potential Challenges to the Group

As a member becomes hyperaroused, a contagion of hyperarousal may result; all members may become prepared for danger, leading to lack of emotional safety in the group. Aggressive behavior or agitation in one member may trigger others, and may result in intimidation and alienation. Shutdown of verbal and cognitive abilities accompanies hyperarousal, leading to confusion, frustration, insensitivity to others, and inability to use therapy appropriately. Difficulty in expression and reception of information increases the likelihood of misunderstandings among members.

If tolerance for aggressive comments, postures, or intimidation were to become a norm in a group, it would undermine the group's need for safety, and would work against the expression of more vulnerable feeling. Individuation and differentiation among members would likewise be compromised. While PCGT ground rules exclude aggressive behavior, facilitators need to be aware of the potential for both group and members to subtly acclimate to an environment of hyperarousal, which undermines the focus and aim of the group therapy and the capacity for being in the present. This pattern can occur if a high level of arousal in one or more members occurs frequently and goes unaddressed. For individual members, chronic hyperarousal may have long-term effects on memory, and constitutes a health risk (e.g., increased susceptibility to high blood pressure, heart attack, gastrointestinal problems, compromise of immune functioning, and premature aging).

Interventions to Consider

Facilitators monitor arousal levels in the group, and comment on a member or the group feeling agitated or "charged" (or whatever term the group prefers, as long as it is neither judgmental nor idealizing). Facilitators act early in the group's development to address expression of aggression and agitation. Unaddressed, intimidating actions can interfere with development of cohesion and trust, the foundation for healthy connections to the group (see subsection on anger). Facilitators encourage taking time to "breathe out" and reduce tension in the group. Facilitators may informally educate members on the effects of hyperarousal, in terms of group process, as well as the risk to mental and physical health. As hyperarousal in the group is recognized, attended to as a PTSD symptom, and kept to a minimum in the group process, members will gradually become more aware of their own responses, and often start to self-modulate with support from the group.

Numbing

Numbing also interfaces with expression of feelings and sharing of experiences in group. Numbing may contribute to alexithymia, and also interferes with empathy among members. In terms of group process, members may experience a delayed reaction to issues discussed in group, due to numbing of emotional response during group. If unprepared for this delayed response, members may feel distrustful or unsafe about disclosure of potentially emotional material that could overwhelm them later, especially as they may not be aware of the significance of an issue at the time of discussion.

Potential Function

Numbing may serve a protective function during a traumatic event, allowing action uncomplicated by emotion. Later, it may prevent the individual from being overwhelmed by the implications of the trauma, as well as by the stressors of everyday life.

Potential Challenges to the Group

Numbing maintains the status quo, and reduces empathy within the group. It fosters a sense of emptiness, increasing risk of depression. When feelings are inaccessible, members feel disconnected from a sense of community, and also from a sense of purpose and meaning.

Interventions to Consider

Facilitators may rely on reflective listening, which extends to reflection of nonverbal cues and body language, in order to help restore contact with feelings. They may help group members to label numbing as a symptom of PTSD, while encouraging a sense of safety about moderate levels of emotion. Therapists may also enlist the group in identifying feelings, and in developing reconnection among members. As members speak frequently about their feelings in a safe environment, there is opportunity for "successive approximations" to emotion. Members may at first use general terms for feelings (e.g., "I had that blah feeling"), and refine the capacity for expression over time, as facilitators accept any reference to emotion as an expressive communication. In telehealth settings, facilitators need to be even more aware of nonverbal behaviors, given the limitations of telehealth platforms. Engaging silent group members, along with enlisting the group's awareness of withdrawn members, can help break through numbing symptoms and resulting interpersonal patterns, thus allowing for greater awareness of emotion in group and in the members' personal lives. Overwhelming current life situations can be buffered by the cohesion of the group. Members can be supported in engaging in strategies suggested by other group members that can help to build confidence and reduce feelings of anxiety or inadequacy.

Avoidance and Numbing

Potential Function

Avoidance serves a protective function following a traumatic event, reducing exposure to trauma reminders. Distress and hyperarousal symptoms may also therefore be reduced, at least in the short-term. If hyperarousal has potential for loss of control, avoidance is again protective. It is worth considering that reminders of trauma would be very distressing for most people, and avoidance strategies may be considered a natural response to reduce overwhelming affect.

Potential Challenges to the Group

Avoidance may start with certain trauma reminders, but can generalize to situations that may limit involvement in activities and relationships. Avoidance can extend to people with certain characteristics that are not in and of themselves risky. Avoidance can also affect level of commitment to the group, to the point of missed sessions, or dropping out from the group altogether. Even to join a group for survivors of trauma means countering avoidance, as the presence of other survivors can initially be a trauma reminder. PTSD groups often show inconsistent attendance and attrition, as well as evading of issues within the group; and it can be considered an act of courage to commit to a group that is offered for survivors of trauma, which naturally challenges avoidance. Avoidance may also manifest itself in group content and discussion. Topics of a more superficial nature, and the group's ongoing energy devoted to such themes, may represent a group-as-whole act of avoidance.

Group participants may confuse avoidance strategies and positive coping. Both may decrease or eliminate strong negative emotions or intense reactions to stimuli. They are therefore similar in the reduction of a negative experience for the individual, yet occupy opposite ends of a response continuum. At one end, avoidance strengthens behaviors that interfere with functioning, and increases the symptoms themselves, through negative reinforcement (as reduction of an aversive state). Avoidance behavior can be seen as an attempt by survivors to turn off the negative cognitions and emotions with which they struggle. However, this process is not selective; both numbing and avoidance constrain the entire spectrum of an individual's experience, positive and negative. The expression of avoidance behaviors and numbing reactions diminishes

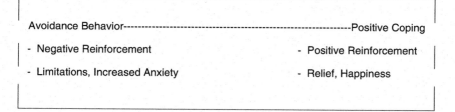

Figure 5.1 Continuum of Action from Avoidance to Positive Coping.

interactions with both negative and positive experiences. At the other end, positive coping refuels the self with positive self-gains (see Figure 5.1).

Avoidance has significant negative consequences. For example, individuals may avoid social interactions to prevent the experience of a panic attack, the expression of anger or hostility, or the feelings associated with some other negative emotional state. The avoidance results in the individual isolating from family and friends, usually the people that mean the most to the individual. Similarly, some individuals turn to drinking alcohol or using other substances to manage negative emotional states. Avoidance and numbing create a negative coping loop associated with the experiencing of psychiatric symptoms, thereby maintaining the symptom structure and impeding psychological recovery.

NUMBING FEELS GOOD - WHAT'S WRONG WITH THAT?

Positive coping is associated with positive self-gains/positive reinforcement. These interventions also reduce the negative condition but do so by engaging in an activity that is followed by a pleasant outcome. As stated previously, it is natural to make choices to turn away from negative experiences. For example, we may turn to a different station on the television or radio, so we do not have to listen/watch an unwanted selection offered by the station. Such behaviors may be considered a personal choice – one that does not particularly interfere with functioning. Such preferences or decisions are choices that do not interfere with the rest of life or result in painful experience, as avoidance and numbing tend to.

Interventions to Consider

Facilitators may need to "go in the shallow end" when it comes to avoidance (but not avoid it!). They may normalize avoidance as a common and understandable symptom of PTSD. The present-oriented environment can encourage a sense of safety from which members can approach more challenging levels of involvement that might include triggers (e.g., going to new places). Facilitators may enlist the group to share ways that some members have overcome avoidance of certain places and people. Facilitators may also assist group involvement by predicting avoidance after an emotional disclosure or conflict in the group, allowing members to express feelings that would otherwise lead to avoidance. When the group is engaged in superficial conversation for a period of time, redirecting the group to earlier educational sessions as a reminder of symptoms and trauma-related challenges may help the group to reconnect with more personal and meaningful topics. Process comments to the group, for example, wondering aloud about a group's focus on "red herring" themes, may also help the group acknowledge and address this pattern. Once avoidance and numbing give way to more affirming choices, the positive coping becomes a pleasant experience that refuels the self. The survivor surmounts the presence of the trigger associated with the index trauma by engaging in a behavior that reduces the impact of the trigger and is followed by a positive outcome. It is an effort that opens the individual to pleasant cognitions and emotions rather than numbing and turning them off. Surmounting not only terminates the negative affective state but also refuels the survivor's resources. It may be used to refuel the self even in the absence of a symptom trigger. For example, taking walks, listening to music, meditating, or engaging in some other positive coping activity extends psychotherapy to life outside the group.

Reexperiencing Symptoms

Group members are likely to be experiencing some degree of intrusion from the trauma during group and in their lives. For some, intrusive recollections may be a rare occurrence, while for others, intrusive symptoms may be prominent, including dramatic and disturbing flashbacks. Reexperiencing represents one of the concrete ways in which survivors with PTSD are removed from the present. The experience of group may be punctuated by sensory experience from the past, resulting in inattention, confusion, and increased hyperarousal. Often group members fail to reveal their intrusions, due to embarrassment and to avoidance strategies. Facilitators can expect that discussion of PTSD symptoms and current experiences will at times inadvertently trigger intrusive recollections, or even flashbacks for some members. These experiences are often followed by emotional numbing.

Facilitators may suspect reexperiencing if a member appears distracted or becomes suddenly hyperaroused. Indirect evidence of frequent reexperiencing in the group process can also be seen in repeated expression of a sense of helplessness, irritability, and loss of group focus.

Potential Function

Reexperiencing maintains the message of the trauma and readiness to respond to trauma. It reduces the focus on everyday life and maximizes attention to catastrophic past events. This intense focus, while painful, can put daily life stressors into a perspective in which they all but fade into the background. The past may have that "bigger-than-life" feel that dwarfs current life difficulties and the accompanying anxieties.

Potential Challenges to the Group

The effect of reexperiencing on the group process is significant, as members *must experience the group* in order to benefit from it. Remaining in the past works against the advantages of the group. Members may begin to avoid the group if they find themselves triggered, and are likely to remain isolated and defensive within the group. If the past looms large, it can feel "beside the point" to address the situations in everyday life that are the main focus of the group.

Interventions to Consider

Facilitators may note the nonverbal cues suggesting reexperiencing, and may reach out to members to help them return to group (e.g., *"John, are you with us? You seem to be somewhere else – do you want to come back in with the group?"*). Members sometimes suspect that they are "really crazy" when they reexperience, so normalization of these symptoms as common to PTSD is important to help group members with issues of shame and stigma. The group focus itself is an intervention for re-experiencing, as members are helped to re-orient to the present. Basic grounding techniques are useful in this context (see "grounding" in chapter four). As focus on current life is maintained, attentional patterns gradually change, and members can become more fully involved in group, and in their own lives. The group can be enlisted to help members manage the anxieties of everyday life, for example, through sharing similar feelings of being overwhelmed by demands, and through problem solving and working out solutions that increase members' confidence.

The Constellation of Issues Associated with Traumatic Experience

Issues such as loss of meaning, loss of predictability (and accompanying helplessness), loss of community/sense of alienation, sense of personal endangerment/loss of safety, and shame can result in automatic patterns in communication and interpersonal relating that may miss some of the nuances in everyday interactions.

Potential Function

These attitudes and ways of relating provide protection, and plans for action (or withdrawal) in a chaotic, unpredictable world. The individual is protected from the shock of disillusionment, and from the hurt and shame due to disappointment and loss of hope.

Potential Challenges to the Group

Members may present with loss of sense of agency, or cynicism, when it comes to recovery and therapeutic change. The sense of helplessness, common in PTSD, can be both a carryover of the traumatic experience, and a trigger for reexperiencing. In the group, members with these predominant feelings and beliefs may be passive, or may actively express frustration and alienation, even enlisting other members to share this perspective. Sense of shame can result in avoidance, and also may motivate scornful or disdainful statements in the group.

A related pattern that may emerge is: "*confusing comprehension (understanding from personal experience of the traumatic event) with the ability to help*," leading to withholding feelings, situations, and needs when sharing them. Members may state that they do not wish to share thoughts and feelings with family, friends, or even other group members, and the facilitators. They may state that their decision not to share is due to the inability of the other to understand their thoughts and feelings, as the other has not experienced the traumatic event(s). This pattern may arise even in groups of individuals with similar trauma histories. It may present in other ways:

- Members may not wish to "bring down" the other group members by sharing their own distress. They may instead sit quietly in the group meeting, or perhaps fail to attend a session.
- Members may believe that, as the index event cannot be changed, the memories and emotions associated with the event will also never change, so the sharing of emotions and thoughts is a useless exercise.

Interventions to Consider

Facilitators may help members put a voice to these ideas and feelings, identifying them as common in survivors of trauma. Rather than exploring their origins, they help them connect with present-day experience.

The group may be enlisted, as members may offer alternative viewpoints. Facilitators may also represent the negative side of the ambivalence, or use paradoxical interventions to gently challenge rigid patterns of belief. For example, "So there's really nothing you can do." If the member is unable to identify a counter-example (e.g., 'Well, there is not

MUCH I can do, but I can always ... [identifies an action]"), the group can be enlisted to provide more balanced options. Similarly, if the group invests in a shame-based or disdainful stance suggesting the pointlessness therapy, facilitators can make whole-group process comments (e.g., "There seems to be no point, yet everyone would love to gain help from this group.").

When members equate "inability to comprehend with the inability to help," one of the tasks of the facilitators is to clarify that others' inability to fully understand does not prevent them from aiding. For this strategy to work, facilitators suggest that members may be able to receive help, but must be open to identifying how the other may provide aid. The past cannot be changed, but the distress and pressure that members currently experience *can* be relieved. Members do not have to share the details of a nightmare, or the intrusive memory of the index trauma. A healthy option might be to say to the other, "I am having some difficulty right now, but if you do *this* it would really help me." The requested assistance may be for a few moments of solitude, or to go on a walk together, or to share in some other activity to help mitigate distress. These actions require members to be introspective and honest with themselves and to ask the significant other for a specific type of aid. Such requests often serve to decrease the distress of the significant other also, while aiding the person making the petition.

Facilitators may point out that we often find it distressing to observe someone struggling with unknown concerns. We may further believe, as the concern has not been shared, that we are somehow the cause of the conflict. The question may be posed to the group: "When you see your significant other struggling and becoming upset, how do you feel watching their distress and not being able to offer help?" Members frequently respond that they also feel distress in that circumstance, which supports the facilitators' suggestion to share rather than engage in actions that support avoidance or numbing. This discussion suggests that the act of not sharing may actually be more hurtful than sharing. Facilitators may also make this analogy: When members see their primary care physician for an ailment, they must offer information concerning their distress from the ailment to the physician so that appropriate care may be provided. The physician and the client then manage the ailment together. It is not necessary for the physician to have experienced the symptoms to provide the needed care. In PCGT, when a member does not wish to share distress with the other group members, facilitators may ask the group members whether they themselves have had similar concerns, and how they managed it. Facilitators may ask the group, "When you are having a bad day, is it better to avoid group or attend group?" The group will typically support the identified member or members attending group when struggling with symptoms, sharing distress to relieve the burden.

From Rage and Aggression to Emotion

Anger is one of those natural emotions that are again "grist for the mill" in PCGT. In contrast, rage (like terror) reflects a bodily state of very high arousal, in which the mid-range emotions are blocked by fight-or-flight response. Rage tends to communicate aggression even in the absence of aggressive actions. Aggressiveness or rage may be conveyed through body posture, gesture, voice volume, intensity of eye contact, and/or verbal content (e.g., violent images and words, stories of aggressive behavior or aggressive wishes ("I'd like to wring their necks!")). It may be driven by hyperarousal, in which case it may be unintended (although still essential to address). Reexperiencing may also evoke aggression, for example, a flashback incorporating physical or verbal aggression intended for another place and time. At the same time hyperarousal (see "Hyperarousal" subsection) can signal risk for aggression or intimidation. Longstanding hyperarousal may fuel use of aggression in the interest of achieving power and control that appears otherwise unavailable – especially given the sense of helplessness commonly experienced when triggered. A member may also be accustomed to behaving aggressively at work or at home, and therefore not recognize or acknowledge its impact on others. Intense sense of shame or sense of helplessness can also lead into aggressive behavior.

Potential Function

Aggression can be a strategy for restoring sense of power when feeling helpless or humiliated (or at risk for either of these). It can be a way of establishing control in a feared or untrusted situation, including group. Intimidating actions may say to facilitators and group members: "Keep a distance; don't offend me; (don't hurt me)." Aggressive communication can be a protection against vulnerable feelings. It may also channel intrusive traumatic experience as a reenactment in the group.

Potential Challenges to the Group

While rageful or aggressive communication may indirectly express a sense of vulnerability, this pattern intrudes on others in order to secure a sense of physical and emotional safety. As a result, other members and facilitators may find themselves "walking on eggshells." Fear and loss of safety in the group affect the intimidating member as well as other members. Members may feel triggered or retraumatized. One resulting dynamic can be an affirmation of and identification with the power of rage and aggression, as an inoculation against powerlessness (which, as a human dynamic, can potentially draw in the facilitators as well as members). This pattern throws off the balance in the group, leaning the power in the group toward more aggressive members and others identifying with them, while undermining the group as a whole. Unchecked, this pattern can lead into premature pseudocohesion (see next subsection topic) and scapegoating of members who are not "on board" with aggressive behavior. Facilitators may be co-opted or unofficially "demoted."

Interventions to Consider

It is important to adhere to and remind members of the group guidelines, which proscribe intimidation and other aggressive actions. A direct approach includes setting limits (emotional and physical safety need to be secured as a priority). Verbal body reflection can be useful here, as with venting, for example, reflecting the physical signs of arousal. Labeling the presence of hyperarousal and its potential contagion can increase the group's awareness, which can be helpful not just in the moment but in the personal lives of members. Once limits are set, facilitators can reframe the aggressive stance in terms of its motivating factors (e.g., overcoming sense of helplessness; responding to shame/embarrassment, etc.) and potential advantage (e.g., asserting control). Basic clinical tools when encountering aggression or rage, in addition to the above, include interrupting (e.g., "I see you are very agitated, so I am going to interrupt you here..."), and redirecting (e.g., "I notice you are becoming very agitated. Can you take a moment and think about what the trigger might be?"). In early sessions, facilitators enlist the group once the aggression has ceased by checking in to see where the group's level of arousal, anxiety, fear, and reexperiencing might be. Typically, other members may be triggered to traumatic experiences; the facilitators then engage the group in basic grounding (looking around the room, smelling a pleasant scent, touching or holding a soothing object, breathing out (see chapter four subsection), and then discuss reaction to the instance of aggression, while refocusing on the present. In later sessions, group members may more immediately express discomfort with aggression in the group as a violation of group norms, and register reactive hyperarousal or feeling triggered, which is a prompt for the member introducing aggressiveness or rage into the group to self-check. At the later stages of group, if group members do not spontaneously react, it may be that the group does not feel safe enough for doing so – in which case, the facilitators again take charge of the situation to restore safety to the group and check in with members. It is very important for the group as a whole to have a voice after an instance of aggression, in order to offer an opportunity to express reaction in a non-aggressive fashion, and to restore capacity for mid-range emotions that may have been temporarily abridged due to arousal in the group.

Mutuality Versus Premature "Pseudocohesion"

Journalist Chris Hedges (2002, *War is a Force that Gives us Meaning*) notes a human tendency for those exposed to trauma to bond in a kind of merger that lacks mutuality and individuation – while true relationship involves individuals coming together with all their differences. Similarly, Parson (1985) notes that some groups of Vietnam veterans with PTSD develop a "too early cohesion" that is for all intents and purposes counter-therapeutic, potentially leading to "therapeutic impasses, intensification of symptoms, acting-out and even the demise of the group." This early appearance of cohesion represents a form of pseudomutuality[2] that prevents differentiation and avoids true intimacy and sharing of feelings. Parson sees this phenomenon as based on "feelings of narcissistic endangerment," "paranoid defenses in the group's social structure," and "general fragmentation-prone functioning" secondary to trauma and accompanying "loss of self-cohesion" (suggesting, as does Hedges, that the individual as a whole person is lost in this process). This accelerated "pseudocohesion"[3] enacts a variety of trauma-related issues (e.g., loss of trust and safety, authority issues) and sends the group members into an alliance that may often ignore, demote, or co-opt the facilitators. The group develops an "us-versus-them" mentality (Tajfel, 1978), or entrenched ingroup-outgroup stance that supports the status quo against change, and discourages connection to the world outside the group. Reexperiencing and hyperarousal can intensify this pattern.

Potential Function

One of the main functions of this pattern is to counter shame, especially in the context of having symptoms, and of needing to be in therapy, in addition to the sense of injury from the trauma itself. In any group in which members have significant symptoms, it may be a natural occurrence to go through a period of over-identification within the group, and alienation from others outside the group. Merging obviates the need for change, as though all members are fine just the way they are as long as they belong to the group. The shared history of trauma can become a banner under which members unite, eschewing potential and need for change. Family members and old friends may be seen as "the other," the "uninitiated," who don't share the experience and can never truly understand its impact (as noted earlier in this section under The Constellation Of Issues Associated With Traumatic Experience). The truth behind this pattern – that members will not see the world in quite the same way after trauma – is overgeneralized as justification of trauma-based beliefs and actions.

Potential Challenges to the Group

This pattern may result in loss of trust, stagnation, immobilization of therapy within the group, and a loss of sense of agency in group members, as the group becomes polarized and dominated by one point of view rather than offering a space for each individual. It also may camouflage real issues within the group to which this pattern may be a reaction, for example, a member whose issues or actions are known to members but not to the facilitators. For example, members may become aware of a problem with another member during their pre-group/waiting room interactions, or due to being acquainted outside the group. Members may know before the therapist does that another member is, for example, "using" prior to coming to group; suspected of a compromising legal problem; borrowing money from group members; asking to borrow medication. If facilitators are not "clued-in" concerning the member's actions, the facilitators may appear to be unconcerned, unperceptive, or irrelevant. The group may then functionally "demote" the facilitators in a pattern that either protects or targets that member, while deflecting group processes that would lead to individuation or change.

Interventions to Consider

It is easier to head off this pattern early when it is less entrenched than when it is in full force. Inflexibility and crystallization of severe or trauma-based beliefs may signal that the group is moving toward premature cohesion. These signals warrant early intervention, especially when a subset of group members express aggressive feelings that may intimidate other members, or when a contagion of hyperarousal emerges in the group. Facilitators rely on a variety of skills in intervening; the aim is: 1) to address the issues that precipitate these early signals, in order to avert this pattern; and 2) to diffuse this pattern once it begins to develop. Early on, facilitators emphasize both the individuality of the members and the fact that they have in common the experience of trauma. Facilitators provide education about trauma and express hope for change. As this pattern can develop when the group members have a "secret" that the facilitators do not share (as described previously), or when facilitators miss something like a frequently intoxicated member or a member taking advantage of others (leading to loss of trust in the facilitators), facilitators need consider the legitimate sources of this phenomenon and reassure members of their willingness to address difficult situations in the group. If the pattern becomes entrenched, possible interventions include:

• A cautious paradoxical approach in which facilitators reflect the negative side of potential ambivalence (e.g., "So there's really no point in making any changes").

- Respectful confrontation (identifying the pattern; countering assertions cheerfully, with counterexamples) and education (e.g., reminding members about group guidelines and the purpose behind them, and about the potential power of the group should all members engage in a productive process).
- Overt setting of limits (e.g., if a member is being scapegoated), with review of group purpose and guidelines. It is always preferable for the facilitators to take on criticism than to allow a member to be targeted (which leads to further loss of safety and trust within the group). When confronting and setting limits, it is important to do so in a non-shaming manner, so as not to intensify the entrenched position of the group. Shame can be diffused by facilitators presenting as human beings (as well as professionals), who care about doing therapy, and who are aware of their own imperfections and limitations. Therapists need not overdisclose in order to achieve this effect, but can communicate these qualities through therapeutic style and manner of expression. Gentle use of humor can be helpful. If the group is allied with one facilitator over another, the allied facilitator needs to support the non-allied facilitator and endorse and value the contributions of the "other" facilitator.

Moral Injury

Moral injury[4] refers to specific reactions to sense of moral betrayal, which may occur in one or several identifiable domains (Barnes, Hurley, & Taber, 2019; Litz et al., 2009; Griffin et al., 2019; Shay, 2010). McCann and Pearlman (1990) included moral injury in their emphasis on "frame of reference" disruption and emergence of concomitant existential issues. Moral injury as currently defined may occur across several domains: acts of omission or commission that violate the survivor's values and moral beliefs; acts of others that violate moral and ethical code of the survivor (e.g., "betrayal trauma"; Freyd, 1996) and systemic conditions or acts of omission or commission that violate needs, promised actions/protections, or responsibilities of the overarching organization, governmental body, or agency – to which the survivor is witness or falls victim.

Potential Functions

A focus on moral injury may represent an important attempt to maintain an ethical stance after disillusionment by the interpersonal aspects of the traumatic experience(s). High standards and personal dignity may have restorative significance, and may also counter a sense of annihilation encountered during the trauma. Moral stance can be an important aspect of personal identity.

Potential Challenges to the Group

Once a survivor anticipates potential betrayal, there is opportunity for reenactment, suspicion, amplified distrust, sense of helplessness, and jumping to the conclusion that the moral violations are recurring in current situations. Of course moral and ethical violations may actually occur in the individual's life, and such events may be especially evocative – needing particular attention in group to avoid a reactive response that will dig the individual in deeper, precipitating an entrenched response with little opportunity for resolution. When the survivor was also a perpetrator of a moral violation, or when the context is one in which the survivor assumes responsibility despite having had no control over the actions of others or agencies (but wishes such action had been available), resulting actions may include self-recrimination, self-punishment, and self-sabotage. There may be a sense of having no right to successes when others suffered the indignities of moral violation – as well as a sense that successes and happiness in current life violate ethical standards by failing to perpetually remember and honor the violations of the past (see "Keeping a Vigil").

Interventions to Consider

As established in prior chapters, PCGT does not delve into the past, but works with impact of past experience as expressed now. There are treatments directly addressing moral injury (Litz, Lebowitz, Gray, & Nash, 2016) on an individual basis. In PCGT, facilitators work in the present while informing themselves in a trauma-aware fashion, in order to facilitate progress in the areas of potential injury. As these themes emerge in the group, facilitators utilize the group as a legitimate shared body of normative experience that offers an alternative to the violations of the past. Facilitators therefore need to identify any patterns undermining the trustworthiness of the group, which could be a trigger for members in this regard. The facilitators may identify common patterns that can be present in any group that may represent moral and ethical divides (the approach will depend on stage of group, and overall group functioning toward individuation and mutuality). Present-oriented themes to address may include:

*   *Making amends for acts of commission or omission by the survivor* (e.g., through volunteering, engaging in civic projects, helping neighbors)
*   *Countering past moral violation committed by authority structures:* engaging in positive social action that contributes to the larger community (e.g., recycling committees, human rights organizations, welcoming committees, local government, advocacy, or spiritually based groups).

- *Developing resilience when acts of others are the source of moral injury*, by:
  - ○ Defining one's own values and living by them to the extent possible
  - ○ Recognizing when standards are too high to fulfill (developing flexibility)
  - ○ Striving to give others the benefit of the doubt, and developing perspective-taking
  - ○ Regarding the motivations of others (i.e., not assuming the worst; putting oneself in the shoes of the other)

As the domains of moral injury almost exclusively involve interpersonal trauma, corrective experience in the group as a whole is valuable in helping the survivor overcome fears and assumptions about self and others, as well as to diminish reenactments of these issues that may arise in everyday social groups (whether family, work, school, friendships, or organizations in which the individual is involved). Facilitators may draw attention to positive experiences in the PCGT group as examples of effective group membership and potential to experience something other than or beyond injury in current life.

Keeping a Vigil

Following trauma, a sense of "keeping vigil"[5] (Wattenberg et al., in Schein et al., 2006) may interfere with return to life-as-usual, including life in the present; "major needs that emerge in the aftermath of trauma may potentially come into conflict initially with therapy, based on this sense of vigil." Vigil can be related to survivor guilt, and to moral injury (Litz et al., 2009, 2016). It is a focus that honors the past through continual attention to it, often with the ideal of "never forgetting," and therefore preventing future trauma. These values are meaningful and important; yet at the same time, if they pervade all times and places of the member's life, they detract from the essential messages of current life and current relationships, depriving the survivor of meaning in the present.

Potential Function

Keeping a vigil honors the past and may even represent warning about how to attain a better future at a systemic or cultural level (e.g., the "Never forget" caveat embodied in the USC Shoah Foundation founded by Stephen Spielberg in 1994, which chronicles the horrors of the Nazi holocaust through acknowledgment, commemorative ritual, and creative acts educating community about the human and moral losses and warning against recurrence).

Keeping a vigil may honor the dead. It may honor the figurative "death" of the survivor's innocence, and other aspects of self harmed by the trauma; and it marks the time of the member's disillusionment and (often) near-destruction/annihilation. The sense of vigil says, "I am still here," and "I am here for others who are not here," as well as, "I was witness to inhuman acts when there seemed to be no moral authority, no deity, to protect from this degradation" (Johnson et al., 1995). Keeping a vigil offers a sense of control in the face of helplessness. It may reclaim a sense of meaning when normal meaning was lost. It may create a sense of continuity for those who have died or who have not fully survived. It creates a sense of safety by assuring to never again being caught off-guard. The larger-than-life pattern of the mission in sense of vigil may serve to transcend the near-annihilation at the time of the trauma, and reduce the sense of vulnerability.

Potential Challenges to the Group

In the aftermath of trauma, survivors may be unwilling to allow themselves to relax again, hesitating to embrace what seems like a false sense of security. Going on with life may also appear to betray experiences of horror and loss during the trauma, invoking survivor guilt and sense of moral injury. Sense of vigil may lead to struggles at work or with family members around moral issues. Survivors with a strong sense of vigil may feel torn between the commitment to current life and the need for continuing remembrance to restore meaning lost during the trauma. Yet being only partially present in current life distances them from family, friends, and deeper relationships.

These patterns in group may serve to underscore the enormity of trauma, and may suggest that the present focus and therapy itself are dwarfed in its shadow. Members occupied by a sense of vigil may hesitate to accept feedback from the group, feeling that investment in current life may be acceptable for others but not for themselves. It can be difficult to accept help when the main focus is on the vigil and not on the individual's needs and current life. These patterns may emerge in group for members with a primary focus on sense of vigil:

* The need to protest injustice and to advocate, while supported by the group, can limit intimacy if it is the main focus. These patterns can occur:

   * *Venting in a political style* rather than engaging in more personal dialogue
   * *Returning to details of the trauma* as testimony to the injustice (which are then redirected by the facilitator)

- *Endorsing a parallel path* (honoring the occurrence of trauma) to the group's present-day agenda, which may challenge the group's focus and leadership. Group members may struggle with *despair and depression* related to the senselessness of the original trauma, reified by the sense of vigil. Members may share in entrenched existential issues (e.g., loss of meaning, hopelessness). And the vigil itself can be exhausting.
- *The Need to Remember and Represent* those who cannot speak for themselves (survivor guilt). The survivor can have a sense of being undeserving of happiness and progress in life, as though even being alive (and reasonably "OK") is a form of disrespect to others who suffered (or to the suffering self). A sense of betrayal from the original trauma may suggest the absence of any protecting spiritual presence. The burden then falls to the survivor to take on responsibility for the remembrance of these individuals and not falter until things have been put right. Group members may be half-hearted about therapy of any kind, and may even feel a need to continue suffering in order to honor those lost to the trauma.

Interventions to Consider

Identifying the sense of vigil, and positively reframing the themes embedded within it, allows facilitators to honor members' concerns without concurring with the ways they play out in everyday life. Because vigil harkens back to specific events, it may be necessary to head off trauma disclosures within the group.

Members may not be aware of the theme of keeping a vigil, which the facilitator may connect with some of the PTSD symptoms identified in the early sessions. For some, this awareness may be enough to shift this pattern. This awareness can be enhanced by reminders of the time frames of past and present, and the potential for intrusion of the past into the present while the group is working on being aware and involved in everyday life. In addition, facilitators may work on "successive approximations" to moving from vigil toward investment in the present:

- As with moral injury, members may be supported toward positive social action and observances related to sense of vigil, while encouraged toward investing in their current lives. Members may set aside respectful periods of acknowledgment, and to integrate observances into current life so that it is possible to "take breaks" from the vigil and create access to the present. Thoughtful, planned spiritual observances may be a part of this process.
- Amplification of an entrenched vigil-devoted position (e.g., "So your vigil requires every bit of your attention and energy; your family and

friends need to accept that you will not be involved with them in a serious way") can allow the survivor to correct the facilitator's absolutism, and to recognize that the options may not be "black and white."

- Reframing in terms of sacrifice can provide acknowledgement, while inviting/giving permission to limit the sacrifice (e.g., "When is it enough sacrifice?"). It may even be considered that an exclusive focus on the vigil limits opportunities to connect with others who would resonate with the member's concerns.

Responses to Stressors and Crisis (See Also Section on Hyperarousal)

High levels of current stress, and crises, are common in the lives of human beings and in any group. They can occur more frequently for a subset of survivors of trauma (e.g., group members who are first responders and therefore more prone to loss and injury; those who are caregivers within their families; those in complicated work environments; those in complicated relationships; and those who have secondary contexts related to being survivors, from medical comorbidity to legal or financial stressors). Survivors of trauma run the gamut of response to stressors, with some particular variations based on trauma:

- Hyperarousal symptoms can intensify the sense of crisis, often accompanied by panic episodes. Hyperarousal symptoms can engage fairly quickly ("from zero to 100 in a second," in common parlance) and may persist for a prolonged period).
- History of trauma may lead to diminished response to risk or stressors (from an "I've seen so much worse" perspective)
- Some survivors self-protectively distance from potential stressors that could trigger sense of helplessness and hyperarousal (and concomitant panic or rage).
- Post-traumatic growth (Tedeschi & Calhoun, 2004) may help some survivors take a long view, to become less reactive to the "stings and arrows of outrageous fortune," from a "this too shall pass" perspective. Stressors and related arousal may occur, followed by finding ways to move on, and "make the best of things."
- Response to significant life stressors may also involve becoming accommodated to crises and living in crisis mode – whether with relative indifference to seriously challenging events, or with sensitized reaction to each stressor. Some survivors may thrive in a crisis and feel most comfortable when responding to highly stressful situations, appreciating being the person to whom others can turn to in an emergency.

Facilitators are likely to encounter the full range of possible crisis areas among group members: interpersonal (whether family, partner, child, or work, or even neighbor/acquaintance); financial; legal (including divorce); housing-related; work-related/education-related; environmental; and medical. In addition, it is not uncommon to have members in group who are in a high-stress profession (e.g., firefighter, trauma nurse, police officer), who are literally handling crises in their jobs, and potentially more hyperaroused and crisis-prone because of these circumstances (encountering more trauma, and a greater number of trauma triggers). As suggested previously, some survivors of trauma are drawn to high-stress jobs, for a variety of reasons that may be related to trauma or simply circumstance (e.g., tending to be a caretaker or rescuer; being in the military; being qualified for high-stress positions due to having been in the military; becoming accustomed to the "rush of adrenalin" having been placed in a caretaker role as a child or teenager, and maintaining that role into adulthood (e.g., survivors of an abusive or neglectful childhood)). These contexts and stress-response patterns are "grist for the mill" in PCGT. Note that if a group member is at current risk (e.g., living in an unsafe environment) or recently victimized, additional resources and supports may be needed, to be determined in collaboration with the group member.

Potential Function

High-stress or crisis-prone contexts tend to be "bigger than life," and this quality enters the group as well. The sense of high arousal and crisis interact with sense of meaning. Whether the source of high stress or crisis is a job or life circumstance, it may convey immediate meaning that supersedes other meaning in the lives of survivors (Hedges, 2002). It lends urgency and importance to issues discussed in group, and to the group members as well as the group itself, which the facilitators are likely to experience. As members engage in high-end struggles and share them in the group, the sense of helplessness is invoked, and then diminished as the group process imbues the group and members with a sense of empowerment – which tends to be intensified by the arousal in the group (merging with the "bigger-than-life" quality). There may be a strong sense of camaraderie generated by interactions spurred by intense energy in the group. Small anxieties, slights, and insecurities take a back seat to these high-end situations and reactions, experienced as petty or trivial by comparison to the larger issues at hand.

Potential Challenges to the Group

When crises and high arousal are prominent in a group, the sense of urgency can block more differentiated communication and actions.

Feelings, or at least subtle feelings, and interpersonal sensitivity may be suppressed; alexithymia may be exacerbated (and along with that, communication in the individual's life is likely to be less effective). Being in crisis mode reinforces an action orientation to life, which can lead to impulsive decisions or acting on anger. Insularity may evolve that separates the group member from the community as a whole. Members who are in a caretaker or rescuer role may carry the role into group and find it difficult to be vulnerable or to ask for help from others. For members who are often in crisis, other group members or facilitators may end up in a reciprocal, "rescuer" role. For members who are inured to crisis, the everyday life concerns and vulnerabilities of others may appear inconsequential, or weak. For members whose post-traumatic growth (Liu et al., 2017; Schubert, Schmidt, & Rosner, 2016; Tedeschi & Calhoun, 2004) tends to lead them toward positive attributions and moving on, frequent crises in the group and high associated levels of arousal may evoke helping responses and, if not resolved, frustration and challenges to meaning-making in the group. As arousal is contagious, members are likely to share in hyperarousal, and can more easily be triggered to traumatic experience. While intense arousal in group may be energizing initially, periods of crisis or high arousal tend to be followed by exhaustion or numbing.

Interventions to Consider

Facilitators again find themselves walking a line between acknowledging the crises in members' lives, and helping members reduce the emotional temperature in the room. As high level of arousal does not lend itself to problem solving, experience of emotion, nor to differentiation among members, facilitators engage the level of affect related to the crises or stressors (whether elevated or suppressed) and intervene early on. As discussed in the subsection on hyperarousal in this chapter, verbal body reflection can be helpful in assisting members in returning to a connected and less aroused state, through making them aware of their level of affect and the physiological signs of this arousal. The practice of self-observing can in and of itself help to reduce arousal if it is not extreme. Because intense affect can be contagious for the facilitators as well, facilitators note their countertransference, and use their own excitement or exhaustion as a cue to work with the group toward a level of arousal that facilitates a calmer, meaningful discussion and responsiveness to issues at hand. The group can be enlisted to reflect on the "feeling in the room," and to problem solve in the moment how to return to the present in affect as well as in subject matter. Group members may benefit from being reminded of the education provided early in the group sessions, or may expand the education with further information on the impact of high arousal on thinking, higher processes, planning, and experience of feelings. As with many issues explored by the group, members can be encouraged to discuss what happens at home when the intensity level is heightened.

Transitions in the Context of Disability, Access to Work, and PTSD

PTSD symptoms that interfere with ability to work incur roughly the same secondary issues as other psychiatric disabilities. The stigma and shame often associated with psychiatric diagnosis can be intensified when those symptoms may at least temporarily affect capacity to support oneself through employment. A formal disability designation may occur in the context of workers' compensation, Social Security disability, or specialized disability source such as medical disability from an employer, or compensation from the Veterans Administration. While PTSD is among the diagnoses that validate individuals for experiences of extreme stress, it is a "double-edged sword" in that the diagnosis (when shared) is also revealing of an extreme experience that likely involves helplessness, betrayal, and victimization. While some may see any vulnerability as weakness, others may feel relieved to have a diagnosis that explains distressing symptoms. These are issues that members are likely to bring to the group. Members may be in different places regarding this issue. Some may not be dealing with a disability designation, while others may be supporting themselves on disability, or in the process of working toward obtaining disability, or working their way back into a work environment. A portion of members in a group may be going through transitions with work that affect them financially and in terms of lifestyle.

Potential Function

While it can be a source of stigma, a PTSD diagnosis or identification as a trauma survivor has earned respect in many communities. This identification can be both limiting and potentially inspiring. Both within and outside the group, survivors of a shared trauma may create their own subgroups in order to fend off alienation and disconfirmation in the society at large.

Potential Challenges to the Group

Given the very real symptoms associated with the disability, it may appear daunting or paradoxical to consider more fully joining a non-trauma-based community. After going through the struggles that necessitated the disability status (e.g., job loss, loss of relationships, income, and sometimes, housing), survivors may become discouraged about "getting out there" and trying again, especially after pursuing the disability process. Individuals can feel "stuck" in terms of the diagnostic label, yet fearful that progress will mean premature discontinuation of disability supports. In addition, for members who have found a trauma-based community, stretching out toward new communities may result in fear of losing or even betraying the community of other survivors.

In the group, the impact of these concerns may manifest in expressed doubt about the potential for recovery and therapeutic change. Members may tend to believe that the facilitators are naïve in embracing that "recovery is real." They may suspect that facilitators cannot really appreciate what the members have to lose in moving more fully into a community that could involve work, or even connection with others who are not survivors of trauma. There can also be a "plexiglass ceiling" experience for survivors with disabling symptoms: the closer one gets to the chosen goal, the more clearly the barriers are revealed.

Interventions to Consider

Facilitators typically find themselves walking a fine line between appreciation of members' limitations, and instillation of a realistic sense of hope for reduction of symptoms and access to the life members would choose for themselves. Facilitators also need to make sure that their own values are not infusing heavily into the expectations for the group, whether belief in the advantages of work over disability, or belief that members cannot work and should not give up disability. Helping members talk about their fears is useful, as is validating their hopes. Group members' tendency toward negative self-evaluation can be reframed as indication of high standards (and can be a clue to the values of group members). It can be helpful to dispel naïve views that relapses cannot recur, or that things will always be within one's control and get better and better (as survivors of trauma, group members are aware that these notions are unrealistic). An array of services may become available for individuals with a psychiatric disability designation. Community supports outside the group such as vocational counselors, vocational rehabilitation, and supported employment/education can be particularly useful. As members approach the "plexiglass ceiling," it is important to validate how much clearer the barriers are at this point, and to acknowledge feelings, fears, and hopes in this critical period. Identifying members' strengths, even in the ways they made it through challenging symptoms and circumstances in the past, can be helpful in building a recovery trajectory. Facilitators can enlist group validation around these issues, which can be especially meaningful in acknowledging these struggles and providing support for overcoming these challenges. Motivational interviewing (Miller & Rollnick, 2012) strategies are useful in this context. The Recovery Movement (Gagne et al., 2007; Resnick, Fontana, Lehman, & Rosenheck, 2005; Klee et al., 2017, on the peer support movement) and the psychosocial rehabilitation model (Anthony, 1993) have been powerful countervailing forces supporting the belief that relapse can indeed be part of recovery (and by extension, that disability can be a phase of a journey into post-traumatic growth; Tedeschi & Calhoun, 2004). The recovery movement and the psychosocial rehabilitation approach were born out of the need for reinfranchisement of individuals with psychiatric disabilities, including PTSD, to create viable avenues for membership in the larger society, with tenets of valuing the essential person, advocating for meaningful roles independent of disability, and offering the potential to work again through processes of reasonable accommodation and "supported employment" (Mueller et al., 2019).

Suicidal and Homicidal Thoughts, Feelings, and Actions

Members may sometimes express suicidal and/or homicidal ideation. Such feelings and thoughts (or even urges) may be a response to a sense of helplessness, hyperarousal, guilt, reenactment of the trauma (e.g., a sense of annihilation, a wish to die during the trauma), and depression that often accompanies PTSD. It may be that the survivor sees life as so changed that it is not worth living.

Potential Function

For survivors of trauma, a sense of helplessness can lead to thoughts of suicide. There can be a sense of there being "no way out." For survivors whose alexithymia and numbing make it hard to endorse everyday life occurrences and to develop skills at dealing with them, preoccupation with suicide or harm to others may be a respite from feeling inadequate and out-of-place in dealing with current life concerns. Homicidal thoughts and actions also may be seen as a way of taking action in the face of helplessness, especially in situations in which the survivor feels cornered, and may therefore be triggered to the trauma. Secondarily, expressing suicidal or homicidal thoughts can become a way of communicating distress, if the survivor expects to be dismissed or ignored. In addition, suicidal or homicidal thoughts and feelings can for some become a refuge from everyday life challenges (e.g., dealing with financial problems or relationship issues). Like the trauma itself, suicide and homicide are "bigger than life" issues that blow the necessary small tasks of life "out of the water."

Potential Challenges to the Group

Naturally the ultimate risk of suicidal or homicidal urges is to actually commit the act and result in loss of human life. Related risk factors:

- Individuals with PTSD are also often subject to depression.
- Sleep loss associated with PTSD can trigger hypomania and mania in individuals prone to bipolar disorder.
- Mood disorders can exacerbate the risk for suicide.

IMPACT ON THE GROUP

Members who have experienced losses may feel responsible for a suicidal member, and may be triggered to previous losses. The sense of emotional safety may be reduced, and sense of helplessness may increase. Members may focus on the risk potential of one of the members, and disregard their own current concerns. In the presence of a member raising homicidal thoughts, the sense of physical and emotional safety may be diminished, as other members may be triggered to their own experiences with violence. Members may also feel indirectly (or directly) threatened by a member who expresses homicidal urges, and feel the need to manage the individual to preserve safety (and therefore, they may be less likely to bring up personal concerns).

Interventions to Consider

The risk of suicide, self-harm, and harm to others must be judiciously evaluated in order to determine degree of actual risk. Common tools generally are crisis line numbers, risk assessments, and safety plans. If the risk issues remain at a manageable level, they will be important topics for the group to address. When there is a realistic likelihood that a member may act on such thoughts, feelings, and urges, concrete intervention outside the group is naturally required (e.g., evaluation for hospitalization, psychiatric assessment for change of medication). When a group member is in crisis and shares it with the group, it is important to reassure the group that the facilitators will take necessary action (rather than leave it to the other members to handle). Members also need to know that facilitators will not overreact to the mere mention of suicidal or homicidal thoughts (as the group members may fear being psychiatrically hospitalized unnecessarily and potentially without their consent), yet will take them seriously. The facilitators must walk a fine line between clinical risk concern (responsibility for directing the member to an appropriate level of care), and attending to the group process. A member expressing suicidal or homicidal urges may be helped to learn through the group to express the feelings underlying suicidal or homicidal ideation. Reflective listening can help to pull for what may be making the individual feel helpless (or what feels intolerable in the individual's life). The group can be enlisted in exploring themes around helplessness, and to provide a validating but balanced view concerning the situational concerns of the suicidal member (e.g., getting through a divorce; filing for bankruptcy;

being evicted; legal problems; "anniversary" reactions). Often, normal-izing the circumstances as something others have experienced can suggest potential for getting through to the other side of the crisis without re-sorting to suicide. In the case of an attempt, or hospitalization related to risk, it is important to help the group process feelings of helplessness about the group's limited power to protect its members. Members can be assured that resources are out there to help when anyone is at risk. It is also an opportunity to explore unspoken issues in the group, such as other members' urges to act on suicidal or homicidal feelings.

Self-Medication and the Interaction of PTSD and Substance Use

Substance abuse is not an automatic rule-out for PCGT, although the group's focus is more general and PCGT is not a dual diagnosis treat-ment such as Seeking Safety (Najavits, 2002). A referral to concurrent or alternate care may be made, depending on the level of substance de-pendence. In the context of trauma, substance use may be seen as self-medication. It can become an issue in and of itself, beyond the usage for attempting to ameliorate symptoms or dispel disturbing memories. Concerns around substance use range from violation of the group rules concerning intoxication in group, to usage that affects group member-ship through missed sessions or inattention (e.g., being hungover or being uncomfortable sober; see section on "Missed Groups and Inattention"). It may also be "grist-for-the-mill" as a group issue in its impact on current life.

Intoxication

Concerning coming to the group after using non-prescribed substances or overusing prescribed substances, members are aware by the first session that the guidelines specify being free of psychoactive (nonprescribed) substances in group, and that members appearing "under the influ-ence" will respectfully be asked to leave the group. Ambiguous situations may also occur, for example, an intoxicated member may evade detec-tion; mild intoxication may be suspected but not clear; and a member may have a change of medication that makes it difficult to distinguish over-medication from self-chosen overuse of prescribed medication.

POTENTIAL FUNCTION

The appearance of substance abuse within the group suggests the extent to which current life requires something to take the edge off it (e.g., for managing hyperarousal and/or reexperiencing, as well as life stressors). Substance use may also constitute a reenactment, if the trauma involved substance use or intoxication. Individuals who come to the group intoxicated, or even hungover, or who miss sessions due to intoxication, may be "hedging their bets" – checking out the group from a safe distance while maintaining this "standby" self-treatment. An episode of intoxication may also communicate external stressors that the member has not yet shared, or may communicate the degree to which substance dependence has a central role in the member's life. As it is a violation of group guidelines that could end the member's involvement in the group, it may also be a way to leave the group without addressing the reasons for leaving.

POTENTIAL CHALLENGES TO THE GROUP

The presence of intoxication disregards the group guidelines, although that may not be what is intended. Facilitators may also be seen as enabling the intoxicated member if intervention is not evident. If undetected by facilitators, an episode of intoxication in the group can create a divide between facilitators and members, and a burdensome secret for members. The smell and other sensory presentations of intoxication can trigger some members whose trauma included alcohol in a prominent role. Diminished emotional safety and trust may pull for merger in the group rather than individuation among members (see section on "Premature Pseudocohesion"). If a member is removed due to intoxication, this event can generate shame issues that need to be addressed so that other members are not lost to the group. Authority issues are likely to emerge. Group members may express anger that the intoxicated member has been asked to leave the group, complaining that facilitators are being "too hard" on this individual (while they may later express feeling reassured by facilitators' protective action). Depending on what facilitators can share when a member goes into a "detox" or "rehab" unit, members may be mystified and concerned about the member's absence from the group. Group members may also be realistically concerned about risks to health and safety for a group member using alcohol or drugs regularly.

Interventions to Consider

If a member does arrive at the group intoxicated, the facilitators take steps to assure the safety of the member and group, and evaluate with the member and the member's treatment team what steps are needed (and whether the member can return to group vs. seek alternative treatment for substance dependence). It is important to minimize shame for the entire group (including the intoxicated member), reassure group members, and process feelings resulting from the event. Facilitators assure members that they are taking the necessary steps and following up concerning the member, without stating more than the member wishes to have shared with the group. Facilitators are transparent about privacy and confidentiality guidelines. The group will need to process the incident in the same or next session, and welcome the member back to the group if the member returns. It is important for the group to process the way in which the facilitators respond to the intoxication incident. Setting reasonable limits as determined in group guidelines models for members that they can set limits in their own lives.

Missed Groups and Inattention Related to Self-Medication

Members may be adherent to group guidelines regarding intoxication, yet miss sessions due to using substances frequently, or appear inattentive in group. Members who rely heavily on alcohol or drugs (or other addictive patterns) may feel alienated from other group members who do not share this reliance, or who have chosen to end a prior pattern of substance dependence. They may be torn between the group's therapeutic norms, and the norms of a primary social group that shares a value of substance use.

POTENTIAL FUNCTIONS

As with the previous discussion of self-medication, this pattern of use underscores the value of immediate although temporary relief from PTSD symptoms (which contrasts with psychotherapy). Patience Mason (1990), who writes from the perspective of a family member of someone with PTSD, notes that despite the apparent harmful impact that self-medication may have on relationships, work, and life in general, no one but the trauma survivor can determine whether the "cure may be worse than the disease" at certain points in time. Hers is a reminder to practitioners (as well as significant others) that we can offer options for change but are not responsible for making decisions for group members. Self-medication may intensify and support numbing reactions (as well as avoidance – see "Avoidance" section), which may in turn serve as a protection from the group's challenging emphasis on mid-range emotions and tolerance of "softer" feelings.

POTENTIAL CHALLENGES TO THE GROUP

Members actively self-medicating may be less available to both their own mid-range emotions and the experiences of others, reducing the empathy quotient in the group. In addition, frequent missed sessions can reduce the intimacy level of the group, and the trust among group members. Misunderstandings can arise when missed sessions prevent development of a shared group history. In addition, for some members, use of substances can be the basis of a "peak experience" that offers relief from emotional numbing.

INTERVENTIONS TO CONSIDER

One obvious intervention is to offer self-medicating members alternate or concurrent treatment (e.g., Seeking Safety or a Dual Diagnosis group or individual treatment in addition to or in place of PCGT), to be determined collaboratively by the member and the treatment team (and processed with the group and the member, as the member considers moving to a different treatment modality). Assuming the member remains in the group, inattention can be addressed as limiting connection within the group (and likely in the member's personal life), linked to patterns of numbing and avoidance. Facilitators may broaden the topic to disconnection as a general group issue, to create a sense of commonality across different sources of disconnection. Enlisting the group allows other members to offer encouragement based their own experiences with substances and recovery. For members for whom use of substances serves the generation of peak experiences, facilitators can take the opportunity to encourage sharing and discussion of the role and meaning of peak experiences in their lives. This is an instance in which a motivational interviewing approach allows members to explore options and make personal choices after clarifying discussion in group (see chapter four on motivational strategies).

Substance Dependence as an Issue for Group Discussion

Members in a PCGT group may not all be "clean and sober," but able to benefit substantially from the group. Self-medication may be an issue that does not lead to sporadic attendance, inattention, or distractibility, yet is "grist for the mill" in terms of impact on relationships, health, work, and/ or lifestyle, and personal recovery.

POTENTIAL FUNCTIONS OF SELF-MEDICATION

Prior sections above explore the possible functions of use of substances to self-medicate. As above, the pattern of use may serve to titrate intimacy, facilitate social comfort, and connect the individual with a community in which substances play a prominent role.

POTENTIAL CHALLENGES TO THE GROUP

Self-medication may mask symptoms that could be addressed through alternative means (e.g., practicing yoga, Tai Chi, or meditation, increasing level of exercise, and making full use of the group to address symptoms and other sequelae of trauma affecting current life). It may prevent the self-medicating member or members from developing more nuanced coping strategies.

Facilitators again enlist the group. Members who have overcome substance dependence are likely to share strategies, and function as role models. Acknowledgment of the advantages of self-medication affirms the member's choices while not endorsing or enabling them.

ADDRESSING RELAPSES

For members who have achieved a level of sobriety, and then relapse in response to current stressors (whether life events, or anniversary reactions/other triggers), it is important that the group feel safe and non-shaming so that members can bring up setbacks and losses. Group support can be especially important for a member who has relapsed. Facilitators may want to reflect on the well-worn adage that "relapse is part of recovery," as members in relapse may express that they are now "back to 'square one.'" It may be particularly helpful for the group for facilitators to assist members in exploring the substance abuse "triggers" and any connection to symptoms and issues related to trauma.

Missed Group Sessions (Sporadic or Prolonged Absences)

There are a variety of issues that may lead to inconsistent attendance or attrition for individuals living with histories of trauma.

Potential Functions

Absences modulate the level of intimacy in group, and obviate the need to develop a level of trust and sense of safety. Members may also have difficulty individuating within the group, or have mixed feelings about a pull to merge with the group. In addition, some members may feel they need to solve problems on their own, and see dependency on a group (or therapy in general) as a weakness that makes them vulnerable all over again (as they likely felt during the trauma). Another function of missing sessions is to not overwhelm the group or facilitators, if there is a belief that one's personal issues are too much for any one setting or person(s) to handle.

Potential Challenges to the Group

Repeatedly missed groups can result in fragmentation in the wholeness of the group, and may precipitate demoralization of members and facilitators. It is more difficult for the group to develop mutuality and intimacy, as well as trust, when a member or members are inconsistently present. Frequently missed groups may appear to suggest that the issues of members are too big to be "held" by the group. The missing member, as well as the group, has less opportunity to experience the corrective potential of the group. Sporadic group attendance may incline the group toward less nuanced coping strategies such as avoidance, due to fewer opportunities to practice more subtle communication skills and interpersonal strategies.

Interventions to Consider

Facilitators may educate the group regarding the value of utilizing the group even when it is moderately uncomfortable or unfamiliar. They may also validate concerns that can lead to missed sessions (e.g., difficulty tolerating differences of opinion; feeling slighted or not met where one is; finding that emotions come up that are difficult to manage; not wanting to trust the group enough to fully enter). There can be unexpected issues, such as a member having family, medical, or work difficulties preventing attendance, that require problem solving and understanding. While facilitators can encourage members to try to schedule medical and other important appointments around the group time whenever possible, they also demonstrate support for the members' outside commitments (the group being a support for the person's life, rather than a replacement for it). It may help to predict that members will occasionally have mixed feelings about coming to group, while at the same time encouraging discussion of these feelings in the group. It is generally the rule of thumb to enlist the group in a non-shaming manner; absences and reactions to absences are processed in the group so that members can share common reactions to the intimacy of the group, and similar feelings of wanting to evade or avoid closeness or intense emotion. Acknowledgment of these issues enhances authenticity in the group and models that it is possible to address them without loss of identity, esteem, or agency. It also demonstrates that the group is capable of handling issues as they arise for members, and that no one's issues are too great for the group.

Need for Validation, and Risk for Loss of Empathy (Empathic Rupture)

Need for validation is central for survivors of trauma. The traumatic experiences themselves, and often the aftermath, have been deeply invalidating. Empathy and mutual validation among members are fostered in the group early on, as members identify with each other over shared experience of symptoms and patterns related to being survivors of trauma (presented and discussed in the early sessions of PCGT). This early empathy may be based largely on identification regarding similarities, even though there will be variations on these themes. As group cohesion develops through members sharing personal experiences in their lives, members further identify with each other at first, then gradually begin to differentiate as individuals – each partaking in the group and serving distinct roles within it. As members discuss their specific feelings and situations, recognition of members' individuality deepens. Members feel a bond based not only on sameness, but on mutual caring, new respect for each other as distinct individuals, and a friendly curiosity about the other. As differences are accentuated, there is also greater opportunity for conflict of values, perspectives, and lifestyles to surface. Differences over strongly held beliefs may be expressed as members begin to relate more genuinely, which is both an opportunity and a challenge to level of em- pathy in the group. Members become less predictable to each other as they express greater individuality. Divisions of opinion may pique interest and deepen the interaction, yet may be experienced as confusing and unsettling. Members may be abrupt or blunt when they first venture to formulate responses to other members and the facilitators. Yet at this time in the group's trajectory, members' sensitivity to invalidation may increase given that they area taking risks to relate more personally. This increased vulnerability can sensitize already sensitive issues and exacer- bate susceptibility to shame (Ginzburg et al., 2009). The group's devel- opment toward individuation offers both opportunities for enhanced empathy and mutuality, and a risk of disconnection and empathic rupture.

Potential Function

If the group remains uniform in belief, a sense of certainty is upheld, and members do not need to deal with ambiguities. Rejection of differences in viewpoint may protect sense of self from threat. The threat may also be that of increased intimacy in the group, or sense of annihilation when personal beliefs are disconfirmed.

Potential Challenges to the Group

For members, the group is both a potential support and a complex in- terpersonal learning environment. Following periods of intense bonding, recognition of differences may leave members again feeling alone and isolated with their experience of trauma. For some, differences around strongly held beliefs may feel invalidating, especially concerning values learned under conditions of extreme stress. A comment by the facilitators that appears critical or misses the mark, even if intended as supportive, can engender a loss of emotional safety, resulting in shame and anger – entering the territory that has sometimes been referred to as "narcissistic injury." The term "narcissistic injury" was derived from analytic litera- ture and now applies to a pattern in any therapeutic process that may occur if a comment (or interpretation) by the therapist is made too early, too abruptly, or too forcefully. In group, it can also apply to comments by other group members (in any group there can be one or two members who speak bluntly or forcefully, and in trauma groups, these roles may be accentuated). The resulting disconnection is usually accompanied by hurt, sense of outrage, and loss of sense of emotional safety. This may become the territory of "empathic rupture," and if not repaired, "empathic failure." There may even be a sense of betrayal as the group's connection develops more facets and less uniformity (and as facilitators support this differentiation). When conflict occurs, members may be tempted to be absent for the next session, or even to drop out of group, due to:

• Fear of escalating into aggression due to difficulty managing hyperarousal
• Guilt over hurting others through blunt communication
• Fear of being vulnerable to emotional hurt
• Fear of embarrassment over defensive reactions

Hyperarousal is often a mediator of loss of empathy within the group, because it makes it difficult to correct or clarify a misunderstanding. Members (and even facilitators) may learn to avoid potentially upsetting issues in order not to trigger conflict and accompanying arousal and anger.

Interventions to Consider

Facilitators monitor interactions that are potentially triggering and work toward lowering the "emotional temperature" of the room, in order to restore a sense of progress through issues that arise and reframe them in a more nuanced fashion. Because traumatic experiences often involve shame – even if it is simply over having been helpless, or caught off-guard – shame-related sensitivities require facilitators to lead with an abundance of respect, and broad acceptance of members as persons (and to model these attitudes for the group). Facilitators walk a fine line between supportive validation of members' feelings, and helping them "test the limits" through considering other viewpoints about the world and oneself. Facilitators cannot avoid occasional misunderstandings in the group, but can approach them with interest and transparency. Facilitators can model humility rather than blaming or shame; who has not at one time or another said or done the wrong thing? These approaches can be helpful in diffusing or diminishing risk for empathic rupture or loss of empathy:

• Facilitators monitor interactions that are potentially triggering and work toward lowering the "emotional temperature" of the room, so that members have access to their higher processes in managing progression toward differentiation in the group. They use redirection, reframing, and informal grounding to address this need.

- Facilitators emphasize group norms of respect and support, and model these attributes through their actions (embedding them also in the group's guidelines).
- Facilitators support members' strengths through acknowledging their individuality, their abilities, and their potential for a contributing role in the group.
- Facilitators reframe differences and disagreements in terms of the value of each individual's concerns, and explain and interpret the statements of conflicting members to each other rather than let the argument develop beyond a useful level (protecting the group from interference related to hyperarousal).
- If charged interchanges occur, facilitators interrupt rapidly, and diffuse them, in order to preserve a sense of emotional safety, and sufficient calm to allow new interpersonal learning in the group.
- Facilitators connect the concerns raised in group with interpersonal issues in the members' lives, and support generalization to life outside the group (e.g., "Does this happen at home? How do you usually deal with it?").

The Protector/Rescuer/Caretaker Role and Trauma

In most groups there may be a member who assumes the role of caretaker or rescuer as a kind of "assistant therapist," and may partially bypass the role of group member in doing so. In trauma groups, this pattern may be intensified due to trust issues, moral injury, or difficulty "switching gears" from an authoritative role (whether in current life or during past trauma). To complicate things, survivors of trauma may themselves be healthcare professionals or first responders.

Potential Function

This pattern protects the member from becoming too vulnerable too soon, and prevents uncomfortable experiences of vulnerability and potential shame. From this elevated vantage point, the member can check out the group and assess safety, as well as whether the group members or facilitators will address the pattern and invite full membership into the group. The caretaking member may protect the group from the facilitators, and the facilitators from the group members; in doing so, trust issues and authority issues are diffused through taking the facilitators "off the hook" regarding their own roles. Sense of helplessness is diminished for this member, through the sense of agency inherent in this role. Intimacy is limited in the group, as this role does not involve much personal disclosure except as a role model. An underlying issue may also be that this group member feels undeserving of care, or has not experienced consistent care in early life. There may be a history of deprivation, and/or a pattern of meeting one's own needs through others. At a group level, this role becomes entrenched when it serves a purpose for the whole group – that is, when the caretaking member is performing this role on behalf of the group because the group is not ready to trust facilitators, or when there is an unidentified problem in the group.

Potential Challenges to the Group

While this member can evolve into a very useful role of reaching out and supporting others, the challenge is that if this role becomes entrenched, and the facilitators do not address it, there will be a member who does not need to share as a full group member and who is excluded from the risks others take in making themselves vulnerable. Some members may allow this member to represent them instead of taking full membership of the group themselves, while others will resent the authoritative role and eventually confront the member (e.g., "*You're* not a therapist, why don't *you* say something about yourself?"). If facilitators have not already addressed the pattern, the caretaking member may be caught off-guard and defensively "double down" on this role. As the pattern expresses a polite distrust of the facilitators (as well as the group), facilitators may feel "de-skilled" in the group as members look to the caretaking member as an authority. Members may also feel "de-skilled," as another member is taking part of their responsibilities within the group. Sense of emotional safety is diminished by the experience that another member's protection is needed, and by the lack of exchange of disclosure and mutual vulnerability.

Interventions to Consider

As long as facilitators do not feel threatened and can graciously share their power (as they do generally with the group, as facilitators), the caretaking member can generally be helped to move into a genuine role as both helper and group member. This is really a whole-group intervention. As this encouragement is transparent in the group, group members can be relieved of the responsibility for either following the caretaking member, or challenging this role. The facilitators also demonstrate that they can be trusted to assert their own roles, rather than abdicate to the caretaking member and tacitly agree that they are not fully engaged in their facilitator roles.

It is essential not to shame or disenfranchise the caretaking member, who may feel more vulnerable than is apparent. It is also important to be aware that the roles members take in groups really do not belong to any one member, although a member may be drawn to one role more than another. For example, if the caretaking member is out sick for one week or two, another member will typically take on the role. Even if some members resent the caretaker's elevated position in the group, they may identify with the member as well; if that member can be "demoted," so can they. The caretaking member's actions can be reframed as "working too hard," which may resonate with the member, who is likely to be feeling drained by taking on care of others and not receiving much care in return. The group can be enlisted to "help the member out" (e.g., by being assertive, offering feedback and support to others, not depending on the caretaking member for these actions). The member can be asked about what it is like to be in this role, and whether it repeats in the member's personal life. This line of discourse gives other members an opportunity to identify with the member, to share similar stories, and to ask questions of the member and facilitators. Facilitators can also take the "heat" off the caretaking member by asking the group what it is like to take risks, share feelings, and be more vulnerable. These actions can be reframed as courageous (which they are). If the caretaking pattern is quite entrenched for both group and caretaker, facilitators may represent the "other" side of presumed ambivalence (e.g., empathize with reasons for maintaining this role, even though it is draining and results in the member getting less out of the group). Facilitator's suggestion that the group may need the member in that role gives the group the opportunity to relieve the caretaking member of that responsibility. Ultimately, if the member's role becomes less entrenched (i.e., more balanced between caretaking and participating in the group), there is opportunity for the member to gain real skills in reaching out to others, and to allow for exchange and greater spontaneity as sources of replenishment.

Common Patterns in Group Therapy and PCGT

Sharing the Space Versus "Monopolizing"

Facilitators will find that, as in any group, certain group members are more talkative than others. There may be a member who typically responds first in agenda setting, and provides feedback to other members when someone expresses a personal concern, taking charge while others are quiet. In most groups, this member can serve as a role model for others, as long as the role becomes more fluid (and shared) as the group progresses. However, a pattern may emerge in which a group member holds forth on a topic (whether relevant or irrelevant) in such a way that therapists and group members cannot readily interject or redirect. If members do not shift toward sharing the group "space," there are several ways facilitators may intervene.

Potential Function

A monopolizing pattern protects members from feeling too intimate and vulnerable. It may protect secrets, keep the group under control, and maintain emotional safety for group members who are not sufficiently trusting of the group or facilitators to contribute. If one member takes charge in the group, the other members do not need to develop trust in each other or the group leaders. This pattern may reflect the loss of trust in authority or helping figures experienced by many survivors of trauma, as well as a sense that personal feelings are unacceptable or shameful.

Potential Challenges to the Group

The group may allow a single member to take charge and to speak for them and appreciate that they are relieved of the responsibility to participate. At the same time, they are likely to feel bored and alienated. The member who monopolizes also loses out due to not really being able to get feedback of a meaningful nature. Additional impact includes:

- Loss of trust in group facilitators (if monopolizing continues unchecked)
- Tacit agreement among group members to avoid sharing personal information or feelings, leading to stagnation of the group
- Frustration and sense of helplessness among members

Interventions to Consider

- Respectful interruption, redirecting.
- In early group sessions: maintaining group structure; reinforcing agenda setting.
- Mid- to later groups: enlisting the group in taking responsibility for level of contribution by group members. If one person does all the talking, are the other members participating in this pattern by not assuming a place in the group themselves? Facilitators may reframe that the monopolizing individual is "working too hard" – and ask other group members to help take the monopolizing member "off the hook" – which underscores the contribution of all members to a working group.
- Respectful process comments addressing trust, and emotional safety in the group.

Transforming Boredom

Groups do not need to be entertaining. Most groups have lulls, or focus on topics that are important yet not necessarily fascinating. However, if the facilitators dread the group because the atmosphere is so stulti-fying, there is an entrenched pattern that can be addressed in order to engage the group at a more meaningful level. Such would be the case if group conversation consistently focuses on matters that appear to be trivial, to the exclusion of real issues of significant import (e.g., three members in a group are going through divorce, yet for four weeks in a row they devote their energy in group to discussion the fashion choices on certain television programs). Discussion may appear overly concrete (e.g., giving each other directions to their favorite restaurants), or very abstract (e.g., discussing details of economic theory in a manner devoid of emotional content). In either instance (whether a concrete topic or an abstract one), there is little opportunity for the group to progress in regard to personal issues, and a high likelihood that members will also be bored. Facilitators can empower themselves with a variety of inter-ventions that can find the strengths in the boring group, and use these strengths to shift the pattern.

Potential Function

As with monopolizing, boredom generated in the group may:

- Titrate intimacy in the group
- Maintain the trauma-based need for fending off distressing issues and obviating the need to develop trust in the group and in the facilitators
- Prevent attention to loss of meaning and other issues that may be overwhelming, by focusing on superficial issues
- Maintain neutrality in order to avoid emotion, conflict, or the hyperarousal characteristic of PTSD, thereby assuring greater safety in the group
- Express ambivalence about therapy, and potential for recovery
- Cover over a rift or secret in the group (e.g., a member's intoxication that has not been detected by facilitators) or an unaddressed issue between two members of the group

Potential Challenges to the Group

- Superficiality within the group interactions
- Missed opportunity to address pressing personal issues
- Missed opportunity for interpersonal learning
- Sense of stagnation of the group, loss of spontaneity
- Inconsistent attendance (group members are assured of not missing much)
- Greater likelihood of attrition

Interventions to Consider

Facilitators may actively weave the apparently superficial or irrelevant themes into more meaningful discussion. For example:

- Facilitators can spin off the theoretical discussion by finding themes parallel to the members' lives (e.g., costs/benefits analysis in economics as applied to life choices)
- Facilitators may reframe the group's focus on less meaningful matters as a strength (with all sincerity, as there are often strengths embedded in "boring" or apparently unproductive discussions). They can then shift the discussion to topics that are more emotionally challenging. For example, "This discussion shows how much intelligence and intellectual ability there is in this room. If you could move this focus, like a flashlight, to illuminate aspects of your own life, where would you focus your thoughts and ideas?" Discussion may then ensue in which either a more personal topic is selected, or members discuss how difficult it is to apply these abilities to personal situations, and what the barriers might be. In either case, facilitators support members' strengths, and express faith that members can solve problems in their own lives as opposed to withdrawing into neutrality or passivity.
- Depending on the relationships in the group or phase of the group, facilitators may use gentle humor to agree with the avoidant side of ambivalence about therapy involvement (e.g., "It's a good thing we all watch the same shows; if we didn't we would have to check out our own fashion statements – not to mention the stories of our own lives!").
- Facilitators comfortable with a paradoxical approach might prescribe or amplify the pattern. For example, in the group described previously, in which members persisted in discussing fashion exhibited in a television program, the facilitators might propose a "fashion day" for the group; the "win-win" of this intervention is that members will either reject this idea and switch gears to more personal issues, or take up this icebreaker idea with creativity or humor – which will also move the group toward greater intimacy as members personalize and share their fashion statements (preparing the group for greater intimacy, mutuality, and interpersonal comfort in future discussions)
- Process comments, which can run the gamut from mild paradoxical intention, to direct reflective observation of the pattern, to drawing the issue onto the facilitators themselves, for example.
- "I notice the group topics have been less personal for the past few weeks. Does this mean that everything is going OK for everyone?"

- "I notice we are staying away from more personal topics lately. Is there something behind all this that we need to talk about? Is there a problem we are not addressing that is making it feel less safe in the group?"
- "I notice we are not getting to personal issues of late. I wonder if you-all are feeling uncomfortable with us as facilitators – something we might have done, or said, or not said. Are we missing the boat in some way?"

"That Doesn't Work for Me": Addressing Roadblocks to Problem Solving

Problem solving is not always a linear process. Problems may defy solution – and with gathering urgency – even when there appears to be a reasonable path to resolution. It is not unusual in any group for a member to convey a sense of urgency about an issue that feels intolerable. There may be pressure for the group to provide an immediate "cure" or "fix" that will relieve the sense of helplessness, and solve the problem instrumentally. Group members and even facilitators may feel propelled to tell the member in need what to do, given what appears to be a straightforward plea for help. However, the advice often falls short for the member presenting the problem: the path advised has already been tried, the suggested solution feels inaccessible, relying on others to help solve the problem accentuates a sense of helplessness.

Potential Function

This pattern can reflect a sense of helplessness in the current situation that conjures trauma-related feelings of helplessness (a problem that cannot be solved in the present). Or the complaint may be a form of protest that "this should not be happening." There may be a sense of moral betrayal in the occurrence that makes it difficult to resolve with concrete action. The sense of inadequacy in the group as a result of being collectively unable to solve the problem means that the group and facilitators now understand more about the member's experience of life. For the member experiencing the insoluble problem, while lack of useful assistance can add to frustration, it can also create a sense of "being in the same boat" with the group members, who are eventually equally "stumped" by the problem. The member may also regain a sense of autonomy and self-respect through not relying on others to solve the problem that initially appeared to need urgent fixing. The willingness of others to engage around fixing the problem may nevertheless be reassuring, especially if assistance was not forthcoming during or after the trauma.

Challenges to the Group

If the problem is too big for the member, it may end up appearing being too big for the group. If the member's intention in presenting the problem, even urgently, is to express how frustrating and overwhelming the member's life is – that one more problem is just too much to solve – or how unfair the situation is, group members' and facilitators' advice may be largely beside the point. There is a fine line to walk, because to miss the intense need of a member undermines the sense of efficacy and caring in the group, while to venture into problem solving when the member largely needs empathy results in a sense of inadequacy when the problem solving does not yield results. The group must take the problem seriously, showing interest in its solution, especially when it is presented with urgency. Yet the subsequent derailing of the problem-solving attempts can leave the group and facilitators feeling useless and demoralized. Members who need a sense of agency to combat their own sense of helplessness may be frustrated and withdraw or become irritable. Recovery and therapeutic change may be cast into doubt if urgent and thorny problems cannot be resolved. The member whose problem "stumps" the group is likely to continue to feel powerless – a feeling that may resonate through the group as a common trauma-related theme. And the sense of urgency may upstage the needs of other group members.

Interventions to Consider

While many therapies lay out step-by-step problem-solving methods, these may be less useful in this situation than recognition of the non-linear processes involved in developing satisfying conclusions to issues. Facilitators can walk that fine line by modeling compassion about the loss of empowerment represented in this member's concerns, validating the member's sense of the enormity of the issue and the frustration around it not being solved (e.g., "I see you wish you could solve this problem more easily; you can see by the group's response that this problem is really very challenging"). Here the facilitators also take a "one-down" position, modeling that it is possible to tolerate the uncertainty and sense of inadequacy. By acknowledging that the issue is not easy, and by not engaging to try to quickly fix the issue, the facilitator demonstrates willingness both to be helpful, and to accept and validate the member's need to be heard at the moment. This process acknowledges that 1) feeling inadequate is acceptably human; 2) if the facilitators can feel inadequate and still exhibit legitimate and transparent authority, then members may be able to accept their own humanity after the helplessness engendered by the trauma. Note that the trauma itself is not identified in this process, yet the process itself reclaims a sense of empowerment.

In terms of actual problem solving, it is always useful to ask the member what might be helpful – which might spare the group the attempt at problem solving for which the member is not fully prepared. Refocusing on the feelings of the member can advance both the member and the group, while continuing to respect that an issue that looks easy to resolve may not be. Given the member not being prepared for the solutions offered, the facilitators may enlist the group by asking whether other members have encountered issues that seemed to have no satisfactory solution (and what that was like for them). Deepening the process through expression of feelings may assist with actual problem solving, once the emotions and values involved are clearer. Facilitators may then take a strengths-based approach, pointing to small successes (and appreciating successes that members may have regarded as inadequate, or even as failures). They may ask other group members to identify the strengths they see in the group member, and the skills used that allowed the group member to show up for session, thereby enhancing a sense of agency and resilience. Motivational interviewing strategies can be informally applied, e.g., reflective listening combined with emphasis on positive potential over fear and doubt (e.g., "You are so worried about this issue, which you say is like "'the story of your life' – yet you are intent on solving this problem"). Facilitators also support the group's efforts to help, and may reframe rejected solutions as "brainstorming," and compassionate action, even in the face of the requesting member's unresolved problem. This relabeling connects the group and its members, and may help the group as a whole, as well as the member sharing the problem, feel a greater sense of empowerment in the group while the problem is a "work in progress."

Approaches to Venting

Clients new to psychotherapy may overestimate the extent to which it is an opportunity to vent, to "let off steam," to "get out feelings" vehemently in a torrent of words, with little opportunity for exchange or feedback. Venting suggests a "pressure cooker" theory of emotion – that venting prevents a later explosion – a common understanding of emotion culturally. Therefore it is not surprising that new group members may identify with this approach to feelings.

While not specifically associated with PTSD, venting may reasonably be assumed to express high arousal, frustration, and anger (and may also drive further arousal when hyperarousal is already present, rather than releasing the proverbial "pressure valve"). When arousal is already high, stressors can appear to build toward explosiveness, especially if the survivor's strategy is to stave off any stressor that could potentially lead to reactivity; and yet stressors continue to occur, resulting in that proverbial "perfect storm." While it may be momentarily satisfying to vent, venting has not been identified as an effective strategy for preventing outbursts. As Leonardo DaVinci has been reported to have said: "Where there is shouting, there is no true knowledge."

Potential Function

Venting carries an urgency that communicates a helpless feeling. It suggests an expectation of being disregarded unless the point can be made right here and now. It can momentarily act as self-defense against shame and shaming circumstances. It may be seen as an alternative to vulnerability, especially given a forceful mode of expression. The blustering persona of someone who relies heavily on venting can ward off intimacy and create a greater sense of safety, through keeping others at bay. A member may also use venting to "ground" to the issues of current life, using a list of current complaints to keep focused away from the trauma. At a group level, frequent venting suggests that the group as a whole is fending off vulnerability and closeness, most likely as a way to manage trust issues.

Potential Challenges to the Group

Venting has its place in psychotherapy as an opportunity to speak one's mind, especially for individuals who have had little opportunity to do so. At the same time, as a form of expression, it limits the engagement, exchange, and mutuality of more connected discourse. In a group for survivors of trauma, loud, aggressive speech can be a trigger for reexperiencing. Other members, as well as the facilitators, may feel intimidated; sense of safety in the group may be diminished. This pattern may block some of the benefits group can have for alexithymia, and diminishes opportunity for interpersonal learning if it dominates the group in place of more nuanced communication.

Interventions to Consider

Education about therapy and about PTSD can be helpful in shifting from venting to more flexible forms of communication. The group guidelines include "no intimidation," which can be applied to venting if it veers from vociferous complaint into aggressiveness (see next topic, "Anger Is an Energy"). The direct approach can be useful; for example, interrupting ("I am going to interrupt you here"); descriptive body reflection ("I notice that you are leaning forward, you are pointing your finger, your voice is getting loud, and your face is turning red"); redirecting ("try sitting back, take a moment, and see if one feeling besides anger comes up, that you can share with the group"); setting limits (e.g., on voice volume, amount of time devoted to venting); enlisting the group ("Let's see what the group can tell you; (to group): if you were in that same situation, how would you feel? What would you do?"). Facilitators may also represent the "other" side of the ambivalence (e.g., emphasizing the value of maintaining a list of complaints in order to stay focused), allowing the group and member to pose the alternative. In addition, the reliance on group structure can limit opportunities to vent, as group members set an agenda and allocate time to members' issues.

If agenda setting revolves around opportunities for venting (suggesting trust issues and low tolerance for intimacy in the group), facilitators have an opportunity to weave in discussion of trust; for example, "I notice we have been focusing a lot on the difficulties with parking, and have come up with some great ideas about how to advocate for more parking spaces. We, as facilitators, have also made the facilities management aware of your concerns. Today we are revisiting this issue, and I would like to ask whether you feel we haven't done enough. Is there more you feel we should be doing? (discussion ...) ... If we can't solve the parking problem, what would that mean about the group, and about us as the facilitators?"). The discussion can then field the issues, for example, from feeling the facilitators are not taking the group's concerns seriously, to whether facilitators recognize the unfairness of having to enter the group in an anxious or agitated state after coming in late due to parking issues. The discussion can be expected to lead to recognition of unidentified issues – for example, that one group member cannot make it in earlier due to being a caregiver, and fears being judged by the facilitators and group, while another group member worries about not getting enough time from the group if parking problems result in lateness. If a member or members actually do question whether the facilitators are taking the problem seriously, the facilitators have an opportunity to clarify their actual views of the situation, as well as to express concern that the parking issue may be interfering with discussion of personal issues that are closer to home for the members.

From Shame-Based Reactivity to Acknowledgment: Addressing Stereotypes, Bias-Related Boundary Trespass, and Other Forms of Disparagement

Group members enter the group with whatever biases they have. Survivors of trauma are not more susceptible to bias than others; however, trauma groups may be particularly sensitive to communications that register stigmatizing categorical labeling, given shame- and esteem-related issues characteristic of PTSD (American Psychiatric Association, 2013; Ginzburg et al., 2009; Resick et al., 2016). The group environment, through emphasizing respect and acceptance, is for most members a stimulus for taking a broad view and questioning entrenched stereotypes.

Race and ethnicity issues may arise in group, requiring the facilitators to reflect on their own conscious and unconscious bias. For some members of minority groups, experiences of power dynamics in the dominant culture have led to exploitation and trauma. Intergenerational trauma, as well as recent events related to social injustice, may invoke feelings of distrust, rage, and helplessness within the group, as the setting may represent a microcosm of past and present macro-, mezzo-, and micro-aggressions and trauma. Similarly, LGBTQ individuals may be particularly vulnerable to exploitation and oppressive dynamics (Toseland, Jones, & Gellis, 2004). As in most groups, comments and actions based on bias or stereotypes may occur, and can challenge group cohesion and mutual respect. Themes of marginalization, oppression, and stigmatization can lead to group attrition and devaluation of minority members of group.

Shame-related issues in the group may be suspected when there are incursions into disrespect toward facilitators or other members. Externalized shame may appear as disdain, scornfulness, dismissiveness, or disparagement (Lewis, 1971; Lewis, 1995; Searles, 1965). These are all "grist for the mill," and once addressed in terms of respect for self and others in the group, usually resolve in favor of the work of the group. When externalized shame-based attributions target the group or other group members, it may be that the member has had past negative group experiences, or has felt significantly alienated in past primary groups. Moving into relation with a group may feel more unsafe for this member than for others.

Potential Function

These patterns serve to preserve the status quo for a member flouting group boundaries or engaging in negative attributions toward groups of others. The group may be moving too fast for the member (or for the group itself, as expressed by this member), leaving a sense of inadequacy, confusion, or fear that this pattern then counters (slowing the group down, reducing sense of intimacy and concomitant vulnerability). These actions may create greater distance for the member and group, and reassure the member (and group) that facilitators will set boundaries and limits. These patterns also distract the group from loss of meaning through creating distractions. These actions draw out the facilitators, inviting greater transparency; members can more clearly see where group members are "coming from" when they are put in the position of addressing these issues. Uncertainty about the facilitators is at least partially relieved through opportunity to observe their styles of responding.

Potential Challenges to the Group

Respect for boundaries is important for all groups, and particularly so when members' boundaries have been violated by trauma. Issues related to self-esteem and shame may occur in any group, and may be reflected in behavior concerning the boundaries of the group, other group members, and facilitators. Clarity about boundaries is all the more important because of the misapprehension of therapy in popular films, television, and fiction (specific instances are too numerous to mention). Facilitators may find occasions on which they must clarify their roles, affirming that they are unavailable for friendship or romance with group members. These issues are common to many clinical situations, including groups addressing trauma. In some instances, boundary trespass simply signals a need for education and information, while on other occasions it may represent disregard of boundaries due to:

- A wish that a personal relationship with a group facilitator would be a "cure" (which also suggests devaluing of the member's own sense of agency and the group's capacity to help)
- Cynicism about therapy and therapeutic boundaries, and concomitant devaluing of the facilitator and the group, related to disillusionment from the trauma
- Shame-based attribution regarding the gender, gender-orientation, or ethnicity of the facilitator or other members, reflected in disregard for interpersonal boundaries (i.e., targeting the identity of the facilitator or another member to re-create the shame the member felt as a result of the trauma)
- Envy or shame-based rage toward facilitators due to the assumption that the facilitators have been spared the trauma to which the members has been subject
- Feeling inadequate, or intruded on, in relation to the intimacy level in the group; pushing the group and facilitators away (e.g., making others feel uncomfortable or intruded on, whether intentional or not; repelling the facilitators and members to reduce personal discomfort)
- Feeling unsafe regarding the group's invitation to vulnerability (related to trauma history)

Incursions on boundaries range from direct overtures toward facilitators or members, to overly familiar comments, or modes of address (e.g., calling a facilitator or member "sugar"), to offensive sexual or ethnic jokes, to explicit description of sexual exploits, to veiled or outright ethnically or racially biased remarks. Toseland et al. (2004) observed that racism, if not addressed in the early stages of group, can result in a pattern of stereotyping in the group, accompanied by dynamics "representative of less mature development" in group interactions (p. 21), suggesting a risk akin to premature pseudocohesion. Many group members, or the group as a whole, may feel offended or embarrassed by these shame-based actions. Group topics will tend to be more superficial. Slowing the group down may leave members ready for greater meaningful interaction bored or frustrated. Members may feel unsafe when fellow members are disrespectful or biased. Individuality may be undermined for the group due to loss of safety. If the member engaging in these actions has had negative experiences in past groups, there is a risk that this member will be scapegoated or excluded.

Interventions to Consider

Assent to the group guidelines will minimize boundary incursions, yet facilitators need to address such instances when they do occur, in order to restore the emotional safety of the group. Facilitators are tasked with taking a stand to model valuing of persons and protecting boundaries, while affirming rather than shaming the challenging member or members. Expeditiously addressing responses that are racist, culturally biased, or stereotypic is essential to obviating a hurtful process in the group that could potentially trigger members to traumatic memories. Interventions are respectful and transparent, and as noted by Chang-Caffaro and Caffaro (2018), call for self-awareness, cultural sensitivity, and courage. For facilitators, taking a relational approach within a social justice framework affords opportunity to appreciate inherent cultural and ethnic identities of group members as they intersect with group dynamics. Facilitators encourage mutual support, and can educate and guide members toward respectfully acknowledging differences, including shared and divergent values. Allowing group members to develop curiosity regarding each others' ethnic and racial heritages and personal experiences around these identities helps the group differentiate and develop toward mutual concern and support. Useful facilitator skills include setting limits, redirecting, education, reframing, enlisting group, "listening between the lines" (especially for shame issues), process comments supporting meaningful discussion and differentiation (and countering tendency toward premature cohesion), honoring personal and cultural differences, and transparency with oneself regarding potential implicit and explicit bias.

Summary

There are many interventions and strategies from which present-centered facilitators may draw, as dictated by their preferences and training as therapists. Facilitators are encouraged to use interventions within the PCGT approach with which they feel comfortable, rather than trying to fit a particular mold. As therapy is a dynamic process, a particular intervention may work well on one occasion but not another, depending on stage of group development, group membership and culture, style of facilitators, presence of other issues confronting the group, etc. Facilitators rely on their flexibility, creativity, and range of skills in responding to these dynamics. The next chapter augments this manual through description of mechanisms underlying the experience of trauma and recovery from trauma, and how to think about "the present" in this context.

Notes

1 This and chapter four incorporate updates and revisions of the Special Topics section of the original Present-Centered Group Therapy Manual utilized in research. As indicated in chapter one, modifications to optimize the original framework have been based on developments in the field, further experience and reflection on the utility of PCGT, and theoretical integration. The manual itself is in the public domain and can be obtained through the book authors, or, regarding the original manual used in CSP-420, the Veterans Administration's National Center for PTSD Executive Division in White River Junction, VT.
2 'Pseudomutual' refers to "...a family relationship that has a superficial appearance of mutual openness and understanding although in fact the relationship is rigid and depersonalizing." https://dictionary.apa.org/pseudomutuality (American Psychological Association (2020))
3 The term "pseudocohesion" is used to suggest a "pseudomutual" bond that: 1) is not based on the needs and expression of the individuals within it; and 2) short-circuits the "getting to know" process and trust-building that would gradually create a cohesion based on mutuality.
4 Moral injury was added as an important development in the trauma field. Moral Injury overlaps with PTSD, but is not a symptom of PTSD. It has been shown to be more prevalent for certain sources of trauma (e.g., severe and repeated or ongoing trauma). Research in this area has developed since PCGT originated, but its clinical aspects were noted in the original handout of secondary features related to PTSD (under discussion of "Feelings of Guilt," chapter three, Appendix B, Handout for Sessions Two and Three, item number 6).
5 "Keeping a vigil" is newly added to this manual, as a clinical concept describing a trauma-related phenomenon that can contribute to difficulty focusing on the present.

References

American Psychiatric Association. (2013). *Diagnostic and statistical manual of mental disorders* (5th ed.). Arlington, VA: American Psychiatric Association.
American Psychological Association. (2020). *APA dictionary of psychology.* Retrieved from website https://dictionary.apa.org/. Washington, D.C.: American Psychological Association.
Anthony, E. J. (1968). Reflections on twenty-five years of group psychotherapy. *International Journal of Group Psychotherapy, 18*(3), 277–301. DOI:10.1080/00207284.1968.11508370.
Anthony, W. A. (1993). Recovery from mental illness: The guiding vision of the

mental health service system in the 1990s. *Psychosocial Rehabilitation Journal, 16*(4), 11–23. https://doi.org/10.1037/h0095655

Barnes, H. A., Hurley, R. A., & Taber, K. H. (2019). Moral injury and PTSD: Often co-occurring yet mechanistically different. *The Journal of Neuropsychiatry and Clinical Neurosciences, 31*(2), 98–103.

Chang-Caffaro, S., & Caffaro, J. (2018). Differences that make a difference: Diversity and the process group leader. *International Journal of Group Psychotherapy, 68*(4), 483–497.

Chinman, M., George, P., Dougherty, R. H., Daniels, A. S., Ghose, S. S., Swift, A., & Delphin-Rittmon, M. E. (2014). Peer support services for individuals with serious mental illnesses: Assessing the evidence. *Psychiatric Services, 65*(4), 429–441.

Freyd, J. J. (1996). *Betrayal trauma: The logic of forgetting childhood abuse.* Cambridge, MA: Harvard University Press.

Gagne, C., White, W., & Anthony, W. A. (2007). Recovery: A common vision for the fields of mental health and addictions. *Psychiatric Rehabilitation Journal, 31*(1), 32–37. doi.org/10.2975/31.1.2007.32.37

Ginzburg, K., Butler, L. D., Giese-Davis, J., Cavanaugh, C. E., Neri, E., Koopman, C., … Spiegel, D. (2009). Shame, guilt, and posttraumatic stress disorder in adult survivors of childhood sexual abuse at risk for human immunodeficiency virus: Outcomes of a randomized clinical trial of group psychotherapy treatment. *The Journal of Nervous and Mental Disease, 197*(7), 536–542. doi:10.1097/NMD.0b013e3181ab2ebd

Griffin, B. J., Purcell, N., Burkman, K., Litz, B. T., Bryan,C.J., Schmitz, M., Villierme, C., Walsh, J., & Maguen, S. (2019). Moral injury: An integrative review. *Journal of Traumatic Stress, 32*, 350–362.

Hedges, C. (2002). *War is a force that gives us meaning.* New York, NY: Public Affairs.

Johnson, D. R., Feldman, S. C., Lubin, H., & Southwick, S. M. (1995). The therapeutic use of ritual and ceremony in the treatment of post-traumatic stress disorder. *Journal of Traumatic Stress, 8*(2), 283–298.

Klee, A., Chinman, M., & Kearney, L. (2019). Peer specialist services: New frontiers and new roles. *Psychological Services, 16*(3), 353–359. http://dx.doi.org/10.1037/ser0000332

Lewis, H. B. (1971). *Shame and guilt in neurosis.* Madison, CT: International Universities Press.

Lewis, M. (1995). *Shame: The exposed self.* New York, NY: Simon and Schuster.

Litz, B. T., Lebowitz, L., Gray, M. J., & Nash, W. P. (2016). *Adaptive disclosure: A new treatment for military trauma, loss, and moral injury.* New York, NY: The Guilford Press.

Litz, B. T., Stein, N., Delaney, E., Lebowitz, L., Nash, W. P., Silva, C., & Maguen, S. (2009). Moral injury and moral repair in war veterans: A preliminary model and intervention strategy. *Clinical Psychology Review, 29*(8), 695–706.

Mason, P. (1990). *Recovery from the war: A guide for all veterans, family members, friends and therapists.* High Springs, FL: Patience Press.

McCann, I. L., & Pearlman, L. A. (1990). *Psychological trauma and the adult survivor: Theory, therapy, and transformation.* New York, NY: Brunner/Mazel.

Miller, W. R., & Rollnick, S. (2012). *Motivational interviewing: Helping people change.* New York, NY: Guilford Publications.

Mueller, L., Wolfe, W. R., Neylan, T. C., McCaslin, S. E., Yehuda, R., Flory, J. D., ... Davis, L. L. (2019). Positive impact of IPS supported employment on PTSD-related occupational-psychosocial functional outcomes: Results from a VA randomized-controlled trial. *Psychiatric Rehabilitation Journal, 42*(3), 246–256. doi:10.1037/prj0000345

Najavits, L. (2002). *Seeking safety: A treatment manual for PTSD and substance abuse.* New York, NY: Guilford Publications.

Parson, E. R. (1985). Post-traumatic accelerated cohesion: Its recognition and management in group treatment of Vietnam veterans. *Group, 9*(4), 10–23.

Resnick, S. G., Fontana, A., Lehman, A. F., & Rosenheck, R. A. (2005). An empirical conceptualization of the recovery orientation. *Schizophrenia Research, 75*(1), 119–128.

Resick, P. A., Monson, C. M. & Chard, K. M. (2016). *Cognitive processing therapy for PTSD: A comprehensive manual.* New York, NY: Guilford Publications.

Schein, L. A., Spitz, H. I., Burlingame, G. M., & Muskin, P. R. (2006). *Psychological effects of catastrophic disasters: Group approaches to treatment.* Binghamton, NY: Haworth Press. https://search.proquest.com/docview/42443652?accountid=28179

Schubert, C. F., Schmidt, U., & Rosner, R. (2016). Posttraumatic growth in populations with posttraumatic stress disorder – A systematic review on growth-related psychological constructs and biological variables. *Clinical Psychology & Psychotherapy, 23*(6), 469–486.

Searles, H. F. (1965). *Collected papers on schizophrenia and related subjects.* Madison, CT: International Universities Press.

Shay, J. (2010). *Achilles in Vietnam: Combat trauma and the undoing of character.* New York, NY: Simon and Schuster.

Tajfel, H. (Ed.) (1978). The achievement of group differentiation. *Differentiation between social groups: Studies in the social psychology of intergroup relations.* (pp. 77–98). London: Academic Press.

Tedeschi, R. G., & Calhoun, L. G. (2004). Posttraumatic growth: Conceptual foundations and empirical evidence. *Psychological Inquiry, 15*(1), 1–18.

Toseland, R. W., Jones, L. V., & Gellis, Z. D. (2004). Group dynamics. In C. D. Garvin, L. M. Gutiérrez, & M. J. Galinsky (Eds.), *Handbook of social work with groups.* (pp. 13–31). New York, NY: The Guilford Press.

Wattenberg, M.S., Foy, D.W., Unger, W., & Glynn, S. M., (2006). Present centered group therapy (PCGT): An evidence based approach to trauma with adults. In Shein et al. (Eds.), Psychological effects of catastrophic disasters: Group approaches to treatment. Binghamton, NY: Haworth Press.

Part II

Present-Centered Group Therapy Practice: Theory, History, and Applications

6 The Present in Embracing Today: Time Frame, Mechanisms, and Trauma Recovery

Melissa S. Wattenberg, Daniel Lee Gross, and William S. Unger

The Present in Embracing Today: Time Frame, Mechanisms, and Trauma Recovery

A moment can define a person's life. This is the legacy of trauma. It is not that a moment *must* define a life, although it almost certainly invites re-definition. But it *is* that trauma has a magnetic quality drawing a person back to it, over and over, again and again. And it *is* that trauma tends to derail what came before, to leave a gaping hole in a person where the known self and world used to be. And it *is* that trauma tends to disconnect the current moment, and disengage movement toward the future.

How do PTSD symptoms alter connection with life in the present? And how do survivors reconnect? One of the challenges to recovery is that traumatic memory transcends time. The memories seize attention as though occurring in the moment, mediated by hyperarousal, and perpetuated by the wish to es-tablish predictability and control (Foy, 1992) across all times. The horrific events refuse to fall into sequence, intruding into the present with accom-panying arousal when no actual risk is present – leaving neutral or positive persons, places, and situations appearing suspect, or dangerous. Traumatic memories appear unbidden, taking over current sensation, attention, and state of mind, as though occurring in the present. Survivors may state these in-cursions verbally or through behavior, for example, "When was I in Vietnam? Yesterday!" Or, "I'm not hoarding, I know what it's like to go without, in the camps." The occasion of trauma introduces a challenge to our cognitive schemas, overwhelming the ability to take in, sort, and apply new information in order to adapt to change in circumstance (Janoff-Bulman, 1992; McCann & Pearlman, 1990). Winnicott (1989) is quoted (Alford, 2013, pp. 146–147) as saying, "trauma ... implies a breaking of faith... Trauma is the destruction of the purity of individual experience by a too sudden or unpredictable intrusion of actual fact." Alford elaborates: "Trauma undermines our confidence in the stability of the world, not just the external world, but the inner world. Our trust in the world is violated... The traumatized... carry an impossible history within them...PTSD is knowledge of the terrible vulnerability of the self in the world. One's faith in the stability of the world is not easily restored once the world's solidity is shattered in such a way that it is experienced as a somatic as well as cognitive event. Hypervigilance and exaggerated startle response are, in a larger sense, quite realistic. Once we realize that our world can be broken in a moment, everything changes. All the development we have undertaken since birth, … people and culture, all our actual relationships that support us in a woven web of flesh and love and expectations met over and over again until the world seems stable and predictable can be shattered in a flash...." For survivors working toward healing in the aftermath of trauma, these are significant challenges: How might it be safe to reconsider patterns of action learned under conditions of extreme stress? What might it mean to be more alive and alert to the present, more available for integrating new and non-traumatic experience, allowing traumatic experiences to fall into perspective? It is in these contexts that we discuss embracing today.

Defining the Present

The positive track record for PCGT invites further consideration of the present focus, what it is (as "the present" can mean a variety of things), and what is useful about it in the group. In keeping with the broad context in which present-centered group therapy was historically developed, the term *present-centered* refers to a focus on, and availability to, everyday life. This "present" may include recent experience, personal identity, relationships, work and ongoing tasks, as well as future concerns – and not simply that elusive "moment" that is a snapshot in the flow of life (as may be utilized in mindfulness approaches (e.g., Mindfulness Based Stress Reduction, Carmody, 2015; Acceptance and Commitment Therapy (ACT), Walser & Westrup, 2007; Hayes et al., 2013; Dialectical Behavioral Therapy (DBT), Linehan, 2014; DBT-PTSD for complex PTSD, Bohus et al., 2019; Bormann et al., 2018; Davis et al., 2019). Yet even in the context of mindfulness, these snapshots occur over time. Mindful "moments" are captured within the flow of time, in which the "moment" could be as long as a breath, or as short as an eye-blink.

The definition and derivation of the word "present"[1] indicate meanings from "being 'at hand'" to an "instant," to "contemporary." Each of these meanings is auspicious for survivors of trauma managing symptoms that profoundly distract from being available to the company of friends, family, and community. Survivors of trauma report disruption of the present, from momentarily being distracted, to spending months or more preoccupied by traumatic memories.

The Present as Connected to Space

"The present" as formally defined can suggest a personal presence ("being there"), and can also reference the "portion of space around someone," suggesting a sense of place, or environment, as part of the present. This conceptualization of the present as including surrounding space lends itself well to groups, which "create a space" for healing, and invite members to "be here now." This concept of a present connected to "place" also highlights what can be a missing piece for survivors. It is not uncommon for survivors to express a sense of hovering over their current lives rather than being in them – feeling disconnected from both the people and the places around them. Intrusive symptoms can disconnect survivors from the spaces they would otherwise inhabit, whether in their homes, at work, or in connecting with the larger world around them. The focus on the present in PCGT, then, includes reconnection with not only the current time frame, but also relationships and activities, the places in which the relationships and activities occur, and the potential for developing comfort and investment in places not yet explored.

The Present and Personal Narrative

The concept of "the present" is reflected again in our language regarding time and tenses,[2] allowing for a beginning, middle, and endpoint in personal history – distinctions that can be disrupted for survivors of trauma. Our Western linguistic systems encourage distilling the hypothetical moment that separates the past from the future, to develop a coherent narrative of life and experiences across time. For survivors, this time frame may also be disrupted by intrusions, while the practice at being in the present (and sharing events in the present across the time frame of the group) that is characteristic of PCGT encourages development of a current-day narrative. While development of a trauma narrative is beyond the scope of PCGT, the experience of reconnecting with the current time frame, as broadly defined, offers a foundation from which disparate experiences can be catalogued and set in their place in time. It is notable that some survivors of trauma at completion of PCGT have reported being appreciative for this opportunity to "work on their trauma," despite never having discussed the details of their trauma. Group discussion of trauma-related symptoms and issues can lead to diminished trauma-based thinking (and feelings), allowing a more robust present and future, and an improved placement of the past in the sequence of time.

"Flow" in Time and Awareness in the Present

For trauma treatment and recovery, and for PCGT, the capacity to be aware and available in the moment includes being present enough to enjoy, appreciate, and notice nuances in current life in a way that informs future action and development of meaning. Csikszentmihalyi (1990, 1997) suggests advantages to being "in the flow" as a return to awareness that feeds optimal creativity and (future) performance. Csikszentmihalyi's focus on optimal experience may appear ambitious for group treatment of PTSD, in which reconnecting with the present is intended to be re-storative; yet survivors may take the opportunity to move toward and achieve the optimal as well.

Availability to the Present as Respite from Suffering

To Csikszentmihalyi, being "in the flow" can be an antidote to suffering, and a respite from existential challenges, including "social controls": "...the universe was not designed with the comfort of human beings in mind... It seems that every time a pressing danger is avoided, a new and more sophisticated one appears on the horizon... The four grim horsemen of the Apocalypse are never very far away... In our lifetime we exert little influence over the forces that interfere with our wellbeing" (*Flow*, pp. 8, 9). He advocates for a form of independent thought that is relatively devoid of expectation and "social controls," and tied to being in the present: "The most important step in emancipating oneself from social controls is the ability to find rewards in the events of each moment. If a person learns to enjoy and find meaning in the ongoing stream of experience, the burden of social controls automatically falls from one's shoulders." These pronouncements apply as well to recovery for survivors of trauma, for whom social controls, or failure of social controls to protect, may be implicated in the original trauma (Ford, 2019, Keynote Panel: Charting a Course Forward for the Traumatic Stress Field – International Perspectives *(Ford, Julian, PhD; Herman, Judith, MD; Armour, Cherie, Professor; McFarlane, Alexander, MD; Mwiti, Gladys, PhD))* – and for whom experiences of connection and spontaneity, distinct from the trauma, may be enlivening and empowering.[3]

PCGT offers the present not as a respite (which it may not always be), but as potentially lively and intricate current life. In place of distracting intrusions that revisit and reify past traumatic experience, PCGT directs and redirects movement toward ongoing, developing, and new experiences. In this sense, the present is several things: it is a time frame, a place in time; it is a portal, a way into accurate perception of surroundings and events, in which to mine information relevant to functioning; and it also suggests movement toward and within such surroundings and events, orienting and reorienting, toward contact and connection. Across these embodiments of the present, the group offers a therapy space in which there is room to move and create change.

Potential for "Corrective Experience"

In present-centered group therapy, the group itself becomes the medium for what may be considered a "corrective experience" centered in current life. There is no structured induction into the present. Members are educated about the group format and present focus, and are encouraged to assist each other in maintaining this focus. PCGT approaches PTSD symptoms and associated issues through a combination of PTSD education (more formal in the first three groups), trauma-aware guidance from facilitators, and experience of cohesion and engagement in the group.

How Does Being in the Present Help?

To address this question, it is useful to explore both how PTSD can affect the time frame of the present, and how the group process in PCGT, with reduced interruption from traumatic memories, can be instructive and restorative. Schema theory is useful in two contexts if not more: 1) understanding of cognitive-emotional schemas disrupted by trauma (McCann & Pearlman, 1990); and 2) extent to which PTSD symptoms of reexperiencing and hyperarousal (along with avoidance and other symptoms) disrupt the schemas for time frame of the present (see Table 6.1 for summary of PTSD symptoms and relationship to time frame violation). These two sets of concepts are intertwined:

- Violation of the current time frame maintains trauma-based schemas. New information from the present is at least partially blocked by sensory experience from the past. Insufficient access to the present means that there is little opportunity for trauma-based schemas to recalibrate. Without ready and consistent access to current life, survivors are repeatedly bombarded with experiences from the past that reinforce the trauma-based schemas.
- In PCGT, the present-day focus allows trauma-disrupted cognitive-emotional schemas to gradually recalibrate. Due to repeated emphasis on the experience of current living, and away from reexperiencing and trauma details, hyperarousal is less activated (even if still relatively high in comparison to that of to non-trauma-survivors). Under these conditions, schemas that have been disrupted by trauma and maintained by PTSD symptoms of arousal, reexperiencing, and avoidance now have opportunity to access new information that was previously blocked or minimally available. As these opportunities are established in the group, members' emotions, ideas, current experiences, and assumptions about life and relationships are available to be shared and explored.

Role of Mid-Range Emotions

As discussed throughout this book, PCGT emphasizes mid-range emotions – not just high end experiences of rage, terror, or "freeze" response that are hallmarks of physiological states related to hyperarousal, but the more subtle, "meat-and-potatoes" of daily life such as uneasiness, hurt, envy, happiness, contentment, discomfort, annoyance, and satisfaction. These nuanced feelings offer information about everyday life occurrences, needs, preferences, and decisions. Without access to these emotions, survivors of trauma have a

Table 6.1 Relationship of PTSD Symptoms (Referencing DSM-5, American Psychiatric Association, 2013) to Violation of Time Frame

Symptoms Related to PTSD	Relationship of Trauma to Time Frame of the Present
Distressing, recurrent, intrusive memories of the event(s)	Directly violates time frame of the present
Recurrent distressing dreams/ nightmares with content and/or affect related to the traumatic event(s)	Directly violates time frame of the present
Flashbacks/reliving/dissociative experiences (feelings, sensations, or actions representing recurrence of the traumatic event(s))	Directly violates time frame of the present
Reactivity to reminders/triggers: intense or prolonged distress and or physiological activation in response to internal or external cues reminiscent of an aspect of the traumatic event(s)	Directly violates time frame of the present
Efforts to avoid distressing memories, thoughts, feelings, as well as external reminders (e.g., people, places, activities, objects, contexts, and conversation topics) associated with the trauma	Attempts to protect time frame of the present; partially infiltrates time frame of the present through avoidance actions
Inability to remember an important aspect of the traumatic event(s)/ dissociative amnesia	Protective of time frame of the present against traumatic memories
Pervasive negative beliefs or expectations about oneself, others, or the world; persistent negative emotional states (e.g., shame, guilt, fear, anger, horror); inability to experience positive emotions	Infiltration of past time frame into functioning in the present (carry-over of "lessons of trauma" specific to past events, overtaking feelings, experiences, and potential lessons from current life)
Preoccupation with blaming self and/or others regarding the causes and consequences of the traumatic event(s)	Infiltration of past time frame into functioning in the present through preoccupation with the wish to undo the trauma ("if only ("I," or "other(s)") had/had not ...) – leading to diminished engagement in the present

Table 6.1 (Continued)

Symptoms Related to PTSD	Relationship of Trauma to Time Frame of the Present
Markedly diminished interest and/or participation in significant activities; feelings of detachment/ estrangement from others	Infiltration of trauma into the time frame of the present, leaving the present pale in comparison and less accessible than the past
Reckless or self-destructive behavior	If secondary to hyperarousal, or reexperiencing: direct violation of time frame as though still in the midst of trauma, where risk-taking may have been expected. If a form of avoidance through distracting risk-taking: protective of the time frame, while also displacing time frame through avoidance-based actions not grounded in the present. If secondary to trauma-based negative feelings or beliefs (including blame): infiltration of past time frame into current living, obscuring nuances in current life
Hypervigilance, including potential for irritable behavior and angry outbursts, exaggerated startle response, sleep disturbance, diminished concentration	Directly violates time frame of the present through sense of urgency/danger based in the trauma, as though past is present (with need for being "tuned in to danger" rather than nuances of current living and relationships)

"blind spot" when it comes to navigating situations and relationships under non-emergency conditions. Discussions in trauma groups often revolve around frustration and weariness regarding negotiation of daily life (especially relationships with family members, and others who are not survivors of trauma). It is exhausting and confusing to operate without the necessary cues from the emotions of everyday life. The difficulty of experiencing or expressing emotion, the "alexithymia" common in PTSD, pinpoints what can be a longstanding disconnection from feelings contributing to this issue. Alexithymia can mean either of these experiences (see below).

Alexithymia

* *Difficulty putting feelings into words*

    * Related to hyperarousal and concomitant shutting down of higher cognitive processes

- Related to overwhelming experiences that defy description, and distrust of inner experience

- *Difficulty experiencing emotion*
  - Related to emotional numbing/inability to experience positive emotions, and, potentially, avoidance of feelings related to trauma
  - Related to intrusive experiences that trigger hyperarousal and distract from current circumstances, including mid-range emotion

As members actively discuss their experiences in the present, group feedback and guidance from facilitators introduce new perspectives for understanding and evaluating those experiences. Much of the group involves discussion of feelings, which may start out awkwardly; however, as facilitators meet them where they are and walk them through feeling choices and successive approximations of emotion, facility with emotion increases. The emergence of the more subtle, nuanced emotions, supported by group, helps to counter the impact of hyperarousal. Empathy, and both nonverbal and verbal affirmation from other group members, is validating, and motivates further reflection and expression. From there, the group works toward transfer of these gains to life outside the group, which involves fine-tuning and situation-specific application of developing emotion skills.

The Nature of Past and Present in PTSD

PTSD Symptoms and Time Frame (See Table 6.1)

The nature of PTSD creates a reverse image of what it means to be in the present, through its interruption of the present and injection of the past at certain intervals. This reverse image is of being centered in the current life – a life that, while not perfect, could be filled with subtle feelings and observations, intermittent sense of wellbeing, caring about personal struggles of the moment, connecting more spontaneously with people and places, and valuing current goals and activities. Because the intense and complex learning context in PTSD reflects a natural process, survivors of trauma may not realize that their current life is as disrupted as it is – even if it pales in comparison to memories of trauma.

Attention and connection to the present are key aspects of recovery, while PTSD symptoms (DSM-5; American Psychiatric Association, 2013) disrupt this attention and connection to everyday life. While disruption occurs in most disorders, PTSD is among the few involving incursion into the present by a specific past time frame. This incursion from the past takes up space. It interferes with new learning, offering up the past to relearn again and again. Hyperarousal mediates this process by shutting down higher processes and engendering a flight/fight/freeze response. The resulting trauma-based sense of immediacy and danger overwhelms current time frame cues. The survivor picks up cues to danger signaled by hyperarousal, and may feel as though the traumatic event(s) were recurring. Because danger information acquired under conditions of high arousal is particularly well learned (Pitman, 1989), the sense of recurrence of trauma is compelling. Those who survive a trauma tend to reflexively relearn what they already know (the traumatic past). When encased in this recursive process, there is very little remaining attention and energy to accommodate new information in the current world. If not interrupted, this closed loop of danger cues and traumatic memories overrides current life, replacing major chunks of the present. Genuine experience of the moment is diminished. The "mid-range" emotions that are essential to navigating daily life are blocked. Impact on all domains of life (from relationships to enjoyment to work) may be profound.

The diagnosis of PTSD as first established in 1980 identified these three primary elements, all affecting capacity for connection to the present:

- Intrusive memories invading the present through nightmares, flashbacks, and/or intrusive memories, as well as emotional or physiological reactivity to reminders
- Arousal distracting from connection with present-day cognition, interactions, and transactions
- Avoidance interrupting engagement in the present, and numbing interrupting emotional connection in the present

As PTSD has evolved through the editions of the DSM (Diagnostic and Statistical Manual of Mental Disorders, 5th Edition, 2013; also, DSM-III, 1980, and DSM-IV-TR, 2000), impact on beliefs/values, attributions, and mood has been incorporated. Table 6.1 charts the manner in which PTSD symptoms reflect disruption of the time frame of the present. Impact ranges from taking the survivor *out* of the current time frame (as with reexperiencing symptoms and hyperarousal), to interrupting, diminishing, or altering connection to current life. As with any list of symptoms that appear as discrete items, it is important to remember that functionally they are not linear. Within a person, these symptoms co-occur, interact, and affect each other.

- For Criterion B, Intrusions, each symptom directly "violates" the time frame (inserts sensory information from the past traumatic event into the present), whether through imagery or emotional and/or physiological reactivity related to the past event.
- For Criterion D, Alterations in Cognitions and Mood, "Persistent negative emotional states" may represent a more subtle form of emotional reexperiencing, and as such, directly violate connection with the present and introduce the past trauma into the present. Items 1 and 2, concerning altered beliefs, expectations, and cognitions, may result from trauma-related affects invading the present, especially if

they manifest intermittently (e.g., when the survivor is triggered). Otherwise, they may represent ways of making sense of a post-trauma world. Items 5, 6, and 7 each describe different modes of diminished connection, and are labeled as instances of "infiltration" from the past. The implication is that longstanding intermittent disruption of the present by traumatic memories, related affects, and hyperarousal can keep the individual "on tenterhooks," resulting in fatigue, and long-term distraction from current life.

- For Criterion E, "Marked alterations in arousal and reactivity associated with the traumatic event(s)," items 1 and 3 (irritability and angry outbursts, and hypervigilance) are characterized as violation of the time-frame by trauma-related affects, and are probably associated as well with reexperiencing, even if without related content. Items 4, 5, and 6 (exaggerated startle response, problems with concentration, and sleep disturbance) are characterized as indirectly violating time frame, with the explanation, "still 'tuned in to danger'" – suggesting that the entire criterion of arousal and reactivity revolves around trauma-based threat perceived as active in the present.

Experience of Time Frame Disruption Related to Trauma History

Survivors experiencing disconnection from the current time frame, as well as their families, friends, and providers, will notice this sense that life in the present is sometimes missing or interrupted. Key examples of this trauma-related phenomenon are identified below, with implications for therapeutic response.

"Loosed" from Time

The survivor knows that the trauma is a past event. In that sense, the trauma has its location in the past. However, as indicated in this chapter's opening reference to the impact of trauma, its powerful and often less-than-completely-integrated meaning leaves it poorly hinged to its own time sequence, and therefore, easily brought forth by even peripheral reminders – leaving the survivor in uncertain time. Given the threat to safety inherent in the original trauma, the loss of predictability and control at the time of the trauma, and the survivor's awareness that life can be uprooted, it can happen that even an associated sensory cue such as weather, a small sound, or a flash of light will conjure the traumatic event. Reactivity to such peripheral cues is honed, and reinforced, by the need to react quickly in order to preserve safety (as was not possible during the original trauma). The pattern of accompanying hyperarousal, followed by relief generated by evasive action in response to the trigger, creates a largely closed system in which the trauma is repeatedly vanquished (only to appear again). Attention and response to the present-day meaning of current and recent life events are diminished, and sometimes absent. Here is where survivors of trauma may note that it is hard to attend to "small talk," or to relate to the emotions that others are experiencing, or to attend family gatherings. Surrounding life may seem insubstantial in comparison to the traumatic past.

Implications for Treatment and Recovery

While therapeutic response to intrusive memories can take many forms, there is clear value in shifting toward focus on significant current non-traumatic situations, which may then promulgate new learning in place of old patterns. Awareness of triggers, prioritizing of relationships, and turning attention toward mid-range emotions can begin to secure a sense of safety and meaning in the current time frame. Ongoing discussion of feelings among members is likely to result in reduced alexithymia, which will aid in the "small talk" situation and facilitate social connection. As the member has greater access to current life, there is opportunity for "trauma triggers" to become less formidable and more manageable.

Time Travel

Even if the survivor has been able to label and catalogue the traumatic event, placing it in its proper place in time, the *direction* of time can also be experienced as altered in PTSD (as fictionalized in Vonnegut's Slaughterhouse Five: "Billy Pilgrim has come unstuck in time" (Vonnegut, 1969, chapter 2, p. 23); Vonnegut was, notably, a survivor of a German POW camp during World War II. Rather than experiencing diminished connection to the surrounding world as a result of reexperiencing, the trauma survivor tunnels into the past in response to an otherwise non-threatening reminder. The capacity to keep in good contact with information from the present, including new learning, communication with loved ones, and nuanced observation of the surrounding world, is temporarily eclipsed, while old knowledge from the trauma is repeatedly rehearsed and relearned.

Implications for Treatment and Recovery

PCGT persistently refocuses and redirects away from the traumatic past, reintroducing the present to help the survivor return to current life. If time travel appears to be occurring in the group, the facilitators or other members will notice the nonverbal cues, and encourage return to the room. Establishing reliable present-day touchstones for cuing current life are important in preventing "time travel," and facilitating return to the current time frame if it does occur. These may be a familiar object, a safe place, or a pleasant scent that overrides the sensory cues within the intrusive memory. In group discussion, other members are likely to share similar experiences, and provide their strategies for addressing them. Again, practice at being in the present within the group facilitates developing new skills for responding solidly and accurately to available time cues of the present. The survivor can be encouraged to develop a sense of agency in place of helplessness in response to this phenomenon, developing strategies to reengage the present rather than "go along for the ride."

Living "Out of Time"

Hard-to-integrate traumatic events can take on a larger-than-life presence, as though existing outside of time, much as spiritual or peak events are said to do (Eliade & Trask, 1959; Buber, 1970). As in peak and spiritual experiences, unique, arcane knowledge distinguishes and separates trauma survivor from others in everyday life who have not shared that experience. However, spiritual or peak events such as the birth of a child, or a profound spiritual awakening, typically do not share the degree of intrusive quality, sense of helplessness, and distress characteristic of traumatic memories. In addition, peak and spiritual experiences seem to cooperate with being placed back into the flow of time and the context of meaning, while traumatic events tend to hover, leaving an overlay of apprehension and doubt across the present landscape – as though "waiting for the other shoe to fall." Present-day life can feel flimsy, more of an illusion than a reality. This overlay of trauma awareness colors relationships and action in the present, muting the intensity and significance of current experience while the survivor has one foot in that larger-than-life place. The survivor may even gravitate toward current activities that pull for intensity and transcendence of the mundane, and may feel a sense of worthlessness or pointlessness if not acting in this mode.

Implications for Treatment and Recovery

Among the potential approaches to breaking through this out-of-time orientation, PCGT offers a steady practice of valuing the details in daily life (as validated through group discussion), offering the survivor a chance to expand appreciation of the smaller, less "high-end" pleasures in life, and assuring that, for example, "being a star," a "rescuer," a "guru," or adventurer are not required in order to have value.

Post-Apocalyptic Time Frame / Profound Alienation

Influenced by subtle rather than overt intrusions, and intensified by loss of meaning, this phenomenon can also have profound impact on functioning in everyday life. In this construction, events are set in time, but there is essentially a double take at being in the current life (often accompanied by a hesitance regarding investing in this life). In an extreme form, survivors of trauma may feel that "I am already dead.... I died in Iraq" (as fictionalized in the films, Jacob's Ladder, 1990, and *Enemies, a Love Story (1989)*). Many others feel they *should* have died, if others actually did die during the trauma (see "survivor guilt" in chapter five). The world after trauma may seem colorless, undependable, and confusing, while the trauma-laden world is compelling (as depicted in the ending of *The Hurt Locker*, 2009). Having lived through the trauma, the survivor may feel aimless, or displaced. There may be a sense that the world is not as it should be (see also moral injury, chapter five) – and as such, difficult to endorse. The time frame dislocation raises existential issues, as characterized by Beckett's existential paradox (1965): "I can't go on.... I'll go on." The survivor may feel that, given the inability to prevent the trauma, everything now is "beside the point." Even if the survivor can "go on" and be effective in this post-trauma world, it may not seem worth the investment of time, energy, and commitment to this world. This post-trauma orientation can also reflect difficulty saying good-bye to others who died traumatically, or a part of self that perished due to the trauma. Loss of the old self ("I am not who I used to be") may diminish the sense of potential effectiveness in the post-trauma world, leaving the survivor feeling "less than," or "like damaged goods." Paradoxically, the survivor may also feel "better than" others who have not seen trauma, or see the current world "less than," given the potential for trauma.

Implications for Treatment and Recovery

The present focus does not deny the traumatic past, and does not automatically resolve it. It does not promise there will be no further traumatic occurrences. Instead, it provides an environment in which members connect and share the struggle to establish meaning and connection. In PCGT, the active group environment, and modest structure, create a setting allowing survivors to reconnect gradually with the world around them, at their own pace. It is likely that members will share existential issues, and recognize they are not alone. This connection can then serve as an opportunity to establish a foothold in current life, and from there, to work toward potentially safe spaces and places in the community.

Schema Theory, PTSD, and PCGT

Schema Theory

The generally robust relationship between past learning and present experience is embodied in schema theory (*The Psychology of the Child*, Piaget, 1950; *Cognition and Reality*, Neisser, 1976; *Image and Mind*, Kosslyn, 1980). These concepts have been applied to PTSD in a variety of clinical and evidence-based approaches and subsequent research, among them *Cognitive Processing Therapy for Rape Victims* (Resick and Schnicke, 1996); with many editions since for a variety of populations); *Treating the Trauma of Rape* (Foa & Rothbaum, 1998); *Schema Therapy* (Young et al., 2003); *Seeking Safety* (Najavits, 2002). In articulating the processes involved in natural cognitive, emotional, and behavioral functioning, schema theory has implications for the recovery process (Janoff-Bulman, 1992; McCann & Pearlman, 1990).

While early in the field of psychotherapy, treatment of anxiety and phobias appeared to be fairly easily addressed from understanding of straightforward associations (with therapy working to create new associations to replace the old dysfunctional ones), PTSD's deep cut into so many aspects of experience, emotion, and belief has demanded a more complex set of interventions and concomitant theory. Generally, the application of schema theory to trauma revolves around the horrific "index event" violating expected norms regarding predictability and control, resulting in a tragic outcome.

*General Definition of Schemas, and Their Application
to Understanding Trauma*

Schema theory began not as a way to understand disruption, but as a model for the fundamental work of operating in the world. Schema theory describes the integrally connected nature of past and present in the process of learning and adaptation. This integration is automatic for the most part, and often independent of conscious awareness. Past experience is organized and catalogued so as to inform current action and plans for future action, embedded in complex patterns for potential action (schemas), geared to be flexibly responsive to the ambient world in a (typically) seamless, coherent, and fluid manner, with capacity for nuanced accommodation to circumstance. Embedded in psychological schemas are behavioral patterns, thoughts, feelings, beliefs, attitudes, social and relational nuances, and expectations, all contributing to a capacity to operate, largely effectively, in the world. According to the precepts of this widely accepted cognitive model, incorporation of past learning is essential to ongoing and future learning, toward managing complex physical and social environments (Janoff-Bulman, 1992; McCann & Pearlman, 1990; Resick et al., 2015). In this context, the past is not so much a problem as it is a resource, or, more commonly, "just a part of life" – something we can take for granted, rejoice and sorrow in, and build upon.

Schemas can be described in brief as intersecting, complex response systems operating across a variety of contexts, which allow individuals to flexibly apply previously learned patterns of knowledge to new or novel situations in an iterative process – repeatedly recalibrating in response to new information, so that new learning can be readily incorporated and applied. In a perpetual process of highly articulated assimilation and accommodation sequences (Piaget, 1950), schemas digest new information toward adaptation to new situations, as well as potential other relevant new situations.

The academic study of knowledge processes had embraced "information processing" (to eventually include computer modeling of complex thought), leading into incorporation of schema theory, as information processing models were insufficient. The utility of this theory can be described through consideration of complex tasks from playing a piano to playing chess, to developing a really good tennis serve, to choreography of a complex and smoothly executed dance routine. While all movements, actions, and preparations for action can be considered within a stimulus-response framework – and here the intention is not to replace but to enhance the original behavioral constructs – all of these complex actions involve a level of automatic action and smooth sequences of steps and transitions that in a stimulus-response model would look like a series of choppy movements. Or would take too much time. The example given by Neisser and many others, is that of the master chess player who has at disposal not only the moves and arrangements of the current game, but that of many games and many arrangements of possible moves that can be taken into consideration flexibly, at any relevant moment. This accelerated application in thought, considering many possible maneuvers and potential future sequences in a moment's reflection, suggests complex cognitive processes.

These theories have been similarly applied to development of mastery of a musical instrument, in which the learner initially plays individual notes, and then chords, followed by learning a flow of notes and chords that lead smoothly into each other, into which a variety of expressive emphases can be placed with precision and the appearance of spontaneity. Piano virtuosos have at their fingertips not only a particular piece as a whole (and the various ways it can be played), but the experience of studying and playing many other pieces, the history of that composer and the composer's repertoire and intentions, and those of other composers of that time period and other time periods, while simultaneously integrating emotion and expression into the piece.

Schema theory has been used to capture such complex, coordinated actions, which each person in one way or another must partake in, in our learning and execution of complex and skilled tasks in our own lives. It suggests that we develop integrated patterns out of our initial simple steps – which perhaps were even initially not that simple, but also based on past learning, for example, through assimilation and accommodation. The more thorough our learning, the more flexibly and quickly we can apply the related schemas, and the more easily we can accommodate it for new learning. New learning involves the schema or complex of schemas being available to alteration in response to the world (accommodation). Ultimately, in schema theory, everything we do, all of our actions, are achieved through our application of our old knowledge patterns to new situations, and continual adjustment of our information to be able to respond flexibly to the next situation. From mailing a letter to driving a car, we are engaging in a highly complex, fluid, and organized process. And then there are schemas within schemas, for example, of what we need to get done in a day, which might organize both driving and mailing a letter, and many other tasks that need to be planned out and executed.

Trauma theorists have posited disruption of natural and effective schemas by trauma, suggesting that psychological trauma can overwhelm healthy/flexible functioning, replacing it with trauma-biased patterns of cognition (and accompanying emotion and action). The traumatic impact interrupts the give-and-take of the normal schematic processes, due to a combination of hard-to-integrate material that does not match existing schemas, and accompanying hyperarousal that demands an emergency response in the moment (rather than mobilization of complex recalibration of schemas). Existing schemas do not fully digest the meaning of the traumatic experience in a way that allows accurate incorporation, and application (i.e., through activating a selective process, and applying it to largely recognizable, relevant circumstances). As discussed earlier in this chapter, trauma experience can alter the interrelationships in processing past and present experience (as well as future experience). This alteration is much of what we address in our treatment and recovery efforts.

The functional interference from PTSD symptoms involves intrusion from tragic, unpredictable, and uncontrollable prior experience, which then misinforms current experience, and distracts from nuanced attention to everyday life. The initial "shattering" of expected patterns leads into a set of rudimentary, makeshift recalibrations of schemas post-trauma, which tends to validate an excess of vigilance as instrumental to re-establishing and preserving safety. The survivor becomes increasingly alienated from the current world. As the survivor becomes "tuned in to danger," the stress response is heightened, resurrecting the traumatic past, through symptoms of hyperarousal, reexperiencing, altered beliefs and emotions, and avoidance. These powerful reactions override attention to non-trauma-related information in the present, resulting in both disconnection from the current time frame, and overlearning of trauma-related information (e.g., amplifying a sense of danger, and the need for hypervigilance), leading to entrenched trauma-based attitudes and beliefs.

Janoff-Bulman (1992) identifies the "Just World Hypothesis," the naïve but common (and natural) belief that being a good person will provide safety, as if being in a "state of grace." A traumatic event violates this expectation, leaving the individual at a loss in terms of schemas for operating in a "just world." The subsequent makeshift reaction in the urgency of the trauma (especially while hyperarousal limits higher cognitive processes from functioning optimally) is either to modify schemas (a largely accommodative response to the traumatic situation) or impose already existing schemas (a largely assimilative response) in order to restore functioning as rapidly as possible. Given the need to quickly restore functioning under cognitively limiting conditions, survivors' schematic responses will be less nuanced, cruder, less articulate than in a peaceful or relaxed context in which schemas are tending to initially take one side or the other of the "Just World" belief system; either the trauma survivor must not be a good person, or else the world is not a good or safe place. Healthy recalibration of schemas post-trauma would allow a gradually more sensitively honed response with more subtle and reasonable modifications that are less absolute and less rigid. For example, an eventual understanding that one has only partial predictability and partial control, in a world that is pluralistic, neither all good nor all bad, is perhaps the best way to restore full functioning. Capacity to fully activate useful schemas after a trauma depends on many factors, including past trauma, and quality of social support, especially in the immediate aftermath of the trauma. However, the common avoidance symptoms characteristic of PTSD, and the tendency for hyperarousal to resume with any reminder of the trauma, mediate against approaching and reexamining the trauma "triggers" in order to better evaluate the origin of the reactivity and recalibrate for more flexible functioning. Therefore, many survivors remain "stuck" in trauma-based thinking and accompanying hyperarousal. There is a strong risk of maintaining the original schematic adjustments made in the immediate aftermath of the trauma, rather than further calibrating toward integration of traumatic events and recovery.

Some theorists emphasize errors in assimilation and accommodation (Resick et al., 2015), while others emphasize violation of the foundation on which "natural" or previously developed schemas are based (e.g., "naïve" need to believe that one is a good person in a "just world"; as above, Janoff-Bulman, 1992). Whatever the specific mechanisms behind this disruption, the result is the disconnection from the time frame of the present, and relearning of the traumatic past, with loss of corrective information from present-day cues. This loss of important relevant feedback translates into concomitant loss of engagement, for example, in the contexts of relationships, work, and general orientation to life and healthy living.

- Resick et al. (2015) identifies Safety, Trust, Power and Control, Esteem, and Intimacy as schemas to address in Cognitive Processing Therapy (each across dimensions of "self" and "others")
- The education provided in PCGT includes some of these themes, identified as "issues associated with PTSD" (see chapter three) – as well as some that are now associated with PTSD symptoms (e.g., esteem; "Persistent and exaggerated negative beliefs or expectations about oneself, others, or the world")

- McCann and Pearlman (1990) identify these schemas as disrupted by trauma:

- Frame of reference (meaning, causality, hope, locus of control)
- Safety
- Trust/Dependency
- Independence
- Power
- Esteem
- Intimacy

The therapeutic factors of group psychotherapy (Yalom 1995) map easily onto a present-centered approach, inviting group members toward awareness in the present, more flexible and nuanced functioning, and attention to current life. Table 6.2 shows Yalom's therapeutic factors of group therapy in relationship to both PTSD symptoms, and the trauma-based schema disruptions identified by McCann and Pearlman. The group therapy factors have particular relevance for PTSD, as indicated in this table. One caution is that, while the therapeutic factors are described as especially relevant to specific symptoms and certain schemas, the generally salutary nature of these factors means that they may also have impact on symptoms and schemas not specifically identified. Similarly, the schemas that may be disrupted by trauma, as identified by McCann and Pearlman (1990), also are broad categories of impact, and are not necessarily independent of one another. A therapeutic factor with notable relevance to one set of schemas may resonate across others as well. The intention of Table 6.2 is to draw attention to the consonance of these therapeutic factors with the needs and concerns of survivors, rather than to limit the field of application or suggest a strict one-to-one correspondence.

The trauma-awareness in PCGT is essential to making the therapeutic factors accessible. This awareness is braided into PCGT through education in the early sessions, and attunement to these issues and their manifestation throughout the group. The blending of the therapeutic factors with trauma awareness allows development of cohesion and connection in individuals who might otherwise feel too alienated to continue the group, too much at a loss regarding emotional expression, or too overwhelmed by reexperiencing.

In addition to trauma awareness, and the benefits of group treatment in combination with this awareness, a key component of these sessions (as well as the earlier sessions) is the consistent focus in the present and redirection away from incursions from the past. As discussed earlier, this focus is essential to creating a consistent "place" in the present for each member, as a platform from which desired changes and choices in each person's personal life can be made without being interrupted or overcome by trauma-based schemas (i.e., action patterns, including beliefs, thoughts, feelings, habits, and behaviors). Maintaining this focus over time allows a natural process of recalibration of these schemas through activation of awareness in the present, which begins to inform responses to life in place of trauma-based information. This recalibration can take a variety of forms.[4]

Table 6.2 Yalom's (Yalom, 1995) Therapeutic Factors as Relevant to PTSD and Schemas Related to Trauma

Therapeutic Factors	Therapeutic Factors and PTSD Symptoms (DSM-V, APA, 2013) and Related Issues	Therapeutic Factors and Schemas Disrupted by Trauma: Frame of Reference, Safety, Trust/ Dependency, Independence, Power, Esteem, and Intimacy (McCann & Pearlman, 1990)
Instillation of hope	Addresses discouragement and despair related to distressing and persistent symptoms, and specifically counters negative alterations in cognitions and/or mood	Helps to restore *frame of reference* (hope, meaning, causality, and locus of control). Frame of reference schema directly identifies hope among its aspects, which also is essential to creating meaning.
Universality	Reconnects to sense of community. Counters sense of alienation, and detachment	Has broad impact, especially on frame of reference (reduces alienation, creates sense of connection ("we're all in the same boat") and meaning. Secondarily, this sense of connection and meaning can contribute to restoring sense of safety, begin to establish trust, build esteem, and provide a sense of common experience that supports intimacy and perspective-taking.
Imparting information	Shared knowledge "levels the playing field" and activates empowerment and awareness in the present, which helps to counter avoidance symptoms and trauma-based alterations in mood and cognition.	"Knowledge is power": helps to restore power and independence schemas

(Continued)

Table 6.2 (Continued)

Therapeutic Factors	Therapeutic Factors and PTSD Symptoms (DSM-V, APA, 2013) and Related Issues	Therapeutic Factors and Schemas Disrupted by Trauma: Frame of Reference, Safety, Trust/ Dependency, Independence, Power, Esteem, and Intimacy (McCann & Pearlman, 1990)
Altruism	The altruism evoked in group serves an empowering function in the context of moral injury (see chapter five). Taking action for the sake of others also helps to overcome avoidance, challenges alienation and detachment, and counters blame and shame.	Altruism's impact on the frame of reference schema: helps to restore meaning and create new meaning; adjusts locus of control through empowerment; enhances sense of agency (power schema, independence schema). Esteem of self and others may be enhanced through giving to others.
Corrective recapitulation of primary family group	In the context of trauma, the recapitulation may apply not only to the family group, but the interpersonal aspects of the traumatic event or its aftermath. The group provides opportunity for a different and potentially corrective interpersonal experience. Impact on symptoms may be seen in: • Reducing dependence on avoidance, given the emphasis on engagement in the "here and now" • Countering detachment and lack of interest • Experiencing being in a group with other trauma survivors while engaging in the group offers a new experience	As trauma-based reactions and interactions become evident in the context of the group, this awareness offers opportunity for recalibration. The frame of reference is encouraged to shift from trauma-based to non-trauma-based life, restoring a sense of meaning that takes into account new information gleaned from the group. Members again have opportunity to reaffirm capacity for intimacy and reduce alienation. As confidence increases though this process, esteem for self and others also can be expected to shift. Group interactions provide a source of trust as the

(Continued)

Table 6.2 (Continued)

Therapeutic Factors	Therapeutic Factors and PTSD Symptoms (DSM-V, APA, 2013) and Related Issues	Therapeutic Factors and Schemas Disrupted by Trauma: Frame of Reference, Safety, Trust/ Dependency, Independence, Power, Esteem, and Intimacy (McCann & Pearlman, 1990)
	to survivors of trauma. While members may be reminded of their trauma initially just through joining a group for survivors, the novel experience of being in a non-trauma situation with other survivors gradually counters reexperiencing and arousal. • As members experience the absence of trauma in the group, they have opportunity to gradually reconsider trauma-based thoughts, feelings, and beliefs.	group process becomes supportive and robust.
Social learning	Group members who have become isolated, withdrawn, or detached, or who have relied on avoidance strategies, can learn from other survivors either through example and through group problem solving.	Development of these skills can help to increase power (interpersonal effectiveness) and intimacy (closeness/ connection); esteem for self and others is also likely to be enhanced through investing in mutual social learning.
Imitative behaviors	Group members act as role models for each other when it comes to symptom management and interpersonal life. There is a "fake-it-'til-	Independence and power may be enhanced through practicing behaviors observed in others (enhancing sense of agency); locus of

(*Continued*)

Table 6.2 (Continued)

Therapeutic Factors	Therapeutic Factors and PTSD Symptoms (DSM-V, APA, 2013) and Related Issues	Therapeutic Factors and Schemas Disrupted by Trauma: Frame of Reference, Safety, Trust/ Dependency, Independence, Power, Esteem, and Intimacy (McCann & Pearlman, 1990)
	you-make-it" implication that trying out potentially adaptive behaviors can result in effective behavior change, which in turn improves access to engagement in current life.	control (within frame of reference schema) may adjust, in addition, due to increased sense of agency as a result of trying out actions that work for others.
Interpersonal learning	Development of perspective-taking can reduce alienation and tendency to blame others, enhancing capacity for connection in current life. The experiences of others, and others' reports of positive results from specific strategies for managing situations and symptoms, can have impact on management of reexperiencing symptoms and an array of arousal symptoms (e.g., sleep, angry outbursts, hypervigilance).	Interactive exchanges with others that result in useful learning will enhance esteem for self and others, as well as sense of intimacy. Learning from other members as peers, rather than the facilitators, can enhance power and independence (increasing sense of agency), as well as modifying frame of reference through greater locus of control within self. As others become a source of education, trust and dependency schemas may shift toward enhanced capacity for trusting and relying on other group members (to later generalize outside of the group).
Group cohesiveness	Connection with the group in the moment, and being able to count on it over time, offer the	Cohesion is one of the most powerful interventions in a group. It enhances sense of

(Continued)

Table 6.2 (Continued)

Therapeutic Factors	Therapeutic Factors and PTSD Symptoms (DSM-V, APA, 2013) and Related Issues	Therapeutic Factors and Schemas Disrupted by Trauma: Frame of Reference, Safety, Trust/ Dependency, Independence, Power, Esteem, and Intimacy (McCann & Pearlman, 1990)
	benefit of grounding the group members in the current time and place, and countering feelings of detachment, alienation, and estrangement from others.	safety in the group, restores trust and the capacity to allow dependency, and promotes a sense of agency as members become part of something larger than themselves. Cohesion directly creates a safe sense of intimacy. The liveliness of a cohesive group stokes a sense of immediate significance, contributing to frame of reference a renewed sense of meaning.
Catharsis	In terms of emotional expression, PCGT emphasizes "mid-range" emotions. While not the high-end emotional release often implied by catharsis, this aspect of group helps to reduce alexithymia, enhancing experience of and expression of emotions.	Capacity to experience, express, and integrate emotion helps to restore sense of intimacy (through interchange with others, and also, increasing awareness of self through ongoing discussion of feelings).
Existential factors	Group members can diminish the sense of alienation through sharing it, and exploring new meanings. This factor can assist with the tendency to blame self and others, and other absolute or polarizing attributions. Acceptance becomes available	This broad function of group has direct impact on frame of reference (addressing hope, meaning, causality, and locus of control). Other schemas may be secondarily affected by this shift frame of reference. For example, a recalibration to

(Continued)

Table 6.2 (Continued)

Therapeutic Factors	Therapeutic Factors and PTSD Symptoms (DSM-V, APA, 2013) and Related Issues	Therapeutic Factors and Schemas Disrupted by Trauma: Frame of Reference, Safety, Trust/ Dependency, Independence, Power, Esteem, and Intimacy (McCann & Pearlman, 1990)
	through acknowledging that there may be no special reason certain things – like trauma – have happened, and that only limited control and predictability are achievable. Acceptance of being able to "go on" despite horrific experiences can also have positive impact on moral injury and the need to keep a vigil (both described in chapter five).	account for existential factors allows for partial control, and partial trust. A shift in the schema for independence may occur that acknowledges that the survivor cannot control everything, yet can still function independently and interdependently. Expectations in general are likely to shift toward greater flexibility and acceptance, allowing greater range of nuanced responses that enhance overall functioning.

- For some group members, there may be a sense of completion and resolution of the trauma itself, even though details of the trauma have not been discussed.
- For others, the trauma may settle partially or completely into the past.
- Others may experience greater clarity in portions of their lives, even if trauma-based intrusions persist but are better managed.
- Still others may find more of a life alongside trauma symptoms, including meaningful activities and relationships and/or a more positive view of life and its meaning (this response may be consistent with post-traumatic growth (Tedeschi & Calhoun, 2004).
- Practice of expression of feelings in the group is likely to result in greater awareness of emotion, and improved ability to express emotion (reduced alexithymia).

PTSD and Recovery

Recovery, PTSD, and Relationship to PCGT

SAMHSA (Substance Abuse Mental Health Services Agency) identifies recovery as "A process of change through which individuals improve their health and wellness, live a self-directed life, and strive to reach their full potential." Present-centered group therapy is consistent with the basic values and characteristics of this approach. The *individualized, person-centered* approach within PCGT supports a sense of *empowerment, purpose,* and *hope,* in keeping with recovery principles (Ellison, Belanger, Niles, Evans, & Bauer, 2018, p. 91; italicized are key recovery components identified by SAMHSA that show "greatest concordance" in a systematic literature review on recovery). The manual as updated has adopted the language of recovery and psychosocial rehabilitation, emphasizing personal goals, and the context of participation in community and relationships (as determined by the individual survivor), in addition to symptom management and problem solving. While any symptom focus could be seen as pathologizing, the intent is to the contrary. The sharing of clinical criteria demystifies the mental health "label," and allows posttraumatic stress disorder and related trauma-based conditions their roles as descriptors that attempt to capture the real human toll of traumatic experiences – albeit in a medically based compendium of psychiatric conditions. The inclusion of this diagnosis transformed the field in 1980 when PTSD was introduced into the Diagnostic and Statistical Manual of Mental Disorders (American Psychiatric Association, 1980, DSM-III), as documentation of the impact of human suffering (see also chapter seven). Through sharing of the symptoms and issues common to survivors of trauma (including definitions consistent with the medical establishment's view on these "lived experiences"), members are empowered to orchestrate their own recovery in collaboration with providers (and beyond providers as they continue in their lives following the group).

When we talk about interference from PTSD symptoms, it is important to have an eye toward what healthy functioning looks like. The definition will differ person to person; however, from a psychosocial rehabilitation/recovery perspective (Anthony et al., 1993; Gagne et al., 2007; Resnick et al., 2005; Resnick and Rosenheck, 2006; Resnick and Goldberg, 2019) , effective living includes: a meaningful life; access to enjoyment, as well as productivity; being able to respond flexibly to new situations and adapt to developmental stages of life; and in these contexts, capacity to meet challenges in new ways, communicate in such a way as to enhance interpersonal functioning and connection, and ability to use strengths to overcome impact of symptoms (Deegan, 2005; Davidson, O'Connell, Tondora, Staeheli, & Evans, 2005). In 2006, SAMHSA's website (https://store.samhsa.gov/system/files/pep12-recdef. pdf) characterized recovery as *"a journey of healing and transformation enabling a person with a mental health problem to live a meaningful life in a community of his or her choice while striving to achieve his or her full potential."* The 2019 update, influenced by a whole health approach, states that recovery is: "A process of change through which individuals improve their health and wellness, live a self-directed life, and strive to reach their full potential" – and follows that with a variety of "guiding principles" that cover a meaningful life in community: "Hope; Person-Driven; Many Pathways; Holistic; Peer Support; Relational; Culture; Addresses Trauma; Strengths/Responsibilities; Respect." These dimensions, applied to PTSD, suggest again that recovery takes place across "many paths," is highly individualized and collaborative, is multifaceted (and nonlinear), incorporates/respects the individual's strengths, culture, relationships, and acknowledges the trauma.

Application of Recovery to Trauma

Davidson (2005) describes trauma recovery briefly as represented in current research and practice, followed by general tenets of psychosocial rehabilitation:

> "…one of the defining characteristics of trauma is that it leaves the person forever changed as a result, having neither the same sense of personal identity nor of the world at large that existed prior to the event (Herman & Kallivayalil, 2018; van der Kolk, McFarlane, & Weisaeth, 1996)….Admittedly a gradual process…recovery is a process of moving the trauma and its immediate effects from the forefront of the person's awareness (the 'figure'), where it exerts considerable control over his or her day-to-day life, into less prominent domains on the periphery of the person's awareness (the 'ground') where it is largely under the person's control or is at least no longer considered intrusive….recovery…often involves growth and an expansion of capacities…in which the person finds her or himself able to rise to the challenge and reclaim a meaningful and gratifying life despite, or beyond the limitations of, the disorder."

This discourse on recovery highlights both the philosophy of a recovery journey rather than a specific outcome, and incorporates references to schema theory, as useful in describing PTSD and related recovery. When it comes to pursuit of functional goals consistent with the re-covery model and psychosocial rehabilitation, loss of engagement in current life poses both an obstacle to be overcome, and an opportunity for posttraumatic growth in the process of finding meaningful ways to connect, post-trauma.

Challenges to and Opportunities for Recovery

The idea of mobilizing recovery in PTSD begs several questions: What is the "full functioning in a community of one's choice," toward which recovery from PTSD may lead? Given that safety is a predominant concern for trauma survivors, what is the value of moving toward a broader set of values, and personal development, given a potentially threatening world? What intrinsic processes can be engaged to guide recovery and posttraumatic growth? While the answer to these questions will vary person to person – what overarching restoration to health might be anticipated in recovery from PTSD symptoms and trauma-based beliefs, attributions, and patterns? What might best reflect the goals of individuals toward overcoming PTSD? The absence of PTSD symptoms, while likely a relief, may not be sufficiently motivating, especially when the symptoms can be experienced as protective. Behaviorist Ogden Linsdley's "Dead Man's Test" (per the 1991 report of his statements in 1965) is often applied to functional goal-setting and behavior change. It states that, "if a dead man can do it, it isn't behavior and you shouldn't waste your time trying to produce it." For example, a dead person can stop smoking; but a dead person cannot run faster because of stopping smoking. Wanting to run faster without getting winded represents what the dead person can't do, which the living person might identify as a goal, and may then choose to stop smoking as a means to this desired outcome. Applying this "test" to PTSD: a person's PTSD symptoms could cease; yet what is the motivation for the living person? What would lead a trauma survivor to choose to live in a non-trauma-based way, following disillusioning and real (and hard-to-integrate) experiences that provide disturbing information about self, others, and the world? What motivation might justify integration of horrifying experiences in a way that is meaningful and integrates into the individual's schemas, to inform accurate perceptions of ongoing life? In this book's manual sections, special attention iss given to adhering to the "dead person test" (Lindsley, 1991) when discussing symptom management. In PCGT, the context of a change in behavior to manage symptoms, and the intention underlying the change, are primary. Symptom management occurs in the context of the person's life, and has impact and ramifications; a "dead person" can stop having symptoms but cannot have a fuller life with better relationships. Coping more effectively with a distressing symptom may produce greater intimacy with others, freedom to access new places, and improved peace-of-mind. For each individual, the motive behind change in a behavior will be distinctly connected to that person's life and circumstances. While more explicit in this updated manual, PCGT has always been applied to current circumstances and personal functional goals and roles (and the intersection of symptoms, goals, desired roles, and circumstances).

Intersection of the Cycle of PTSD Model, Drive Theory, and Maslow's Hierarchy of Needs

An additional consideration concerning the role of PCGT as a treatment for PTSD comes from a review of the cycle of PTSD symptoms and what has been referred to as "a failure to recover" following a traumatic event (Monson & Fredman, 2012). The symptoms of PTSD are hypothesized to interact in a self-sustaining system comprised of hyperarousal, emotional numbing, avoidance behaviors, and reexperiencing symptoms. This model suggests that the expression of hyperarousal leads to emotional numbing and avoidance behaviors, with each of these actuating the occurrence of reexperiencing symptoms. The presence of reexperiencing symptoms triggers hyperarousal, thereby maintaining the cycle. Treatment directed at reducing the expression of any of these symptoms interrupts the cycle and breaks the chain of PTSD symptoms.

PCGT offers therapeutic gain through facilitating a sharing by participants of positive coping skills as a means of providing relief from the arousal or heightened stress levels associated with PTSD. This conceptualization is consistent with drive theory as an explanation for symptom development and maintenance. Briefly, it postulates that the presence of an activated drive state (e.g., high arousal) will tend to elicit actions directed at decreasing that drive state. Such arousal-reducing actions may run the gamut in terms of how functional they are in a broader social context, and how much effort is required in order to achieve the desired effect. Yet the reduction of the heightened drive state reinforces the expression of these related actions, irrespective of their utility socially and in the long run. Maslow's hierarchy of needs (see Figure 8.1) may contribute to an understanding of how these drive states are activated in PTSD. Maslow (1943) identified physiological and safety needs as the first two levels that must be met in order to move toward fulfilling the next levels of need. High drive levels related to trauma are consistent with threat at these first two levels. Following the experience of trauma, vulnerability in respect to these physiological and safety needs stokes reactivity at these levels, resulting in corresponding actions, and perpetuation of the PTSD symptom cycle. Actions stemming from this reactivity are consistent with survival needs, rather than needs for belonging, esteem, or self-actualization; they may therefore appear out-of-step in the larger context of the survivor's life. Yet this self-sustaining symptom pattern is driven by the sense of threat to these basic needs, and accompanying arousal. By finding alternate methods for decreasing the overall, underlying arousal level through PCGT, this cycle is reduced or eliminated.

The work done in PCGT is directed toward a decrease of PTSD symptoms, with members often identifying reduction of arousal symptoms as a high priority. As the group facilitators guide the members' work on the identification of trauma-based reactions and related behaviors, reduction of arousal and stress underlying such behaviors becomes the key to the therapeutic problem solving and sharing process of PCGT. The member-identified techniques and strategies become a means of reducing symptom expression by decreasing the overall arousal associated with these symptoms. The sharing of skills contributes to breaking the cycle of PTSD symptoms. An example of this process may be seen in the sharing of controlled breathing or mindfulness skills, which group members often have learned in other contexts (although not part of the PCGT protocol, members may briefly share such techniques that they find useful for managing nightmares, sleep disturbance, intrusive idea-tions, or other PTSD symptoms). In the exchange of an array of coping skills, members commonly disclose that they have experienced relief from the broader experience of PTSD symptoms. The utilization of the iden-tified and shared skills by PCGT members acts as a PTSD-specific treatment intervention. The reduction of overall arousal breaks the chain of PTSD symptom expression and improves the overall quality of life for the group members.

Summary

Present-centered group therapy (PCGT) provides trauma-aware group treatment focused on the experience of living day-to-day life. Originally developed as an alternative to exposure-based therapy (as described in detail in chapter one), PCGT offers a person-friendly modality in which to organically develop strategies for embracing the current time frame. This "embrace" centers around: understanding and managing symptoms; handling problems, difficulties, and challenges; developing and improving relationships; and recognizing and making use of opportunities in everyday life, including pursuit of personal goals. In terms of schemas disrupted by PTSD (see Table 6.2), the modest structure, present-orientation, and in-tegration of trauma education and awareness create an opportunity for recalibration of trauma-based schemas. A key source for this recalibration is the ongoing direction and re-orientation to the present, and attention to interruptions in the present. The point of intervention may aim at re-experiencing symptoms, or hyperarousal, and will likely extend to avoid-ance, and altered cognitions and mood. The group offers practice at being in the present rather than tunneling into the traumatic past, and also, at operating at a reduced level of hyperarousal, with focus on mid-range emotion, problem solving, and strategizing as a group (which cannot readily occur in a state of hyperarousal). As a reparative experience (as noted in the "Recovery" section above), the present-focus offers a kind of "figure-ground reversal," in which the present shifts into position as "figure," allowing intrusions and arousal levels from trauma to shift into the background, connected to past experience. This approach continues to respect and validate the importance of the trauma history, while working with survivors to validate their present, and their right to engage actively in their current lives. As group members practice this focus in the company of each other, they support this shift. Through this process, survivors of trauma have occasion to gradually move toward fuller and more enlivened, spontaneous, engaged lives.

The next two chapters offer a broad context regarding the practice of present-centered group therapy. Chapter seven details the intersecting history of the field of trauma recovery, and group therapy for trauma, from which PCGT ultimately developed. Chapter eight considers adaptation of PCGT for a variety of settings that treat survivors of trauma, with key points on how to implement and deliver treatment (including telementalhealth).

Notes

1 "Present:....as a noun, 'the present time' (11c., Modern French présent) and directly from Latin praesentem (nominative praesens) 'present, at hand, in sight; immediate; prompt, instant; 'contemporary,' from present participle of præesse 'be before (someone or something), be at 'hand,' from prae- 'before (see pre-) + esse 'to be' (from PIE root *es- 'to be'). Meaning 'being there' is from mid-14c. in English......'this point in time' (opposed to past and future), c. 1300, 'the present time,' also 'act or fact of being present; portion of space around someone,' from Old French c. 1300, 'the present time,' also 'act or fact of being present; portion of space around someone,' from Old French present (n.) from Latin praesens 'being there' (see present (adj.))." (https://www.etymonline.com)

2 While our language divides time up in such a way that we categorize our experiences (past/present/future), there are languages that are purported to approach time differently – and which underscore the cultural dependence of concepts of time that we endorse in mainstream western culture. For example, Whorf (1956) identified that the Hopi language divides experience into categories of "manifest" and "unmanifest" rather than past-present-future, with everything from prior events to concrete objects and defined relationships as "manifest," and everything future or abstract as "unmanifest." A future trip down the river, an idea for constructing a new building, and an emotion would all be "unmanifest." The past, a rock, and one's physical space would be "manifest." Whorf commented that the resulting continuous experience of time would render the adage, "Tomorrow's another day," meaningless. While his conclusions have been challenged, and the realities of Hopi language may be more complex, Whorf characterized the time in Hopi culture as a flow, with events embedded in it. It may be worthwhile to consider various cultural constructions of time in understanding and treating loss of time frame in the context of trauma. However, trauma and its impact are universal human phenomena, despite varied expression across cultures reported in the literature (Sakamoto and Couto, 2017).

3 These observations are pertinent to the time in which this book is being written, given the context of the global pandemic of 2019–2020 (including its sometimes complex social context), and the racial violence occurring and exposed to scrutiny during this period. The latter has increased acknowledgement of the reality of racial and ethnic bias, from so-termed "microaggressions" to criminal acts, including those committed by representatives of the state. Present-centered group therapy, given its open-ended discussion format, offers a context in which to support survivors of trauma around racial and ethnic identity that may have been targeted under traumatic conditions, and may continue to be triggered by local and world events and ongoing life. In the context above, access to the current moment and current life can serve as a foundation for focused consideration and discussion of options, and development of creative and collaborative responses (mediating against polarization). Additionally, as the concept of being in the moment applies to both facilitators and group participants, we as facilitators can take a moment in our own lives to find a measure of freedom, and develop avenues

for positive action. The pandemic has led providers of PCGT to experience being in the "same boat" as group members in the need to respond to circumstances in the moment (which has spurred innovations in use of virtual treatment, including in the practice of PCGT; see chapter 8). Again, as being in the moment (or not) pertains to facilitators as well as group members, it has been incumbent upon our practitioners to move themselves into the moment, as well as to experience the impact of the shared pandemic circumstances, and the resonance of world events.

4 These potential outcomes are based on clinical experience in PCGT groups, rather than on the research literature, although the research literature (see chapter 2) does report positive evidence for PCGT.

References

Alford, C. F. (2013). *Trauma and forgiveness: Consequences and communities.* Cambridge: Cambridge University Press.

American Psychiatric Association. (1980). *Diagnostic and statistical manual of mental disorders* (3rd ed.). Washington, D.C.: Author.

American Psychiatric Association. (2000). *Diagnostic and statistical manual of mental disorders* (4th ed. TR). Washington, D.C.: Author.

American Psychiatric Association. (2013). *Diagnostic and statistical manual of mental disorders* (5th ed.). Washington, D.C.: Author.

Anthony, W. A. (1993). Recovery from mental illness: The guiding vision of the mental health service system in the 1990s. *Psychosocial Rehabilitation Journal, 16*(4), 11–23. https://doi.org/10.1037/h0095655

Beckett, S. (1965). The Unnamable (Three novels by Samuel Beckett: Molloy, Malone dies, The unnamable). New York, NY: Grove Press.

Bigelow, K., Boal, M., Chartier, N., & Shapiro, G. (Producers), & Bigelow, K. (Director). (2008). *The hurt locker* [Motion picture]. U.S.: Summit Entertainment.

Bohus, M., Schmahl, C., Fydrich, T., Steil, R., Müller-Engelmann, M., Herzog, J., … Priebe, K. (2019). A research programme to evaluate DBT-PTSD, a modular treatment approach for Complex PTSD after childhood abuse. *Borderline Personality Disorder and Emotion Dysregulation, 6*(1), 1–16. https://doi.org/10.1186/s40479-019-0099-y

Bormann, J. E., Thorp, S. R., Smith, E., Glickman, M., Beck, D., Plumb, D., … Heppner, P. (2018). Individual treatment of posttraumatic stress disorder using mantram repetition: A randomized clinical trial. *American Journal of Psychiatry, 175*(10), 979–988. https://doi.org/10.1176/appi.ajp.2018.17060611

Buber, M. (1970). *I and Thou.* New York, NY: Scribner.

Carmody, J. (2015). Mindfulness as a general ingredient of successful psychotherapy. In B. Ostafin, B. Robinson, & B. Meier (Eds.), *Handbook of mindfulness and self-regulation* (pp. 235–248). Springer.

Csikszentmihalyi, M. (1990). *Flow: The psychology of optimal experience.* New York, NY: Harper & Row. p. 8, 9.

Csikszentmihalyi, M. (1997). *Finding flow* (Vol. 131). New York, NY: Basic Books.

Davidson, L., O'Connell, M. J., Tondora, J., Staeheli, M., & Evans, A. C. (2005). Recovery in Serious Mental Illness: Paradigm Shift or Shibboleth? In *Recovery from severe mental illnesses: Research evidence and implications for practice* (Vol. 1, pp. 5–26). Boston, MA: Center for Psychiatric Rehabilitation.

Davis, L. L., Whetsell, C., Hamner, M. B., Carmody, J., Rothbaum, B. O., Allen, R. S., ... Bremner, J. D. (2019). A multisite randomized controlled trial of mindfulness-based stress reduction in the treatment of posttraumatic stress disorder. *Psychiatric Research and Clinical Practice, 1*(2), 39–48. https://doi.org/10.1176/appi.prcp.20180002

Deegan, P. E. (2005). The importance of personal medicine: A qualitative study of resilience in people with psychiatric disabilities. *Scandinavian Journal of Public Health.* https://doi.org/10.1080/14034950510033345.

Eliade, M., & Trask, W. (1959). *The sacred and the profane: The nature of religion.* New York: Harcourt, Brace & World.

Ellison, M. L., Belanger, L. K., Niles, B. L., Evans, L. C., & Bauer, M. S. (2018). Explication and definition of mental health recovery: A systematic review. *Administration and Policy in Mental Health and Mental Health Services Research, 45*(1), 91–102. https://doi.org/10.1007/s10488-016-0767-9

Foa, E. B., & Rothbaum, B. O. (1998). *Treating the trauma of rape: Cognitive-behavioral therapy for PTSD.* New York, NY: Guilford Press.

Ford, J., Herman, J., Armour, C., Mcfarlane, A. C., & Mwiti, G. (2019). *Keynote panel: Charting a course forward for the traumatic stress field – International perspectives.* Boston, MA: ISTSS.

Foy, D. W. (1992). *Treating PTSD: Cognitive-behavioral strategies.* New York, NY: Guilford Press.

Gagne, C., White, W., & Anthony, W. A. (2007). Recovery: A common vision for the fields of mental health and addictions. *Psychiatric Rehabilitation Journal, 31*(1), 32–37. https://doi.org/10.2975/31.1.2007.32.37

Hayes, S. C., Strosahl, K. D., & Wilson, K.G. (2012). *Acceptance and commitment therapy: The process and practice of mindful change (2nd edition).* New York, NY: The Guilford Press.

Herman, J. L., & Kallivayalil, D. (2018). *Group trauma treatment in early recovery: Promoting safety and self-care.* New York, NY: Guilford Publications.

Janoff-Bulman, R. (1992). *Shattered assumptions: Towards a new psychology of trauma.* New York, NY: Free Press.

Kosslyn, S. M. (1980). *Image and mind.* Cambridge, MA: Harvard University Press.

Lindsley, O. R. (1991). From technical jargon to plain english for application. *Journal of Applied Behavior Analysis, 24*(3), 449–458. https://doi.org/10.1901/jaba.1991.24-449

Linehan, M. (2014). *DBT skills training manual.* New York, NY: Guilford Publications.

Litz, B. T., Berke, D. S., Kline, N. K., Grimm, K., Rusowicz-Orazem, L., Resick, P. A., ... Peterson, A. L. (2019). Patterns and predictors of change in trauma-focused treatments for war-related posttraumatic stress disorder. *Journal of Consulting and Clinical Psychology, 87*(11), 1019–1029. https://doi.org/10.1037/ccp0000426

Marshall, A., & Kassar, M. (Producer), & Lyne, A. (Director). (1990). *Jacob's ladder* [Motion picture]. United States: TriStar Pictures.

Maslow, A. H. (1943). A theory of human motivation. *Psychological Review, 50*(4), 370–396.

Mazursky, P. (Producer and Director). (1989). *Enemies: A love story* [Motion picture]. United States: 20th Century Fox.

McCann, I. L. , & Pearlman, L. A., (1990). *Psychological trauma and the adult survivor: Theory, therapy, and transformation.* New York, NY: Brunner/Mazel.

Monson, C. M., & Fredman, S. J. (2012). *Cognitive-behavioral conjoint therapy for PTSD, Harnessing the healing power of relatonships.* New York, NY. Guildford Press.

Najavits, L. (2002). *Seeking safety: A treatment manual for PTSD and substance abuse.* New York, NY: Guilford Publications.

Najavits, L. M. (2015). The problem of dropout from "gold standard" PTSD therapies. *F1000prime Reports, 7.* https://doi.org/10.12703/P7-43

Neisser, U. (1967). *Cognitive psychology.* New York, NY: Appleton-Century-Crofts.

Neisser, U. (1976). *Cognition and reality: Principles and implications of cognitive psychology.* New York, NY: W H Freeman/Times Books/Henry Holt & Co.

Online Etymology Dictionary. https://www.etymonline.com, Harper, D. from circa 1995 to present.

Piaget, J. (1950). *The psychology of intelligence.* London: Routledge.

Pitman, R. K. (1989). Post-traumatic stress disorder, hormones, and memory. *Biological Psychiatry, 26*(3), 221–223. 10.1016/0006-3223(89)90033-4

Prochaska, J. O., Norcross, J. C., & DiClemente, C. C. (1994). *Changing for good: A revolutionary six-stage program for overcoming bad habits and moving your life positively forward.* New York, NY: Harper Collins.

Raskin, N. J., & Rogers, C. R. (2005). Person-centered therapy. In *Current psychotherapies* (pp. 130–165). Pacific Grove, FL: Thomson Brooks/Cole Publishing Co.

Ready, D. J., Mascaro, N., Wattenberg, M. S., Sylvers, P., Worley, V., & Bradley-Davino, B. (2018). A controlled study of group-based exposure therapy with Vietnam-era veterans. *Journal of Loss and Trauma, 23*(6), 439–457. https://doi.org/10.1080/15325024.2018.1485268

Resick, P. A., & Schnicke, M. K. (1996). Cognitive processing therapy for rape victims: A treatment manual. InJ. R. Conte (Ed.), Through interpersonal violence: The practice series. Thousand Oaks, CA: Sage Publications.

Resick, P. A., Monson, C. M., & Chard, K. M. (2016). *Cognitive processing therapy for PTSD: A comprehensive manual.* New York, NY: Guilford Publications.

Resick, Patricia A., Wachen, Jennifer Schuster, Mintz, Jim, Young-McCaughan, Stacey, Roache, John D., Borah, Adam M., Borah, Elisa V., Dondanville, Katherine A., Hembree, Elizabeth A., Litz, Brett T., Peterson, Alan L. Resick, P. A., Wachen, J. S., Mintz, J., Young-McCaughan, S., Roache, J. D., Borah, A. M., ... Peterson, A. L. (2015). A randomized clinical trial of group cognitive processing therapy compared with group present-centered therapy for PTSD among active duty military personnel. *Journal of Consulting and Clinical Psychology, 83*(6), 1058–1068. https://doi.org/10.1037/ccp0000016

Resnick, S. G., Fontana, A., Lehman, A. F., & Rosenheck, R. A. (2005). An empirical conceptualization of the recovery orientation. *Schizophrenia Research, 75*(1), 119–128. https://doi.org/10.1016/j.schres.2004.05.009

Resnick, S. G., & Goldberg, R. W. (2019). Psychiatric rehabilitation for veterans and the evolution of the field. *Psychiatric Rehabilitation Journal, 42*(3), 207. https://doi.org/10.1037/prj0000383.

Resnick, S. G., & Rosenheck, R. A. (2006). Recovery and positive psychology: Parallel themes and potential synergies. *Psychiatric Services, 57*(1), 120–122.

Sakamoto, I., & Couto, S. (2017). Group work with immigrants and refugees. In C. D. Garvin, L. M. Gutiérrez, & M. J. Galinsky (Eds.), *Handbook of social work with groups* (pp. 360–383). New York, NY: Guilford Press.

Steenkamp, M. M., Litz, B. T., & Marmar, C. R. (2020). First-line psychotherapies for military-related PTSD. *JAMA.* https://doi.org/10.1001/jama.2019.20825.

Tedeschi, R. G., & Calhoun, L. G. (2004). Posttraumatic growth: Conceptual foundations and empirical evidence. *Psychological Inquiry, 15*(1), 1–18.

van der Kolk, B. A., McFarlane, A. C., & Weisaeth, L. (Eds.). (1996). *Traumatic stress: The effects of overwhelming experience on mind, body, and society.* New York, NY: Guilford Press.

Vonnegut, K. (1969). *Slaughterhouse-five: Or, the children's crusade, a duty-dance with death.* Chapter 2, p. 23. New York, NY: Modern Library.

Walser, R. D., & Westrup, D. (2007). *Acceptance and commitment therapy for the treatment of post-traumatic stress disorder and trauma-related problems: A practitioner's guide to using mindfulness and acceptance strategies.* Oakland, CA: New Harbinger Publications.

Whorf, B. L. (1956). *Language, thought, and reality: Selected writings of Benjamin Lee Whorf.* Cambridge, MA: MIT Press.

Winnicott, D. W. (1989). The concept of trauma in relation to the development of the individual within the family. In C. Winnicott, R. Shepherd, & M. Davis (Eds.), *Psychoanalytic explorations* (pp. 130–148). London: Karnac Books.

Yalom, I. D. (1995). *The theory and practice of group psychotherapy.* New York, NY: Basic Books.

Young, J. E., Klosko, J. S. & Weishaar, M. E. (2003). *Schema therapy: A practitioner's guide.* New York, NY: Guilford Press.

7 Group Psychotherapy and Treatment of Trauma: A History

Daniel Lee Gross and Melissa S. Wattenberg

Group Psychotherapy and Treatment of Trauma: A History

Present-centered group therapy (PCGT) has been strongly influenced by a lineage of treatment approaches beginning in World War II that evolved into the evidenced-based treatments of the last two decades. An understanding of the evolution of group treatment of post-traumatic stress disorder (PTSD) can offer the clinician a useful frame of reference. While separate histories of group therapy and trauma therapy are well-documented in books and journals, the marriage of the two has been less frequently examined. Understanding the fits and starts of this unique history across emerging schools of thought and socio-political movements, culminating in their eventual influence on clinical practice, can add nuance to the practitioner's perspective on the treatment options currently available for treating PTSD. Appreciating the historical context of trauma-related treatment can shape the practitioner's conceptualization and approach. The retrospective exploration of trauma-related group treatment (TRGT) also underscores the absence of evidence that one singular treatment approach – in the past or present – completely and consistently addresses all manifestations of PTSD, including highly challenging symptoms, co-occurring disorders, concomitant psychosocial losses, and existential concerns. History, in this context, favors a broad view with an array of interventions, and may serve to inoculate against a "one-size-fits-all" approach, as cautioned by Maslow (1966): "If all you have is a hammer, everything you look at will be a nail" (p. 15).

The themes that carry across the history of group treatment for PTSD include both an array of treatment choices (including past- and present-oriented), and the survivor's need for validation by others with shared experience (as occurs in effective group treatment). The converging history of the recovery movement (Kurtz, 2014) and the related psychosocial rehabilitation model (Anthony & Farkas, 2009) have informed group treatment as well in ways consonant with the lessons in the PTSD field: it is essential to start with the individual as a person, to make a collaborative assessment of the individual's needs from a trauma-aware perspective, and to restore faith in oneself, others, and the world.

Current Status in the Field

Over time, group treatment, PTSD interventions, and recovery in general have moved from a narrower perspective (with the risk of limiting interventions) to a broader, more nuanced understanding where a variety of accepted evidence-based "doors" provide accessible treatment tailored to survivors of trauma. This development in the field of trauma treatment has been especially important given the many manifestations of PTSD, and the importance of empowerment and personal choice for trauma survivors who have experienced disempowerment.

At the same time, while an array of approaches is available to treat PTSD, residual tensions remain among practitioners regarding the value of "uncovering" or "exposing" traumatic memories vs. working with survivors in present-oriented modalities. That is: do trauma survivors need to recount, in detail, the traumatic memories and events in order to recover from PTSD symptoms? Or can PTSD symptoms be treated through an approach focusing instead on coping and managing current symptoms and present-day living? Despite many accepted non-trauma-focused treatments for PTSD, from mindfulness-based stress reduction (Carmody & Baer, 2008) to seeking safety (Najavits, 2002), this age-old tension persists and must be addressed in order to understand the meaning of what appears to be a split within the field. Case in point: when we have presented together on PCGT at national conferences for group therapists, often some conference attendees have challenged whether it is possible to treat PTSD without the option of delving into, unearthing, and processing the traumatic events. In treating a population for whom choice is important for the survivor, some clinicians may feel a parallel sense of being disempowered when a treatment protocol – even a flexible one like PCGT – limits some of the clinicians' choices in the interest of maintaining a consistent contract with group members. Theoretical orientation also contributes to these differences; for some practitioners coming from either a strict analytic or strict cognitive behavior therapy (CBT) perspective, a present-centered approach may appear irrational, counterintuitive, even paradoxical. In one of our recent presentations, differing camps among participants argued their points. One position was that focusing on traumatic incidents in group is the sine qua non for effective trauma treatment. Others maintained that focusing on traumatic memories can lead to hyperarousal contagion and therapeutic impasse. That afternoon's robust exchange mirrored the dialectical process that occurred across the genesis and evolution of TRGT (and PCGT in particular), leading to a point in our current understanding of trauma and its sequelae that allows for both trauma-focused and present-oriented approaches, depending on the client's preferences and clinical indications.

Models in Conflict

The debate of whether or not to uncover traumatic memories is emblematic of past and present rivalries between treatment paradigms. Rothstein (1980) described theoretical rivalry as "paradigm competition" and attributed the process of competition as an impetus for psychotherapeutic innovation. Borrowing from Kuhn's theory of paradigmatic evolution, Rothstein embellished on Kuhn's (1970) principles by applying psychoanalytical themes. Dogma (or what Rothstein described as narcissistic investment in established therapies) would eventually become questioned and revised, leading clinicians to develop innovative psychotherapeutic evolution in theory and technique. As Rothstein states, "The consistent awareness of the therapeutic limits of psychoanalysis has led its practitioners to seek modifications that would yield more favorable results" (p. 391). Such recurrent paradigmatic tensions in TRGT history have served as the catalyst for clinical generativity. At the same time, these historical tensions remain alive and well in the current trauma field.

Historical Rejection of Trauma Impact

Even if he didn't explicitly use Rothstein's terms, Erwin Parson (1984) attributed the "conspicuous barrenness" of literature on the topic of group treatment for trauma (p. 153) to paradigm conflict, pertaining to another rift in the field (concerning the validity of the PTSD diagnosis, a relatively new diagnosis at that time). According to Parson, this tension rested between two perspectives: the predisposition perspective and "condition of the event" perspective. Predisposition theorists posited that pre-existing characterological vulnerabilities or deficits led to succumbing to the traumatic nature of the event. Condition of the event proponents argued that intrinsic factors of the event itself led to the distressing psychological sequelae. Competition between these two schools of thought, according to Parson, gave "some useful explanation for the reasons the literature on the group treatment of combat veterans and other survivors of trauma is virtually nonexistent, despite the fact that reactions to catastrophic events is not new" (p. 154). His observations pointed to the recent history at that time of discounting trauma and re-configuring in Freudian terms some weakness in the individual based, on developmental history, as the primary issue to address in therapy. Research following the war in Vietnam, however, provided evidence of more direct impact of traumatic events on development of PTSD symptoms. Keane and colleagues (1989) identified that the relationship between duration and intensity of combat exposure best predicted PTSD symptoms, as opposed to other historical factors. Even after the diagnosis of PTSD was established by the American Psychiatric Association in the *Diagnostic and Statistical Manual of Mental Disorders, Third Edition*

(DSM-III) in 1980 (APA, 1980), it took over a decade for this perspective on trauma to fully take hold in the field.

The literature devoted solely to the historical arc of TRGT, from its inception to current modalities, is relatively lean, considering the pre-valence of trauma-based group therapies provided in private practice, community clinics, hospitals, and other mental health settings. This chapter provides a brief overview and consideration of how the friction of paradigm competition bore therapeutic fruit in this ever-developing field. To be sure, the distillation of TRGT history in this chapter underscores the immensity and complexity of the topic, a rich and epic narrative deserving a book of its own.

Underpinnings: The 1940s

Early writings on TRGT can be traced back to the early 1940s. Bion (1961) created his theory of group therapy while treating World War I veterans in England, although his writings do not reflect a formalized treatment ap-proach targeting trauma or its sequelae. Nonetheless, his concepts laid the groundwork for later clinicians, whose writings in trauma treatment bor-rowed from Bion's pioneering theories (Klein & Schermer, 2000; Parson, 1984). One of the earliest recorded moments of TRGT treatment occurred in 1944 (Rome, 1944). Rome noted how group therapy led to de-stigmatization and emotional release with active duty military personnel. A year later, Dynes (1945) discussed how group therapy with soldiers provided a "better adjustment of the patient in their disabilities and home environment" (p. 34). Carl Rogers and Robert Neville (Erskine, 2013), while at the University of Chicago, developed a non-directive treatment of war neurosis in 1945. Borrowing from Harry Stack Sullivan's interpersonal theory, Rogers and Neville created a group approach emphasizing "a democratic process of equality and encouraging group members to share their traumatic stories and feelings with each other. By telling these stories over and over again while receiving empathic responses, the traumas of war were healed" (p. 264). Sparked by the needs of the hour, these therapeutic innovators spontaneously responded to a set of symptoms not yet catalogued within a single diagnosis; their incipient templates would later leave their mark on evidenced-based approaches.

In a separate context influencing the zeitgeist of the 1930s and 1940s, social worker Grace Coyle (1937) of the Settlement House movement noted in her book *Studies in Group Behavior* (1937) the importance of cultivating an esprit de corps among immigrants when assisting their adjustment to a new environment and helping them access resources. Her work identified use of groups as a powerful tool. While her groups were not intended specifically as therapy, some of the same benefits accrued. And while the target of her work was not trauma, it is likely that there were many trauma survivors among the immigrants assisted within this movement.

Slow Start and Early Developments: The 1950s

TRGT gradually advanced in the 1950s. The general lack of documented TRGT can be understood in the context of the peripheral status of group treatment across these years and the lack of a formal diagnosis addressing trauma. In his book *American Therapy: The Rise of Psychotherapy in the United States,* Jonathon Engel (2009) noted that group therapy slowly grew to be recognized as a viable treatment option, and by 1956 it was a "marginal but accepted approach to psychotherapy" (p. 126). Individual psychotherapy remained the dominant mode of treatment. Engels continued: "some 1,000 therapists across the country counted themselves as group practitioners, and a variety of social work and psychology programs had begun to mentor students in the practice" (p. 126). There is a remarkable exception: *Traumatic War Neuroses Five Years Later* (Futterman & Pumpian-Mindlin, 1951). Here, the authors described psychoanalytically informed approaches for the treatment of what was then referred to as "war neurosis." In a case study combining individual and group treatment for a 26-year-old combat veteran, the writers described the following case:

> The veteran's presenting complaints were anxiety, irritability, rapid heartbeat, combat dreams, headaches, fears of riding in elevators and of the dark, and an obsessive fear of killing his child. He was seen both in individual and in group therapy ... in one dramatic group session he spoke of throwing a hand grenade into a fox hole and later finding a dead German soldier in it ... in the individual session that followed, he became aware of the relation between his childhood insecurity and inability to express hostility on the one hand and his combat breakdown on the other. (pp. 404–405)

This clinical scenario would be recognizable to today's clinician, from the somatic experience to the impact of past trauma. Even more salient in today's debate in TRGT is the author's focus towards identifying and treating traumatic memories. The next decade would usher in a wave of revolutionary theories that would not only dramatically change the course of psychotherapy, but also result in a broadening temporal shift of focus, to include the present as well as the traumatic past.

The Rise of Group Therapy and Trauma-Related Approaches: The 1960s

The 1960s blossomed into a therapeutic "rich time" (Erskine, 2010). Therapeutic trends, such as Eric Berne's (1966) modified psychodynamic groups, Fritz Perls' (1967) concept of therapy in the group, and the emergence of encounter groups influenced TRGT into the 1970s.

Encounter groups in particular relied on provocative measures that would later be deemed traumatizing and shaming to group participants (Engel, 2009; Erskine 2010; Yalom & Leszcz, 2005). For example, in Schutz's book, *Elements of Encounter* (1973), group guidelines consisted of the following: "Men are encouraged to wrestle rather than fight with their fists," and to "take off your clothes when it feels right" (p. 64). However, Schutz also advocated for a "here and now" approach, stating, "this helps you to stay with feelings and avoids your going off into safer areas invested with less real emotional energy" (p. 63). Schutz's and Perls' emphasis on here-and-now approaches, although radical at the time, would later be streamlined into TRGT theory and practice. Their eschewing of exploration of past traumas, and instead embracing of present concerns, planted the seeds for the advancement of non-trauma-focused treatments for PTSD. Not all institutions warmed to the iconoclastic therapies of the 1960s, although even in large, traditional organizations such as the Veterans Administration (VA – Now the Veterans Health Administration (VHA)), paradigmatic shifts were afoot.

In their article "Persistent Stress Reaction After Combat," Archibald and Tuddenham (1965) contraindicated present focus in their work with veterans at the VA: "the current emphasis on the 'here and now' in psychotherapy in conjunction with the combat veteran's tendency to avoid discussing his traumatic combat experiences may easily create a tacit agreement between the therapist and the veteran to avoid the subject" (p. 480). In a prescient show of endorsement, the authors campaigned for group treatment over individual therapy at a time before clinicians used group therapy as a widespread modality for trauma:

> We feel that group therapy has advantages over individual therapy for men with combat syndrome. Our hypothesis is simple: combat was experienced in a group setting and can best be abreacted in one ... we deliberately recreate a "band of brothers," and foster the abreaction which they have hitherto assiduously avoided. (pp. 480–481)

Here, quite possibly, is the first endorsement of not only group treatment as the preferred modality for treating trauma, but also the remarkable emphasis of intentional use of interpersonal rapport as a therapeutic element in the recovery process. This description is reminiscent of the pioneering work of Coyle (1937) in the settlement houses, suggesting the ameliorative impact of "esprit de corps" (noted earlier in this chapter) in facilitating adjustment for immigrants. Decades later, Yalom wrote of how positive outcomes in group therapy rested on group cohesion (Yalom & Leszcz, 2005). Within the annals of TRGT, however, Archibald and Tuddenham's case study represented a first in many respects, including the use of group dynamics to address avoidance. Group solidarity as an intervention for trauma treatment took further root within the political shifts in the next decade and beyond, evolving into an indispensable, recurring factor in the changing tides and currents of TRGT history.

Activism and Advocacy: The 1970s

By the beginning of the 1970s, the creative waves of group experimentation fueled by the urgency of activism profoundly shaped the direction of TRGT. Vietnam Veterans Against the War created "rap groups" in New York City in 1970 in response to the shortcomings in available mental health care for Vietnam veterans (Galloucis & Kaufman, 1988). Rap groups originated from the self-help movement and tended to be informal and supportive rather than formally clinically driven (Parson, 1984). Galloucis and Kaufman (1988) underscored the distinction: "although there was an important therapeutic element, the emphasis was on communality and shared commitment" (p. 93). Veterans' grass roots advocacy spurred by the lack of mental health resources overlapped temporally with the "battered women's movement" (Walker, 2006) and the women's rights movement in which small non-clinical focus groups were common. These movements co-created a watershed moment in the history of TRGT. Group support spurred by the women's rights movement awakened the public's awareness of sexual assault and trauma, leading to newfound group approaches.

Beginning in the early 1970s, rape crisis centers began treating women (Herman, 1992). Within a decade, the number of available clinics grew in scope and accessibility. Paralleling the grass roots action of Vietnam veterans, feminist activists created alternatives to the paucity of treatment within the mental healthcare system (Herman, 1992). As the awareness of sexual trauma grew for women, so did the recognition of child abuse. TRGT emerged as a treatment approach for survivors of sexual abuse, as exemplified in Tsai and Wagner's group treatment of adult survivors of childhood sexual abuse (Tsai & Wagner, 1978). By weaving group and individual treatment approaches, the authors targeted reduction of guilt/shame and provided education regarding the sequelae of trauma. The cumulative impact of treatment targeting the traumatic effects of sexual trauma continued to shape the arc of TRGT (Herman, 1992; Resick & Schnicke, 1992). Herman's *trauma recovery group* in the late 1970s, following research for her book *Father-Daughter Incest* (Herman & Hirschman, 1981), was based on observations of just a few groups in different parts of the therapeutic community treating adult survivors of childhood sexual abuse at that time (Mendelsohn et al., 2011). This group became the foundation for later treatment developments that eventually included preparatory and post-intensive groups that were not focused on trauma details; however, this early iteration was focused on trauma narrative. The inclusion criteria set for this group initially were: positive regard for group therapy, ability to function on a daily basis, and ongoing contact with an individual therapist (Herman & Schatzow, 1984).

With public awareness of trauma came more unconventional group practices. Engel (2009) described psychotherapy in that era as "balkanized ... the dominant triad of psychodynamic, cognitive, and humanistic therapies splintered repeatedly" into what he described as "recapture" therapies. Recapture therapies "aimed to help clients and patients recapture lost memories, relive past traumas, face repressed memories, and admit to base trusts of their own histories" (Engel, p. 179). Primal scream therapy and rebirthing therapy exemplified such therapies. Blurred boundaries between facilitator and group members in addition to controversial techniques such as wearing diapers and acting out childhood traumas led to, in Engel's words, "bizarre and even tragic outcomes" (p. 179). As standardized treatment evolved and incorporated research and outcomes, these unorthodox therapies began to wane in their stronghold as accepted treatment approaches for trauma.

A landmark moment in the advancement of group therapy occurred with the publishing of Irvin Yalom's first edition of *The Theory and Practice of Group Psychotherapy* (Yalom, 1970). Yalom's seminal contribution to group treatment, like Bion and Coyle several decades before, provided a valuable framework for group development and dynamics of group technique. Based on research, Yalom created a systematic and comprehensive tome on group treatment, weaving elements of psychoanalysis and modern concepts, including here-and-now approaches. In his fifth edition written with Molyn Leszcz, Yalom and his coauthor questioned the more controversial elements of encounter groups and, without outright dismissal, addressed the potential toxic effects of encounter techniques (Yalom & Leszcz, 2005). Their theory and concepts continue to inform current schools of thought in TRGT. Today's clinicians would be hard-pressed not to witness Yalom's therapeutic factors of universality or instillation of hope (as well as other identified therapeutic factors) when conducting trauma-related group sessions.

Diagnosis and Advancement: The 1980s

Unfolding clinical developments in the 1980s led to significant shifts in theory and practice of TRGT. Evidence-based approaches began to edge out older, traditionally psychodynamically oriented treatment approaches (Engel, 2009). Evidenced-based group treatment could be understood through MacGowan's (2008) definition: "a process of the judicious and skillful application in group work of the best evidence, based on research merit, impact, and applicability, using evaluation to ensure that desired results are achieved" (p. 3). The dominance of evidenced-based approaches can be attributed, in part, to the establishment of diagnostic criteria, prevalence estimates, and increased research funding (Norton et al., 1995) for mental health diagnoses and treatment. Other factors included the federal government as a "dominant purchaser of psychotherapy services through its Medicare and veterans' health programs as well as through the many private insurers it contracted on behalf of its civilian employees" (Engel, 2009, p. 190). In 1980, the *Diagnostic and Statistical Manual of Mental Disorder, Third Edition* (DSM-III) defined the first diagnostic criteria for PTSD, sparking new interest in trauma treatment (Galloucis & Kaufman, 1988). Psychodynamic approaches for group trauma treatment continued in clinical settings, although clinicians, such as Parson (1984), acknowledged how the multifaceted problems of trauma survivors underscored the limitations of psychoanalytic group approaches. Herman and Schatzow (1984) continued to provide a ten-session group for incest survivors, which found a home at the Victims of Violence program in Cambridge, MA, in the mid-1980s (Mendelsohn et al., 2011). The group began with introduction and establishment of ground rules, followed by middle sessions devoted to goal definition, storytelling (trauma narrative), and goal achievement, followed by consolidation of therapeutic gains in the termination phase.

Increased awareness of survivor guilt and the impact of substance abuse experienced by survivors of trauma (Parson, 1984; Galloucis & Kaufman, 1988) widened the repertoire of options for clinicians. Challenges to treatment included:

- Psychosocial disruption across many dimensions (e.g., family issues, employment issues, loss of income)
- Loss of interpersonal skills related to avoidance, hyperarousal, and alexithymia
- Distressing cognitive-emotional patterns (e.g., survivor guilt, shame, self-blame)
- Existential issues and loss of meaning
- Re-experiencing-induced disconnection and reactivity
- Commonly co-occurring disorders (e.g., depression, panic with agoraphobia, and substance abuse or dependence)
- Secondary trauma (due to poor or inadequate community response following the trauma)
- Delayed onset of symptoms
- Fluctuation of symptoms in response to environmental triggers (Parson, 1984; Galloucis & Kaufman, 1988)

The presenting client concerns expressed upon arrival in treatment broadened the needs to be met by clinicians, calling for a much fuller repertoire of options. Beysner (1985), for example, blended gestalt therapy and CBT in a group treatment for veterans in order to recapture the present and engage the trauma survivor despite the powerful influence of past events drawing survivors away from current issues and personal life.

CBT advanced as an evidenced-based approach for TRGT. The field of trauma called for targeted yet comprehensive approaches, including group treatment. CBT was a natural fit, offering specific and measurable interventions and outcomes. CBT groups focusing on trauma gained prominence in the 1980s (Parson, 1984) and by the late 1980s were established as promising in the treatment of PTSD (Galloucis & Kaufman, 1988; Resick, Jordan, Girelli, Hutter, & Marhoefer-Dvorak, 1988). The rising use of exposure therapy, behavioral rehearsal, and cognitive restructuring (Foa & Rauch, 2004; Foy et al., 2002) gave credibility to CBT groups as potentially effective, research-supported treatment for trauma. However, as with psychodynamic therapies, these focused CBT treatments also encountered challenges in effectively treating the sequelae of trauma. By the end of the 1980s and beginning of the 1990s, CBT approaches infused schema theory (Neisser, 1976) from the academic literature on cognition as an augmentation of CBT. The complexities of trauma treatment expanded cognitive theory and compelled clinicians to address the multifaceted issues inherent in prolonged or complex PTSD. As TRGT branched out into further variations over the next two decades, this sprouting of CBT to include more complex cognitive processes enhanced TRGT approaches.

Beyond Diagnosis and Establishment: The 1990s

TRGT grew exponentially in the 1990s. In Judith Herman's landmark work, *Trauma and Recovery* (1992), the author found the diagnostic criteria for PTSD insufficient and defined a syndrome specific to prolonged, repeated traumas: complex post-traumatic stress disorder. An innovator in this developing field, Herman, along with her team at the Victims of Violence Program, drew on her earlier work with incest survivors (Herman & Schatzow, 1984) to inform a more heterogeneous and elaborate three-stage group treatment model intended to mirror the trauma recovery process: safety and self-care in the introductory phase (a non-trauma-focused intervention aimed at establishing control, and literally helping survivors create safety); a trauma-focused phase (remembrance and mourning); and a third phase (reconnection) focused again on the present and creating connection with life beyond trauma. The refining of PTSD-related concepts by pioneers in the field, and dissemination of theories and recommendations for PTSD treatment, resulted in a proliferation of group treatments. Time-limited interventions such as cognitive processing therapy (CPT; Resick et al., 1988; Resick & Schnicke, 1992), integrated cognitive therapy, and schema theory (Janoff-Bulman, 1992; McCann & Pearlman, 1990a). Lisa Najavits (2002) created Seeking Safety, an evidence-based, present-oriented approach for treating the struggles of dually diagnosed survivors of trauma (PTSD and substance dependence) from a CBT perspective. As treatments proliferated, Johnson et al. (1994) reflected on a shift in the field from "first-generation" (trauma-oriented) treatments to "second-generation" programs focusing on "the present and future rather than the past, on involvement with family and community rather than fellow veterans, and on relationships outside of the Vietnam/trauma circle" (p. 227). However, group therapy focused on trauma continued to be a strong interest in the field, leading to the VA Cooperative Study 420's development of a prolonged-exposure-based group (Trauma-Focused Group Therapy (TFGT)), for which PCGT was developed as a comparison (Schnurr et al., 2003, detailed in chapter one).

The expanding media coverage of natural disasters and traumatic aftermath, accompanied by calls for a therapeutic helping response, compelled group therapists to alleviate suffering through TRGT modalities. The devastating destruction of Hurricane Katrina in 2005 and the concomitant impact on survivors underscored the need to address not only the immediate psychological aftermath of trauma, but also the painful ongoing effects and anniversary reactions. Debriefing groups were introduced typically on-site (e.g., at schools or disaster relief centers) either during a prolonged trauma, or in the immediate aftermath of a disaster, using trauma-focused interventions. Support groups in the aftermath of a disaster differed from debriefing groups in that care, often on-site, extended for months or years after a disaster (Dembert & Simmer, 2000, p. 240), with a less targeted, broader life focus. Dembert and Simmer's two-prong intervention illustrated the implementation of TRGT within disaster relief programs, integrating debriefing and support sessions within one treatment modality. While too numerous to cover exhaustively, examples and applications of TRGT during the 1990s included AIDS support groups, chronic and terminal physical illness supports, groups for traumatization in children, clinical and self-help groups for adults abused as children, formal and informal supports for "battered women," programs for survivors of rape, and groups for survivors of political persecution and torture (Klein & Schermer, 2000; Classen & Yalom, 1995).

The potential toll on therapists providing trauma treatment gained attention in the decade of the 1990s. McCann and Pearlman (1990b) observed that clinicians providing repeated, intense trauma-focused treatment began to experience PTSD symptoms similar to those of their clients, leading the authors to describe the phenomena as "vicarious traumatization." Similarly, countertransference received renewed attention from mental health professionals working in the trauma field. Of the various definitions of countertransference, Saakvitne (2005) offered a succinct definition: "the response the therapist has to a group, members of the group, and the group's dynamics" (p. 146). The author described how the impact of delivering trauma treatment could create a Gordian knot intertwining the two themes, with countertransference creating susceptibility to vicarious trauma, and, reciprocally, vicarious trauma impeding the clinician's ability to access countertransferential awareness. Peer consultation and support were recommended to intervene in this process, and engender greater insight and awareness. Others saw counter-transference as embodying useful information for the group facilitators. Taking a psychodynamic object-relations stance, Weinberg, Nuttman-Shwartz, and Gilmore (2005) viewed the clinicians' reactions in trauma groups as opportunities:

> … therapists dealing with trauma and disasters should be able to contain all the projected parts and emotional detritus, elaborate it within themselves, and return these projections to their source in a way that advances group members' development. (p. 198)

Aware of the potentially harmful effects on the provider, clinical experts throughout the decade recommended ongoing use of supervision, consultation, therapy, and peer-clinician support as a means to mitigate vicarious trauma and effectively explore countertransference (McCann & Pearlman, 1990b; Saakvitne, 2005). McCann and Pearlman (1990b) designed a weekly treatment meeting protocol, devoting the first hour to case consultation and the second to how therapists responded psychologically to survivors, describing the latter hour as "feelings time" (p. 145). That the tentacles of trauma wrapped around the practitioner as well as the survivor leant further credibility concerning the impact of trauma, contributing to the robustness of this field and underscoring the vulnerabilities at play for both the provider and the client.

Age of Dissemination: The 2000s

The 2000s harkened further blossoming of TRGT approaches and innovations in the trauma field. A literature review by Shea et al. (2009) noted TRGT options that included psychodynamic, interpersonal, process, present-centered, exposure, imagery rehearsal, feminist insight model, feminist empowerment, substance abuse, and process-oriented treatments. Klein and Schermer (2000) attributed the ongoing growth of TRGT to the effects of living in a global community and the widening dissemination of PTSD treatment. Their computer search of the literature identified three articles in 1970, eight in the 1980s, and 19 in the 1990s. They observed accordingly that, "the literature on trauma and groups has increased exponentially over three decades" (p. 40). In 2000, researchers compared the relative effectiveness of TRGT among supportive, psychodynamic, and cognitive behavioral modalities, leading the authors to state, "positive treatment outcomes were reported in most studies" (Foy et al., 2000, p. 170).

Present-centered group therapy was developed in 1997 and reported in a scholarly journal for the first time in 2003, in the context of a VA

Cooperative Studies Program 420 (CSP-420), the largest controlled trial on treatment of Vietnam Veterans by the VA National Center for PTSD enlisting ten sites (Schnurr et al., 2003). As a part of that study, Dr. Shea originated and collaboratively developed PCGT as a non-specific treatment control to test the effectiveness of trauma-focused group therapy (TFGT) in Vietnam veterans with PTSD (see chapter one). PCGT was devoted to establishing rapport, providing PTSD and related education, problem solving, and addressing interpersonal difficulties and group interactions (Schnurr et al., 2003). TFGT, by comparison, implemented elements of prolonged exposure therapy, cognitive restructuring, psychoeducation, relapse prevention, and skills development. Results from the CSP-420 study concluded both PCGT and TFGT were effective treatment for PTSD (see chapters one and two).

The catastrophic September 2001 attack on the World Trade Center Towers in New York City generated even wider usage of trauma-focused interventions and trauma-related bereavement groups (Phillips, 2009). In light of the immediate need, the American Group Psychotherapy Association and the Eastern Group Psychotherapy Society funded by a grant from the *New York Times Company Foundation* and the New York City Mental Health Association, came together to educate practitioners about group trauma treatment. This collaboration culminated in a large conference (held in May 2002 in New York City) presenting a wide variety of evidence-based group treatments (American Group Psychotherapy Association 2002). These treatments were then further disseminated in a series of smaller training venues and publications (e.g., Foy et al., 2004) and eventually in a text for group practitioners treating survivors of catastrophic disasters (Schein et al., 2006). The aftermath of Hurricane Katrina in 2005 led to group interventions and the sponsoring of wellness workshops provided by the World Council for Psychotherapy and the Louisiana Group Psychotherapy Society, producing TRGT interventions that continued to address anniversary reactions and related psychological sequelae (Nemeth et al., 2012). One such approach utilized CBT for treating children in schools and communities affected by Hurricane Katrina (Jaycox et al., 2010). TRGT diversified into further creative paths incorporating equine therapy (Kinney, Eakman, Lassell, & Wood, 2019), Acceptance Commitment Therapy (Casselman & Pemberton, 2015), and mindfulness-based approaches (Bremner et al., 2017; O'Malley, 2015; Polusny et al., 2015; Stephenson, Simpson, Martinez, & Kearney, 2017)

As TRGT evolved, the literature began to address specific needs of survivors of trauma, and to consider the importance of sequencing treatment interventions. While the cognitive processing therapy (CPT) manual developed during this time period adhered to a prescriptive, schematic approach (Resick et al., 2017), it began with education about trauma and PTSD. Versions were developed to meet the needs of specific populations (e.g., veterans). Herman's (1992) well-established group treatment model for trauma described in the previous section continued to be one of the few models articulating a therapeutic course involving stages of treatment (as noted, beginning with safety and self-care – including meditation, yoga, and trauma education – prior to delving into intensive trauma-focused content), and then followed by a present-oriented, post-intensive group reconnecting the survivor to everyday life.

Seeking Safety (Najavits, 2002) introduced a present-focused approach integrating substance abuse and PTSD treatment, in a versatile model to be delivered in either individual or group therapy. Borrowing from Herman's blueprint, Najavits' design has enfolded safe coping skills, case management, and interpersonal skills. Najavits has also emphasized the need for flexible options and further research on optimal treatment levels and staging.

The earlier friction between treatment approaches diminished in the 2000s, while options for comprehensive and compatible frameworks for treating PTSD developed, with increasing recognition of the role of the survivor in collaboratively choosing a workable treatment approach. Rothstein (1980) advocated for a similar outcome, one that would embrace various viewpoints rather than supplanting one paradigm over another, observing that paradigms are "imperfect and improvable" (p. 394). Following suit, residential treatment programs embodied dialectical integration in the 2000s to salubrious effect. The Real Life Heroes program (Kagan & Spinazzola, 2013) adopted a wide ranging, patterned approach blending storytelling, trauma-focused, present-oriented, and family therapy elements for traumatized youth. In a similar fashion, the VA PTSD residential programs (Menefee et al., 2016) designed a patchwork of trauma-focused interventions, present-centered skills, dialectical behavioral therapy, and Seeking Safety modalities using group therapy formats.

Group and Individual Treatment

Whereas clinicians historically weighed the pros and cons of individual or combined therapy (Gans, 1990), Herman and Schatzow (1984) required combined therapy as a criterion for commencing trauma-focused treatment. Suzanne Phillips (2009) addressed integrating individual, couples, and group therapy within a trauma-centered framework. By noting the "complex and circuitous" (p. 104) recovery process, Phillips advocated for the interplay of combined modalities and viewed the blending of combined treatment as synergistic. The decision to separate or combine treatment remained an organic, unfolding process (described here in the context of a disaster):

> In the aftermath of such disaster, what people need as a group, and what they psychologically need as individuals from the acute stage to long term recovery is complex, fluid, and at times as unexpected as the disaster itself. (p. 89)

Some TRGT manuals, such as those for CPT, do not comment regarding considerations of combined treatment within the context of delivering trauma-focused content (Resick et al., 2017), and related studies indicate individual CPT to be more effective than group CPT (Dubovsky, 2016). In the CSP-420 study by Schnurr and colleagues (2003), both treatment conditions (PCGT and TFGT) included ongoing case management to address any issues that might interfere with group treatment. Throughout our time providing PCGT, we sometimes combined individual CPT or other individual work with PCGT. On more than several occasions, a cross-pollination of recovery unfolded: the PCGT was supportive of individual therapy, while individual CPT therapy led group members to process their insights with their peers in PCGT (without changing the open-ended, present-oriented focus of the group). However, PCGT has been offered with and without accompanying individual therapy based on a collaborative approach underscoring the client's choice of treatment options.

Current Time Frame

The growing array of TRGT options in 2020 has fortified the field with substantial choices of group modalities for PTSD. Research elaborating facets and nuances of PTSD has pushed the field of PTSD treatment in corresponding ways, yielding advanced implementation of treatments specific to symptoms and concomitant psychosocial issues. Group treatment for trauma can be expected to remain a formidable modality for trauma survivors.

This promise is even more salient in 2020, in the context of the massive corona virus outbreak. Notably, as of the writing of this chapter, the world is experiencing the collective trauma of coping with a pandemic. The devastating path of the COVID-19 virus will require innovative, efficacious interventions, including trauma-aware interventions. Expansion of group treatments and modes of delivery can be expected to develop in response to this crisis. Remote video conferencing is already in use, and clinicians are rapidly shifting from office to telework and telehealth platforms (see chapter eight for specifics regarding telehealth approaches) as they provide both individual and group support for PTSD. On a professional note, one of the authors started telehealth sessions for a PCGT cohort that began in physical closeness in a clinical room prior to the outbreak of COVID-19. While some treatment modalities may not translate well into a telehealth platform, particularly during a global crisis, PCGT is geared to respond to the moment and to deliver clarification and support through the group process itself. The group members' willingness to shift from office to videoconferencing in order to continue PCGT not only speaks to the resilience and commitment of trauma survivors, but also to the compelling, adaptive nature of PCGT in the face of ongoing, threatening world events.

A proliferation of variations on telehealth treatments with increasing nuance and specificity can be anticipated, which will maximize access to treatment and traverse as yet unknown paths towards recovery.

Summary

A retrospective gaze into the dynamic history of TRGT can help clinicians appreciate the variety and range of modalities available to today's clinician. The historical roots, subsequent debate, and clinical advances have yielded a substantial array of treatment options. PCGT lands at a crossroads in the field of trauma treatment, reifying the essential benefits of group therapy to meet the needs of trauma survivors. As a recovery-friendly and adaptive modality, PCGT provides a bridge for helping clients move from surviving to thriving.

The next chapter covers a range of potential applications and adaptations of PCGT, and suggestions for implementation. A section on telehealth interventions has been included in chapter eight, as two of the authors have been successfully providing PCGT through virtual modalities (teleconferencing and video).

References

American Group Psychotherapy Association & Eastern Group Psychotherapy Society. (May 2–4, 2002). Conference, *Psychological effects of terrorist disasters*, with financial support from the New York Times Company Foundation. New York City.

American Psychiatric Association. (1980). *Diagnostic and statistical manual of mental disorders* (3rd ed.). Washinton, D.C.: Author.

Anthony, W. A. & Farkas, M. D. (2009). *A primer on the psychiatric rehabilitation process*. Brookline, Massachusetts: Boston University Center for Psychiatric Rehabilitation, College of Health and Rehabilitation Services.

Archibald, H. C., & Tuddenham, R. D. (1965). Persistent stress reaction after combat: A 20-year follow-up. *Archives of General Psychiatry, 12*(5), 475–481. doi:10.1001/archpsyc.1965.01720350043006

Berne, Eric. (1966). *Principles of group treatment*. New York, NY: Oxford University Press.

Beysner, J. K. (1985). Multimodal inpatient treatment of Vietnam combat veterans with posttraumatic stress disorder. *Psychotherapy in Private Practice, 3*(4), 43–47.

Bion, W. (1961). *Experiences in groups, and other papers*. New York, NY: Basic Books.

Bremner, J. D., Mishra, S., Campanella, C., Shah, M., Kasher, N., Evans, S., ... Carmody, J. (2017). A pilot study of the effects of mindfulness-based stress reduction on post-traumatic stress disorder symptoms and brain response to traumatic reminders of combat in operation enduring freedom/operation Iraqi freedom combat veterans with post-traumatic stress disorder. *Frontiers in Psychiatry, 8*, 157.

Carmody, J., & Baer, R. (2008). Relationships between mindfulness practice and levels of mindfulness, medical and psychological symptoms and well-being in a mindfulness-based stress reduction program. *Journal of Behavioral Medicine, 31*(1), 23–33.

Casselman, R., & Pemberton, J. (2015). ACT-based parenting group for veterans with PTSD: Development and preliminary outcomes. *The American Journal of Family Therapy, 43*(1), 57–66.

Classen, C., & Yalom, I. D. (1995). *Treating Women Molested in Childhood* (1st ed.). San Francisco, CA: Jossey-Bass.

Coyle, G. (Ed.). (1937). *Studies in group behavior.* San Francisco, CA: Harper and Brothers Publishers.

Dembert, M. L., & Simmer, E. D. (2000). When trauma affects a community: Group interventions and support after a disaster. In R. H. Klein & V. L. Schermer (Eds.), *Group psychotherapy for psychological trauma* (pp. 239–264). New York, NY: Guilford.

Dubovsky, S. (2016). Individual treatment beats group therapy for PTSD. *New England Journal of Medicine, Journal Watch*, Dec 9.

Dynes, J. B. (1945). Rehabilitation of war casualties. *War Medicine, 7*, 32–35.

Engel, J. (2009). *American therapy: The rise of psychotherapy in the United States.* New York, NY: Gotham Books.

Erskine, R. (2010). Relational group psychotherapy: The healing of stress, neglect, and trauma. *International Journal of Integrative Psychotherapy, 1*(1), 1–10.

Erskine, R. (2013). Relational group process: Developments in a transactional analysis model of group psychotherapy. *Transactional Analysis Journal, 43*(4), 262–275.

Foa, E. B., & Rauch, S. A. M. (2004). Cognitive changes during prolonged exposure versus prolonged exposure plus cognitive restructuring in female assault survivors with posttraumatic stress disorder. *Journal of Consulting and Clinical Psychology, 72*(5), 879–884. https://doi.org/10.1037/0022-006X.72.5.879

Foy, D. W., Glynn, S. M., Schnurr, P. P., Jankowski, M. K., Wattenberg, M. S., Weiss, D. S., … Guman, F. D. (2000). In E. B. Foa, T. M. Keane, & M. J. Friedman (Eds.), *Effective Treatments for PTSD* (pp. 155–175). New York, NY: Guildford Press.

Foy, D. W., Ruzek, J. I., Glynn, S. M., Riney, S. J., & Gusman, F. D. (2002). Trauma focus group therapy for combat-related PTSD: An update. *Journal of Clinical Psychology, 58*(8), 907–918. http://dx.doi.org/10.1002/jclp.10066

Foy, D. W., Unger, W. S., & Wattenberg, M. S. (2004). *Group interventions for treatment of psychological trauma module 4: An overview of two evidence based group approaches to trauma in adults* New York, NY: *American Group Psychotherapy Association.*

Futterman, S., & Pumpian-Mindlin, E. (1951). Traumatic war neuroses five years later. *The American Journal of Psychiatry, 108*(6), 401–408.

Galloucis, M., & Kaufman, M. (1988). Group therapy with Vietnam veterans: A brief review. *Group, 12*(2), 85–102.

Gans, J. S. (1990). Broaching and exploring the question of combined group and individual therapy. *International Journal of Group Psychotherapy, 40*(2), 123–137.

Herman, J. L. (1992). *Trauma and recovery: The aftermath of violence – from domestic abuse to political terror.* New York, NY: Basic Books.

Herman, J. L., & Hirschman, L. (1981). *Father-daughter incest.* Cambridge, MA: Harvard University Press.

Herman, J. L., & Schatzow, E. (1984). Time-limited group therapy for women with a history of incest. *International Journal of Group Psychotherapy, 34,* 605–616.

Janoff-Bulman, R. (1992). *Shattered assumptions: Towards a new psychology of trauma.* New York, NY: Free Press.

Jaycox, L., Cohen, J., Mannarino, A., Walker, D., Langley, A., Gegenheimer, K., ... Schonlau, M. (2010). Children's mental health care following Hurricane Katrina: A field trial of trauma-focused psychotherapies. *Journal of Traumatic Stress, 23*(2), 223–231.

Johnson, D., Feldman, S., Southwick, S., & Charney, D. (1994). The concept of the Second Generation program in the treatment of post-traumatic stress disorder among Vietnam veterans. *Journal of Traumatic Stress, 7*(2), 217–235.

Kagan, R., & Spinazzola, J. (2013). Real life heroes in residential treatment: Implementation of an integrated model of trauma and resiliency-focused treatment for children and adolescents with complex PTSD. *Journal of Family Violence, 28*(7), 705–715.

Keane, T. M., Fairbank, J. A., Caddell, J. M., Zimering, R. T., Taylor, K. L., & Mora, C. A. (1989). Clinical evaluation of a measure to assess combat exposure. *Psychological Assessment: A Journal of Consulting and Clinical Psychology, 1*(1), 53–55. https://doi.org/10.1037/1040-3590.1.1.53

Kinney, A. R., Eakman, A. M., Lassell, R. & Wood, W. (2019). Equine-assisted interventions for veterans with service-related health conditions: A systematic mapping review. *Military Medical Research,* 6, 28. https://doi.org/10.1186/s40779-019-0217-6

Klein, R. H. & Schermer, V. L. (Eds.). (2000). *Group psychotherapy for psychological trauma.* New York, NY: The Guildford Press.

Kuhn, T. S. (1970). *The structure of scientific revolutions* (2nd ed.). Chicago, IL: The University of Chicago Press.

Kurtz, L. F. (2014). *Recovery groups: A guide to creating, leading, and working with groups for addictions and mental health conditions.* London: Oxford University Press.

MacGowan, M. J. (2008). *A guide to evidenced-based group work.* London: Oxford University Press.

Maslow, A. (1966). *The psychology of science: A reconnaissance.* New York, NY: Harper and Row.

McCann, I. L., & Pearlman, L. A. (1990a). *Psychological trauma and the adult survivor: Theory, therapy, and transformation.* New York, NY: Brunner/Mazel.

McCann, I. L., & Pearlman, L. A. (1990b). Vicarious traumatization: A framework for understanding the psychological effects of working with victims. *Journal of Traumatic Stress, 3*(1), 131–149. https://doi.org/10.1007/BF00975140

McNally, R., & Breslau, N. (2008). Does virtual trauma cause posttraumatic stress disorder? *The American Psychologist, 63*(4), 282–283.

Mendelsohn, M., Herman, J. L., Schatzow, E., Kallivayalil, D., & Levitan, J. (2011). *The trauma recovery group: A guide for practitioners.* New York, NY: The Guilford Press.

Menefee, D., Leopoulos, W., Tran, J., Teng, E., Wanner, J., Wilde, E., ... Day, S. (2016). Inpatient trauma-focused treatment for veterans: Implementation and evaluation of patient perceptions and outcomes of an integrated evidence-based treatment approach. *Military Medicine, 181*(11), e1590–e1599.

Najavits, L. M. (2002). *Seeking safety: A treatment manual for PTSD and substance abuse.* New York, NY: Guilford Press.

Neisser, U. (1976). *Cognition and reality: Principles and Implications of Cognitive Psychology.* New York, NY: W. H. Freeman and Company.

Nemeth, D., Kuriansky, J., Reeder, K., Lewis, A., Marceaux, K., Whittington, T., ... Safier, J. (2012). Addressing anniversary reactions of trauma through group process: The Hurricane Katrina anniversary wellness workshops. *International Journal of Group Psychotherapy, 62*(1), 129–142.

Norton, G. R., Cox, B. J., Asmundson, G. J. G., & Maser, J. D. (1995). The growth of research on anxiety disorders during the 1980s. *Journal of Anxiety Disorders, 9*(1), 75–85. https://doi.org/10.1016/0887-6185(94)00029-A

O'Malley, P. G. (2015). In veterans with PTSD, mindfulness-based group therapy reduced symptom severity. *Annals of Internal Medicine, 163*(12), JC9. https://jamanetwork.com/journals/jama/fullarticle/2422542

Parson, E. R. (1984). The role of psychodynamic group therapy in the treatment of the combat veterans. In J. Schwartz (Ed.), *Psychotherapy of the combat veteran* (pp. 153–220). New York, NY: Spectrum Publications.

Perls, F. S. (1967). Group vs. individual therapy. *ETC: A Review of General Semantics, 24*(3), 306–312.

Phillips, S. B. (2009). The synergy of group and individual treatment modalities in the aftermath of disaster and unfolding trauma. *International Journal of Group Psychotherapy, 59*(1), 85–107. https://doi.org/10.1521/ijgp.2009.59.1.85

Polusny, M., Erbes, C., Thuras, P., Moran, A., Lamberty, G., Collins, R., ... Lim, K. (2015). Mindfulness-based stress reduction for posttraumatic stress disorder among veterans: A randomized clinical trial. *Journal of the American Medical Association, 314*(5), 456–465.

Resick, P. A., Jordan, C. G., Girelli, S. A., Hutter, C. K., & Marhoefer-Dvorak, S. (1988). A comparative outcome study of behavioral group therapy for sexual assault victims. *Behavior Therapy, 19*(3), 385–401.

Resick, P. A., Monson, C. M., & Chard, K. M. (2017). *Cognitive processing therapy for PTSD: A comprehensive manual.* New York, NY: The Guilford Press.

Resick P. A., & Schnicke, M. K. (1992). Cognitive processing therapy for sexual assault victims. *Journal of Consulting and Clinical Psychology, 60*(5), 748–756. https://doi.org/10.1017/bec.2017.2

Rome, H. P. (1944). The role of sedation in military medicine. *U.S. Navy Medical Bulletin, 62*, 525.

Rothstein, A. (1980). Psychoanalytical paradigms and their narcissistic investment. *Journal of the American Psychoanalytic Association, 28*(2), 385–395.

Saakvitne, K. W. (2005). Holding hope and humanity in the face of trauma's legacy: The daunting challenge for group therapists. *International Journal of Group Psychotherapy, 55*(1), 137–149.

Schein, L. A., Spitz, H. I., Burlingame, G. M., & Muskin, P. R. (2006). *Psychological effects of catastrophic disasters: Group approaches to treatment.* New York, NY: Haworth Press. https://search.proquest.com/docview/42443652?accountid=28179

Schnurr, P. P., Friedman, M. J., Foy, D. W., Shea, M. T., Hsieh, F. Y., Lavori, P. W., ... Bernardy, N. C. (2003). Randomized trial of trauma-focused group therapy for posttraumatic stress disorder: Results from a department of veterans affairs cooperative study. *Archives of General Psychiatry*, *60*(5), 481–489. doi:10.1001/archpsyc.60.5.481

Schutz, W. (1973). *Elements of encounter*. Big Sur, CA: Joy Press.

Shea, M. T., McDevitt-Murphy, M., Ready, D. J., & Schnurr, P. P. (2009). Group therapy. In E. B. Foa, T. M. Keane, M. J. Friedman, & J. A. Cohen (Eds.), *Effective treatments for PTSD: Practice guidelines from the International Society for Traumatic Stress Studies* (pp. 306–326). New York, NY: Guilford Press.

Stephenson K. R., Simpson, T. L., Martinez, M. E., & Kearney, D. J. (2017). Changes in mindfulness and posttraumatic stress disorder symptoms among veterans enrolled in mindfulness-based stress reduction. *Journal of Clinical Psychology*, *73*(3), 201–217. https://doi.org/10.1002/jclp.22323

Tsai, M., & Wagner, N. N. (1978). Therapy groups for women sexually molested as children. *Archives of Sexual Behavior*, *7*, 417–427. https://doi.org/10.1007/BF01542487

Walker, Lenore E. A. (2006). Battered woman Syndrome: Empirical findings. *Annals of the New York Academy of Sciences 1087*: 142–157. Web.

Weinberg, H., Nuttman-Shwartz, O., & Gilmore, M. (2005). Trauma groups: An overview. *Group Analysis*, *38*(2), 187–202. Web.

Yalom, I. (1970). The theory and practice of group psychotherapy. New York, NY: Basic Book.

Yalom, I., & Leszcz, M. (2005). *The theory and practice of group psychotherapy* (5th ed.). New York, NY: Basic Books.

8   PCGT Applications, Implementation, and Treatment

William S. Unger and Daniel Lee Gross

PCGT Applications, Implementation, and Treatment

Present-centered group therapy (PCGT) was developed for PTSD that may occur following exposure to traumatic combat experiences during military service. Even within the veteran population in which PCGT has been most frequently utilized, PCGT has been offered to veterans with military sexual trauma, childhood sexual assault, and other early life traumas, as well as traumas suffered while off station during military service. PCGT may also be applied in a broad array of clinical and educational settings involving services for trauma survivors. Included in these settings are community mental health clinics, private group or individual psychotherapy programs, forensic units, mental health recovery settings, inpatient and residential psychiatric programs, partial hospital settings, intensive treatment settings, college counseling centers, and university training programs, in addition to the Veterans Administration, the Department of Defense, and sexual trauma treatment centers. It may be further argued that PCGT should be considered as a treatment for all trauma survivors. Such applications would be open to males and females, children, adolescents, and the elderly, as well as groups of first responders, survivors of terrorist attacks, torture victims, and diverse and cross-cultural populations.

With the increased recognition in the DSM-5 (*Diagnostic and Statistical Manual of Mental Disorders, Fifth Edition*; American Psychiatric Association, 2013) concerning trauma-related disorders, the treatment of survivors of trauma requires diverse offerings for appropriate clinical care. Educational institutions, program directors, and other treatment settings have come to understand that clinicians must have a quiver of services available to meet the needs of a diverse clientele. This chapter reviews considerations for implementation of PCGT in a wide range of clinical settings as the utility of the protocol reaches far beyond the diagnosis of PTSD. Present-centered group therapy offers a flexible treatment approach that can easily be adapted to meet the needs of survivors across settings, trauma-related diagnoses, and individual needs. In PCGT, the identified index trauma is not shared with group members; rather the impact of the event(s) on the individual's quality of life is central to the group work. Group members may each have a similar index trauma, as is often the case with military personnel. However, treatment groups in the research reviewed in chapter two have also been composed of mixed groups of trauma survivors including combat trauma, military sexual trauma, motor vehicle accidents and other traumatic experiences suffered during military service. Therefore, PCGT may be composed of individuals struggling with the psychiatric consequences of a variety of life-changing events. PCGT's flexibility includes that it may also be useful as an adjunctive service to other group or individual treatment programs, as well as a stand-alone treatment. PCGT is also an accessible modality; differing cultural experiences and values may readily be incorporated into present-centered group therapy, given that a focus of the model is on the participant's life experiences, as well as the sharing of strategies used by the group members (which are richer when including a variety of perspectives and backgrounds).

In a broader context, the focus of the PCGT treatment remains on symptom management and an understanding of how symptoms have impact on the individual's quality of life. Group participants develop an understanding of how their symptoms may be related to some of their problems, and learn to identify, talk about, and deal with them more effectively. Trauma disclosure has not been an aspect of PCGT. The role of the facilitator has been, and should remain, on the facilitation of shared positive symptom management strategies offered by group participants. The presentation and endorsement of positive symptom management techniques from one's peers in the group enhance group cohesion. This group support can serve to decrease the pull toward avoidance that diminishes the participants' quality of life. The options for the wider use of PCGT may include a focus on symptom management and improved overall wellness for individuals presenting with an array of trauma- and stress-related disorders and other clinical concerns. A number of clinical considerations for the broad implementation of PCGT are included in the following sections.

The Role of Trauma in the Development of Psychiatric Disorders

PTSD was the first diagnosis to include the identification of an experienced trauma in the development of chronic psychiatric symptoms (*Diagnostic and Statistical Manual of Mental Disorders, Third Edition*, American Psychiatric Association, 1980 (DSM-III)). Subsequently, the *Diagnostic and Statistical Manual, Fifth Edition* (APA, 2013) introduced an entire diagnostic class of trauma and stress-related disorders. This class has included disorders that occur throughout the life span with both short-term and chronic presentations. Broadening this class supports the role of trauma in the development of a broad range of psychiatric symptoms. Included in this new class of disorders are *other specified trauma- and stressor-related disorder*, and *unspecified trauma- and stressor-related disorder*, for symptom presentations that occur following a trauma but do not meet the full criteria of a specific member of this class. The decision to include these two conditions acknowledges that the impact of trauma may be broad and may manifest with a wide range of psychiatric symptoms.

Based on data from a large nationally representative sample of people participating in the National Comorbidity Survey (NCS), 60 percent of men and 50 percent of women reported they have experienced a traumatic event at some point in their lives. The majority of these individuals have been exposed to two or more traumatic events (Kessler, Sonnega, Bromet, Hughes, & Nelson, 1995). A 90 percent lifetime incidence of a traumatic event was reported for individuals with a psychiatric diagnosis (Mueser & Rosenberg, 2001). Many of the individuals with a history of an index trauma develop psychiatric symptoms that differ from those of PTSD. Approximately 90 percent of individuals accessing public mental health services have a history of multiple trauma experiences (National Executive Training Institute [NETI], 2005).

Following the attack on the Twin Towers in New York City in 2001, PTSD was only one of the psychiatric disorders that were observed in the general population. Other diagnoses including anxiety disorders, mood disorders, and substance-use disorders were also identified within the group of trauma survivors. For individuals without a diagnosis of PTSD, the symptoms presented were clinically associated with that index traumatic event.

In most clinical settings, individuals presenting for mental health services receive a broad intake evaluation as the usual standard of care during the initial clinical encounter. Across clinical settings, it is not uncommon to find that despite a thorough evaluation for the presence of high intensity stressors and a trauma history, clients may deny that they have experienced such events. The report of trauma exposure often occurs once the client becomes engaged in psychotherapy. Given this initial hesitation to disclose trauma, the actual incidence of traumatic events may be even greater than that reported in the research cited previously. In light of the growing recognition of the role that trauma can play in a variety of psychiatric conditions, interventions that are at least trauma-aware have become the cornerstone of any effective therapy program.

PCGT may readily serve individuals with symptom presentations associated with a variety of trauma-based disorders, and with a variety of index trauma events, in a broad array of clinical settings. While PCGT was originally developed in the context of treatment of PTSD, a mental health disorder with symptoms directly associated with the experience of an identified index trauma, it focuses on the present day rather than the trauma or specific PTSD trauma experiences. As the presence of an index trauma has been reported for a significant number of individuals seeking mental health care, and the incidence of trauma in the general population is significant, a wide range of individuals presenting with psychiatric symptoms may benefit from PCGT.

Heterogeneity of Index Trauma, and Trauma-Based Diagnosis, in PCGT Groups

Whether the diagnosis is PTSD or another trauma-related disorder, much of the clinician's work in PCGT is to facilitate group members' sharing the positive strategies they have utilized to cope with the psychiatric consequences of the index trauma. Individuals with different traumatic events may therefore be placed into the same group. To date, trauma groups run in the Department of Veterans' Affairs Trauma Recovery Clinics have often been comprised of veterans with varied sources of trauma (including combat, sexual assault, catastrophic accidents, and other traumas associated with military service), and who may also have multiple co-occurring disorders. These group members may, in addition to PTSD symptoms, have diagnoses such as depression, panic disorder, and/or substance dependence, among others. Therefore, PCGT group work broadens into the management of other psychiatric symptoms associated with the index trauma, in addition to PTSD. Given effective use in these contexts, heterogeneous PCGT groups composed of individuals with different index traumas and different trauma-based psychiatric diagnoses may readily benefit from being in the same group. Here again, it is the role of the PCGT clinician to facilitate the sharing of member-developed techniques, as members collaboratively generate healing solutions to their own and others' trauma-related distress, across the presenting diagnoses within the group. The group is enlisted and guided to work together in the sharing and developing of solutions to decrease symptom burdens and to improve the overall wellness and quality of life for each individual and for the group as a whole. This process differentiates PCGT from other more structured models of therapy that present the clinician's advice and engaging in the prescripted interventions and exercises as the agents of symptom change.

Consideration for Implementation

General Group Therapy Management Skills as Applied in PCGT

The PCGT clinician utilizes the same general tool set as do leaders of other group protocols. Clinicians listen carefully to the comments, questions, and remarks of the group members. During the delivery of other group formats, but especially when offering skill-based treatment groups, the leader may have a session-by-session structure for implementation of the treatment protocol. Such a guideline exists for PCGT, but it does not provide the offering of manualized techniques. The group clinician facilitates the sharing and promotes an open forum for the expression of concerns and distress by group participants. When providing group treatments other than PCGT, clinicians most typically respond to these concerns by engaging group members in some therapeutic frame and offering a selection of positive symptom management alternatives for the presented concerns. The clinician engages as a contributor to the problem-solving process.

One of the key differences for facilitators when offering PCGT is the understanding that it is contraindicated, or at least unnecessary on most occasions, for the clinician to suggest solutions to the identified concerns. This difference is significant for professionals trained largely in structured cognitive-behavioral or behavioral interventions. As mental healthcare providers, we have put great emphasis on our education and preparation. The term *caregiver* implies the provision of services to assist with the challenges faced by our clients. We have been instructed and have practiced at providing the help needed to those who come to us for care. The PCGT clinician offers care but does so by utilizing a different perspective. The interventions offered for care do not come directly from the clinician. Rather, they are provided and shared by the group members in response to the problems presented by their peers. As noted by Yalom (1995), "... group cohesion is the analogue of relationship in individual therapy" (p. 47). The clinician does not offer direct aid but facilitates the sharing of problems with the group. The clinician understands and trusts that the presenter's concerns are not unique but are consistent with those of the other group members. The group engages in joint brainstorming and problem solving of the identified concerns. The presenter is provided positive coping behaviors from the other participants to address the identified issues. The clinician's role in the provision of care is to facilitate group sharing and problem solving concerning the identified issues as well as the sharing of management strategies to address the barriers to the implementation of the techniques offered.

The experience of group brainstorming and effective problem solving often empowers the group members to take an active role in managing their own wellness. Identifying and sharing one's own skills reinforces the self-activating behaviors associated with positive coping and self-care. The individual learns to trust that they are capable of effectively managing seemingly overwhelming distress. The PCGT clinician provides aid by guiding and activating the process of self-care.

The PCGT Clinician's Dilemma in Group Management

As noted, the PCGT clinician utilizes many skills that are common applications in other group therapy approaches. Having been trained as an active problem solver for clients seeking assistance with mental health concerns, the transition to PCGT is not without difficulties. This may be especially true for clinicians with experience in offering skill-based treatment protocols consistent with cognitive-behavioral or other structured forms of group therapy. The PCGT clinician maybe required to alter a long-standing mindset and response pattern. Clinicians in their training and professional experiences have often acquired an arsenal of interventions that are available for the client's use. The desire to assist is a core aspect of the clinician's persona. As care providers, it is our desire to directly respond to the client's distress, and this value can be a significant challenge in the delivery of PCGT. It is understood that this dilemma also arises in the delivery of group treatments other than PCGT, including more structured and stepwise protocols that offer techniques in a standardized and prescribed manner. The clinician, in the service of non-PCGT approaches, often struggles with the content of a group meeting and may wish to offer another approved intervention prior to the designated time for the intervention as described in the protocol manual.

In PCGT, following the presentation of a participant's struggles, the clinician responds to the client's distress by eliciting a problem-solving response from the other group members. The PCGT clinician provides care through promoting the group response, which may offer unique and creative ways to positively manage the presented concern. The mechanisms for the clinician's facilitation of the group response are not proprietary to PCGT. A more complete discussion is offered in chapters four and five. The PCGT clinician makes extensive use of general listening skills in the communications with the group members. These skills focus on non-problem-solving responses from the clinician in relation to group members, and include paraphrasing, reflecting, and use of clarifying questions. The PCGT clinician works at promoting the engagement of the group in shared brainstorming of problem solving, based on each participant's experience with the positive strategies they have used to successfully manage their psychiatric symptoms. During this process participants often offer the core cognitions and emotions associated with their own traumas, stemming from the impact of the trauma on their own physiological responses and safety needs (see later section in this chapter on Maslow's hierarchy of needs, as related to trauma, for a fuller discussion (1943)). The commonality of these needs across the group promotes a sense of trust and sharing among the participants, enhancing the PCGT impact.

The Role of the Clinician and the Relationship as the Vehicle for Change

Initial Engagement

As noted in Section 1, the therapeutic relationship and development of a working group cohesion are the two key concerns for the clinician in the implementation of PCGT. The following sections offer considerations for specific programmatic challenges across a variety of settings. It is important to keep in mind the extent to which trust issues are central for survivors of trauma. Survivors often experience a significant degree of anticipatory anxiety related to the potential disclosure of their trauma experiences, and a subsequent increase of PTSD and related symptoms when approaching treatment. It is not uncommon for someone to present for treatment services and drop out after the initial intake interview or following the completion of a comprehensive clinical assessment. If they do remain for mental health services, they may approach any additional appointments for treatment planning or psychotherapy with great caution.

To promote engagement in psychotherapy, it is essential to partner with those seeking mental health services, and to offer the assistance that meets their needs. The development of trust is a key aspect of treatment, and begins with clarity concerning the purpose and focus of options for care. Establishment of a trusting relationship is the conduit to clinical engagement in any treatment for trauma. For PCGT, trust in the relationship with the facilitators is initially the vehicle for enlisting engagement with the group; the group cohesion and engagement then become the source of therapeutic change.

Transparency about the nature of the group is essential. Group members need to be recruited with the understanding that the group will revolve around mutual sharing of symptom management techniques, and not about traumatic experiences. The utility of this approach and the role of group members must be conveyed to the potential members. The task of implementing an intervention relies, to a great extent, on the development of a therapeutic relationship with our clients. We may offer the best evidenced-based treatments available but fail to engage the individual therapeutically, even if the individual joins the group. The initial development of a therapeutic relationship drives the engagement and therefore the opportunity for progress in psychotherapy. This early development of a therapeutic relationship is the conduit for change; it is not the mechanism of change, but it provides the trust essential for the development of group cohesion, which then becomes the vehicle for change.

The role of the clinician includes the need to manage physiological needs and safety concerns in order to promote sharing within the group. Individuals suffering from a lack or loss of basic physiological requirements such as food, shelter, and sleep will have more difficulty with their interactions with other group members. For example, members may be currently food-insecure, housing-insecure, or living in an unsafe environment or neighborhood, and these circumstances must be addressed either through the group or through additional referrals in order to create safety within the group. Each participant must also feel physically and emotionally safe during the group process. Promoting a sense of personal safety within the group must be adequately addressed, beginning with the guidelines of mutual respect that must be maintained, and that must be enforced should violations occur during PCGT. These guidelines are presented in the initial session (see chapter three), and are essential to the process of PCGT.

Given the role in promoting group cohesion and the sharing of positive symptom management strategies, the facilitator supports the equal value of each group member, in terms of both the validity of the issues they present, and the utility of their self-generated mechanisms for relief of symptoms. This respect and equal valuing of members contributes to the development of a positive working group cohesion. This working group cohesion provides the robustness of connection that enhances the adaptability of PCGT in a broad spectrum of settings. Regardless of setting, once a group has been gathered together and meetings for PCGT have begun, the guidelines, progression, and mechanism for the provision of PCGT remain the same. What may vary, dependent on setting, are the specifics of referral, recruitment, and implementation processes, which will be addressed in the section on Application and Implementation in Specific Settings.

Application of PCGT in Heterogeneous and Diverse Populations

Group diversity is not a limiting factor for PCGT. It is important to note that cultural and clinical differences exist in even the most homogenous of group settings. Whether group members have similar or different cultural backgrounds, they can share their coping strategies and benefit from diverse perspectives on symptom management. One of the roles of the PCGT clinician is to take the individualized aspects of client diversity and seamlessly integrate them into the group process. Here the facilitator guides the group to the core physiologic and safety concerns associated with the content shared during the PCGT, and thereby establishes a sense of understanding and cohesion among the participants.

The diversity of cultural backgrounds, age, religion, gender, gender preference, socio-economic status, and other characteristics of group members is embraced by the PCGT clinician and enhances the group. Group members bring viable strategies for managing symptoms and life situations to other group members, both independent of their backgrounds, and because of their backgrounds. The role of the group facilitator is to promote this sharing across these differing perspectives. A diversity of cultural experiences and values can be readily incorporated into PGCT, given that the protocol is focused on these current symptoms and life situations with which members are grappling, and the problem solving that they offer to the group. Each individual group member presents with a unique complexity of experiences that may manifest in subtle expressions of cognition and emotion, which contribute to the range of perspectives from which members can benefit. The group's proposed interventions do not need to be uniform in the ways members apply them. Members may retool and modify the strategies according to their personal preferences and needs, while still preserving the underlying mechanism of the proposed strategy. This flexibility in application parallels other adaptable treatments; for example, in the application of mindfulness, the mechanism of the intervention is identical across a variety of possible practice styles. The opportunity for flexibility in PCGT makes it accessible, as well, across heterogeneous sources of trauma, and a variety of cultural affiliations, as long as members can "fine-tune" the intervention to their individual needs. The role of the group facilitator remains flexible, yet consistent, with a focus on guiding the sharing by group members and the individualized utilization of the positive coping strategies offered.

For the facilitator, the recognition of diversity, and the group's influence on the members' experiences, should be understood, and not underestimated. Chang-Caffaro and Caffaro (2018) described the complex challenge of clinicians maintaining a clinical eye on social justice perspectives in group therapy. They advocated for use of self-awareness, cultural sensitivity, and courage, adding, "these facilitation skills, comparable to group therapy skills, but in addition inclusive of a critical consciousness and awareness of one's own personal bias and prejudices, are not simple to master" (p. 485). Each individual brings their own perspective and truth to social interactions. Experiences are colored by the tint of the lens by which we all view life events. In groups with a broad base of diversity, the range of these individual perspectives can appear daunting to the group facilitator. However, it is important for the clinician to place these differences in the broader context of human cognitions and emotions. While the aspects of an event and individual differences (be they biological or experiential) may vary considerably, the core thoughts and emotions associated with the traumatic experience may be very similar. All clients can experience fear, anger, frustration, love, hate, as well as many other basic emotions. In addition, their thoughts associated with traumatic experiences in particular may function as core beliefs: "It was my fault, I am to blame, I should have done something else, or no one cares about me." As important as diversity is to our understanding, in the process of valuing diversity we should not fail to acknowledge that all of us have the same basic daily life needs (as represented in discussion of Maslow's hierarchy, below). We are all human beings with similarities concerning our core thoughts and feelings; we all have essentially the same basic wants and needs as we move through our lives. The contextual cues associated with an experience may differ, but they frequently lead to similar human responses.

Trauma and the Self

A brief consideration of Maslow's Hierarchy of Needs hypothesis (1943; see Figure 8.1) is offered to assist with an understanding of this perspective

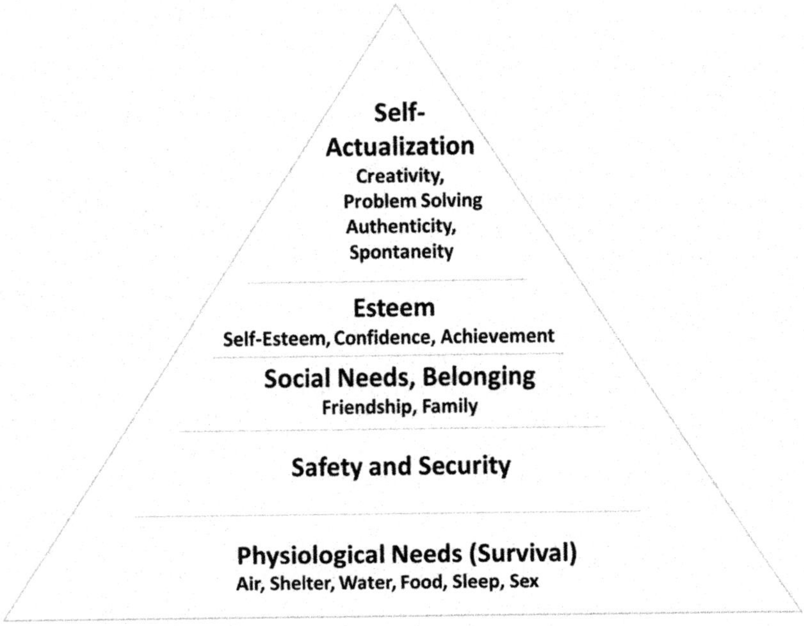

Figure 8.1 Maslow's Hierarchy of Needs (Based on Maslow, 1943).

(see also discussion in chapter six, Intersection of the Cycle of PTSD Model, Drive Theory, and Maslow's Hierarchy of Needs).

Physiological and safety needs comprise the first two steps of the hierarchy that are required for the further development of the self. During the experience of a trauma, significant challenges concerning physiological and safety needs are presented to the self. Cognitions and emotions associated with these challenges may develop into the core beliefs, self-statements, and reactivity in response to reminders of the event. These thoughts and reactions originate at the level of those basic needs, rather than at the next levels of need in the hierarchy.

Commonalities Despite Differences

Concerns regarding cultural diversity, to the extent that they involve group affiliation and sense of belonging, correspond to the more advanced need levels of Maslow's hierarchy. These advanced levels of need are, of course, extremely important to the work of the facilitators, especially as members move toward social connection. However, the feelings and thoughts connected with trauma stem from the two basic levels, and tend to serve as a common thread for group members despite cultural differences.

Differences Despite Commonalities

Despite the common bond of the violation of physiological and safety needs and their sequelae, cultural factors may create distinctions even in the ways that trauma-based thoughts and reactivities are experienced. Across the broad spectrum of human experience, certain social, cultural, ethnic, or religious groups may have encountered challenges at these first two levels more frequently, either personally or intergenerationally. Differences in the "loading" of such life experiences may greatly influence the cognitions and emotions associated with the trauma. Some members may have experienced more recent traumatic events, or more recent traumatic reminders, which can set members apart (especially if these events are culturally related, and the group is composed of culturally diverse members). Awareness of these factors is very important for facilitators, who can guide the process toward acknowledgment of both commonalities and distinctions, and toward comfort in sharing despite differences.

Appreciation of Commonalities and Distinctions in Group

An appreciation for the role of the shared core beliefs established due to threat from the trauma at those first two levels (physiological and safety needs), as noted previously, must not be dismissed, even in the context of variation in trauma "loading." These thoughts and emotions are basic to the nature of the trauma experience and must not be underestimated or neglected. They represent the basic challenges encountered by all survivors of trauma regardless of the nature of the actual traumatic event and its role in the subsequent development of psychiatric symptoms. While current and past "load" at these levels may differ, the experience of threat to safety and physiological needs is fundamental, and a source of commonality once members share and connect at the level of their resulting symptoms and self-appraisals that are deeply rooted in the trauma.

At the same time, as the group evolves, recognition of members as individuals becomes central, and facilitation of mutual respect of differences (rather than emphasis largely on commonalities) becomes key. By the middle sessions of the group, members begin to differentiate around personal characteristics beyond the trauma, which may include cultural background and identity. In terms of Maslow's levels above, members may focus on needs for belonging, esteem, and/or self-actualization, in each of which cultural factors may play a role. While trauma history remains the commonality among members, their differentiation allows greater range of feedback and original ideas. Facilitators need to immediately intervene with any eruption of bias-related actions or comments in the group as this differentiation occurs (see chapter five, sections entitled: From Shame-Based Reactivity to Acknowledgment: Addressing Stereotypes, Bias-Related

Boundary Trespass, and Other Forms of Disparagement). Members may be more open with each other once they feel accepted for their differences as well as similarities. Shared problem solving becomes more meaningful as interactions are based on members' successes and "'misses" – what worked and what did not – and their recognition of each other as individuals with something to offer, in addition to their shared history of suffering. Members' perspective-taking, their ability to put themselves in someone else's shoes, can be expected to increase for many members as they share their unique perspectives. In this sense, members may develop greater appreciation for experiences beyond their own. As facilitators model acceptance and interest regarding each member, the modest structure of PCGT offers opportunity for members to develop appreciation for the lives of others, including those with differing values, beliefs, identity, cultural backgrounds, and experiences.

Diversity of Diagnosis

As the experience of a trauma is a core aspect of not only PTSD, but also an entire class of disorders in the DSM-5, these shared core beliefs and emotions may be approached from the therapeutic frame of PCGT. In addition, PCGT may be useful with other groups of survivors regardless of the assigned diagnosis or treatment setting. Sakamoto and Couto (2017) noted the limitations of PTSD criteria when working with refugees: "PTSD does not accurately reflect the complicated individual and social repercussions of persecution, war, torture, and the trauma of resettlement" (p. 374). These authors question the efficacy of using western, trauma-focused group treatments for refugees, and instead recommend community-led support groups that focus primarily on socialization, reestablishing meaningful bonds, and regaining trust in the community. These observations are consonant with the utility of PCGT with survivors of trauma across diagnostic and cultural identities.

Application and Implementation in Specific Settings

In addition to Veterans' Healthcare Systems, other potential settings for use of PCGT may include, with relevant adaptations: community mental health clinics, private group or independent psychotherapy practices, college counseling centers and university training programs, trauma specialty programs, the Department of Defense, forensic units, mental health recovery settings, inpatient and residential psychiatric programs, partial hospital settings, intensive treatment settings, and sexual trauma treatment centers. Accordingly, potential applications of PCGT would be open to a diverse clientele including male and female adults, children, adolescents, and the elderly, as well as groups of first responders, survivors of terrorist attacks, and torture victims. Due to its flexibility, PCGT may also be adapted to a variety of cultural contexts and populations.

General Programmatic Procedures

Prior to the initiation of a PCGT program, a process of the identification and selection of group members is necessary. These services include the development of referral and assessment procedures in the selection of participants. For example, in considering client preference: candidates seeking highly structured and/or skill-focused interventions, as well as those interested in trauma-focused work, would be best served by other clinical applications; those preferring a supportive, less structured approach, or who prefer to address present-day issues, may be good candidates. The actual referral can be made once preferences and pre-conceived ideas of therapy and past experiences are more thoroughly explored. The actual programmatic implementation of referral and assessment procedures may vary significantly based on differences in staffing, physical environment, and available system resources. The following discussion offers some general considerations about referrals and assessment and is not offered as a suggestion to adopt a specific intake protocol. As always, the process of therapy begins with a referral and continues into the clinical assessment. Enrollment in PCGT follows established guidelines for group involvement.

Referral

Education of referral sources remains the gold standard to group enrollment. Colleagues, in addition to other professional and non-professional referral sources, should be well informed regarding the nature of PCGT. This remains true for institutions, the community, or private practice settings. The focus of the group should be clarified for referral sources and potential group members: it is facilitator-led sharing by participants of positive coping and problem-solving strategies for individuals with a history of a traumatic experience. The mention of the term *trauma* frequently creates concerns for potential group members regarding whether they will be required to disclose information concerning the index trauma. Although some clinical settings may assess trauma exposure and ask for descriptions of traumatic events during the intake and assessment process, such a disclosure is not a requirement of PCGT and it should be made clear to potential group members that sharing traumatic experiences is not part of PCGT. As stated earlier, transparency about the nature of group offerings is essential. Confusion and lack of clarity regarding the role of group members may contribute to early termination by the potential client during the pretreatment contacts with the provider or at the start of group meetings. As such, well-intentioned but unclear information to the client is a disservice to the potential client, the clinician, and all those involved in the referral process.

Number of Members

The identification of clients for PCGT is very much like the referral process for the other individuals in our clinical practice. In group settings, the number of participants enrolled generally follows a guideline of four to nine individuals (varying somewhat by setting). This number allows for appropriate interaction between group members to achieve treatment gains but remains intimate enough to ensure adequate access to time in group for client service needs. Fewer than four individuals may prohibit the development of a therapeutic landscape for the sharing of varied perspectives for symptom management. A greater number of participants may also hinder this process by not allowing adequate collaboration due to inequitable process time in the group.

Assessment

The inclusion of a life stressor and trauma history is a core aspect of the bio-psycho-social assessment procedure common in most psychiatric settings. A detailed account of the event(s) is not necessary for enrollment in PCGT as a disclosure of the event is not an aspect of the treatment protocol. However, the identification of a trauma events(s) is necessary. In the past, a diagnosis of PTSD has been a required element in the development and the research utilizing PCGT. However, as discussed earlier PCGT has utility in the treatment of all symptoms associated with a trauma history. It therefore follows that the identification of a trauma and how the associated symptoms impact the client's quality of life are important components of the assessment protocol.

Post-Assessment Treatment Planning

Following a referral and the completion of an initial intake evaluation, a common practice is to schedule a follow-up meeting for shared treatment planning between the clinician and the client. During this meeting, the clinician presents the findings and service recommendations to the client. The clinician then co-develops the treatment plan for psychotherapy with the client. There are many choices regarding the presentation of these options, with most having the client decide whether to move forward with a trauma-focused treatment or with a non-trauma-focused intervention. The trauma-focused therapeutic approach directs the focus of symptom changes to the additional processing of cognitions, emotions and memories associated with the index trauma. These techniques typically have all participants repeatedly share the details of the traumatic event(s). Treatments that do not focus on an index event include trauma-specific interventions such as Cognitive Processing Therapy and protocols with a non-disclosure aspect such as PCGT. The options presented are not mutually exclusive and both can be offered as potential directions in the overall timeline of the treatment plan. Of course, the final decision always rests with the individual. The following metaphors may be used to assist potential group members in the decision-making process, which can then assist the clinician in collaboratively creating a treatment plan for the next phase of treatment.

USE OF METAPHORS IN TREATMENT CHOICE DISCUSSION

The previous discussion reviewed general conceptual concerns, the referral and assessment processes, and treatment planning associated with PCGT. Potential group members are often put off by technical presentations of the offered clinical services. The following metaphors are presented as considerations and potential tools to assist with the description of mental health protocols and the mechanisms of psychotherapy. They may assist with clarifying, "how things work" and the participant's understanding and expectations of the therapy process. These metaphors are provided to promote understanding regarding the requirements and benefits of treatment by simplifying the description of the individual's involvement in psychotherapy. These metaphors may be utilized as guides to informed consent to treatment, which is a cornerstone of the therapeutic relationship.

Computer Metaphor An explanation of how psychotherapy can aid the individual may assist with enrollment. Many individuals consider treatment like having a problem with their computer and they call the technical center for aid. In a perfect world, the technician/therapist immediately answers the call, looks at the computer/person seeking aid, and makes the needed repairs and the problem is resolved. However, that is not how life works. One often finds that in making such a call that the lines are busy and you are put on hold. You may have to make multiple attempts to reach the technician as you are informed they are busy with other individuals and you will receive service from the next available representative. You may have to hang up due to your own schedule limitations and call again later.

When a technician does join your call, you are asked to start your computer, run the problematic program, describe the issue and follow the directions given to you. At times, the advice will be confusing, and will require a number of attempts before you can implement the instructions. Following the intervention, you are asked to restart the computer and re-assess the problem. Sometimes the problem remains and other directions are provided to resolve the issue. In certain instances, despite numerous attempts the problem continues for unknown reasons. At other times, the problem returns after a few days. The process may seem haphazard and frustrating. However, as the problems remain, you continue to make attempts to resolve the issues. With additional work and the completion of the processing, your machine is operating within the needed parameters. During the process of resolution, you have learned how to manage these problems should the issues return. This does not preclude the occurrence of other problems, but the added skills will also assist with addressing the new issues.

Pressure Cooker   Following a presentation of available treatments, this writer often offers the client two metaphors as aids to decision making and to assist with an explanation how engaging in psychotherapy may help to improve their symptom burden. The first metaphor offers a non-trauma-focused approach. The client is likened to a pressure cooker on a stove with the "fire of life" turned on underneath the vessel. The fire of life represents the challenges and stressors associated with the client's past and present life experiences. The pressure cooker cannot turn the fire of life off, that is, "life happens." As the life events progress, stress increases on the individual. The steam and pressure continue to develop across time.

Despite the constant and growing pressure, it is often the case that the individual attempts not to display weakness or signs of emotion to others, and thereby shuts off the pressure valve. For trauma survivors this pattern may be connected to the index trauma(s) and feelings of vulnerability. The turning off of the valve is an effort not to show vulnerability or helplessness in the face of a stressor. The internalization of stress also develops, in part, as an attempt to prevent placing a burden of distress on another. The client tries to avoid or numb out, thereby not showing signs of weakness. These attempts effectively turn down or close the pressure valve at the top of the vessel, which results in an increase of internalized pressure.

These avoidances may continue until the pressure valve is effectively turned off, not allowing any of the steam to be released in the effort to manage and not present signs of weakness. Someone glancing at the pressure cooker from the outside of the stove may, in fact, not notice that steam is not being released. However, during this time, the internal pressure continues to build. The numbing and avoidance may provide a short-term reduction of distress from the "fire of life" and thereby reinforce these avoidance behaviors. The individual has been working very hard to present as being OK. However, this strategy is not sustainable and leads to an increase of symptoms.

The clinician then presents a question to the client, "If the fire of life is on underneath and the valve is turned off, what will eventually happen?" To this the client responds in some fashion that, "It will explode." This response is confirmed by the clinician with the addition of a comment noting that managing psychiatric symptoms is therefore not a matter of strength but the use of positive coping interventions. Even if the steel were thicker or stronger, the same result would eventually occur. Therefore, the management of symptoms is not a matter of strength, it is a matter or managing the steam/pressure by keeping the valve open as wide as possible with symptom intervention strategies. The more positive management interventions that are available, the greater the opening of the valve and the more relief that occurs from the release of the pressure. In fact, if there were enough symptom management interventions utilized such that the top of the vessel could be removed, there would continue to be steam rising due to the presence of the fire of life underneath, but no internalized pressure would develop as the vessel was completely open. So, one set of treatment strategies targets the acquisition of symptom management or intervention techniques to prevent closing the valve and the accumulation of pressure. These strategies do not require a focus on the index trauma for the client to move forward with mental health goals. PCGT is one such technique in the clinician's treatment options.

Infected Wound Metaphor (Trauma-Focus Explanation) To help the client understand this set of approaches the metaphor of an infected wound may be presented during treatment planning. It may be paired with the use of the pressure cooker metaphor to present differing treatment options. The pressure cooker is consistent with non-trauma-focused psychotherapies and the infected wound offers an understanding of trauma-focused interventions.

The individual is informed that everyone experiences psychological challenges and significant stressors during their lifetime. We also all experience numerous cuts and scrapes beginning with our early childhood. For most of these injuries, physical and psychological, we essentially literally or psychologically wash it off, put a bandage on it, and move forward with our lives. In fact, the common wisdom we receive from others is to, "forget about it and get on with our lives." This wisdom may in fact be adequate for most of the emotional and physical challenges we face day to day. However, there are instances in which this wisdom does not work as the injury becomes infected. Just attempting to move forward or, "forget about it" is insufficient. In these cases, we may attempt to change the bandage, wash the wound, use a bigger bandage, or perhaps even tighten the bandage to support the wound. None of these options treats the infection. These interventions may make the infected wound feel better for a short period of time. The wound may be less sensitive to touch, so we may be able to put the injury out of our thoughts briefly. However, if the infection remains, we eventually do something to aggravate the injury or trigger a memory, and we experience significant pain.

Clients often tend to use this same strategy to manage psychological traumas. We attempt to numb ourselves, stay busy with our daily routine, attempt to distract our thoughts away from the trauma, use alcohol or other substances to "self-medicate," or engage in an array of avoidance strategies to cover over, forget, and bandage up our trauma. However, none of these interventions offers an effective treatment for the source of our pain, which is the infection/trauma experience. The healthy choice is to unwrap the injury and wash the wound repeatedly until the infection is gone. This is often a painful process. Taking off an old bandage hurts, opening the wound hurts, getting the disinfectant and washing the wound repeatedly to clear the infection also hurts. This is much like the process of repeatedly debriefing the client on the index trauma in an attempt to access the details of the event. However, the pain during treatment, which may be intense, is not associated with the infection but with the healing process. Once the infection is removed, the wound can heal. The infection/toxin is gone. There may always be a scar/memory from the injury, on our body and in our thoughts. Like the scar, the memory of the index trauma remains, but the infection and overwhelming painful affect are gone. The memory will never be totally removed, but the impact of the infection no longer prevents us from moving forward with our thoughts, emotions, and lives. Our thoughts associated with the traumatic event will never be happy or pleasant, but we no longer need to make use of the maladaptive avoidance behaviors and numbing strategies to live our lives.

Wounded Arm Metaphor (Presented-Centered Explanation)   Another wound metaphor may be used to describe the process of PCGT. Group members come to the group with wounds that have not healed, perhaps a wounded arm. The PCGT group offers a safe environment for the wound to heal and is like keeping the wound clean and protected by a bandage so that the body's natural healing processes can begin to work. As the wound heals, it can be uncovered now and then, and the support offered from group members can be applied to the arm wound as a healing ointment. As the wound continues to heal, the bandages can be removed and the individual can use the arm more actively, with more confidence that the arm will not be seriously reinjured, even if it is stiff and hurts a bit at first. Problem solving offered by group members helps individuals to safely experiment in exercising the arm in ways they might have before they were wounded even though the arm will continue to carry the scar. The wounded arm becomes stronger as the internal strength of the body's natural healing processes supported by the external healing ointments and safe experimentation combine to strengthen and improve the functioning of the arm.

Metaphor of Refueling a Car   Two individuals driving a car pull over with the fuel near empty and the vehicle running, "on fumes." Person A (numbing/avoiding) pulls over to the side, turns off the engine, and feels relief from the concern that the vehicle is running out of fuel. This provides a brief respite from the concerns. However, these concerns return once an attempt is made to restart the vehicle and move forward with life. The vehicle comes to a halt shortly thereafter and cannot go further due to a lack of fuel.

Individual B pulls over, stops the vehicle and walks to go get gas to put fuel into the tank, which is a bit of a chore. This refuels the vehicle and is a positive coping behavior that supports the individual. It provides the energy to manage similar triggers effectively in the future. When the vehicle is restarted, it can move forward without the concern of being stuck with an empty tank.

Considerations for Clinical Settings

General referral and assessment protocols are presented in the following sections. These services will be offered with varied procedures based on numerous variables including space, staffing, and programmatic requirements. Systems that offer interpersonal warmth and convey caring and compassion during initial contact with clients help to present reassuring safety cues.

The following discussion presents considerations across several different clinical settings to assist with managing the identified concerns during the process of PCGT. A comprehensive list of mental health programs is beyond the scope of this chapter. The selected program types offer a crosscut of the potential contexts, issues, and logistics regarding the implementation of PCGT, which may be extrapolated to related settings. Many of the issues discussed within each of the identified programs are not limited to that organization and overlap programmatically across the venues listed. Generally applicable approaches to implementation are presented first, followed by specific settings. The relevant highlights for each setting are provided, rather than revisiting instructions that significantly overlap multiple settings, in an effort to avoid unnecessary repetition. A key consideration for each setting is how the group relationship and group cohesion may be developed and maintained within each clinical environment and programmatic structure.

Program-Specific Considerations: Outpatient Mental Health Settings

COMMUNITY MENTAL HEALTH CLINICS

Approximately 90 percent of individuals presenting for services at a community health center reported a history of trauma exposure (Cusack, Frueh, & Brady, 2004). SAMHSA, in a 2019 eSolutions newsletter, indicated that 90 percent of individuals presenting at public behavioral healthcare settings have a history of at least one lifetime traumatic event. Clients presenting for psychiatric treatment services at a community mental health program present for many different reasons. Following assessment, and during a meeting with the client for joint treatment planning, decisions concerning the timeline for starting treatment services are critical. In many outpatient community settings there may be a wait time for establishing a core number of participants for a group prior to the onset of the first PCGT meeting. If the clinician conducting the assessment is not the leader of the PCGT treatment, having a "warm handoff" with that clinician is suggested (especially important given trust issues common for trauma survivors). During this meeting, the clinician completing the evaluation introduces the PCGT facilitator. A presentation of information concerning the group follows, which includes a timeline for the group meetings and a possible follow-up appointment to address the client's additional questions or concerns prior to the start of PCGT.

The warm handoff with the PCGT group facilitator also allows for a brief introduction of the clinician and helps to address the anticipatory anxiety associated with enrollment into group treatment. For trauma survivors, the unknown is often seen as unpredictable, uncontrollable, and therefore unsafe. Addressing the safety concerns is a critical aspect of recruitment for PCGT, especially in a general community mental health setting that is not specialized for treatment of trauma and perhaps not programmatically designed to manage these needs on a routine basis.

An advantage of community mental health settings is that "wrap-around care" may be available – and certainly a variety of treatment modalities will be available. Other services agreed upon during the treatment planning session may be initiated, including medication management and individual or couple-based interventions. These may start prior to or in conjunction with PCGT. The overall mental health treatment needs of the participant are the primary concerns, and the timing of services would be determined collaboratively. PCGT may be offered as a component of the individual's overall treatment plan, or as a stand-alone service. The initiation of additional services shortly after the treatment planning meeting is always recommended, when possible, especially those services not managed by PCGT (e.g., medication, or case management). This setting has distinct advantages in being able to apply the best practice model of coordinated care when initiating PCGT, promoting both safety and therapeutic gain.

As staffing levels in managed care and community mental health can vary, should there be a delay in engagement in treatment services or PCGT participation, maintaining some degree of contact with the identified clients is recommended. These contacts may include additional follow-up meetings with the potential group participant, as permitted by the clinician's schedule and the financial resources of the client. An additional option may be the scheduling of brief telephone or telehealth contacts prior to the start date of the initial PCGT meeting to check on the status and continued interest of the participant, as well as to provide updates concerning the progress of group enrollment.

In community settings, it is not unusual to have group referrals who reside in the same neighborhood. Ensuring privacy and confidentiality may be a significant challenge. Group members may participate in the same worship groups, community and school organizations, and have children who interact with each other in several different settings. For example, children may attend the same community and school functions. They may have mutual friends and neighbors and share a network of social connections. Such repeated and ongoing interactions result in varying degrees of familiarity, and emphasize the necessity for guidelines for privacy and confidentiality regarding information shared in PCGT meetings. Confidentiality is essential for the group members' comfort with self-disclosure and sharing during group meetings, which is critical to the therapeutic processes of PCGT. A discussion of these potential barriers is needed in the context of establishing adherence to the agreed-upon guidelines for confidentiality and mutual respect during the initial contact with the potential group member, during the first group meeting, and as needed during the delivery of PCGT.

UNIVERSITY COUNSELING CENTERS AND TRAINING PROGRAMS

The offering of PCGT in the university setting may present many of the advantages and challenges noted in the community mental health clinics. In addition, advantages for PCGT may be a familiarity with providing evidence-based groups and, often, access to other resources such as medication management and individual therapy. Challenges include concerns regarding privacy and confidentiality, as would be the case for any group provided within a circumscribed community. Group members may have varying degrees of social interactions associated with life on campus. Some members may reside in the same dormitory, be involved in school organizations or services, be classmates, or be members of the same athletic teams. As discussed in the mental health clinic section, this concern can be managed through group selection, and through insisting on confidentiality, while alerting prospective group members that they may recognize other group members (e.g., from classes, etc.). The user-friendly qualities of PCGT (its flexibility, and relative ease of training and implementation), as well as its reliance on group interaction, make it an ideal treatment for trauma survivors in university settings.

DEPARTMENT OF DEFENSE (DOD) SETTINGS

The individuals involved in the provision of service to our country have placed themselves into a career with highly structured protocols and lines of authority. Military service can place the service member at high risk for trauma, including stressors related to military action, trauma related to accidents, and interpersonal trauma including military sexual trauma. A service member's choice to volunteer for additional duties is respected and greatly valued, yet may incur greater risk for trauma and its psychological impact. Mental health programs offered by the DoD are designed to meet the needs of those who serve in extreme conditions, as well as to enhance the overall health of service members, and to support the optimal functioning leading to retention of personnel. Participation in treatment following a traumatic event or incident may be mandatory, or voluntary but encouraged (as with "first responders").

PCGT offers a viable treatment option in the context of mandatory participation in mental health services. Exposure-based protocols may not be the primary option for individuals that are soon to be redeployed. Such individuals may agree to attend treatment, but not engage in the imaginal or trauma-focused aspects of the therapy, thereby dampening the potential for therapeutic gain. PCGT allows for the sharing of trauma-relevant skills for the management of daily stress and symptoms associated with prior military experiences. It utilizes a supportive present-day orientation to the daily high demand and stress of military service without a detailed debriefing of traumatic events. This approach can bolster the management of psychiatric symptoms as well as the rigors of routine military life. In addition, PCGT provides an outlet for expression of feelings and ideas, with opportunities for individuation in the act of sharing positive resolutions to group concerns that are consistent with a military focus on "mission first." These benefits may not be readily available in another setting. Military mental health emphasizes strength-oriented language, which is consonant with PCGT's focus on sharing positive coping skills and the mission to move forward by promoting individual and group wellness.

Challenges Related to Stigma of Being in Therapy, and Privacy   The DoD has taken care to minimize potential stigma associated with participation in mental health programs, as well as to protect confidentiality. However, documentation concerning an individual's treatment remains within the organization and has the potential of being accessed when, "deemed necessary." Also, within the ranks of service, the seeking of mental health services may potentially be seen as a sign of weakness, or of the individual being unreliable, especially during high-stress events or conflicts.

In an attempt to decrease the potential for stigma, especially following incidents involving large numbers of personnel, the DoD has made participation in mental health services mandatory for all involved in the event. As they are "ordered" to engage in the mental health programs, service members can engage in treatment without the stigma of seeking help for perceived emotional instability or some personal weakness. Mandatory group participation may begin at the assessment process with all unit members being instructed to participate.

PCGT facilitators should keep these constraints in mind when approaching referrals and assessments, as well as in the provision of PCGT. Support for participation in mental health services from the command structure that extends through the ranks is essential to making the services truly accessible. The limits of confidentiality within the organization should also be clarified at all levels of the organizational hierarchy, and must be transparent to the participants. The military is also subject to roughly the same challenges as university counseling centers and other close community treatment settings, in that referrals may be initiated for someone from the same unit, barracks, or worksite. This concern should be addressed as described in the community mental health section, yet with greater emphasis on the potential stigma and how to manage it. Additional concerns relevant to DoD personnel may also be found in the following subsections regarding mandatory and voluntary participation; while there can be a downside to someone feeling forced into treatment, the advantage, again, is that members can participate without negative attributions from others and/or themselves. The role of the PCGT clinician is then to work on genuine engagement while acknowledging and assisting with the processing of the mandatory nature of the referral. The offering of a range of mental health services, including PCGT, may help to restore a sense of choice for the individual and enhance participation.

Command Structure, Hierarchy, and Group Composition The PCGT facilitator should have an understanding of the potential impact of the command structure and hierarchy on the therapy process when constructing groups, with a strong consideration for developing groups comprised of individuals with similar levels of responsibility. Given the hierarchical nature of the military structure, the strong distinction between officers and enlisted personnel, and the circumscribed roles based on rank, the opportunity to share openly would be limited in a group were it heterogeneous regarding rank.

The facilitators would do well to have a rule of thumb about how to implement and initiate the group when disparities in rank exist among members, for example, adding to group guidelines, and addressing this issue specifically in the initial individual orientation meetings. If service members of significantly varied ranks must be in the same group, it is important for the group to acknowledge it and work out a shared plan for handling the disparities in rank when in the group, as well as following completion of the group. The impact of group sharing on post-treatment relationships is of concern. Ultimately, procedures agreed upon and established by military leadership prior to the start of PCGT may be needed to obviate potentially negative impact of disparities in group. Such an agreement needs to be clear to all members of the group, and should include a course of action regarding violations of guidelines for mutual respect and confidentiality during and following the completion of PCGT.

HOMOGENEOUS GROUPS FOR MILITARY SEXUAL TRAUMA (MST)

MST is an event experienced by both men and women. A further consideration includes the potential that group members may have experienced prior sexual assaults as an adult and/or during childhood. It is suggested that PCGT groups be homogeneous with regard to gender and, as possible, the source of the trauma. Survivors of MST may be included in PCGT with a thought toward differences in the frequency and intensity of the assaults. For a PCGT group devoted to survivors of MST, the recency of the assault and the ongoing risk of additional events may require additional services that directly address current safety.

SEXUAL ASSAULT TREATMENT PROGRAMS

PCGT groups for survivors of sexual assault tend to be organized by gender. Although the type of assault may appear similar, the actual traumatic event may vary significantly. Some traumas may be associated with a single event with a single perpetrator of the same or different gender. Others may be repeated assaults by different individuals or groups of individuals. Still other events may include a physical assault in addition to the sexual attack. The focus of the PCGT clinician remains consistent with care to be taken to maintain the present focus rather than discussing details of the assault, while fostering the sharing of deeply personal information about current life. The guidance from the facilitator in the sharing of positive coping behaviors promotes group cohesion and safety for individuals who often experience difficulty with trust and isolation. The present orientation of PCGT therefore lends itself well to groups that may be heterogeneous as to type and nature of the sexual trauma. As with all psychotherapy for trauma, and with treatment for sexual assault in particular, the return of self-trust is a key to therapeutic gain. Survivors of sexual assault often have cognitions and emotions associated with self-blame and mistrust of their own decision-making process. The guided sharing of PCGT facilitates the return of self-trust by promoting the discussion of the individual's symptom burden and of the interventions used to manage this distress. Trust is further developed in other group members by their openness to receiving these offerings and to sharing their own struggles and successes.

TRAUMA RECOVERY PROGRAMS

Outpatient programs that focus on the treatment of PTSD and other trauma-related disorders frequently offer a breadth of individual, couples-based, group, and intensive outpatient services for survivors of trauma. The advantage of this setting is the availability of trauma-related treatment, of which PCGT is one, and the opportunity to establish sequence and pacing of trauma therapies, coordinating care within the trauma staff team. Relevant aspects of the referral and assessment process have been reviewed in earlier sections of this chapter. Collaboration with the individual regarding the goals of treatment and a discussion of the available options is essential. Trauma symptoms may be expressed across a broad spectrum of behaviors including substance use, and dual service offerings may be required. Some potential PCGT participants are those who express a preference for treatment that does not require a detailed disclosure of the identified trauma. Other individuals may decide on a trauma-focused treatment. A decision may be made to focus on a single intervention or to engage in a number of these psychotherapy options. Services may occur simultaneously or in stages. PCGT may be offered at any stage of treatment, whether in co-occurrence with other psychotherapy interventions, or as a stand-alone therapy. The PCGT facilitator should be aware of the participant's therapy with other clinicians, and share and receive clinically relevant information as needed to enhance the overall quality of the individual's experience concerning their therapy goals. As a specialty clinic may not provide "wrap-around care," the facilitator may need to refer members to services outside the clinic, and coordinate care with other departments.

PRIVATE PRACTICE

Private practice structures may vary considerably. Some clinicians function independently as sole providers in their own practice. Others function in a cooperative multi-provider setting. Still others are an employee of a larger private clinic or mental health program and work with a fee for service agreement. Additional options for private practice exist but the current discussion may be generalized for use in these settings from the identified variants.

The general referral and assessment issues have been previously considered. Established referral sources are always essential for PCGT recruitment and may be especially so for private practice settings. Ongoing outreach to referral sources with the provision of information concerning the nature and purpose of PCGT should occur on a regular basis. This assists with the provision of reminders concerning the offering of PCGT, the timeline for the initiation of treatment, and the education of new staff joining existing referral resources (as personnel changes frequently occur without notice).

In the case of the sole provider, the clinician engaged in the pretreatment services also provides the offering of PCGT. Here, establishing a start date for the group may be a major challenge. The clinician and potential group members share in the decisions involved in mental health treatment planning. Some clients may express interest in engaging in individual psychotherapy services rather than becoming involved in a group therapy protocol. The nature of the offered services is a product of the clinician's skill set developed from clinical training and professional experiences as a service provider. Engaging in individual psychotherapy and case management services may be a part of a comprehensive treatment plan that has included engagement in PCGT.

Once an appropriate number of clients has been identified and a start date has been established, the process of the PCGT protocol follows the guidelines presented in the treatment manual. See also considerations for privacy, confidentiality, wait time, etc., as relevant, in previous section on community mental health programs.

Program-Specific Considerations: Special Treatment-Referred Populations

MANDATORY AND EXPECTED TREATMENT CONTEXTS

Individuals with a trauma history comprise the largest number of individuals accessing mental health, forensic health and drug and alcohol services (Muskett, 2014). Following a disaster, it is also not unusual for mental health services, including group therapy, to be offered to survivors of the incident, sometimes with an expectation of follow-through on treatment (depending on the agency serving the community). Other contexts may also include surviving an event on the job, applying for workers' compensation after a work event, applying for disability, being given an Employee Assistance Program referral, or a living situation that requires being in treatment such as a group home, or halfway house. These settings may also include individuals in law enforcement, following a work-related event, emergency responders (including fire departments, again following an event), and the Department of Defense.

Participation in these groups may be voluntary (while encouraged), but may also be mandatory or required by organizational guidelines. The existence of organizational guidelines that require employees or other service providers to participate in a post-incident debriefing or some other mental health intervention is common. Such incidents include but are not limited to events that occur following a devastating fire for firefighters, a natural disaster or an accident for primary health care providers, or after a shooting/hostage incident for police officers. Individuals involved in the above events or other traumatic occurrences may also be offered group counseling services across a variety of mental health settings.

Mandatory Participation　Forced attendance to PCGT is not recommended, but again, PCGT may be identified as the service of choice for individuals employed in organizations requiring group participation following an index event. Mandatory attendance presents several potential challenges to the work of the PCGT clinician and may have a negative impact on group member participation. Some group members may be open to the treatment, while others, feeling forced to engage in the process, may not. The latter may subsequently attempt to isolate themselves despite the required participation. Such individuals often tend to avoid eye contact, are reluctant to speak spontaneously, or may present in a quiet and reserved manner. Open frustration and irritability concerning attendance may also be directed at the group facilitator or at other group members. Discomfort may arise when group members are coworkers who have long-standing relationships with each other. Concerns regarding confidentiality, privacy, professional status, and the impact that sharing has on the quality of established relationships following completion of the group can have a significant influence on the individual's willingness to participate in the joint problem solving that is essential to the PCGT therapeutic process. It can also be problematic if members of the same group have differing levels of responsibilities and status within their work group. Ideally, group members should be placed into workplace peer groups that are homogeneous with regard to assigned duties and leadership roles. Addressing complicated previous relationships upfront can help diffuse some of the discomfort. To handle disparities in status, facilitators may also establish specific ground rules with those in leadership positions, to be shared with group members and included as additional guidelines for PCGT participation (e.g., "no pulling rank" in the group for managers). For balance, line staff may be reminded to "expect no favored status from supervisors while at work" due to the shared group relationship. Membership in the same work group may also require situation-specific reminders and prompts about confidentiality, for example: no reference to the group when at work; no disclosure to coworkers or supervisors about other members, even if asked; ways to politely say "no" to questions about the group; establishing additional standards for confidentiality, and for management of status within the group. The additional guidelines should also include procedures to be utilized post-treatment so that confidentiality and privacy standards are maintained even when the group has terminated, including avenues of redress if these guidelines are breached or at risk of being breached. It may be workable to utilize human resources prior to and following the period of the group in order to assure adherence to these boundaries.

Mandatory treatment may also include individuals who have been court-ordered to attend mental health treatment. The role of the facilitators is initially to establish the survivor's trust in their ability to support the members, to respond to members' trauma-based thoughts and feelings related to their compromised physiological and safety needs, and to promote group cohesion. Secondarily, trust is further established as group cohesion becomes robust enough to support sharing among PCGT participants regarding positive symptom management strategies. Establishing a sense of equality among group through valuing both their needs and their self-generated strategies for symptom relief is a key aspect of the facilitator's role. The establishment of trust may engender a sense that members are making active choices to participate in the therapy, even though the treatment is mandatory. If there are treatment options from which the survivors can make a choice, the resulting sense of agency is useful for any therapy, and perhaps especially for PCGT, which depends on trust and active engagement.

Voluntary (Expected) Participation Individuals involved in a shared trauma incident may be enrolled voluntarily in PCGT. While these individuals have been involved in the identified event, their experiences during the incident and their symptom presentation may differ significantly. For example, individuals involved in the bombing that occurred during the Boston Marathon could be offered PCGT. Survivors who were located near the explosion and were perhaps injured have a very different experience from the person just a few feet away, someone running by at the time of the explosion, or an individual standing across the street. They were all near the explosion but have different experiences during the event. Despite these significant differences, the physiological reactivity and safety concerns associated with the participant's psychiatric symptoms are similar. These similarities are central aspects of the event.

In work settings, challenges may arise concerning inclusion/exclusion criteria, especially when group enrollment is open or expanded. Not all the individuals in a work setting may be directly involved in a traumatic event. Some coworkers may have been engaged in the provision of off-site support functions to the individuals with direct contact to the incident. Some individuals may also be faced with mandatory enrollment while others are given an option concerning their participation. Under such circumstances, identification and selection of members to form homogenous groups is strongly recommended. The role of the PCGT clinician, as always, is to facilitate sharing among group members, the recognition of the similarities of their experiences concerning physiological and safety needs, and the benefits from sharing the positive coping activities utilized by the group members to help manage their distress.

Program-Specific Considerations: Time-Limited Intensive Recovery Programs

PCGT may be offered to clients recovering from mental health challenges as well as substance use. These programs may vary widely and offer various treatment options including general outpatient, intensive outpatient with daily meetings, residential, and in-patient treatment programs. The duration of these programs may also vary from a week to several weeks. A specific discussion concerning these treatment venues is offered in the identified sections of this chapter.

The inclusion of PCGT offers a treatment that is supportive of existing services and may augment offerings with the inclusion of a treatment for individuals with an identified trauma history. As already noted, a trauma history is an aspect of the life experiences of many individuals seeking mental health care, and this includes those with a history of substance use. As PCGT does not require a disclosure or sharing of the participant's identified trauma, it offers a viable option as a supplemental service for those individuals seeking assistance with the management of symptoms associated with their trauma without trauma disclosure. Many clinicians and clients express concern that a focus on the index trauma during treatment may negatively impact the client's ability to progress with other therapy goals and/or sobriety. The inclusion of PCGT offers a viable protocol for the management of trauma symptoms while addressing these concerns.

SUBSTANCE DEPENDENCE TREATMENT PROGRAMS

PCGT may be offered in recovery settings as an augmentation of other treatment services that target substance use. In fact, in PCGT therapy, substance use is often a topic of symptom management as a response to the presence of trauma triggers. The management of substance use when triggered by cues associated with the index trauma is frequently an aspect of the group work. Facilitators support members in sharing any negative coping behaviors aimed at reducing symptoms, including substance use.

One complication is that survivors of trauma who struggle with substance dependence must cope with "dual activation" of triggers for both PTSD symptoms and substance use. The complicated interrelationship of these triggers may include: 1) trauma reminders (from something in the news, to an anniversary of past trauma) leading to both PTSD symptoms and an urge to "use"; 2) PTSD symptoms in and of themselves precipitating an urge to self-medicate; and 3) triggers for substance abuse (e.g., walking by a bar) leading to substance use, which then in turn may result in increased vulnerability to PTSD symptoms (especially if substances were involved during the index trauma). Even in the face of this dual activation and increased complexity, the basic aspects of physiological and safety needs drive similar responses with regard to the associated cognitions, emotions, and actions. These responses may be shared and addressed in the forum of PCGT therapy.

INPATIENT UNIT

PCGT therapy is a viable option on an inpatient psychiatry unit given the focus on active symptom presentations. Inpatient groups may occur on a daily or weekly basis and may have different participants enrolled in each meeting. The varying enrollment is often subject to the daily census as a result of new admissions and recent discharges. In many settings, participation is influenced by inpatient staff selecting group members based on availability from the day room, other public areas on the unit, and the inpatient bedrooms. The level of participation for group members may also vary depending on medication schedules and other program constraints.

Given this variability in group attendance, PCGT can be adapted and offered as a single session protocol that may be offered repeatedly as needed. Such a group is a departure from the full PCGT protocol, but may be provided in the style of PCGT. The agenda for group meetings may include the rationale for PCGT, a review of the guidelines for mutual respect while attending the group, and brief self-introductions by the clinician and the group members. The limits of confidentiality also require discussion, as the information shared with the PCGT clinician is entered into the medical chart and available to unit staff and other care providers involved in the group member's treatment. There may be considerable scrutiny by unit staff concerning the individual's actions, given the ongoing assessment regarding status on the unit, medication changes, and outcome of the hospitalization. In certain facilities an inpatient staff member may also attend the PCGT meetings, which could lend a comfort factor, or a distrust factor, depending on the relationships of members with that staff member.

The role of the PCGT clinician at the start of each meeting is to present the group members with the purpose of the group, a discussion of confidentiality and group guidelines, an offering of a self-introduction as well as a request for introductions from each participant, and the provision of basic psychoeducation concerning the potential role of trauma exposure on mental health. The process of the PCGT remains consistent with the facilitation of shared concerns and the positive coping strategies as presented by the group participants. The challenges to sharing may also be due in part to the group members having been "selected" by unit staff for participation in the group and the feeling that group attendance is mandatory (see section on "Mandatory or Expected Treatment Contexts" earlier in this section), a distrust of the required participation, and a heightened level of vigilance concerning emotional and physical safety on the unit. The changing nature of group composition also compels facilitators to refocus on group guidelines, safety, and establishing rapport on a routine basis. These issues should be first addressed with the unit staff for feedback and joint development of the needed unit protocols during group meetings.

RESIDENTIAL PROGRAMS

The implementation concerns in residential programs may be similar to those noted for inpatient settings. Individuals may enter or leave group at various times due to differences in admissions and discharge dates. They may also enter the program as a member of a cohort for the duration of their visit. Depending upon the length of the program, PCGT may be adapted to a daily schedule, or for a specified number of days each week. Participants may be assigned to PCGT as a mandatory group associated with the residential program or have it available as an optional treatment offering with voluntary participation as an elective within the residential program (see section on "Mandatory and Expected Treatment Contexts").

Group members may also enjoy varying levels of privileges, with some individuals being allowed to leave the program daily at specified times or having the option of a weekend pass from the unit. PCGT facilitators can help members process the meaning of these privileges and their own trajectories through the program. Related aspects of residential treatment may include peer-led support groups, members at varying stages of residents' treatment, and the democratic process of clients electing peers in leadership roles. The members' relationships outside of the group, and events occurring in the residential milieu, may have a profound impact on their interactions and involvement in PCGT, which can both complicate and enrich the PCGT dynamics. PCGT can contribute to the milieu by supporting members around these issues and provide an outlet for them. The resident leaders may also have an impact on the group, in which their engagement may facilitate engagement of other members. In some instances, the resident leader may tend to act as a co-leader; there is a delicate balance for the facilitator between acknowledging and supporting this leadership role, and encouraging the resident leader to also benefit as a member of the group. Another feature of residential programs is that the group members will also most likely share enrollment in other services offered in the residential program. The facilitator will need to establish the exact nature of confidentiality, involving both not sharing other members' information in other groups, and not sharing other members' actions and statements from other groups.

Residential programs offer the clinician an opportunity to witness PCGT themes like no other treatment setting; the daily observance of trauma related symptoms and behaviors serve as rich material for PCGT agenda setting and problem solving. The emotional intensity may be accentuated due to both the shared living environment, and a higher level of symptoms that may have precipitated the need of a residential placement. While members will vary in communication style in any group, the potential tension between members who are decidedly open and sharing, and others with a tendency to be fiercely challenging or directive, may require reassurance and modulation in the group, guided by group ground rules. The clinician's role is to bring balance and emotional safety to the group interactions, to facilitate group cohesion, and to promote the sharing essential to the PCGT process. In this setting, facilitators need to be informed about extra-group dynamics occurring in the residential environment. Establishing a frame of equality in the PCGT setting, in which group members feel open to share their challenges with personal goals and relationships, is a core component of many psychotherapy groups but is essential to the PCGT treatment format. Facilitators create a balance through selectively engaging reserved or non-participating group members and validating their contributions, as well as supporting the already active members; this balancing of "air time" can help to diffuse the intensity of the group, and bring the day-to-day issues related to trauma-based symptoms to the surface.

INTENSIVE OUTPATIENT

Intensive outpatient-treatment programs (IOPs) may also vary in duration. Some may offer a one-week program, whereas others may enroll participants for weeks at a time. Many of the considerations presented in the discussion of inpatient and residential programs can be applied to this outpatient setting. Group members may have preexisting interactions and relationships that raise confidentiality and privacy concerns for the participants, as they are likely to be going from group to group throughout the day. The offering of booster or reunion groups are also frequently provided by intensive outpatient programs in order to consolidate and/or sustain treatment gains, and may be included in the post-treatment planning following the completion of PCGT.

Length of treatment should remain a deciding factor when implementing PCGT in an IOP. Standard present-centered group therapy (typically at least eight sessions) would require frequency of group and length of program sufficient for completing the PCGT protocol. If the program length or frequency of groups is not sufficient for PCGT, a variant of PCGT may be employed that shares many of the characteristics of PCGT (as indicated in the inpatient section, although the research and usual practice to date has utilized at least eight sessions).

Age-Specific Considerations for PCGT: Children, Adolescents, and Elders

CHILDREN AND PCGT

In addition to the considerations addressed in the previous sections, there are age-specific circumstances with young children that include their developmental comprehension and nature of attendance (mandated or voluntary). Some children may not be able to manage or grasp the cognitive and emotional content of the group, as well as the confidentiality required, reasons for attendance, and educational material. These capacities may be gauged through referring programs, and interview with the child and the caretaker or parent. The identification and discussion with the custodial caretaker is the key to setting the limits of confidentiality. There may also be involvement from child protective agencies; the facilitators should clarify with the children and their parents (and/or caretakers) the limitations of group confidentiality (see the section on "Mandatory and Expected Treatment Contexts"). When engaging children, PCGT aims at the cognitive level of the youngest child in the group, with elaboration as needed for other children. Parents and other adult caretakers may gain information from the child via group discussion, program policy, direct questioning of the child, or non-directed circumstantial disclosure by the child. Such possibilities should be addressed in the pretreatment meetings with the children and the adult care providers. With younger children, parents and caretakers need to be included in the commitment to confidentiality.

ADOLESCENTS AND PCGT

PCGT with adolescents shares many of the general features of therapy with adults, as well as some of the identified confidentiality concerns regarding the use of PCGT with children. The age of the adolescent and considerations regarding legal definitions of self-determination and confidentiality add a level of complexity to the pretreatment meetings with the adolescent and the custodial adult. The teenager may not be open to sharing in PCGT if they believe the adult caretaker will be updated on the information discussed in the group meetings. The limits placed on potential treatment gains by these privacy concerns is a key aspect of the pretreatment meetings with the adolescent and the adult caretaker, in which an agreement about confidentiality can be collaboratively developed (e.g., a parent or caretaker may agree that the teenager's disclosures need not be shared unless there are issues related to risk or a specific behavioral concern). This informal agreement should be made clear to all the participants in treatment planning meetings. It is a general rule-of-thumb that the information shared be kept confidential and not made available to the custodial adult, unless a safety issue arises and a disclosure is required, in order to promote trust and openness in the group. It must also be made clear to the custodial adult that at no time will other group members' information be made available, and that asking about others in the group is off-limits.

With older adults, experience and capacity to apply that experience to helping others may be advantages for a group, while cognitive changes and auditory functioning may be challenges to consider. Some older group members may require the use of hearing aids, which may malfunction or be required but absent during PCGT meetings. Diminished availability of auditory or other cues may affect comprehension of shared information, and unintentional failure to observe guidelines for mutual respect concerning the interruption of other group members while they are speaking. Older group members often report that they speak and interrupt as they may forget their intended response should they wait for the speaker to complete the comment. Such individuals indicate having anxiety concerning forgetfulness as the cause for the seemingly impulsive behavior. These group members may benefit from having a paper and pencil available to make notes concerning their responses, and then be assured that they will have an opportunity to share with the group. The guidelines of mutual respect may require several reviews to address this in-session behavior.

Regardless of the age of participants, be they children, adolescents, or older adults, the role of the PCGT clinician remains consistent with the facilitation of sharing between group members, the recognition of their similarities as well as sharing of their distinct strategies for coping, and an understanding regarding the benefits from the positive coping used by the other group members to help manage distress.

PCGT Implementation and Telehealth Applications

The COVID-19 pandemic's impact on provision of mental health services in 2020 and beyond has required considerable flexibility in the offering of group and individual psychotherapy. General considerations for the delivery of PCGT across a variety of clinical settings apply to this scenario as well. Some clinicians may have extensive experience with working remotely with group members. Others may have little or no experience with treatment over a video or telephone format. Developing a level of confidence with these technologies is strongly recommended prior to engaging in group facilitation. Some clinicians may also question the efficacy of group therapy while utilizing these platforms. Others may have questions regarding the management of risk and safety while working remotely. The difficulty making direct eye contact with group participants may also be disquieting. Introspection of one's own cognitive and emotional reactions regarding the benefits and limitations of telehealth work and the available resources is strongly recommended. The following sections may offer some insight with a review of advantages and challenges associated with the implementation of PCGT when it is applied in a telehealth format.

Distance Intimacy

The realm of telehealth therapy places facilitators and group members into a space of *"distance intimacy."* We step into the group members' worlds, and see their intimate surroundings typically omitted in office visits. Close glimpses into the quotidian lives of group members may offer cues regarding how they experience their PTSD and related problems, and may generate material for group discussion. For example, significant people and pets (cats in particular) who are mentioned but not typically seen in office settings may make routine appearances during telementalhealth appointments. While restricted from group appointments for privacy reasons, family members may accidentally step into a participant's room, giving everyone – facilitators and participants alike – an opportunity to witness interactions that may inadvertently offer therapeutic material for later group discussion (as well as problem solving on the essential task of maintaining privacy). Unwitting disclosures, such as photos and other symbolic objects in the client's intimate living space, allow the clinician to draw a more complex therapeutic portrait based on cues not available in office appointments. Group members who are on their own turf, without the professional surroundings of the group room and its accompanying explicit and implicit rules and expectations, may be observed operating according to their daily habits and rituals. Where else does one begin a session suddenly realizing the participant began the appointment in bed or on a treadmill? How often does the practitioner stop group discussion as a group member shows a litter of puppies barking next to their home computer?

In this context of distance intimacy, we are engaging in highly personal work with the participants across remote settings that share information not available in the group room. This additional information comes to us in the same cognitive and emotional channels but offers a wider bandwidth on the experience. Viewing members' homes brings you into their lives in a very real and highly personal way. It offers the clinician and other group members a broader perspective on previously unknown aspects of the participant's life. These may include fairly stable features such as the physical environment, as well as the perhaps more transient interpersonal ones including friends, family, and pets, or a virtual tour of participant's residence. The actual sharing of such information is a common feature of any therapeutic milieu. However, distance intimacy widens the perspective of this sharing with the addition of auditory and visual data not otherwise accessible, exposing both clinicians and group members to the unexpected. This distant and intimate data offers rich material for group process, particularly for a PCGT setting.

For the PCGT facilitator, the management of unexpected, perhaps surprising and provocative revelations by group members is not unusual. In telementalhealth/videoconferencing, the clinician utilizes the frame of PCGT to facilitate and manage this broader array of information. A group facilitator understands that each group session may have unique and unexpected occurrences once the door to the group room closes. The reverse is true for distance intimacy in that, once the video screen turns on and opens to the meeting, we open the door to the unsuspected: pets appear that help with emotional dysregulation, group members share their safe spaces, or supportive family members converse outside of a hallway. All of these events are impossible to observe in office, but through this lens are witnessed, thereby transporting the clinician into the intimate lives of the group in a distant yet intimate connection.

In this context as well, the role of the relationship is considered a key aspect to the successful delivery of PCGT. In the absence of in-person face-to-face contact, the need to establish and maintain a therapeutic milieu during treatment becomes an even greater necessity. As PCGT's effectiveness relies on interpersonal support among group members, access to both verbal and nonverbal communication is key. This emphasis begins with the referral process and the pretreatment interactions with the clinician facilitating the PCGT meetings. During the pre-group meetings, establishing confidence in the ability to provide effective clinical service, given the realities of telehealth technology, requires clarification of any concerns regarding the security and privacy of the identified format, and the ease of application by the client across a specified timeline. Screening criteria for PCGT may need to consider whether group members wary of technical engagement, or who struggle with cognitive deficits, will adapt to telehealth platforms. The use of coaching to familiarize the potential participants may assist with assessing issues with the use of the technology and the ease of implementation and utilization. The potential participant must feel either safe with these challenges or be willing to anticipate and cope with technical difficulties. Facilitators will need to offer assistance with the management of the telehealth program and provide contact information for technical support. The following sections review treatment factors, handling of technical challenges, and milieu considerations unique to PCGT and telehealth delivery.

Video Versus Telephone, or Both

The ideal environment for PCGT allows for both visual and auditory cues during sessions. Therefore, a video platform is recommended when possible. Facilitators providing PCGT must be able to observe subtle shifts in affect during telehealth sessions. As noted above, present-centered approaches rely on group trust and mutual aid. Some groups may consist of individuals that prefer group meetings via the telephone while others indicate a desire for the use of visual platforms. The decision regarding the use of telephone or visual formats should be considered during pretreatment interactions and meetings with potential participants. Once a format is selected it should remain consistent for the duration of the group. The option for joining group without video may be considered if previously agreed upon by the group. However, group participants may prefer the presence of a group member in voice only presentation to ensure ongoing participation rather than have peers prematurely end treatment due to "technical difficulties."

Inclusion and Exclusion Criteria

Given the safety limits of remote psychotherapy, a number of factors should be evaluated concerning the inclusion of group members. Many of these are also guidelines for admission to outpatient face-to-face groups. Individuals presenting with acute homicidal or suicidal ideation, active psychosis, or acute substance use should be engaged in virtual treatment programs only with specific precautions in place, including ongoing evaluation of safety towards self and others, as well as having respective protocols in place to ensure safety.

Virtual Group Recruitment

Along with the exclusion criteria discussed previously, procedural concerns may rule out certain individuals from PCGT in telementalhealth format. Important considerations involve confirmation of group members' access to a device with camera and WiFi capabilities. Some group members may not have email addresses for accessing telehealth sessions. Clinicians recruiting group members should ask referral sources to first clarify whether prospective group members have the basic technical essentials to participate in telehealth sessions. Some agencies may even have telehealth-related disclosure consent forms, which can detail expectations and inform the client of the pros and cons of telehealth group therapy. Private practitioners may want to create a template for telehealth disclosure forms to be completed by clients before starting PCGT. Recruitment for telehealth PCGT allows group facilitators to break the usual geographical limitations of office sessions. Barriers such as traffic and distance become obsolete, thereby granting clinicians the ability to provide treatment to those previously unable to access treatment. Per licensure standards, group facilitators should adhere to the limitations of where and from whom they will recruit group members, for example, marketing to clients outside of the jurisdiction of their state of practice.

Risk Management and Safety

The development of a safety plan is essential for participation in telehealth protocols, given that the members are not in the room with the facilitators. Group members must agree to give their location at the start of each session and indicate whether they are in a private setting and alone. The safety plan includes emergencies, being late to meetings, having dropped calls/video, and cancellations. The plan considers the unexpected psychological, medical, and environmental needs of the group. The participants should have available, as well as the group leaders, the contact information for local police, fire, and rescue services. Each participant should provide a name for emergency contacts, in the event of an incident or a loss of the remote connection. An assessment concerning access to weapons is also suggested.

Provider Training

It is imperative that providers familiarize themselves with telehealth technology and training before implementing telehealth sessions. Considerations such as using telehealth platforms that protect patient health information (PHI) and abide by HIPPA standards ensure that clinicians adhere to ethical and clinical guidelines. Many platforms offer online training to familiarize users with system specifics and to orient users to the various features of the program. Some platforms also provide contact information for technical support from a live operator who can problem solve connectivity breaks in real time. Group participants should also be made aware of these services when available.

Clinicians should also remain aware that direct eye contact may not be possible during group meetings. The angle of the camera for the participants and the facilitator may be offset and therefore looking at the images on the screen is different than looking directly into the camera. While looking at the camera, the clinician or participant may not observe active movements or facial expressions. With multiple facial images on the screen at the same time, this effect is compounded and multiplied. Quick glances to the camera and back to the facial images of the participants may be needed. However, even during a face-to-face group it is challenging to be aware of the actions of all group members. The utilization of a flexible approach with a focus on the clinical content remains to key to the PCGT process.

Use of Co-facilitator to Manage Interrupted or Dropped Contacts and Connection Difficulties

PCGT warrants co-facilitation for several reasons, one of which is to call group members within the first 10–15 minutes of the session to problem solve technical barriers and to encourage participation. Technical glitches may require group members to call a conference number in order to remain engaged in sessions, leaving facilitators to continually weave between those group members participating through a conference phone line and others joining via telehealth video conferencing. The two group leaders may rotate the responsibility of reaching out to absentees and assisting with technology as needed. In each case, one of the group leaders remains with the active members and continues the facilitation of the PCGT process. This rotation limits the disruption to the flow of the meetings while one facilitator tries to reconnect the missing individual to the session. The resolution of "technical difficulties" may serve to enhance the therapeutic relationship as the leaders are observed to "go the extra mile" to ensure the presence of the participants.

Avoidance symptoms that may typically contribute towards group attrition can be mitigated by facilitators reaching out during the initial check-in to encourage participation. Some group members may struggle with attending group as the interaction focuses on the management of unwanted and negative cognitions and emotions. The presence of technological challenges may be a means to avoid participation, as failure to attend may be placed on the mechanism of attendance. The understanding that a clinician will call after a few minutes may enhance the effort to join the group. This helps to maintain the core of group participants; and avoidance may then be more easily identified as a trauma-based coping behavior to be addressed during the PCGT meetings.

Group Guidelines

Group guidelines for the delivery of telehealth services follow similar rules to those of in-person face-to-face visits, with perhaps the obvious exception concerning the absence of in-person presence. However, some additional considerations must be reviewed with group participants to help ensure that group members are cognitively and emotionally present during meetings. These include being alone and in a private location, no sessions from a public setting, no other technology in use, and no sessions while driving. To minimize distractions, being separate from pets, friends, and family is also required. Group members should be attired as if they were coming to a face-to-face appointment and present themselves as they would at an office visit. Food should not be available, and beverages should be limited. There should be no use of tobacco, alcohol, or other drugs during the meeting, and members are expected to arrive sober. Children should be in a separate location. A plan for management of high conflict during group should be discussed. One or all of the non-speaking group members may have their audio input muted if possible. Group participation in telehealth settings may require group facilitators to help members create novel ways to engage. Group norms such as raising of hands or other non-verbal means to signify participation may help to mitigate common challenges of talking over each other accidentally due to absence of some of the usual cues. Employing a rotation of turns for the individuals talking, or agreeing on an identified word, for example, "next," to indicate the end of a speaker's turn, may assist with the fluidity of the group process.

Privacy

As indicated in several contexts in this section, telehealth can complicate privacy. Appropriate settings for group participation are essential. Some group members with limited means need to find safe surroundings, for example, participation in the group from their parked car to safeguard privacy. The usage of headphones can mitigate problems related to privacy, but may not completely address the unwanted passing of family members or others seen by the group during sessions. Unexpected intrusions, such as a family member unknowingly entering the group members' surroundings may occur; facilitators may need to ask who else is in the client's surroundings, and ask them to take precautionary steps to prevent disruptions and ensure trust and safety.

Confidentiality

Confidentiality, as discussed in the group, involves the usual themes of keeping subject matter sacred within the group experience, along with standard exceptions related to safety and risk. Yet, due to the nature of telehealth, some group members may choose to engage while in a public setting. Underscoring the importance of holding to group confidentiality, including the potential exposure of group members' identity and content, may require ongoing clarification and discussion in order to assure the participants are alone and in a private and safe setting for all meetings.

Confidentiality is a core aspect of trust in all group psychotherapy as well as for PCGT. It is an agreement by group members regarding the non-disclosure of information shared during group with others not in the group. This is typically reviewed at the start of most group meetings during a discussion of guidelines for mutual respect concerning partici- pation. Group members need to trust that what is shared remains within the group. Here confidentiality and privacy intersect. Guidelines require that others outside the group do not have access to the information shared, including visual or auditory signals of members, and that no recording of sessions is permitted. As noted in traditional face-to-face groups, the trust among participants centers on non-disclosure of group content. For the telehealth setting, it includes that no one else is seated in the room off camera, and that even if alone and behind a closed door, someone in the next room cannot hear the auditory portion of the meeting. That the PCGT facilitators can never fully verify the adherence to confidentiality or privacy guidelines may be unsettling to participants, and underscores the need for members to be trustworthy to each other as group members at a level beyond that of an in-person. The facilitation of this trust is a critical element to the PCGT process and should be emphasized and supported as strongly as possible.

Technical Interface

In order for members to benefit fully from the telehealth group, their visual and auditory access must be maximized. For videoconferencing groups a plan for the seating, lighting, and sound should be developed for optimal visual and auditory clarity. For example, it is advantageous for the facilitators to wear solid colors (especially dark colors), avoid stripes and patterns, and set the room up so that they are front-lit against a dark background. The clinician and group members should use names to ad- dress others during the meetings to help members and facilitator track speakers during the virtual session. Eye contact is harder to achieve virtually, and should be discussed. As noted previously, the group members will be looking at a screen with multiple facial images presented simultaneously, and the camera will most often be above these images, creating a different angle for eye contact. As a result, the speaker may not appear to be making eye contact with the group and the group may seem to be looking away or be distracted. The lack of eye contact can hinder the social connection between group members that is essential for the PCGT process.

Telehealth platforms often provide opportunities for group members to add chat comments within the virtual room. Abiding by the age-old rule of "putting actions into words" may mitigate distracting chat discussions.

For example, instead of typing words into the chat forum, facilitators encourage members to voice their thoughts and feelings. Ultimately, providers may need to intervene and ask that group members use the chat function sparingly (or not at all, among members), so that chat does not promote avoidance, sub-groupings, or distraction from the group discussion and process. Addressing the use of chat functions also helps to ensure that group members are cognitively and emotionally present while attending the group.

Provider Role

The provider's ability to convey attunement and empathy to the group is of the utmost importance when facilitating PCGT groups. As noted previously, clear visual (and auditory) access to the providers (including proper lighting in the clinical or telework office) is part of how the facilitators develop a trusting relationship with members despite the physical distance. The context of the virtual contact calls for a modicum of alteration in facilitators' customary social professional behavior. The visual and auditory information may not be presented synchronously, which may be distracting or confusing to other participants. Facilitators are encouraged to limit use of enhanced facial expressions or hand gestures as visual aids during meetings. Repetitive movements should be avoided. For example, repeatedly nodding the head is a typical gesture in in-person sessions, yet may be a distractor given a more focused view of the clinician in a telehealth environment. At the same time, providers should be aware of the potential value of role modeling behaviors to the group, for example, by using "I" statements. The value of authentic use of self may be accentuated in this virtual modality, given the limitation of some of the other cues conveying empathy, reliability, and trustworthiness. Facilitators may own their frustrations when technology breaks down, for example, and may also use themselves to reflect what the group may be feeling (e.g., "What Jan said was so sad, it made me want to cry."), which can foster greater trust between the group and the facilitators. This kind of openness between clinician and members creates rapport in all clinical settings, but perhaps takes on a more important role given the vagaries of Internet connection and camera functioning.

The development of rapport is critical to the delivery of PCGT in any outpatient setting. Maintaining equitable time for each group member may be a significant challenge to the facilitator. An additional consideration in this format is establishing a protocol for speaking, given that nonverbal cues for being about to speak are attenuated. As noted in the "Group Guidelines" section, group members may be muted until recognized by the host/group leader of the meeting, or may be asked to mute themselves when not speaking to reduce ambient noise levels that can accumulate across the multiple connections. Again, participation may require raising a virtual hand or their actual hand while on screen to indicate the intention to speak. This embellished facilitator role of orchestrating the group conversation intensifies the importance of trust concerning the clinician and the relationship with and among group members. Assuring a balance in the "air time" will assist with the development of the sharing and group brainstorming required in PCGT.

Pre-Treatment Technical Check

TEST RUN

A test run can serve as dress rehearsal before the initial session. Technical difficulties will most likely arise during the implementation of telehealth, some of which can be addressed during a group session test run with another provider or other appropriate social contact. An icebreaker session may also be considered with the enrolled group members. Group members new to telehealth may benefit from knowing how to mute their device or to assess the camera and microphone capabilities. Similarly, facilitators would be advised to test out the ability to enter the virtual group room, and have technical support contact available, if possible, to help problem solve unexpected challenges. This support could be from within the organization of the host provider, or from someone accessible to the individual group members, while allowing for privacy and confidentiality.

ACCESSIBILITY/CONNECTIVITY

The devices in use during the appointment should be receiving power or fully charged at the time of the meeting. Weak connection to telehealth sessions can lead to delayed responses and disruptive participation as group members are disconnected and re-enter the group. The determination of group members to take on making this connection as a collaborative endeavor suggests the value of this shared responsibility that may actually work to counter avoidance, providing members with an opportunity for a more active role than is available through in-person group treatment. This pattern may be a function of distance intimacy, as discussed earlier in this section.

Telehealth on Inpatient Groups

This section addresses additional thoughts regarding the innovation of virtual program services on inpatient units, given that inpatients often cannot travel to outpatient group therapies. It should be noted, in the specific context of a pandemic such as COVID-19, that social cues may be diminished by the use of masks by individuals and the staff on the unit.

Nevertheless, there are advantages to telehealth given the need for physical distancing. Setting up telehealth groups on an inpatient psychiatric unit begins with the support of the unit staff and the available resources. On certain units, a single monitor may be the only resource available. In this case, group members are often placed in a linear seating configuration to accommodate the limited view provided from a single screen to the group leaders' device. Group members' masks may affect the quality of the audio during the session, as well as making it harder to identify individuals speaking during the group. Some group members may also be off screen due to limits on the available space for viewing, which also limits access to visual contact during the treatment meetings. Despite advancements in technology allowing the convenience of virtual care, there remain these logistical issues and potential limitations.

Some resource-rich programs may have individual devices available for each of the group member's use during the meetings. This scenario creates an experience similar to face-to-face sessions, in that visual contact is available for each member. The challenge of multiple members each appearing individually (in a manner often described as "Hollywood Squares") is that eye contact is more difficult. As some of the turn-taking cues available in person are less accessible in this modality, facilitators may, as in outpatient groups, want to institute a practice of members stating their names as they are about to speak, and indicating verbally when they are done (e.g., "Over!"). These conventions for virtual practice can organize the flow of conversation and prevent several members from speaking at once.

Anticipation of Use of Virtual Modalities

We are likely to see greater use and concomitant challenges and advantages in using virtual modalities, which have particular utility currently during the COVID-19 pandemic. Other uses involve overcoming travel barriers, and physical limitations preventing safe in-person attendance. Telehealth has also been used to conserve space. PCGT is currently being offered virtually, both through videoconferencing and teleconferencing, with relative success and evidence of positive distance intimacy.

Summary

PCGT was originally developed for PTSD. However, it should be considered as a primary treatment option for all individuals requiring mental health services following a traumatic event. Furthermore, PCGT may also be offered as an adjunct service along with other group or individual treatment programs. The structure of PCGT has great utility as a clinical offering across differing cultural experiences and backgrounds. The focus of the model is on the participants' current life experiences, as affected by trauma-related symptoms, that in turn can be understood in terms of physiological and safety needs that were threatened during the original trauma (see chapter six). PCGT promotes the understanding of group members regarding the common symptoms related to trauma, and addresses these issues through active work within the group on problem solving and mutual support. The group empowers each participant to share positive coping strategies and to learn from their group member peers.

This chapter has reviewed the utility and implementation of PCGT as a treatment for trauma survivors across several clinical settings. PCGT is a generally accessible model that can be readily implemented, with minimal modifications in response to the setting, considerations for recruitment and engagement, and preparation for group specific to the setting. The manual in this book (chapters three through five) can provide instruction on establishing this treatment. The clinician's role in PCGT involves facilitating problem solving regarding strategies for symptom management, and the overcoming of barriers, in the interest of improved life functioning. In this model, group members take a particularly active role in managing their own wellness, which can enhance treatment and recovery across a variety of settings. Members learn to trust that they are capable of effectively managing seemingly overwhelming distress. The PCGT clinician provides aid by guiding and activating the process of self-care and facilitating group cohesion.

Basic processes for referral and assessment have also been reviewed, along with considerations for the implementation of PCGT across a variety of clinical settings. Several conceptual considerations and metaphors are included as tools to guide the clinician in choice of interventions, and consideration has been given to matching survivors to compatible treatments, whether PCGT or other therapies. The importance of transparency, and collaboration with the person referred to treatment, has been underscored as important in any trauma-related therapy, and in PCGT in particular.

References

American Psychiatric Association. (1980). *Diagnostic and statistical manual of mental disorders* (3rd ed.). Arlington, VA: Author.

American Psychiatric Association. (2013). *Diagnostic and statistical manual of mental disorders* (5th ed.). Arlington, VA: Author.

Chang-Caffaro, S., & Caffaro, J. (2018). *Differences that make a difference: Diversity and the process group leader. International Journal of Group Psychotherapy*, 68(4), 483–497, DOI:10.1080/00207284.2018.1469958

Cusack, K. J., Frueh, B. C., & Brady, K. T. (2004). Trauma history screening in a community mental health center. *Psychiatric Services*, 55(2), 157–162.

Kessler, R., Sonnega, A., Bromet, E., Hughes, M., & Nelson, C. B. (1995). Posttraumatic stress disorder in the National Comorbidity Survey. *Archives of General Psychiatry*, 52, 1048.

Maslow, A. H. (1943). A theory of human motivation. *Psychological Review, 50*(4), 370–396.

Mueser, K. T., & Rosenberg, S. D. (2001). Treatment of PTSD in persons with severe mental illness. In: J. P. Wilson, M. J. Friedman, & J. D. Lindy (Eds.), *Treating psychological trauma & PTSD. Vol. 14* (pp. 354–382). New York: The Guilford Press.

Muskett, C. (2014). Trauma-informed care in inpatient mental health settings: A review of the literature. *International Journal of Mental Health Nursing, 23*(1), 51–59. http://mhcc.org.au/media/25362/muskett-2013.pdf

National Executive Training Institute (NETI). (2005). *Training curriculum for reduction of seclusion and restraint.* Draft curriculum manual, National Association of State Mental Health Program Directors (NASMHPD), Alexandria, VA: National Technical Assistance Center for State Mental Health Planning (NTAC).

Sakamoto, I., & Couto, S. (2017). Group work with immigrants and refugees. In C. D. Garvin, L. M. Gutiérrez, & M. J. Galinsky (Eds.), *Handbook of social work with groups* (pp. 360–383). New York, NY: The Guilford Press.

Yalom, I. D. (1995). *The theory and practice of group psychotherapy.* New York, NY: Basic Books.

Index

Note: **Bold** page numbers refer to tables